Contents

Introduction

In the last few years Paris has completed, at enormous expense, a construction programme of new or adapted buildings on an unprecedented scale, and those who have not visited the city since 1985 will be astonished by what has been achieved. With the Pompidou Centre as a precursor, a brief two and a half years has witnessed the completion of the Forum des Halles shopping centre, the Picasso Museum, the Musée d'Orsay, the 'park of the future' at La Villette, the Grand Louvre project, which has increased the museum's size by eighty per cent, and the Bastille Opera House. But perhaps even more important has been the wholesale cleaning and redecorating of major buildings and monuments as part of the 1989 bicentenary celebrations.

The format of *Paris Step by Step* closely follows that of my other books in the series. It treats the visitor as someone who, without precise guidance, will get lost and confused. The city is divided into more than five hundred locations, which are fully described and linked to form nineteen routes. Starting and finishing at a Métro station (*M*), the visitor is led, literally step by step, around the exterior and, when permitted, the interior of each location. Every major point of interest is referred to precisely as it is reached and directions are then given for walking to the next location. In other words, *Paris Step by Step* aims to match, as closely as possible, the services of a personal, knowledgeable guide.

Obviously, few will slavishly follow each route location by location, and the large-scale, interconnecting maps of central Paris show the position of each Métro station so that a route may easily be joined or left when desired.

For the first time in the 'step by step' series, selected bars and restaurants, to suit all purses, are indicated on the maps by the letter R, and up-to-date details about each one are given at the end of the book.

It is appreciated that the reader's knowledge of French will vary from practically nil to fluent, and I would ask those in the latter category kindly to bear with the numerous translations that are given for the benefit of the others. I have decided, however, that the names of locations should always be in French, as these are what will appear on maps and signs; this should cause no difficulties, as few will be unable immediately to appreciate, for example, that Tour Eiffel is French for the Eiffel Tower.

Now, more than ever, is the time for a first or a return visit to this most enchanting of capitals which, if care is taken, can cost significantly less than London or New York.

Bon voyage!

Christopher Turner

Christopher Turner

PARIS
Step by Step

Leaving Charles DeGaulle
Gate 28 — Shuttle bu to RER Station
Gate 30? — Roissybus to Paris Opera

Pan Books London, Sydney and Auckland

This book is dedicated to my friends, Jean-Pierre Vitry, avocat à la Cour de Paris, and his wife, Françoise, who have shown me great kindness and generosity for more than a quarter of a century. Also to their sons, Edouard, Aurélien and Thibault, my godson.

First published in 1991 by Pan Books Ltd
Cavaye Place, London SW10 9PG
9 8 7 6 5 4 3 2 1

© Christopher Turner 1991
Drawings © Benoit Jacques 1991
Maps by Ken Smith
Design by David Pelham and Leigh Brownsword

ISBN 0 330 31618 4

Photoset by Parker Typesetting Service, Leicester
Printed and bound in Great Britain by
BPCC Hazell Books, Aylesbury, Bucks
Member of BPCC Ltd

Christopher Turner has also written
London Step by Step and *Barcelona Step by Step*,
published by Pan Books

Paris and the Parisians

The City

Many readers of this book, who are visiting Paris for the first time but have a prior knowledge of London, will find the differences between the two cities remarkable, considering their proximity. *Vive la différence!* Paris is primarily a city of wide, tree-lined thoroughfares, which run dead straight, frequently ending at a monument or an imposing church façade. Most of the buildings are in the form of balconied apartment blocks, slate-roofed and seven storeys high. They are built, in vaguely Classical style, of a pale gold limestone, which needs regular cleaning to avoid weathering to an all-over grey. An extraordinary number possess ground-floor canopied bars or restaurants which extend across the wide pavements.

Great Classical squares in a miraculously pristine state, and immense vistas, many of which incorporate the beautiful river Seine, with its white bridges, add to the apparent spaciousness of what is one of the world's most densely populated cities. Above all, the quality of being 'lived-in' distinguishes Paris not only from London, but from almost every major city in England and North America, where commerce has taken over and the central area is desolate outside business hours.

The People

The author, who is not renowned for saint-like tolerance or remarkable fluency in the French language, has always found the Parisians to be, in general, kindly, sympathetic and, on a personal basis, extremely generous. However, it cannot be refuted that some visitors express an antipathy towards them. Understandably, the language is a barrier, as the French are not much better at mastering other people's tongues than English-speaking people, but any attempt to communicate in French, however badly, is generally appreciated. Remarkably, a thick English or American accent, resulting in, for example, 'Bon joower je sweez arnglays', is judged to sound most attractive, even sexy! If the reply comes in perfect English it is merely because the Parisian wishes to assist communication; no insult is intended.

However, the great stumbling block is probably the absence of the big, welcoming smile, so favoured by the English and even more by Americans. This does not, however, mean that there is dislike or indifference on the part of, for example, the waiter – it is just that the French are extremely formal people (all that handshaking) and it is considered impolite to grin broadly at a perfect stranger just because he requires service.

It must be admitted that some Parisians claim to dislike the English and Americans because they believe that they dislike them, and as there are English and Americans that feel the same way about the French a pointless, non-stop carousel has been created. In such cases it is important to establish empathy as quickly as possible – quite easily achieved by praising the wonders of French cuisine or the beauty of Paris.

The development of Paris

The Romans captured the Celtic habitation of Lutetia in 52 BC, but only the remains of baths and an arena have survived structurally from their period. Lutetia was renamed Paris *c.* AD 360 after the Parisii, who had stayed on throughout the Roman occupation. Early development was restricted to the Ile de la Cité and the Left Bank, as the Right Bank was marshland (*marais*); temples, however, were built on the hilltop of what is now Montmartre.

Paris fell in 486 to the Franks, whose leader, Clovis, now regarded as the first king of France, became a Christian. The conversion of the Frankish domain soon followed (a century before England) and religious establishments were founded. During the Norman raids of the ninth century both sides of the river were abandoned, the Parisians crowding on to the Ile de la Cité, but in 1148 the first harbour in Paris was opened on the Right Bank, which had recently been partly drained by its monastic landowners.

In the twelfth century Philippe-Auguste's new city wall provided security, and the citizens felt free to leave the overcrowded island; university students began their takeover of the Left Bank. Although Clovis and his Merovingian descendants had ruled from their palace in the Ile de la Cité, it was only in the mid-eleventh century that this became firmly established as the country's premier royal residence. St Louis rebuilt the palace in the thirteenth century, providing accommodation within for parlement and the law courts.

Until the mid-twelfth century, Paris buildings had been designed in the Romanesque style, but Gothic then evolved at St Denis, quickly being adapted at Notre Dame to the High or Early Gothic style. Structures became lighter, with large window areas encouraging the manufacture of stained glass, thus making possible such buildings as the Sainte Chapelle. Turmoil created by the Hundred Years War (1337–1453) and Etienne Marcel's revolt (1357) which was instrumental in royalty abandoning the Ile de la Cité for the Right Bank, meant that little of importance was built in Paris for a long period. Flamboyant, Gothic's next stage, followed; this was much more ornate, and unlike its comparable but short-lived English equivalent (Decorated) remained in vogue until the Renaissance.

For some time the French kings had preferred to live in their châteaux in the Loire valley, but François I returned to the capital in 1526 and encouraged the Renaissance style, particularly with his rebuilding of the medieval Louvre Palace. Renaissance hôtels now began to be constructed in the Marais, a quarter that became even more fashionable in the seventeenth century, following the completion of Henri IV's Place Royale, now the Place des Vosges.

Religious wars in the sixteenth century had restricted church building, but from 1600–40 twenty new churches were erected. In 1616, Salomon de Brosse, with his influential façade to St Gervais-St Protais, introduced Classicism, which was soon adapted to 'Paris Baroque' when Lemercier combined a dome and a portico at the Sorbonne. Secular buildings also adopted the Classical style in the seventeenth century – impressive public buildings, particularly on the Left Bank, reflecting the absolute power of the monarchy.

Louis XIV, having by his victories established the country's security from invasion, began to pull down the Paris wall in 1670 and created the Grands Boulevards along its route. A formal development plan, the city's first, was approved in 1676 and within a period of forty years new streets had expanded the capital's area by almost fifty per cent. However, when Louis XIV vacated Paris for Versailles in 1680 he lost interest in the city, and state-inspired royal projects virtually ceased.

The extravagance of the 'Sun King' had ruined the economy and it was not until 1750 that his grandson Louis XV could afford to recommence public building. Baroque was now abandoned in favour of a return to the 'purer' Classical style.

Many churches were despoiled at the Revolution which, in spite of the state's acquisition of monastic and royal land, led to little new construction of benefit to the Parisians. Napoleon's chief building contribution to the capital was four new bridges and the commencement of the Rue de Rivoli, although the monuments to his victories, notably the Arc de Triomphe, made a greater visible impact on the Paris scene. Early in the nineteenth century, buildings began to imitate, even more slavishly, the detailing of antiquity, and this was the style followed by many of the new churches that were constructed following the freedom of worship which had been restored by Napoleon in 1802.

As in England, the 1830s saw a Gothic Revival, but it never reached such a position of dominance in Paris. Although the industrial revolution attracted migrants to the city, neither housing nor sanitation could cope, 20,000 dying in the 1832 cholera outbreak. Water supplies were soon improved but it was not until 1855 that the real modernization of the capital began, with the commencement of Haussmann's massive scheme for Napoleon III. By the end of the Second Empire in 1870 approximately 20,000 dwellings, mainly of three storeys, had been replaced by 40,000, practically all of seven storeys. However, little of architectural note was designed, apart from l'Opéra , and the loss of many ancient buildings of importance was a catastrophe.

The nineteenth century, which had begun with what is now one of the symbols of Paris, the Arc de Triomphe, closed with two more: the Eiffel Tower and Sacré Coeur; the latter, however, was not completed until 1910. Fortunately, the twentieth century has treated Paris virtually as a 'museum city' and apart from the certain blunder of the Montparnasse Tower and the possible blunder of the Les Halles demolition, most development has been remarkably sympathetic, the emphasis, particularly since Malraux's edict of 1961, being on preservation.

Although throughout its long history Paris has been subjected to siege, occupation and revolution it has not, since the Romans left, suffered wholesale destruction from an alien hand. In addition, the ready availability of stone as a building material has protected the capital from the disastrous fires that destroyed so many timber-built European cities including, of course, London. This is why, in spite of much self-inflicted destruction in the nineteenth century, Paris retains the appearance of a venerable metropolis.

Designers

Outstanding architects, sculptors and decorators whose work is featured in this book.

Anguier, François 1604–69
Anguier, Michel 1612–86
Ballu, Théodore 1817–75
Baltard, Victor 1805–74
Blondel, Merry-Joseph 1781–1853
Bouchardon, Edouard 1698–1762
Boucher, François 1703–70
Boule, André-Charles 1642–1732
Brongniart, Alexandre-Théodore 1739–1813
Bruant (or Bruand), Libéral d.1697
Carpeaux, Jean-Baptiste 1827–75
Chalgrin, Jean-François-Théodore 1739–1811
Champagne, Philippe de 1602–74
Chapu, Henri-Michel 1833–91
Chardin, Jean-Baptiste 1699–1779
Coustou, Nicolas 1658–1733
Coypel, Noël 1628–1707
Coysevox, Antoine 1640–1720
Debrosse, Salomon d.1621
Delacroix, Ferdinand-Victor-Eugène 1798–1863
Delorme, Philibert 1518(?)–77(?)
Desjardins, Martin 1640–94
Du Cerceau, Jacques Androuet 1540–80(?)
Etex, Antoine 1810–88
Fontaine, Pierre-François 1762–1853
Fragonard, Jean-Honoré 1732–1806
Gabriel, Jacques-Ange 1710–82
Garnier, Jean-Louis-Charles 1825–98
Girardon, François 1628–1715
Goujon, Jean 1520(?)–72(?)

Hardouin-Mansart, Jules 1645–1708
Hittorff, Jacques-Ignace 1793–1867
Juste de Tours, Jean d.c.1535
Labrouste, Pierre-François-Henri 1801–75
Le Brun, Charles 1619–1690
Lefuel, Hector-Martin 1810–81
Lemercier, Jacques 1590–1660
Lemoine, Jean-Baptiste 1704–48
Le Nôtre, André 1613–1700
Lescot, Pierre c.1510–78
Lepautre, Jean 1617–82
Le Sueur, Eustache 1617–55
Mansart, François 1598–1666
Mignard, Pierre 1610–95
Oppenard, Gilles-Marie 1672–1742
Pajou, Augustin 1730–1809
Percier, Charles 1764–1838
Perrault, Claude 1613–88
Pigalle, Jean-Baptiste 1714–85
Pilon, Germain 1515–90
Pradier, Jean-Jacques 1792–1852
Puvis de Chavannes, Pierre 1824–98
Rodin, Auguste 1840–1917
Rude, François 1784–1855
Servandoni, Jean-Nicolas 1695–1766
Soufflot, Jacques-Germain 1714–81
Tuby, Jean–Baptiste 1630–1700
Van Loo, Jean-Baptiste 1684–1745
Viollet-le-Duc, Eugène 1814–79
Visconti, Louis 1791–1854

Practical information

Timing a visit

The climate of Paris, like most northern European cities, is
changeable, with summers slightly hotter and winters slightly
colder than London's. Spring and autumn are the best times for a
visit. From late July to early September, many establishments
close for the long summer holiday. At Easter the city is overrun
by tourists, including hordes of school children.

Accommodation

Although possessing 68,000 hotel rooms, accommodation can be
difficult to find in the central area of Paris, at Easter and when the
autumnal exhibitions are held. Hotel information and booking
services, for a fee, are available at Charles de Gaulle airport and
most main-line railway stations (but not Gare St Lazare). The
Office de Tourisme de Paris and its branches in the city also offer
this service. Hotels are graded from one to four stars; lower-
priced rooms, some of which can still be frighteningly basic, are
becoming increasingly difficult to find as soaring property values
lead to upgrading. Unless obligatory, it is always cheaper and
usually more pleasant to eat continental breakfast (*le petit
déjeuner*) at a café rather than the hotel.

Transport

The Métropolitain or Métro

The Métro, the Paris underground railway system, runs until
01.30. Its trains and stations have been modernized in recent
years and the service is now vastly superior to those of London
and New York. The Métro is faster, cheaper, much cleaner and,
above all, more frequent – rarely, even late at night, is a wait of
more than three minutes entailed. A plan of the system is
included in this book on the inside back cover. A traveller must
know the name of the line's terminal station in the direction
travelled, as this, rather than the line's number, will be indicated.
The method works well, except in the case of Charles de Gaulle
Etoile station, from where line 6 southbound and 2 northbound
follow different routes but both terminate at Nation station. If
travelling from the Arc de Triomphe to the Eiffel Tower, for
example, one must be certain that line 6 is taken. In general,
changing lines (*correspondance*) is simple, but may require a
lengthy walk at some stations, in particular Châtelet, Châtelet les
Halles and Charles de Gaulle Etoile, all of which should be
avoided if possible. For most visitors, a *carnet* of ten tickets, each
valid for one Métro/RER journey, is the most economical buy,
but a *carte orange* seven-day central zone season ticket, which
always runs from Monday to Sunday and also includes the bus
system, may be even more advantageous – a passport-size
photograph is required. If a great deal of travelling is planned it
may be advantageous to buy a *Paris Visite* ticket, valid for the
Métro, bus, RER and trains in the Ile de France. These are valid
for three or five days and cover either Paris and its neighbouring
suburbs or Paris and further afield. They may be purchased at the
Paris international airports as well as at mainline and Métro
stations.

The RER system, a rapid service to the suburbs, may be used by
all Métro ticket holders, but an excess must be paid outside the
central zone, e.g. to La Défense or Versailles.

First class accommodation offers no greater comfort but is less crowded in the rush hour. Before 09.00 and after 17.00, passengers with second-class tickets may travel first class.

Buses
Due to their complexity, city bus services are always more difficult for the stranger to comprehend than a rail system. However, no Métro line crosses the Seine between Place de la Concorde and Châtelet (i.e. the most central area of Paris), whereas buses do. Particularly useful is No 27, which runs from St Lazare station, via Avenue de L'Opéra and then follows the *quais* of the Left Bank to Boulevard St Michel and the Luxembourg. Departing also from St Lazare station, No 24 follows the best sightseeing route at a fraction of the cost of a coach tour.

Paris is divided into bus zones and unless some kind of season ticket is held, or the journey is within a single zone, the cost is much higher than the Métro; moreover, unlike the Métro, no change of route can be made on the same ticket, except, of course, with season or special tickets. Tickets are purchased on the bus from the driver and must be inserted (but not season tickets) in the cancellation machine. Always hail the bus, enter at the front and leave at the rear. At some bus stops, queue position tickets are provided from dispensers.

Taxis
Cabs may occasionally be hired in the street or more easily from ranks at designated points; look for the sign 'tête de station'. There are separate day and night tariffs, which are indicated within the vehicle. Supplements are charged for luggage and at railway stations. A tip of 15 per cent is still expected!

Boats
A new service, 'Bat O bus', operates one-hour cruises throughout the year, between Port de la Bourdonnais (Eiffel Tower) and Quai de l'Hôtel de Ville: there are five staging points. *Vedettes* (pleasure boats) operate from beside the Eiffel Tower and the Pont Neuf. *Bateaux mouches*, which leave from Pont de l'Alma, offer lunch and dinner trips. Canal cruises are also available.

Public holidays in France
These are: 1 January, Easter Monday, 1 May, 8 May (VE Day), Ascension Day, Whit Monday, 14 July (Bastille Day), 15 August (Assumption Day), 1 November (All Saints Day), 11 November (Armistice Day), and Christmas Day. Many establishments, particularly shops and banks, close on these days. In addition, self-respecting Parisians vacate the capital from late July to early September for their long annual holidays. In consequence, many of the shops, bars, restaurants and theatres, dependent on their business, are closed.

Foreign exchange
Money can be exchanged at a Bureau de Change every day, with branches at stations and airports remaining open until at least 21.00. However, banks, which are open Monday–Friday, 09.00–16.30, generally offer better rates. Many will find that Eurocheques, now widely accepted, will be the most convenient way of taking money. However, travellers cheques, issued in francs by overseas branches of Crédit Lyonnais, usually offer the most favourable exchange rate. American Express provide by far the best travellers cheques service – available to non-cardholders

from their branches, leading building societies and Lloyds Bank. If cheques are exchanged at an American Express office no commission is charged. Replacement is immediate in the case of loss or theft.

Museums and buildings of historical interest

Visitors familiar with London's free or reasonably priced art galleries and museums are horrified to discover that a fairly hefty charge is demanded to enter most buildings of interest in Paris, and those on a budget will therefore wish to be very selective. However, a one-, three- or five-day museum pass has recently been introduced at 55 francs, 100 francs and 150 francs – this 'Carte inter-Musées' is available from museums and Métro stations. An added advantage is that ticket office queues are avoided. More than sixty museums and monuments in and around Paris now participate in the scheme. Students, pensioners and members of the armed forces are generally offered reduced rates to enter museums, but incontrovertible proof of status and age must be carried as most officials are suspicious of any unsubstantiated requests for reductions. Unless entry is free, admission is generally refused thirty or even forty-five minutes before closing time.

Most museums close on Tuesdays or Mondays; check the opening details in this book for each location. Exhibitions that attract large crowds are best visited during the lunch hour, which is sacrosanct to the French, who invariably spend it . . . eating lunch.

Restaurants

Paris restaurants can be the cheapest, or the dearest, in the western world. Generally, however, the value for money is good, and excellent middle-price establishments, rare in most other northern European or American cities, are to be found in abundance.

Bars/Cafés

Sensibly, Paris bars and cafés open when there is sufficient demand, there being no hypocritical drinking restrictions. Most shut after midnight unless they are situated in entertainment or tourist areas. Those in the business quarter around the Banque de France generally close early and at weekends. Prices fluctuate wildly in a way that puzzles many strangers. The same glass of wine, for example, can cost from 4 francs to 40 francs, depending on the time of day, the situation of the premises, its standard of décor, its popularity and precisely where the drink is consumed – at the bar (the cheapest), seated at a table in the lounge, or on the terrace (the dearest). In general, standard wines cost a good deal less than beer, particularly foreign beers. Spirits are usually expensive, but small tipples of calvados (apple brandy) are a cheap and popular accompaniment to coffee – the coffee usually costs more than the calvados! Ask for a 'café-calva'. See 'Restaurants and Bars', pages 294–304.

Postage

Stamps may, of course, be purchased from post offices (*bureaux de poste*), but also from tobacconists (*tabacs*), which often form sections of a bar or café.

Telephones

Due to vandalism, public telephone boxes in Paris no longer accept coins, only cards, but telephone calls, much cheaper than in the United Kingdom, can usually be made at bars or cafés, where coins are always accepted. Local calls are at a set price, with unlimited time permitted. Every Paris number is now prefixed with a 4, which should be added to all old five-digit figures. Coin boxes also exist within post offices; the central office, open 24 hours a day, is at 52 Rue du Louvre. Many will find it easier, or more economical, to make international calls from here. Room calls from hotels involve a fairly hefty supplement.

Churches/religious buildings

Most churches of interest are described in this book. In spite of recent cleaning, many of their interiors are still rather dark, as Paris had no Wren to insist on the large areas of clear glass that are a characteristic of so many London churches. An oft-repeated formula, of Gothic naves with west fronts and chancels altered later in Classical style, will be noted. Major buildings are open daily but others may close on Mondays and for a fairly lengthy lunch break. In general, weekends are best avoided by visitors. Anglican services are held at Saint George, 7 Rue Auguste-Vacquerie and the American Cathedral, 23 Avenue George V.

Shops

Many small or specialist shops close on Mondays and for an early afternoon break, and also throughout the month of August. Overseas visitors are able to reclaim the government tax on many reasonably expensive items, the amount depending on whether or not one's country is within the EC. Not many bargains are to be found, and the best buys will be food, such as pâtés and cheeses simply because they are difficult to find elsewhere (a problem for American visitors due to their draconian food import regulations). This is why the shopping emphasis in this book is on food.

Toilet facilities

The famous, aromatic Parisian pissotière (for gentlemen only) has virtually disappeared in favour of ultra-modern plastic units (for ladies and gentlemen) which are efficiently sterilized, but which have to be paid for. Cafés and bars have toilets available, but paper is not always provided and visitors are recommended to keep a small supply with them.

Tourist information

Office de Tourisme de Paris, 127 Avenue des Champs Elysées (47 23 61 72). Situated at the Arc de Triomphe end of the avenue, on the south side. The bureau is open daily 09.00–20.00 but during the season its telephone is practically always engaged and personal visits are necessary. Branches are available at main-line stations (not Gare St Lazare) and the Eiffel Tower in summer. 'This Week in Paris', recorded in English, gives up-to-date information 24 hours a day – telephone 47 20 88 98.

Orientation

Paris is divided into twenty administrative areas, known as *arrondissements*, which begin chronologically at the Louvre and then spiral outwards in a clockwise direction. Right Bank (west to east): inner band 1, 2, 3, 4; middle band 8, 9, 10, 11, 12; outer band 16, 17, 18, 19, 20. Left Bank (also west to east): inner band 7, 6, 5; outer band 15, 14, 13.

Numbering of buildings is systematic: it commences at the east end of thoroughfares that run approximately parallel with the Seine and at the river end of thoroughfares that run at angles to the Seine. Odd numbers are always left (in chronological order) and even numbers are always right. Every building, including churches and palaces, fits into the system.

1

Notre Dame, Sainte Chapelle and Conciergerie

The Ile de la Cité (city island), where Paris had its
origins, is fully explored. Notre Dame cathedral and
the Sainte Chapelle, with their brilliant stained glass
are, for many first-time visitors, the most appealing of
the capital's ecclesiastical buildings. The fourteenth-
century Conciergerie retains Marie-Antoinette's
prison cell and, in spite of the recently installed, and
inappropriate, exhibition, evokes more than
anywhere else in Paris the horrific aspects of the
French Revolution. Until the mid-nineteenth
century, much of the medieval appearance of the Ile
de la Cité remained, with more than 100 narrow
streets, picturesque houses and small churches
clustering around the great cathedral and the former
royal palace. Sadly, most were then ruthlessly swept
away by Haussmann's modernization plan, combined
with his wish to open up views of Notre Dame. It has
been estimated that 25,000 residents lost their homes
and now, like the City of London, the Ile de la Cité is
almost uninhabited outside business hours.

Timing: An early start is advisable for there is much
to see, in spite of the small area covered. A bright day
is recommended, as Notre Dame has always suffered
from a lack of natural light. The Musée de Notre
Dame de Paris is open only Sunday, Wednesday and
Saturday afternoons and the Palais de Justice's
judicial courts are closed at weekends.

1

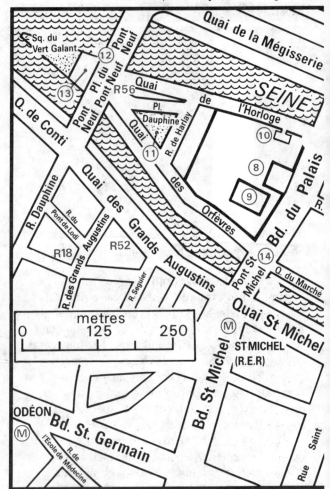

Locations

1 Crypte Archéologique du
  Parvis Notre Dame
2 Place du Parvis Notre Dame
3 Notre Dame
4 Musée de Notre Dame de Paris
5 Rue Chanoinesse
6 Pont Notre Dame

7 Pont au Change
8 Palais de Justice
9 Sainte Chapelle
10 Conciergerie
11 Place Dauphine
12 Pont Neuf
13 Henri IV Statue
14 Pont St Michel

Start *M Cité, line 4 Porte d' Orléans-Porte de Clignancourt. Exit R. First R
Place Louis Lépine. Proceed eastward following, first L, Rue de Lutèce,
which runs south of the square. First R Rue de la Cité. First L Place du
Parvis Notre Dame. Proceed to the centre of its west end; immediately ahead
is the entrance to the Crypte Archéologique.*

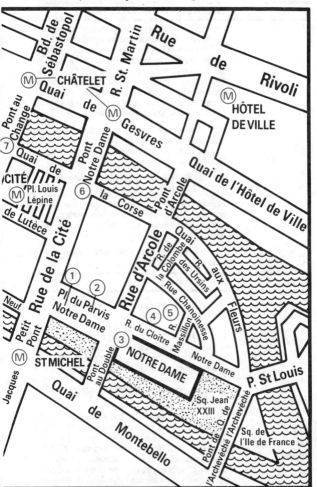

Location 1	**CRYPTE ARCHÉOLOGIQUE DU PARVIS NOTRE DAME**

Place du Parvis
Notre Dame

*Open daily 10.00–18.00 (closes 17.00 October–March)
Admission charge.*

Opened in 1980, the crypt shows evidence of seventeen centuries of development. Lutetia, Roman Paris, evolved on the Ile de la Cité before spreading to the Left Bank.

Foundations of the old Rue Neuve Notre Dame and the 18C Foundlings Hospital of **Boffrand** and **Hardouin-Mansart** have been revealed.

•● *Exit L and proceed to the south-east corner of the Place.*

1

| Location 2 | **PLACE DU PARVIS NOTRE DAME** |

Generally, the most lavish decorative carving on a medieval cathedral was reserved for its west front, and the view of this from the open space which usually fronted the building was known as *paradisus* (heaven on earth) eventually corrupted to *parvis*. Until the demolition of clerical buildings, following the Revolution, and Haussmann's even more comprehensive destruction in 1865, the Place was approximately one-sixth of its present size.

On the south side, a large, bronze monument, made in 1882, commemorates Charlemagne, Roland and Oliver. This occupies part of the site of the medieval Hôtel-Dieu.

Proceed towards the west front of the cathedral.

The Parvis is the official geographical centre of France, and behind the bollards facing the cathedral's portals, a bronze star in the pavement marks the precise central point. All French national highways begin here.

From the bollards (they make useful seats) view the west façade of the cathedral.

| Location 3 | **NOTRE DAME** |

Place du Parvis Notre Dame

The cathedral is open daily 08.00–19.00. Admission free.

Free guided tours in English, July and August daily 10.45, 11.45, 14.30, 15.30, 16.30 and 17.30. (In French throughout the year.) Assemble within the cathedral at the west end of the nave.

Treasury open Monday to Saturday 10.0–18.00, Sunday 14.00–18.00. Admission charge.

Towers and Galerie des Chimières (Gargoyles) open daily 10.00–18.00. Close 17.00 October–March. Admission charge

Binoculars are an advantage as there is much detailing of interest at upper levels.

Notre Dame Cathedral, one of the great masterpieces of Gothic art, dominates the Ile de la Cité, evoking a proud galleon gently sailing down stream. Internally, the building has a stern force that is only partly tempered by its three rose windows, with their vibrant medieval stained glass. It was here that the Gothic style, evolved at St Denis, was first applied to an entire building. Notre Dame remains the most symmetrical in form of the great French cathedrals.

Due to similarities in scale and architectural style, Notre Dame is regarded by many as the 'Westminster Abbey' of Paris. There are, however, major differences that should be borne in mind. Notre Dame was built as a cathedral, not a monastic church. Only rarely has it witnessed coronation ceremonies, most French kings being crowned at Rheims. It was never the royal mausoleum; this was situated at St Denis. Notre Dame was completed structurally during the Gothic period and much original work survives. In contrast, little of the body of Westminster Abbey has escaped alteration or heavy restoration externally. Finally, whereas Westminster's interior is packed with items of great historic or artistic value that can absorb the visitor for many hours, Notre Dame's appeal lies mainly in its unencumbered architectural purity and outstanding rose windows. It is less of a 'museum' than Westminster and will, in consequence, take less time to explore.

History The cathedral was begun in 1163, at the instigation of Bishop Maurice de Sully, as a replacement for two existing cathedrals that stood virtually side by side on the Ile de la Cité. Its architect is unknown. Part of the site of the present Place du Parvis Notre Dame was occupied by the Cathédrale de St Etienne (Stephen), founded by Childebert in the 6C; an earlier Notre Dame stood further east. The latter occupied the position of a Roman temple of Jupiter, a column of which was excavated from beneath the present cathedral's high altar and may now be seen in the Musée de Cluny.

Pope Alexander III laid the foundation stone in 1163 and work began, as usual, with the chancel at the east end. Timbers were obtained from a nearby forest; the Gare de l'Est now stands where its trees grew. Stone was quarried from Vaugirard, Montrouge and the banks of the Bièvre stream. The chancel was ready by 1182, apart from its roof vault, and it was then decided that the cathedral would be consecrated by the Heraclius of Jerusalem, so that east Christendom should also be honoured.

Work immediately began on the transepts, soon to be followed by the nave. By 1208, the cornerstone was laid for the nave's west front and by 1245 its twin towers were completed. It was in 1245 also, that work began on Westminster Abbey; work, however, that was to take not eighty-two but 500 years before a similar stage was reached. Apart from one-bay extensions to the transepts, to bring them in line with the chapels, and the remodelling of the clerestory windows to increase the light, Notre Dame appears today much as its designer intended.

By the reign of Louis XIV, dilapidation of the cathedral had occurred but the greatest damage took place later during the anti-Christian period of the French Revolution. After the fall of Napoléon, the building was even threatened with demolition and it was not until the 'July Monarchy' of 1841 that restoration was put in hand. The work was inspired, partly, by the popularity of Victor Hugo's *Notre Dame de Paris*, first published ten years earlier; excerpts from this book have frequently been filmed under the title *The Hunchback of Notre Dame*. **Viollet-le-Duc**, assisted by **Lassus** and **Boesswillwald**, took twenty-three years to complete his work on the cathedral, during which a *flèche* (short spire), sacristy and much external embellishment, including the famous gargoyles, were added.

Notre Dame has, of course, witnessed many important events. St Louis, on acquiring the 'Crown of Thorns', housed it in the cathedral until the Sainte Chapelle was ready. England's Henry VI, aged ten, was crowned King of both England and France here in 1430. François II married Mary Queen of Scots in 1558. An unusual marriage took place in 1572 between Marguerite de Valois and Henri de Navarre who, because he was a Protestant Huguenot, stood in the cathedral's doorway throughout the ceremony. Charles I of England and Henrietta Maria were married at Notre Dame by proxy in 1625.

During the Revolution, Notre Dame became a 'Temple of Reason' and a ballet dancer, Mademoiselle Maillard, was enthroned as the temple's 'goddess' in 1793. Orgies took place, sculptures were mutilated, and a statue of the Virgin was replaced by one of 'Liberty'. The building was closed to the public in 1795 and used for storage. Napoléon reopened it for worship in 1802, and two years later his coronation took place in the cathedral.

The pope had been invited from Rome for the
ceremony, but Napoléon controversially took the
crown from the pontiff and crowned himself
Emperor, and Joséphine Empress. In 1853,
Napoléon III married Eugénie de Montijo at Notre
Dame.

A Te Deum thanksgiving service for the liberation of
the city followed General de Gaulle's entry into Paris
on 26 August 1944; there was some sniping at the
congregation from Nazi supporters hiding in the
galleries.

More recently, requiem masses have been held in the
cathedral for General de Gaulle, in 1970, and
President Pompidou, in 1974.

Exterior The west front of Notre Dame, apart from
the upper stage of both its towers, was completed by
1230. From ground level upward, it is divided into
five horizontal sections: portals, king's gallery,
windows, grand gallery and towers. Much of the
upper detail can be observed clearly only with
binoculars.

Notre Dame's three west portals are described in
detail when the cathedral is approached more closely.

Buttresses on either side of and between the portals
are embellished, in their niches, with carved figures,
all 19C replacements.

Above the portals runs the **Galerie des Rois** (Kings'
Gallery). The original statues, made *c.*1220, were
damaged at the Revolution and again, in 1871, by the
Communards, as they were believed to represent the
kings of France. In fact, it seems that they were Old
Testament kings, although some early French
monarchs may have been amongst them. Fragments
of many of the originals, discovered in 1977, are
displayed in the Musée de Cluny. The present
twenty-eight kings are all the work of **Viollet-le-Duc**.

Dominating the window stage is the central rose, a
type of window unknown before the Gothic period. It
was constructed with simple, Early-Gothic tracery,
*c.*1220.

Immediately in front of this, a modern Virgin and
Child is flanked by angels.

Figures of Adam and Eve stand in the bays flanking
the rose.

An arcade with ornate tracery, completed in 1250,
fronts the **Grande Galerie.** Its upper stage is
embellished with mythical beasts, the famous
gargoyles of Notre Dame, made in the 19C by **Viollet-
le-Duc.**

It was originally intended that Notre Dame's towers
would be taller and surmounted by needle spires.
However, they remain in the state they had reached
by 1250, the south tower being slightly narrower than
its north counterpart.

•► *Proceed through the gateway in the railings to
approach the west portals.*

Although badly disfigured at the Revolution, the
portals retain some original 13C carving. Most of the
large and easily accessible figures had been 'executed'

or destroyed by the mob, and were restored or, more usually, replaced by **Viollet-le-Duc** in the 19C. It should be remembered that the stonework was formerly gilded, and the figures were painted in vibrant colours.

The most northerly portal L, **Portail de la Vierge** (Virgin) 1210–20, retains the finest original statues.

The large Virgin and Child on the trumeau (central pier) is entirely the 19C work of **Viollet-le-Duc**.

Within the low-level arcades, the bas-reliefs are original but most of the larger figures, in the spandrels, are 19C.

Both doors retain their original, decorative ironwork.

•• *Proceed to the central portal.*

The central portal, **Portail du Jugement Dernier** (Last Judgement), was added 1220–30, following the completion of those on either side. Its subject was a popular theme for west portals, as they were often illuminated by glowing sunsets.

The apex of the tympanum is carved with original figures. Christ in Majesty is attended by an angel holding nails, regarded as a masterpiece of 13C art.

In 1771, the doorways were redesigned by **Soufflot** and the original figure of Christ on the central trumeau column removed; its replacement is by **G. Dechaume**.

At the lower level, the reliefs on both sides are original, although restored in the 18C and 19C. Upper bands illustrate the virtues; below are the vices.

•• *Proceed to the south portal.*

The **Portail de Ste Anne** (St Anne's Portal) was built at the same time as the Portail de la Vierge, 1210–20, but incorporates in its tympanum the oldest carvings in the cathedral; these came from an earlier portal of Notre Dame, made *c.*1165.

Both doors retain their intricately wrought, medieval hinges which, according to legend, were made by Biscornette, a horned devil to whom the ironsmith had sold his soul.

•• *Return from the enclosed forecourt to Place du Parvis Notre Dame R. First R Rue du Cloître Notre Dame. Cross the road to view the cathedral's north façade.*

It should be borne in mind that the surrounding ground has been raised significantly since the cathedral was completed.

The **nave** was built between 1180 and 1208, but remodelled at upper levels when the clerestory windows were extended from 1240 onward. Only the tops of these can be observed externally from here and the change will be more fully described internally.

Originally, the nave was supported by double flying buttresses but these were reduced to single format as part of the 1240 remodelling.

Apart from the extreme west end, chapels occupy

every bay of the cathedral, fitting between the buttresses and forming a continuous wall; they were added to the nave between 1235–50.

All the cathedral's decorative gargoyles are 19C additions by **Viollet-le-Duc**.

•• *Continue eastward.*

The transept (both arms) was built 1182–98. To align with the new wall created by the chapels, its north arm was extended by one bay 1246–*c*.1250 by **Jean de Chelles**. This projects slightly from the chancel's chapels which lie to its east, but not to the same extent as an English transept.

Its **Portail du Cloître** (Cloister) originally led to the canons' cloister, since demolished to form the present street. All the 13C carving, which is exceptional, has survived.

•• *Cross the road to approach the portal.*

Saints, patriarchs, etc. decorate the archivolts.

The lower lintel of the tympanum illustrates scenes from the childhood of Christ.

The portal's central lintel relates the miracle of Theophilus, a 6C deacon, which possibly inspired the Faust legend.

A carved Virgin, considered to be a 13C masterpiece, stands on the central trumeau column.

The tracery of the transept's 13C rose window is more intricate than the west façade's. It is in the High-Gothic style and rests on a range of clerestory windows. Glazing was completed in 1270 and only slight restoration has taken place.

•• *Continue eastward to the chancel.*

Although the **chancel** was built 1163–1182 and marked the commencement of Notre Dame, its chapels were not added until 1296–1330, considerably later than the nave's. They are the work of **Pierre de Chelles** and **Jean Ravy.**

The chancel's flying buttresses were constructed as the chapels were built.

Set in the third bay eastward is the **Porte Rouge** (Red Door), originally reserved for canons of the chapter house, who lived in the maze of narrow streets that once clustered around the north side of Notre Dame.

•• *Cross the road to view its portal.*

This 13C portal, by **Pierre de Montreuil**, is original.

•• *Continue eastward.*

Below the window level of the seven most easterly chapels are panels carved with exceptional 13C reliefs illustrating the Death and the Assumption of the Virgin. The first passed is in the best state of preservation.

Enter the gate R and proceed through Square Jean XXIII, passing the apse.

•• *Continue to the riverside path, turn R and proceed westward to view the south façade.*

This façade is considered to be Notre Dame's finest.

The **flèche**, surmounting the crossing, was designed by **Viollet-le-Duc** in 1859 and constructed of wood encased in lead. It replaced an earlier short spire, destroyed in the 18C.

Protruding from the chancel's south wall is the **sacristy**, built by **Viollet-le-Duc** in 1850. It occupies the site of the archbishop's palace, which was demolished early in the 19C.

The **south transept's** development closely followed that of the north transept; however, its present south façade was built eight years later, in 1258. This was initially designed by **Pierre de Chelles**, but completed by **Montreuil.**

The life of St Stephen is the subject of the transept's **Portail de St Etienne**, a theme that was probably chosen as a reference to the earlier cathedral, dedicated to the saint, which stood on the Ile de la Cité. This portal cannot be approached closely and binoculars are needed to study the detail.

The door retains its 13C ironwork.

● Proceed to the west front and enter the cathedral, usually via the south door (Portail de Ste Anne). Turn L and proceed to the centre of the nave's west end.

Interior At 115 feet, the **nave** of Notre Dame is 12 feet higher than Westminster Abbey's. A congregation of 9,000 can be accommodated, including 1,500 in the galleries. Cleaning in 1987 has revealed a much less gloomy interior than heretofore, but the problem of darkness has never been completely overcome.

Practically all the pillars in Notre Dame are short and rounded, an unusual Gothic feature, which helps to give the cathedral the forbidding strength generally associated with Romanesque buildings.

Their capitals bear little sign of stiff-leaf decoration.

Double aisles encompass the nave and chancel.

*● Proceed to the **inner south aisle's** second bay.*

With a view to increasing the light to the interior, all the nave's medieval glass was replaced in 1756 by clear glass carrying a fleur-de-lys pattern; this was again replaced in the 19C with grisaille (grey pattern) by **Alfred Gerente**, and most of it survives in the chapels and at clerestory level in the most westerly bays on either side.

The nave's glass, in an abstract design, is by **Le Chevalier**, 1964.

*● Proceed to the **outer south aisle's** first chapel.*

Chapelle St Eloi Against the west wall is the poorly lit painting of St Etienne by **Charles Le Brun.** This was presented in 1651 by the Goldsmiths' Company, continuing its tradition of providing the cathedral, each May, with a work of art – a tradition revived in 1949.

● Continue to the next chapel.

Chapelle St François-Xavier The painting of St André, by **Le Brun**, was presented in 1647, also by the Goldsmiths.

1

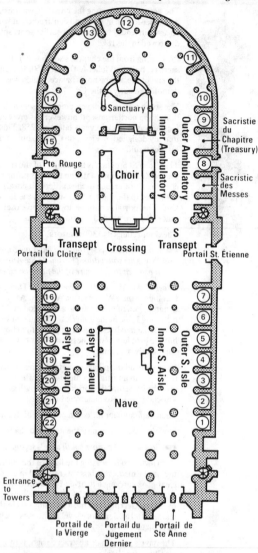

1. Ch. St Eloi
2. Ch. St Francois Xavier
3. Ch. Ste. Geneviève
4. Ch. St. Joseph
5. Ch. St. Pierre
6. Ch. Ste. Anne
7. Ch. d Sacré Coeur
8. Ch. St. Denis
9. Ch. Ste. Madeleine
10. Ch. St. Guillaume
11. Ch. St. Georges
12. Ch. N-D des Sept Doleurs
13. Ch. St. Marcel
14. Ch. St. Louis
15. Ch. St. Ferdinand
16. Ch. St. Clotilde
17. Ch. St. Landry
18. Ch. N-D de Guadeloupe
19. Ch. St. Vincent de Paul
20. Ch. St. Enfance
21. Ch. St. Charles
22. Ch. des Fonts Baptismaux

●● *Proceed past the next two chapels to the fifth chapel from the west.*

Chapelle St Pierre This chapel was originally dedicated to St Thomas of Canterbury (Thomas à Becket). The 16C timber wainscot, carved with figures, was fitted in 1865.

●● *Continue to the next chapel.*

Chapelle Ste Anne A grisaille window was replaced by the present design in 1869.

●● *Continue to the south side of the crossing and proceed to its west pier.*

Attached to this pier, facing south, a tablet commemorates the one million subjects of the British Empire killed in the First World War; most perished on French battlefields.

●● *Proceed to the centre of the **crossing**.*

Upper-level alterations by **Viollet-le-Duc** to the walls encompassing the crossing demonstrate the change made in the 13C to the cathedral's clerestory windows. Like the other Early-Gothic cathedrals of the Ile de France, Notre Dame's walls originally comprised four horizontal elements. Later, to increase light, each small clerestory window was combined with the rosette window below it, thus reducing the four elements to three, the hallmark of the High-Gothic style.

In the 19C, **Viollet-le-Duc** restored the original Early-Gothic design to the most easterly north and south bays of the nave, the most westerly north and south bays of the chancel and the side walls of both transepts.

The crossing had been vaulted by 1267 and, due to **Viollet-le-Duc**'s restoration of the walls, it now appears very much as it did at that time.

Best viewed from here is the north transept's great rose window. The north window, by tradition a gift from St Louis, retains almost eighty per cent of its original glass; it has been recently cleaned and the resulting lighter and brighter, but less sumptuous, colours were a surprise to most. The Virgin, in the centre, is surrounded by Old Testament prophets and kings.

Immediately below the rose is a delicately capricious arcade of clerestory windows. This combination, repeated in many other cathedrals, appears to have been adopted for the first time at Notre Dame.

The **north transept**'s present north wall was not designed until 1246 when it was moved back one bay. This was almost a century after work on the cathedral had begun and, like the south transept's south wall, its appearance is less austere than the rest of the building's.

The **south transept** was vaulted by 1198. Its present south wall, completed by 1258, has a format similar to that of the north transept.

The rose window depicts Christ surrounded by New Testament saints and angels.

●● *Proceed to the crossing's south-east pier.*

A 14C Virgin and Child statue stands against this pier facing west. It was brought from St Aignan, a Romanesque chapel, part of which survives north of Notre Dame in the Rue des Ursins. This statue is notably less stylized than 13C examples in the cathedral.

A slab in the outer aisle's floor L, just before the steps to the south ambulatory, commemorates the conversion to Christianity of the 19C French poet Paul Claudel, 25 December 1886.

•● *Ascend the steps to the south ambulatory and turn immediately L.*

Originally, a high stone screen by **De Chelles** and **Ravy**, completed in 1351, surrounded the entire chancel; as part of the 18C alterations by **Robert de Cotte**, more than half of it was demolished, together with the rood screen; the remainder was cut down. Only the cut-down sections, screening the first three north and south bays of the chancel, survive; they were restored and redecorated by **Viollet-le-Duc** in the 19C.

A door in the second chapel from the transept R leads to the **Sacristie des Messes** (mass vestry), a 19C addition by **Viollet-le-Duc.**

•● *Proceed to the next chapel.*

Chapelle St Denis accommodates the monument to Bishop Alfa, one of several Bishops of Paris from the 18C and 19C to be commemorated in the ambulatory chapels; all are buried in the crypt.

Murals were designed by **Viollet-le-Duc.**

•● *Proceed to the next bay, which fronts the entrance to the* **Treasury** *in the Sacristie du Chapitre.*

Chiefly appealing to those with specialized interests, religious books, vestments and reliquaries are displayed.

•● *Exit and return to the chancel's outer south aisle.*

Immediately ahead, facing the treasury's doorway, are the chancel's gates; these form part of the gilded iron screen that replaced most of its stone predecessor in the early 18C.

•● *Enter the* **chancel** *through this gate and proceed to the centre.*

Best seen from this point is the organ in the west gallery, the largest in France. Although first made in 1753 and enlarged in 1960 it is mostly the work of **Cavaillée-Col**, 1868.

Above it, the west rose window, which the organ partly hides, retains much of its 13C glass; choir stalls were carved with reliefs illustrating the life of Christ by **Jules Degoullons** in 1715. Seventy-eight of the original 114 survive.

Canopied stalls at the west end were reserved for bishops.

•● *Proceed to the* **sanctuary**.

In 1638, Louis XIII dedicated France to the Virgin. The King had been married twenty-three years but was still childless and vowed that the chancel would be redecorated in honour of the Virgin if offspring materialized. The future Louis XIV was born and he later fulfilled his father's vow, commissioning **Robert de Cotte** to reorganize the east end of the chancel, 1708–25. Surviving from this work are the choir stalls already described and the group of figures in the sanctuary: a pietà, figures of angels and the two kings.

Marble, added to the columns, was removed in the 19C.

The six bronze angels against the pillars were made in 1713 and remained in the cathedral throughout the Revolution, miraculously undamaged.

Louis XIV's kneeling figure L is by **Coysevox**, 1715.

Behind this stands the marble pietà *The Vow of Louis XIII*, by **N. Coustou**, with a gilded base by **Girardon**, 1723.

The statue of Louis XIII R is by **G. Coustou**.

•● *Return to the* **south ambulatory** *and continue eastward to the second chapel R.*

Chapelle St Guillaume The 18C 'Visitation' painting on the west wall is by **Jean Jouvenet**.

Against the south wall are much-restored kneeling figures from the monument to Jean Juvenal des Ursins, d.1431, and his wife.

The Comte d'Harcourt, d.1769, lies in this chapel; his fanciful tomb against the east wall was designed by **Pigalle.**

•● *Proceed to the east end of the cathedral.*

Immediately behind the pietà in the sanctuary is the tomb statue of Bishop Matiffas de Bucy, d.1304.

•● *Continue around the apse.*

The north side of the cut-down stone screen L illustrates scenes from the early life of Christ. Two small, toppling figures, at the end of the second group, refer to the apocryphal tale that pagan statues fell as the Holy Family fled to Egypt.

•● *Proceed to the crossing's north-east pier.*

Against this pier, facing west, is the 18C statue of St Denis, by **N. Coustou.**

•● *Continue westward to the last chapel.*

Chapelle des Fonts Baptismaux (baptistery) This contains the Font of Bachelet, designed in the 19C by **Viollet-le-Duc.**

•● *Exit from the cathedral R. First R Rue du Cloître Notre Dame. Immediately R is the entrance to the north side of the north tower, from where the ascent to the Galerie des Chimières (gargoyles) and the summit of the south tower is made.*

Towers There is no lift, and 238 steps must be climbed to the **Galerie des Chimières**. It is possible, however, to halt in a room half-way up, where displays illustrate the cathedral's history. A further 141 steps lead to the summit of the south tower, from which superb views of central Paris are gained.

On reaching the gallery, the visitor is immediately

confronted with the cathedral's best-known gargoyles, the 19C work of **Viollet-le-Duc**; they no longer dispose of rainwater, which is now drained by more effective methods.

From the gallery, in the Place du Parvis Notre Dame below, may be seen, marked by cobbles, the outline of the 6C Cathédrale de St Etienne.

•● *Proceed to the north side of the south tower to view the 'Emmanuel' bell. Await the guide at the door (admission free).*

Notre Dame's great bell, Bourdon de Notre Dame or 'Emmanuel', was the only example in the cathedral to escape melting down at the Revolution. It is one of the world's largest, weighing 12½ tons; the clapper alone weighs almost half a ton. The bell was recast in bronze in 1683 and, allegedly, women threw in gold and silver rings during the casting, which is supposed to give the bell its pure tone. Emmanuel tolls only at Easter and on other solemn occasions, hardly surprisingly as eight men are needed to operate it.

•● *Ascend further steps to the summit of the south tower.*

From here, due to the cathedral's central, island situation and because the tower is not too high, the finest, intimate views of Paris may be gained.

•● *Descend and exit for the north tower R.*

Location 4	**MUSÉE DE NOTRE DAME DE PARIS**

10 Rue du Cloître Notre Dame

Open Sunday, Wednesday and Saturday 14.30– 18.00. Admission charge.

Objects dating back to the Gallo-Roman period, discovered during excavation of the Place du Parvis Notre Dame, are displayed.

Notre Dame's 17C wooden *jubé* (rood screen), presented by Anne of Austria, is exhibited.

•● *Exit L. First L Rue Massillon. L Rue Chanoinesse.*

Location 5	**RUE CHANOINESSE**

It was in this street, by tradition on the site of the present No 10, that Abélard stayed in 1118 when he was teaching Héloïse, the niece of Canon Fulbert. Their passionate romance led to Héloïse's pregnancy, her child being delivered in the convent to which she had been sent.

Until the Revolution, the houses of Notre Dame's canons lined Rue Chanoinesse, their gardens stretching to the quay bordering the Seine. Now, only **Nos 22** and **24**, both 16C, remain. **No 24** is a restaurant, **La Lieutenance**, but its picturesque interior has been preserved (reservations: 43 54 91 36).

•● *First R Rue de la Colombe.*

Beside No 4, La Colombe restaurant, are traces of the **Gallo-Roman wall** of Lutetia.

•● *First R Rue des Ursins.*

Rue des Ursins, built as the first Paris quay, was originally named Port St Landry. Its present level matches the earlier level of the Seine.

•● *Return to Rue de la Colombe R. L Quai aux*

Fleurs. Continue ahead to Quai de Corse and Pont Notre Dame (first R).

| Location 6 | **PONT NOTRE DAME** *1913* |

This modern bridge stands in the same position as the 'greater' bridge of Roman Lutetia; the 'lesser' bridge had connected the south side of the Ile de la Cité with the Left Bank. Burnt down by the Vikings, the Pont Notre Dame was rebuilt in 1413 and became the first bridge in Paris to be given a name. It was also the first thoroughfare in Paris where the buildings were numbered.

•● *Continue westward, following Quai de Corse. First R Pont au Change. Proceed to the centre of the bridge.*

| Location 7 | **PONT AU CHANGE** *1859* |

Charles the Bald established the earliest 'money changers' bridge' in the 9C. Throughout the Middle Ages moneylenders and jewellers operated from stalls erected on it; nowhere else in Paris were foreigners permitted to convert their money into French currency.

The present structure replaced a stone bridge erected in 1639.

•● *Remain on the bridge to view the north side of the Palais de Justice.*

| Location 8 | **PALAIS DE JUSTICE** |

2 Boulevard du Palais

Open Monday–Friday 09.00–17.00. Admission free.

The history of the Palais de Justice, which until the Revolution was known as the Palais de la Cité, is analogous to that of London's Palace of Westminster. Both began as the principal royal residence, sections were later set aside for parliament and law courts, and eventually the sovereign moved elsewhere. In Paris, however, the lawyers stayed and parliament left, whereas in London the opposite occurred.

Although the medieval Sainte Chapelle and Conciergerie are part of the complex, they are more easily comprehended as separate locations and are, therefore, dealt with in that way.

The Palais de Justice serves as the Paris Law Courts and both civil and criminal cases are tried here. With the exception of the late-18C Cour du Mai, parts of the medieval towers and, of course, the Sainte Chapelle and Conciergerie, the present buildings that make up this vast complex were erected between the mid-19C and 1914.

History At the earliest stages in its development, Paris was administered from here, the western sector of the Ile de la Cité; it is known, for example, that the Roman governor's residence was sited on the north side of where the Palais now stands.

In 987, Hugues Capot, the first Capetian, adapted an existing fortress as his residence and, a century later, Louis VI fortified the Palais de la Cité, building a *donjon* (free-standing tower) in the central courtyard. This later became known as the Tour Montgomery and served as the first prison of the palace.

In addition to adding the Sainte Chapelle, St Louis

rebuilt much of the rest of the complex in the 13C and allocated space to parlement.

Charles VII added to St Louis's building, but a new royal palace, the most magnificent seen in France and later to be known as the Conciergerie, was constructed early in the 14C for Philippe le Bel and extended *c.*1353 by Jean le Bon.

François I, the last king to stay in the Palais de la Cité, presented the entire complex to parlement in the 16C.

In 1788, parlement unwisely insisted that the Estates General should be convened; this was done and proved to be a major step towards revolution as, ungratefully, its General Assembly suppressed parlement and, later, even more ungratefully, guillotined its members. The French legal system was then radically altered, the government moved to the Right Bank, and the Palais de la Cité was renamed the Palais de Justice.

Disastrous fires in the 17C and 18C, culminating in the Communard incendiary of 1871, have meant that most of the present complex is relatively modern.

Exterior Viewed from the Pont au Change, the north side of the Palais de Justice, which stretches westward along the Seine, possesses the most interesting exteriors, dominated by rounded, partly medieval towers with conical roofs. Between the towers, however, all the façades are 19C. Elements are described from west to east (R to L).

With its rounded pediment, the **Cour de Cassation**, the most westerly part of the complex, is a Renaissance-style extension, completed by **Duc** and **Daumet** in 1868.

Built by Louis IX, the white **Tour Bonbec** was originally called the Tour St Louis. It gained its present name when prisoners, who were tortured within its walls for information, dissolved into *bonbecs* (babblers). Later, the tower served as a waiting area for those about to be transported to the guillotine. Between January 1793 and July 1794 more than 2,700 prisoners left this tower, via the Conciergerie, for execution.

Lower parts of its fabric are original, but the crenellated upper section is 19C. Recent cleaning has revealed the exceptionally white stonework.

From here eastward stretched the great Conciergerie palace, the original ground floor of which survives, but now at basement level.

Above, the façade is built in 19C Gothic Revival style.

The twin towers, that flank what was the main entrance to the palace, were originally approached by the 9C bridge of Charles the Bald. When built, they both appeared taller than now, as their lower sections, which extend downward to river level, have since been concealed by the construction of the quay; some rooms, originally built on the ground floor, are now 20 feet below street level.

The more westerly of these towers, the **Tour d'Argent**, built early in the 14C by Philippe le Bel, is partly original. *Argent* (silver) refers to its use as a royal treasury. Damiens was imprisoned in this tower in 1757 for his attempted assassination of Louis XV. During the Revolution, the Public Prosecutor Fouquier-Tinville had offices in both towers.

Built as the Tour d'Argent's twin, by Philippe le Bel, the **Tour de César** has a similar history and is, again, partly original. This tower stands on the site of the Roman governor of Lutetia's residence, where visiting emperors were accommodated, hence its name.

The 19C façade between the twin towers and the Tour de l'Horloge on the north-east corner, was built in 14C style, probably by **Marguy.**

Jean le Bon added the square Tour de l'Horloge (clock tower) to the Conciergerie *c.*1353 but it was rebuilt in the 19C.

●● *Return southward from the bridge to view the east façade of this tower from Boulevard du Palais.*

Beneath the clock face, the Latin inscription reads: 'This clock which divides the day into twelve equal parts is a lesson that justice must be protected and the law defended.'

The Tour de l'Horloge houses the world's first public clock, given by Charles V in 1370. Its face is a mid-19C replica of the original, made by **Germain Pilon** for Henri III in 1585. The clock's mechanism has been restored three times; its first bell of solid silver was melted down at the Revolution.

●● *Continue southward along Boulevard du Palais, passing the building's mid-19C east façade. Immediately R are the gates to the* **Cour du Mai***.*

Formerly, in this courtyard, the lawyers' clerks erected a maypole on 1 May in the form of a tree from one of the royal forests, hence its name.

The three wings of the Cour du Mai, the main entrance to the Palais de Justice, were built in 1781–3, following the fire of 1776, by **Desmaisons** and **Jacques Antoine**.

Contemporary with them are the gilded wrought-iron gates and railings, restored in 1877.

Facing west, the courtyard's main façade fronts the Galerie Marchande; its balustrade level sculptures are by **Pajou.**

From the small yard in the north-west corner R, now the Buffet du Palais restaurant, prisoners were led to the tumbrils, watched by the *tricoteuses* (knitting women) sitting on the steps. During the Revolution direct access to the Conciergerie could be gained only from here.

The south wing of the Cour du Mai L, which on its south side adjoins the Sainte Chapelle, was an addition that deprived the chapel of its former situation in the centre of one large open area formed by the Cour de la Sainte Chapelle and the **Cour du Mai**.

●● *Enter the courtyard via the archway R of the gates, ascend the steps and enter the Palais.*

Apart from the Conciergerie, which is a museum, and the Sainte Chapelle, which is also primarily a museum but also an occasional concert hall, the Palais de Justice is entirely given over to the administration of civil and criminal law. Visitors may wander along the corridors and enter most of the courts at will (except the juvenile court). However, little pre-dates the 19C and most visitors find that the area occupying the position of the first floor of the Conciergerie is of greatest interest, even though it was rebuilt after the Communard fire.

Immediately entered is the **Galerie Marchande** (merchant's gallery), once the royal passageway between the palace and the Sainte Chapelle, but rebuilt in the 18C. Until the Revolution, merchants were permitted to sell their wares here.

•• *Turn R and proceed ahead to the Salle des Pas-Perdus.*

The **Salle des Pas-Perdus** occupies the position of the Conciergerie's 14C Great Hall. Rebuilt in 1618, the present chamber is the work of **Duc** and **Dumont**. Plaintiffs and lawyers who, unlike their English counterparts, are no longer bewigged, throng the chamber, which Balzac dubbed 'a cathedral of chicanery'.

Divided by columns into two equal aisles, it is one of the world's largest rooms, retaining the original dimensions of 240 feet by 90 feet.

Immediately beneath lies the ancient Salle des Gens d'Armes of the Conciergerie, seen later.

Against the south wall, R of the entrance, is the anonymous monument to Malesherbes by **J. Dumont**. Malesherbes defended Louis XVI at his trial and was guillotined for his pains in 1794.

Against the opposite wall, at its west end, is the monument to a barrister, Berryer, d.1868, by **Chapie**; the tortoise, mischievously placed beneath the foot of the figure R, alludes to the slowness of legal proceedings.

The **Première Chambre Civile**, reached from the north-west corner, occupies the position of one of the most historic rooms in France. It was originally constructed in the 13C as the private apartment of St Louis, but was also twice rebuilt following fires. In the 17C this was the Grande Chambre or Chambre Doré (gilded) of parlement where Louis XIV entered, booted, spurred and brandishing a whip, to proclaim '*L'Etat c'est moi*' (I am the state). At the Revolution, the chamber became the Salle de la Liberté and the Tribunal sat there, presided over by Fouquier-Tinville. More than 2,700 victims of the Reign of Terror were condemned to death in the chamber, including Marie-Antoinette.

•• *Return through the Salle des Pas-Perdus towards the Galerie Marchande but turn immediately L. Continue ahead to the Escalier Louis XVI.*

This stairway was built for Louis XVI by **Antoine**. Names of old newspaper shops that once stood here are inscribed on the side walls of its central landing.

•• *At the foot of the stairs turn R to the Cour du Mai*

and proceed through the arches ahead to the south-east corner of the Sainte Chapelle's courtyard.

Location 9 | **SAINTE CHAPELLE** *1248*

4 Boulevard du
Palais

*Open April–
September 09.30–
18.30; October–
March 10.00–17.00.
Admission charge.
A combined ticket
admits to the Sainte
Chapelle and the
Conciergerie at a
reduced price.
(Better purchased at
the Conciergerie in
high season when
queues there are
shorter.)*

Many visitors find that the brilliant medieval stained glass of the Sainte Chapelle provides one of their most memorable experiences in Paris. However, the chapel has long lost its *raison d'être*, the altar and organ have been removed, and a sense of emptiness permeates what is, after Notre Dame, the city's most important Gothic building. Evening concerts are regularly held and the stained-glass windows are then floodlit from without – a magical sight.

History The Sainte Chapelle was commissioned by St Louis (Louis IX), partly to serve as a Chapel Royal to his palace that then surrounded it. Primarily, however, it was designed to accommodate the holy relics that he had recently purchased and which were at St Denis waiting for a permanent home. St Louis obtained the 'Crown of Thorns' from Venetian merchants in 1239, by repaying a huge debt owed them by Baudouin, a French nobleman who had become Emperor of Byzantium; Baudouin had given the merchants the relic as surety. Louis bought further 'relics of the Passion' in 1241, including what were purported to be fragments of the True Cross, a nail from the Crucifixion and drops of Christ's blood. The amount paid for these relics was two and a half times the total cost of the Sainte Chapelle. Embarrassingly for the King, another 'genuine' Crown of Thorns came on the market shortly after his purchase; however, plans went ahead for what was to become the most extravagant display pavilion of all time.

It was believed for many years that **Pierre de Montreuil** had been the architect, but recently, stylistic affinities between the Sainte Chapelle and Amiens Cathedral have led experts to suggest that an architect closely connected with Amiens was more likely to have been responsible. In any event, the chapel was built at great speed, taking less than three years to complete.

When consecrated, in 1248, it stood in the centre of the main courtyard of the palace and was linked, at upper level, with the west range of the king's private apartments. Renovations and alterations were made by Charles VIII in 1485.

The Sainte Chapelle survived the palace fire of 1776 but parliament soon added a south wing to the Cour du Mai, against the chapel's north side, thus obscuring this façade from view; a 13C vestry was demolished in the process and the chapel was then used as a storehouse for flour.

During the Revolution, the Sainte Chapelle narrowly escaped demolition. In 1803, it was adapted to house legal archives, resulting in some internal damage which, however, was made good in the mid-19C. The Sainte Chapelle was once more surrounded by blazing buildings in 1871 but survived the conflagration, rescuers arriving before the oil, with which the Communards had soaked the chapel, could be set alight.

England's Richard II was betrothed to Isabel of France in the chapel in 1396.

Although the Sainte Chapelle now serves primarily as a museum and concert hall, one Mass is held each year in May, to celebrate the feast day of St Yves, the patron saint of lawyers: admission by invitation only.

Due to its great height for the area covered, the Sainte Chapelle immediately indicates an unusual purpose. Its lower floor (up to cornice level) was built as a subsidiary chapel for servants of the royal household.

The Haute Chapelle (upper chapel) was the first building to appear to be constructed practically entirely of glass; each of its great windows is almost 50 feet high.

Slender buttresses, ending in finials, support the roof.

• Proceed westward following the south façade.

Protruding from the south wall at its east end is the oratory added by Louis XI in the 14C and dedicated to St Louis.

• Proceed to the south-west corner of the courtyard.

The 15C-style *flèche* was rebuilt of lead-clad wood by **Lassus** in 1854, the third restoration of this feature.

From here can be seen the back of the lead angel which surmounts the apex of the roof at its east end. It was at one time slowly turned by clockwork so that the cross would face all points of the compass.

• Proceed to the west façade.

Charles VIII replaced an existing window with the present Flamboyant rose window *c.*1485.

He also added the upper parts of the two flanking towers, which had been built to accommodate spiral stairways linking the two chapels.

The upper part of the open, two-storey porch is a 19C reconstruction. From its predecessor, a gallery linked the chapel with the private apartments of St Louis on the north side, thus serving as the entrance for the royal family.

Apart from the king, visitors originally approached the upper chapel by an external staircase.

*• Enter the Sainte Chapelle's **lower chapel** from the west front.*

Columns, set out into the room creating narrow aisles, are connected by braces to the wall and support the building, the vault of which is non-load-bearing.

Canons' tombstones, many from the 14C and 15C, form the pavement.

A blind arcade encompasses the area.

This chapel was always painted, but the present 19C work of **Emile Boeswillwald** bears little relationship to the original. There has for long been a movement, so far resisted, to remove completely this garish decoration from both chapels.

*• Ascend either of the spiral staircases to the upper chapel (**Haute Chapelle**).*

Exhilaration, comparable to that experienced on entering Michelangelo's Sistine Chapel, immediately overwhelms the visitor; it is as if one were breaking into a jewelled casket. This upper chapel is the actual Sainte Chapelle and was reserved for the royal family and the most prominent members of the Court.

Its stained glass (excluding the later rose window), made 1245–48 and the oldest to survive in Paris, forms an illustrated bible; 720 of its 1,134 scenes are original.

Bookcases, fitted around the chapel in 1803 to accommodate legal files, damaged some of the lower panes of glass. Their hard-to-distinguish replacements were made by **Lassus** from designs by **Steinheil** during the course of the chapel's restoration under the direction of **Viollet-le-Duc** from 1841–67. The scenes are ranged clockwise from the north-west, most commencing at the bottom of each lancet and 'reading' from left to right upward. The subject matter of each is known, although few visitors will be able to decipher many of them; it is the overall effect that matters. The long sides of the chapel illustrate the Old Testament but end at the first window R on the south side, with scenes related to St Louis acquiring the relics. He is shown receiving them at Sens barefoot, accompanied by his consort and mother.

The windows of the apse, all of which 'read' in lancet order, illustrate New Testament scenes, including the Crucifixion.

As in the lower chapel, the arcades have been garishly redecorated by **Boeswillwald.**

The roof is supported by a cross-rib vault.

Statues of the apostles, each holding one of the chapel's consecration crosses, stand against twelve of the pillars. On the north side, those against columns four, five and six from the west and on the south side, those against columns three, four and five from the west are original: the other six are copies based on the badly damaged originals now in the Musée de Cluny.

In the third bay from the west on the north side, the small niche beneath the windows provided seating for the king and the royal family.

A door in the next bay on the south side leads to the late-14C oratory built by Louis XI. The king was able to watch Mass, unobserved, through the angled grille west of the door.

The west rose window, presented by Charles VIII in 1485, is best viewed from the east end of the chapel; eighty-six panes illustrate the Apocalypse. Its prevailing lemon colour is in strong contrast with the deeper hues of the side windows.

The reliquary stood in the centre of the rostrum at the chapel's east end. Although most of the rostrum was restored in the 19C, some original parts remain. The steps to it L are the originals that the king ascended to approach the reliquary, the key to which only he possessed.

The canopied and bejewelled reliquary was melted

down and its jewels sold at the Revolution. Some of the relics were, however, spared and transferred initially to St Denis and later Notre Dame, where they are now kept. The Crown of Thorns is publicly displayed in Notre Dame cathedral on Good Friday, thus continuing the tradition, begun by St Louis, of revealing the relics to the royal household assembled in the Sainte Chapelle on that day.

● Exit and return to the Boulevard du Palais L. First L Quai de l'Horloge. The first entrance L leads to the Cour de l'Horloge from which, in the north-west corner, the Conciergerie is entered.

Location 10	**CONCIERGERIE** *1313*

1 Quai de l'Horloge

Open June–August 09.30–18.30. April, May, September 09.30–18.00. October–March 10.00–16.30. Admission charge. A combined ticket admits to the Conciergerie and Sainte Chapelle at a reduced price.

All that survives of the great 14C Conciergerie palace, the most remarkable civil architecture in France from the Middle Ages, is its ground floor; the upper floor, twice rebuilt after fires, is now incorporated in the law courts of the Palais de Justice. Marie Antoinette was one of many imprisoned here in the Revolution and her cell may be visited.

History Philippe le Bel added the Conciergerie to the Palais de la Cité complex, 1301–13, incorporating the 13C apartment of St Louis. With its two great rooms, the Salle des Gens d'Armes (Gentlemen at arms) on the ground floor, and the Grande Salle (Great Hall) immediately above, the palace, when built, was acclaimed as the most beautiful building ever seen in France.

The Tour de l'Horloge, guardroom and kitchens were added by Jean le Bon *c.*1353 and the building remained little altered until the fire of 1618 destroyed its upper floor.

Charles V vacated the Palais de la Cité for the Louvre in 1358 and the building then fell under the jurisdiction of a high-ranking official known as the Concierge; this is why the palace became known as the Conciergerie. The entire ground floor was adapted to serve as a state prison *c.*1400.

Charles VII presented the Palais de la Cité complex, including the Conciergerie, to parlement and the lawyers in 1431.

Today, the Conciergerie is a museum and, in spite of its unfortunate new exhibition, evokes more than anywhere else in France 'the Terror' of the years 1793–4, as it was here that the accused were held captive awaiting trial, followed quickly, in most cases, by a humiliating journey in the tumbril to the guillotine. More than half the area is closed to the public.

Interior The present Gothic style entrance to the Conciergerie from the Cour de l'Horloge is modern; at the time of the Revolution the only direct access was from the Cour du Mai. Immediately entered is the **Salle des Gardes**, added for Jean le Bon, *c.*1357 .

Like the remainder of the Conciergerie that is open to visitors, this was built at ground level but now lies 23 feet below the quai, which was constructed in 1611.

A copper band on the pier L, facing the steps, indicates the flood level of 28 January 1910.

Much restoration took place in 1868, but most of the cross-rib vault and decorative capitals to the columns are original mid-14C work.

● *Proceed through the pay barrier to the **Salle des Gens d'Armes** L.*

This chamber became, in effect, the original 'Salle des Pas-Perdus' (lost steps) as prisoners passed through here to the Cour du Mai and their subsequent execution. When built, however, it served as a refectory for the servants of the Court.

Columns, which divide the area of almost 20,000 square feet into aisles, retain their original, early-14C leaf capitals.

● *Proceed beneath the stairs to the **old kitchens**.*

Added by Jean le Bon *c.*1353, but known as the Cuisines St Louis, the kitchens adjoin the Tour de l'Horloge. Up to 3,000 diners, including the royal family, could be catered for.

The cross-rib vault is original.

Four original fireplaces, with separate chimneys, survive in the corners of the kitchen; each had a different function.

● *Return to the entrance to the Salle des Gens d'Armes. Turn L and follow the short **Rue de Paris**.*

This passageway, separated from the Salle des Gens d'Armes by a grille, led to the quarters of the executioner, 'Monsieur de Paris', and thus gained its nickname.

● *Follow the passage to the **Galerie des Prisonniers**.*

The new French Revolution exhibition occupies much of the remaining area. Although of interest, it destroys authenticity in a similar way to the Armouries Museum in the Tower of London.

● *Turn L and proceed to the **prison cell** L.*

It is believed that this is where prisoners about to be guillotined were given their last toilet by the executioner or his son. They were sat on a stool and with collars undone and hands tied behind their backs, the hair was shaved from the napes of their necks; they were then led through a wicket gate in what is now the Conciergerie's restaurant to the registry office (since demolished), and the waiting tumbrils in the Cour du Mai.

From the windows opposite can be seen a courtyard that is entered from the gallery. This was the **Cour des Femmes** where female prisoners exercised. A single tree and moss now grow in this forlorn spot, where Charlotte Corday, assassin of Marat, and Madame Roland took their last walks.

In the corner, separated by a railing, is 'the place of twelve', where the twelve selected for guillotining that day were permitted to say their last farewells.

All the buildings above the lower cornice level of the courtyard are late 19C.

● *Return to the Galerie des Prisonniers and turn L.*

The wall ahead blocks what was the men's exercise yard during the Revolution.

Behind this stood the Parloir (Council Room) to which prisoners were brought from the Tour Bonbec via its spiral staircase.

•● Pass through the low doorway L. Immediately L is Marie-Antoinette's cell.

Marie-Antoinette had been widowed six months, following the guillotining of Louis XVI, when she was brought to this cell from the Tour du Temple, where the royal family had been incarcerated. Five judges and fifteen jurors officiated at her two-day trial. The deposed Queen, who was Austrian by birth, was found guilty of offering to assist the enemies of France, i.e. the Austrian army, which was then only ten days' march from Paris. Marie-Antoinette, 'the widow Capet', was only thirty-eight, but her red hair had gone grey almost overnight, and a contemporary sketch of her on the tumbril, head shorn for execution, presents a pitiful sight.

This cell has now been fitted as a small chapel and a plaque above the altar, commemorating Marie-Antoinette and Louis XVI, was erected by Louis XVIII.

Another cell R is now linked with Marie-Antoinette's; allegedly it was occupied by Danton, and later Robespierre. Each year a wreath is laid here by members of the Robespierre Society, who believe that the Revolutionary leader has been blamed unjustly for 'the Terror'.

*•● Continue ahead to the **Chapelle des Girondins**.*

This chapel became a prison when twenty-two of the moderate Girondins were brought here in 1793.

•● Exit and return to Quai de l'Horloge L. First L Rue de Harlay. R Place Dauphine.

Immediately L is the **west façade** of the Palais de Justice, built 1857–68.

Location 11	**PLACE DAUPHINE**

Contemporary with the Place des Vosges, the triangular Place Dauphine was begun in 1607. Although most of the façades have been rebuilt or much altered, a few original houses of rose brick with stone trims, typical of the Henry IV period, survive.

The east range of houses was demolished in 1874 to facilitate the building of the west façade of the Palais de Justice.

No 14, on the north side, is the least-altered surviving house.

On the south side, **No 25**, the **Hotel Henri IV**, is the only hotel on the Ile de la Cité. One of the capital's cheapest, it is almost always full. However, its facilities at the time of writing were certainly basic.

•● Exit from the west end of the Place R. Continue northward to Pont Neuf, which crosses both arms of the Seine.

Location 12	**PONT NEUF** *1578–1607*

Paris has more than thirty bridges and the Pont Neuf (new bridge) is the oldest of them to have survived. Planned by **Baptiste du Cerceau** in 1578, the bridge, which crosses the Seine at its widest point in Paris, took twenty-nine years to complete. A grief-stricken Henri III laid its foundation stone in 1578 (on the day that his favourite 'mignon', Quélus, died of wounds received in a duel a month earlier). It was said, therefore, that the bridge should be named, more appropriately, the Pont des Pleurs (Bridge of Tears). Work was suspended for many years but the next monarch, Henri IV, insisted on its completion, crossing the bridge when the piers were connected only by wooden planks. Warned that some workers had recently fallen and drowned, Henri proudly retorted, 'But they weren't kings.' Prior to the Pont Neuf's construction, all the bridges in the capital had been lined with houses and shops, but Henri IV insisted that this one should have no superstructures. Also, and again to the King's specification, it was the first Paris thoroughfare to be provided with raised pavements for pedestrians.

The Pont Neuf was opened by Henri IV in 1607 and immediately became the liveliest and most popular promenade in the city.

Although much restored, the basic 16C structure with its medieval-style outline survives; the detailing has always been Classical.

There are twelve arches, each one is decorated with a grotesque head. They are best observed from the areas around the central Henri IV statue.

Traders' stalls were originally fitted into the semi-circular projections and when they were removed in 1854 much of the bridge's animation came to an end.

•• *Proceed to the Place du Pont Neuf in the centre of the bridge.*

Location 13	**HENRY IV STATUE** *Lemot 1818*

Place du Pont Neuf

Between the two sections of the bridge, in Place du Pont Neuf, stands the bronze equestrian statue of Henri IV. An earlier statue, of which this is a copy, had been erected here by the king's son, Louis XIII, in 1635 and Parisians took their complaints to its base following the death of the Grand Dauphin. However, in 1792 it was melted down for cannon.

The present 19C replacement was cast from the bronze of other statues including that of Napoléon from the Place Vendôme column.

Approached by descending steps behind the statue is the **Square du Vert Galant**, where the Vedettes du Pont Neuf embark for river trips. *Vert Galant* (old roué) refers to Henri IV's fondness for the opposite sex. The square is a peaceful haven with grass, trees and seats – ideal for lunchtime picnics in fine weather.

•• *From the south-east corner of Place du Pont Neuf follow Quai des Orfèvres eastward.*

In the 17C and 18C the Quai des Orfèvres was the goldsmiths' and silversmiths' quarter of Paris.

•• *Continue past Rue de Harlay (first L).*

Admirers of Inspectors Maigret and Clouseau will note that **No 36** Quai des Orfèvres is the headquarters of the Préfecture de Police.

•• *Continue ahead to Pont St Michel.*

Location 14   **PONT ST MICHEL** *1857*

The earliest Pont St Michel was constructed in the
14C and rebuilt many times.

●● *First L Boulevard du Palais. First R Rue de
Lutèce, first L. Place Louis Lépine; ahead M Cité.*

2

The Louvre/Palais Royal

The Louvre, the world's most famous museum, cannot be viewed even superficially in less than half a day, and a whole day is necessary to visit every location on this route.

Timing: The Louvre is closed Tuesday. Admission is free Sunday but then, of course, the crowds are greater.

Although the Bibliothèque Nationale is closed on Sunday its exhibitions are open every afternoon.

2

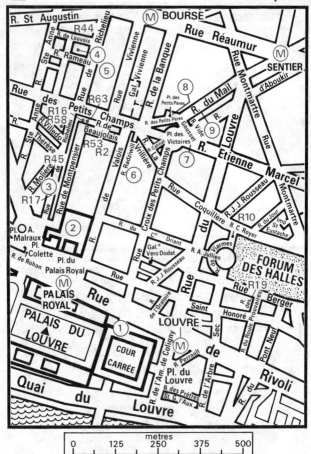

Locations
1 Louvre
2 Palais Royal
3 Fontaine Molière
4 Les Quatre Fontaines
5 Bibliothèque Nationale
6 Banque de France
7 Place des Victoires
8 Notre Dame des Victoires
9 Rue du Mail

Start M *Louvre line 1 Pont de Neuilly/Château de Vincennes. Exit R, immediately crossing Rue de l'Amiral de Coligny, and follow the north façade of the Louvre westward along Rue de Rivoli. First L the archway leads to the Louvre's Cour Carrée.*

Location 1	**LOUVRE**

Open Sunday, Thursday, Friday and Saturday 09.00–18.00, Monday and Wednesday 09.00–21.45. Admission charge but free Sunday.

Direct access points to the museum are from the pyramid in Cour Napoléon and Porte Jaujard, at the museum's south-west extremity. Other entrances, for groups or those with passes, are from Palais Royal Métro station and Passage Richelieu (Rue de Rivoli).

The Louvre, covering forty-five acres, is Europe's largest royal palace; the entire Vatican City would fit into its area three times. Dating from the mid-16C, many of the Louvre's salons have been open to the public since the Revolution and they now accommodate the world's greatest collection of old master paintings, together with antiquities, sculptures and *objets d'art*. For almost a century, the Ministry of Finance, situated in the north range, occupied approximately a third of the complex, but with its progressive evacuation to new quarters in the 1980s the dramatic expansion of the already vast museum became possible. At the same time, a greatly needed information centre and dispersal point for visitors was constructed beneath the Cour Napoléon, surmounted by a controversial glass pyramid.

To avoid exhaustion, many visitors find it preferable to examine briefly the history of the Louvre as a palace, then survey its exterior and finally, possibly on other occasions, enter the museum. Only a trained long-distance walker would now attempt to tour the entire museum in one go – roller skates are not allowed – and many, particularly on their first visit, prefer to make for highlights – *Mona Lisa, Venus de Milo*, etc. – or concentrate on the sections that interest them most. To attempt more than this during one tour might well engender a long-lasting indifference to, or even hatred of, the arts.

The Medieval Palace By tradition, the first building was erected on part of the site of the Cour Carrée (square courtyard) in the 7C. It stood in an area known as Lupara, a Latin name for wolf hunt kennels that may have been adapted in French to Louvre. Other suggestions for the genesis of 'Louvre' have, however, been made. The earliest documented structure was a small fort, built by Philippe Auguste *c*.1190–1223, to bolster the western and most vulnerable part of his defensive wall around Paris.

The castle consisted of four linked blocks forming a rectangle around a courtyard, in the centre of which stood a high *donjon* (free-standing tower). The area covered by Philippe-Auguste's castle would have fitted into less than a quarter of the present Cour Carrée.

In the 14C, the Paris wall was extended westward and as there was, therefore, no longer a need for a fortress at this point, Charles V commissioned **Raymond du Temple** to convert the complex into a royal residence. Work began in 1364 and incorporated a treasury, and a library that was to become one of the most renowned in Europe. Two contemporary illustrations exist of this early palace, nothing of which survives above ground level. However, inside the Louvre extensive sections of low-level structures from that building, which were first excavated in 1865, may be seen in the newly formed crypts.

Even when conversion was finished in 1380 the French kings still preferred to live in their Marais residences.

The Classical Palace In 1537 François I, who had made the Louvre his chief residence in 1528, demolished the *donjon* and replaced the outer wall with a garden. Nine years later he commissioned **Lescot** to rebuild the palace, and a new west range was constructed in Renaissance style. A similar south range was built after the King's death. Catherine de Médicis commissioned a long gallery *c*.1565 to run from the south-west corner of the Cour Carrée to her Tuileries Palace, then under construction further west. Louis XIII decided to quadruple the size of the Cour Carrée, commissioning **Lemercier** to extend Lescot's two wings northward and eastward and add a new north block. Only in 1663 were the last buildings of the Old Louvre demolished, when the important new east block was begun by **Le Vau**; its east façade by **Perrault** incorporated the Louvre's famous colonnade.

Demise and Napoleonic Revival In 1678 Louis XIV and his Court moved to Versailles, building work ceased, and the demise of the great complex as a royal palace began. Tenants were permitted to rent apartments in the Louvre, and the galleries were let to artists, including Coypel, Boucher and the Coustou brothers. Gradually, the palace fell into disrepair until, in 1775, Louis XV's building superintendent, the Marquis de Marigny (brother of the king's favourite, Madame de Pompadour), began its restoration and the completion of unfinished buildings.

Following the turmoil of the Revolution, Napoléon heightened all but the west side of the courtyard and began a new range, which was planned to run eastward from the north end of the Tuileries Palace to the Cour Carrée, but by the time of his deposition this was less than half-finished. Its completion was left to Napoléon III, who also created new courtyards and rebuilt the western section of the south gallery.

Exterior Apart from the Classical outer façades of the Cour Carrée, the Louvre appears to be Renaissance work. However, only the façades of the Cour Carrée, the Petite Galerie and the east section of the Grande Galerie pre-date the 19C.

Although the development of the Cour Carrée took almost 250 years, and the west, south and north ranges were each built in two sections, by different architects, the courtyard façades have always matched the Renaissance style of the first range by **Lescot**. This homogeneity has been disturbed only by Napoleonic alterations to the roofs and upper floors of all except the west range. Since 1986, cleaning of the façades has once more revealed the golden colour of the stone that has been used to build the Cour Carrée since its commencement.

•• *Proceed diagonally ahead R to the south section of the west range (L of its central Pavillon Sully).*

Cour Carrée In 1546 François I, the 'Renaissance King', commissioned **Pierre Lescot**, a canon of Notre Dame and superintendent of the royal palaces, to replace the west wing of the old castle. A year later, when only the foundations were ready, the King died and never saw the realization of what is regarded as the finest Renaissance architecture in Paris. Work

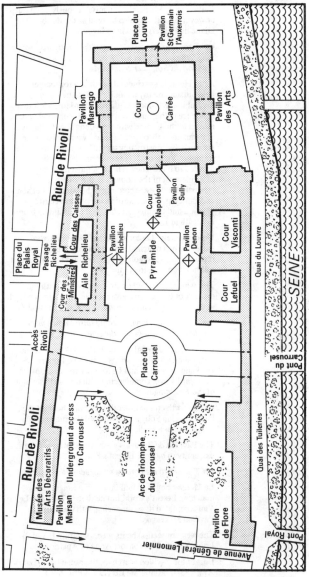

continued, however, and at the south end **Lescot**
added the **Pavillon du Roi** (King's Pavilion) to
accommodate the sovereign's private apartments.
Sculptors **Jean Goujon** and **Paul Ponce** were
responsible for the wing's decorative reliefs,
Goujon's work at upper floor level being particularly
masterly. Happily, this wing has escaped alteration.

Almost every building stage of the Cour Carrée is
commemorated by the inscription of royal cyphers.
Here, the crowned H of Henri II at ground floor level
is surmounted by the double C of his consort

Catherine de Médicis; some mischievously point out, however, that it may also be read as the double D of Diane de Poitiers, the king's favourite.

•● Turn L to the west section of the courtyard's south range, the west end of which adjoins Lescot's earlier Pavillon du Roi, later concealed.

After Henri II's accidental death at a tournament held outside the royal Palais des Tournelles in 1559, his embittered widow Catherine de Médicis left that residence with its unhappy memories for good and moved to the Louvre with her young son, François II. She immediately commissioned **Lescot** to continue his work, by constructing a matching south wing as a residence for herself. However, in 1563 Catherine decided to build a new palace, almost three-quarters of a mile west of the Louvre, in the 'tuileries'. Nevertheless, **Lescot** continued the wing for her son's occupancy as far eastward as the present central pavilion and the architect finished the building before his death in 1578.

Unfortunately, Lescot's delicate mezzanine top storey, which matched that of his west wing, was replaced for Napoléon by **Percier** and **Fontaine** with a full-height floor early in the 19C.

This wing is inscribed on its east pavilion with the cyphers of Catherine de Médicis and her late husband and on its central pavilion with the K of Charles IX.

•● Return to the Pavillon Sully (also known as the Pavillon de l'Horloge), in the centre of the west range.

Louis XIII ordered the demolition of the surviving north and east Gothic wings of the Old Louvre in 1624 and commissioned **Le Mercier** to quadruple the courtyard's size, commencing with the north section of the west range.

At the north end of Lescot's west wing he built the large **Pavillon Sully** and continued the range northward as a replica.

The **Pavillon de Beauvais** was erected at its northern extremity to balance Lescot's Pavillon du Roi.

•● Proceed to the north-west corner of the courtyard.

Le Mercier began to build the north range, still matching **Lescot's** work, but he died in 1654 and **Le Vau** completed it, commencing with the central **Pavillon Marengo**.

The western section bears the monogram LA of Louis XIII and his consort Anne of Austria.

East of the Pavillon Marengo, the range bears Louis XIV's early monogram LB (Louis Bourbon).

•● Return to the south range.

Almost a century after **Lescot's** work had ended, his **south range** was extended eastward as a replica, by **Le Vau**, under the direction of Colbert, finance minister of Louis XIV who was then still in his minority.

Immediately L of the central Pavillon des Arts, the wing bears the early monograms, L and LB of Louis XIV.

•● Proceed to the east range.

Remaining buildings from the Old Louvre were cleared by 1663 and **Le Vau**, assisted by **Charles Le Brun**, began the new east range one year later. The courtyard façade of the east range matches the others.

Only the north bay of this range bears Louis XIV's monogram, possibly indicative of the 'Sun King's' complete lack of interest in the Louvre at this stage, due to his passion for Versailles.

The fountain in the centre of the square is a recent addition.

•● *Exit through the* **Pavillon St Germain l'Auxerrois** *(the east range's central pavilion) to view the Louvre's east façade.*

The Louvre Colonnade Louis XIV held a competition to design this, the Louvre's most important façade and, in 1667, he selected the joint scheme of **Le Vau**, **Le Brun** and **Perrault**. **Claude Perrault** appears to have been chiefly responsible for the colonnade; he was a doctor and the younger brother of Charles Perrault who was to become world-famous in his old age for writing *Cinderella* and other fairy tales. Although a dabbler in the arts and archaeology, Claude Perrault had never designed a building before. Earlier, Colbert had invited the great **Bernini** to come from Rome to submit ideas. Designs were duly presented, the foundation stone laid and Bernini, thanked profusely by the King, returned to Italy. However, his façade was never built, chiefly because it was considered too Baroque and expensive to implement.

When completed in 1670, the harmonious proportions of the façade's great Classical colonnade, in complete contrast to the Renaissance style of the rest of the Louvre, soon established it as a work of quality that was to influence Paris architecture for many years.

A row of statues at roof level, specified by **Perrault**, was never made. He also intended that a moat should be dug in front of the façade to increase its apparent height. This was eventually created in 1967 and, unexpectedly, a partly rusticated basement level was revealed which, believed to be the work of **Le Vau**, contrasts rather unsympathetically with the remainder.

Originally, there were only niches at upper-floor level, but Napoléon pierced them to form windows.

Recurring above them is the double-L cypher of Louis XIV.

A figure of Napoléon, carved on the central pediment during the Empire, was replaced by the present statue of the 'Sun King' at the restoration of the Bourbons.

Above the entrance arch, *Victory distributing laurels* is Napoleonic.

•● *Proceed southward. First R Quai du Louvre. Follow the outer south façade of the Cour Carrée.*

François d'Orléans added the series of rooms, intended for the king, on this side, to harmonize with the east range. The earlier work of **Le Vau** and **Lescot**

was thus hidden, including the Pavillon du Roi.

Immediately L is the east façade of the **Petite Galerie**. Heavily restored by **Félix Duban** in the mid-19C, this was originally built for Catherine de Médicis in 1587, probably by **Pierre Chambiges**, to form a link with the projected Grande Galerie, which was to stretch westward to her Tuileries Palace. After a fire in 1661 necessitated rebuilding, **Le Vau** widened the gallery westward and constructed, on the top floor, the Galerie du Roi (now Apollon).

●● *Cross to the river side of the Quai du Louvre and continue westward.*

Stretching ahead is the eastern section of the long **Galerie du Bord de l'Eau**, originally the Grande Galerie, built for Catherine de Médicis, probably by **Louis Métezeau**, and also restored in the 19C by **Duban**. It reaches as far as the Pavillon Lesdiguières, which faces the Pont du Carrousel. In 1608, Henry IV converted the ground floor into studios and lodgings for artists working at the Louvre, and they remained until expelled by Napoléon in 1806. Richelieu installed the royal mint here in the 18C.

Beneath the cornices, and above the upper floor niches (with statues), appears the H monogram of Henry IV; occasionally the H G monogram of Henry and his mistress Gabrielle d'Estrées is also inscribed, but most examples of these were erased by the King's widow Marie de Médicis. All, however, was heavily restored in the mid-19C by **Félix Duban**.

●● *Proceed to the Pont du Carrousel (first L) and cross to the north side of the Quai du Louvre.*

Flanking the entrance to the Cour du Carrousel is R the **Pavillon Lesdiguières** and L the **Pavillon de la Tremoille**, both the 19C work of **Lefuel**.

The western section of the **Galerie du Bord de l'Eau**, providing the final link with the Tuileries Palace, was originally built for Henry IV by **Du Cerceau** in 1595 but, together with the Pavillon de Flore, threatened to collapse in the 19C, and was rebuilt in 1868 for Napoléon III by **Lefuel**.

Lefuel's work is not a replica of **Du Cerceau**'s; instead, he decided to match the Renaissance style of the eastern section of the gallery.

●● *Enter the **Place du Carrousel** and proceed to the Arc de Triomphe du Carrousel ahead*

Prior to the mid-19C, the area between the Arc de Triomphe du Carrousel and the Cour Carrée was a maze of narrow streets lined with ancient houses; the **Place du Carrousel**, now the Louvre's largest courtyard, was then much smaller. It gained its name from an equestrian display held there in June 1662 to celebrate the birth of Louis XIV's first child.

Towards the north-east corner stands the **Pavillon de Rohan**, built for Louis XVIII, by **Percier** and **Fontaine**, in 1816.

Running westward from this is the wing built for Nalopéon, also by **Percier** and **Fontaine**, 1806–15. This is a copy of the original west section of the Grande Galerie by **Du Cerceau**, which originally faced it; the wing marked the first stage in connecting the north side of the Cour Carrée with the Tuileries Palace. Napoléon was deposed when it was still incomplete and the entirely different façade of the westward section was built for Napoéon III, in Neo-Renaissance style, by **Visconti** and **Lefuel**, 1852–7.

Groups of buildings to the east, on the north and south sides of the Cour Napoléon, were added for Napoléon III by **Visconti** and **Lefuel**. Each group encloses three small courtyards.

Tuileries Palace To the extreme west of the complex, between what are now the end pavilions of the Louvre, formerly stood the Palais des Tuileries. Its name commemorates the tile kilns that stood in the area, and was chosen by Catherine de Médicis, who commissioned the building from **Philibert Delorme** shortly after she had moved to the Louvre; work began in 1564. Six years later, the superstitious Queen was told by a soothsayer that she would die in her new palace and construction was suspended. It was resumed in 1702, under the direction of **Jean Bullant**, and later, **Du Cerceau**, who added the Pavillon de Flore at the south end for Henri IV. In 1665, **Le Vau** and **D'Orbay** had added the Pavillon de Marsin on the north side for Louis XIV.

Louis XVI was effectively held captive in the palace after he had been forced to leave Versailles. From 1793 until 1796, the palace was the headquarters of the Convention. Napoléon chose the Tuileries for his Paris residence, as did his successors – Louis XVIII, who died there in 1824, Charles X, Louis-Philippe and Napoléon III. The Communards gutted the building in 1871, and in 1882 its ruins were demolished. Saved, however, were the two pavilions, which now appear as if they had always belonged to the Louvre: at the end of the south range the **Pavillon de Flore**, rebuilt by **Lefuel** in the 19C and facing it across the courtyard, the **Pavillon Marsan**, remodelled by Lefuel to match it. The latter now accommodates the Musée des Arts Décoratifs. (Page 140).

The site of the old palace and its courtyard was laid out in 1889 to form the Jardins du Carrousel and for the first time the great unobstructed vista from the Louvre to the Arc de Triomphe was revealed. (The Tuileries Garden is described on page 49.)

The **Arc de Triomphe du Carrousel**, completed in 1808, was built as the main entrance to the courtyard of the Tuileries Palace, which lay to its west, and was commissioned by Napoléon to commemorate his victories in 1805. The imperial architects **Percier** and **Fontaine** designed it as a copy, two-thirds the size, of the Arch of Septimius Severus in Rome. It is alleged that the architects suggested a figure of Napoléon for the top, but the Emperor, with uncharacteristic modesty, demurred. Instead, the gilded-bronze horses of St Mark's, Venice, spoils from Napoléon's Italian campaigns, surmounted the arch. These, however, were returned to Venice after Waterloo and the present bronze quadriga was added by **Borio** in 1828 to celebrate the restoration of the Bourbons.

Bas-reliefs on all sides depict six of Napoléon's triumphs.

●● *Proceed eastward to the glass pyramid in the centre of the Cour Napoléon.*

Grand Louvre project In 1981, President Mitterand decided that the entire Louvre Palace should accommodate the museum and the Grand Louvre project was instigated. A vast reception area beneath the Cour Napoléon was created, giving the public direct access to each wing of the three-sided courtyard and areas occupied for almost a century by the Finance Ministry were adapted to museum purposes as it was relocated. By these means, exhibition space has been increased by eighty per cent, thus permitting a more spacious presentation of the paintings and a great increase in the number of sculptures displayed, many of which had long been kept in storage. Some aspects of the project will continue through much of the 1990s, one of the final stages being the restoration of Napoléon III's Second Empire Rooms, for public viewing.

The central pyramid, designed by the American-Chinese architect **Ieoh Ming Pei**, was opened in 1989. It is the focal point of the public information area below and provides the main entrance to all departments.

●● *Enter the museum from the pyramid.*

●● *Alternatively, particularly if queues are long, proceed to the Porte Jaujard entrance in the south-west corner of the museum.*

A free museum plan and up-to-date information is provided in the Hall Napoléon. Exhibits are displayed in galleries that are numbered clockwise, on three floors. Each floor has been allocated a distinguishing colour: ground floor blue, first floor maroon, second floor mustard. Galleries in the Cour Carrée are grouped together as 'Sully' and those in the south range as 'Denon'.

Distribution of works within the galleries is as follows:

Ground Floor
Sully Oriental antiquities 1 – 5 *Code of Hammurabi 2*
Egyptian antiquities 5 – 7 *Seated scribe 6*
Greek, Etruscan and Roman antiquities 7 – 8 *Venus de Milo 8*
Denon Greek, Etruscan and Roman antiquities continued 2 – 5
Sculptures 5 – 10 *Michelangelo's Slaves 10*
First Floor
Sully Greek, Etruscan and Roman antiquities continued and Egyptian antiquities 6 – 8
Objets d'art 1 – 6
Denon Paintings 1 – 10 *Mona Lisa 5*
Greek, Etruscan and Roman antiquities continued 3
Winged Victory of Samothrace 3
Objets d'art 3 *Eagle of Sugerius 3*
Second Floor
Sully French paintings 14C–17C 1 – 4
Denon Paintings 9
Graphic arts 10
Galleries in the north range 'Richelieu' will be opened in 1993 to coincide with the bicentenary of the Louvre as a public museum.

In 1725, the French Royal Academy held its annual exhibition in the Louvre's Salon Carré for the first time and it retained the same venue from 1737 to 1848. However, it was not until the Revolution that the Louvre's works of art were shown to the public when, in 1793, part of the royal collection was exhibited by the National Convention in the Grande Galerie, then called the Musée Central des Arts. Ever since, most of the Louvre has served as a public art gallery.

The present collection evolved in the 16C, during the reign of François I. François, 'the Renaissance king', greatly admired Italian art and looted many choice examples. He also invited artists from Italy to work in France. Leonardo da Vinci was one who accepted, bringing the *Mona Lisa* with him. Later kings added to the collection, as did Napoléon. However, the Emperor's finest acquisitions were plunder and had to be returned after his fall.

Most great European old master painters and sculptors are represented, and there are outstanding antiquities from Egypt, the Middle East, Greece and Rome.

Several interiors of importance in their own right survive, mostly from the Louvre's early development but some from elsewhere.

Salle des Cariatides occupies the ground floor of **Lescot's** first south-west wing of the Cour Carrée (Sully). This ceremonial hall, the oldest room in the palace, is named after the caryatids, by **Goujon**, that support the musicians' gallery. Until 1630, the ceiling was flat with exposed beams. Here, in 1558, Mary Queen of Scots married the future François II. In 1610, the body of the assassinated Henri IV, the only king to die in the Louvre, lay in state in this hall.

Galerie d'Apollon (First floor Denon 3) Originally called the Galerie du Roi, this sumptuous room forms the link between the Cour Carrée and the Grande Galerie; it was rebuilt after a fire in 1661. The gallery, regarded as **Charles Le Brun's** finest interior, is unsurpassed by any of the contemporary rooms at Versailles.

Delacroix painted the ceiling in 1848, with the scene of Apollo's victory over the python.

It is here that the Crown Jewels are displayed, including the crowns of Napoléon and Louis XV.

Leading westward from the Galerie d'Apollon, and now forming the eastern end of the Grande Galerie, is the **Salon Carré** (Denon 4), where the French Academy once held its exhibitions. This was rebuilt by **Le Vau** in the 17C on the site of the late-16C Salle des Ambassadeurs. The wedding banquet for Napoléon's second marriage, to Marie-Louise, was held here in 1810.

The first floor **Grande Galerie** (Denon 5–8), the world's largest undivided chamber, stretches 430 yards along the Seine, from the Salon Carré to the Pavillon de Flore. This lost one-third of its length when the Salle des Etats was formed at the west end in the 19C. The gallery owes its present internal appearance to Napoléon's architects **Percier** and **Fontaine**.

Medieval Louvre crypts (approached from Ground

floor Sully or from the Hall Napoléon, direction Sully).

Opened to the public in 1989 were the newly formed archaeological crypts beneath the Cour Carrée. Visited are the lower sections of Philippe Auguste's 12C fortress, including the *donjon*.

The **Salle Saint Louis**, with its Romanesque columns, was constructed at basement level in the mid-13C and is the only room from the medieval Louvre to survive.

•► *Exit from the Louvre towards M Palais Royal. Ascend to Place du Palais Royal and proceed to its north side facing the Palais Royal.*

Location 2	**PALAIS ROYAL**

Place du Palais Royal

Colonnades, courtyard and garden, all on the north side, open daily 07.00–20.00. Admission free.

Only a fragment of Cardinal Richelieu's 17C palace survives, the remainder having been rebuilt and extended, mostly during the second half of the 18C. The palace itself accommodates government offices and is not open to the public. To the north, its enclosed garden of sublime melancholy provides the fortunate Parisians with a traffic-free haven right in the central business area of their capital. The Comédie Française and Palais Royal theatres form part of the complex.

History In 1624 Richelieu was appointed First Minister by Louis XIII and purchased a mansion, with extensive grounds, not far from the Louvre, then the principal royal residence. Three years later he commissioned **Lemercier** to replace the mansion with a palace. Originally, Charles V's city wall bounded the property to the north but this was demolished and Richelieu was able to extend the grounds. **Lemercier** enlarged the palace 1634–9 and when completed it consisted of a central range with side wings. Courtyards to the north and south fronted the palace; that to the north, the Cour d'Honneur, faced the Cardinal's private park, now the Jardin du Palais Royal.

Richelieu died in the palace, then known as the Palais Cardinal, in 1642 and on his death bed willed the estate to the King. The next year Louis XIII died and his widow, Anne of Austria, now the Regent, together with her son, the young Louis XIV, moved to the palace from the Louvre, which Anne disliked; the building was then renamed the Palais Royal.

In 1652, Louis XIV installed Henrietta Maria, widow of England's recently executed Charles I, in the palace, together with her daughter Henrietta d'Angleterre. The King decided, however, that he and his mother should live in the Louvre. In 1692 Louis XIV gave the palace to Philippe d'Orléans. During the minority of Louis XV, the Regent refused to move to Versailles and lived in the palace, giving '*petits soupers*' (little supper parties) that became notorious for the dissolute behaviour of all concerned.

Extensive rebuilding of the palace for the Regent's son began *c.*1750 under the direction of **Constant d'Ivry**, and it is his work, in spite of subsequent restoration necessitated chiefly by fires, that gave the palace its present form.

In 1780, Duc Louis-Philippe d'Orléans, who then owned the property, was in financial difficulties and, to raise money, commissioned **Victor Louis** to build, around the perimeter of the park, a speculative development of houses, incorporating a ground-floor arcade of shops. The development proved to be a success and what remained of the park became a public garden. Although for much of its subsequent history the palace remained royal property, it was henceforth to be divided into private and public sections. When titles were abolished at the Revolution, the duke adopted the name Philippe Egalité (equality) and he later signed the death warrant of his cousin Louis XVI; however, all this revolutionary zeal failed to save him and he was guillotined with the Girondins in 1793.

After being plundered by the mob, the palace became the Rights of Man Club and later, the Palais Egalité. In 1801 Napoléon allocated the palace to the Tribunale, which sat there for six years.

Louis XVIII returned the property to the House of Orléans in 1814 and Louis-Philippe lived here until 1832, having been proclaimed king in 1830. During his residency, many alterations were made by **Fontaine**.

Jérôme, Napoléon's elder brother and his son, also named Jérôme, moved here in 1851, residing in the palace throughout the Second Empire. The Palais Royal now accommodates the Conseil d'Etat (State Council) and various cultural agencies.

Exterior Through the arcaded wall that faces the Place can be seen the Cour de l'Horloge (clock court). None of its original 17C buildings by **Lemercier** survives but the court, although much rebuilt, presents a homogeneous appearance.

Ahead, the main range was rebuilt by **Moreau-Desproux** in 1763. It was damaged by the Communard fire, and restored in 1876 by **Chabrol**, who renovated most of the palace interiors. Originally, the façade was embellished with the arms of the House of Orléans but this was replaced at the Revolution by the clock.

Fontaine rebuilt the west wing L in 1830, retaining **Moreau-Desproux**'s courtyard façade.

Its south-facing pediment was carved by **Pajou** c.1763.

Originally built by **Lemercier**, the east wing R then accommodated Richelieu's *salle de comédie* theatre. Molière, acting there in one of his own plays, collapsed on stage in 1673 and died shortly afterwards. Ironically, the play was *Le Malade Imaginaire* (*The Imaginary Invalid*). The building then became a *salle d'opéra* where Lully's works were first performed. The wing was rebuilt by **Constant d'Ivry** in 1750, but not as a theatre; further restoration took place after the Communard fire.

•● *Return westward towards Place Colette.*

Immediately ahead, integrated within the complex, is the **Comédie Française**. Originally built by **Victor Louis** for Philippe Egalité in the late 18C, the theatre was rebuilt in 1863 by *Chabrol* as part of his Avenue de l'Opéra scheme. The present building, however, is mostly the work of **Guadet**, 1900.

In 1680, seven years after Molière's death, Louis XIV amalgamated the playwright's old company with that of the Hôtel de Bourgogne and gave the actors the exclusive right to perform in Paris. The company opened their fourth home here in 1799. In 1812, Napoléon, who loved the theatre, awarded them a state subsidy and this is still provided. Officially, the theatre is named the Salle Richelieu, but it is generally known as 'Le Français'. The immense wardrobe still includes costumes made during the reign of Louis XIV.

●● *First R Rue de Richelieu.*

Busts of Racine, Hugo, Molière and Corneille stand against the theatre's west wall.

●● *Proceed first R through the Peristyle de Chartres to the Cour d'Honneur of the palace.*

Controversial, stunted columns and fountains are a recent addition, by **Daniel Buren**, to the courtyard's pavement.

The arcade of the courtyard's east wing is the only surviving part of the cardinal's palace built by **Lemercier** *c.*1640. This is known as the **Galerie des Proues** (prows) because of its 18C nautical decoration, which reflected the late cardinal's position as superintendent of the navy.

The remainder of the range behind was built *c.*1750 by **Constant d'Ivry** and now accommodates the Ministry of Cultural Affairs.

To the south, the façade of the main range was designed by **Constant d'Ivry** *c.*1763; however, its upper storey was built by **Fontaine** who also entirely rebuilt the west wing R (north of the Comédie Française), and added the courtyard's colonnades between 1820 and 1830.

Attic floor sculptures are by **Pajou**.

To the north, the twin colonnades were erected by **Fontaine** in 1831, thus emphasizing the division between the private palace and its public garden.

●● *Proceed to the garden.*

Facing the double colonnade on the lawn, behind the statue of a seated youth, is the Palais Royal Cannon which, although virtually a toy, from 1786–1914 was fired at midday whenever the sun was hot enough to ignite the gunpowder.

●● *Proceed to the south end of the Galerie de Valois, on the east side of the garden.*

In 1780, Louis-Philippe d'Orléans, great-grandson of the Regent, owned the palace, but due to his debts could not afford essential restoration to its theatre. As a money-making venture he commissioned **Victor Louis**, a fellow freemason and the architect of the acclaimed opera house at Bordeaux, to build a speculative development of three-storey houses, with a ground floor shopping arcade, around the perimeter of the palace's park. Originally, all properties were to be rented, but eventually they were sold outright. The scheme, completed in 1786, was an immediate success and the public thronged to the shops and garden.

The façades of the sixty units are identical.

The arcaded galleries take the names of the streets behind them, which were all laid out at the same time and commemorate the Orléans brothers, dukes of Montpensier, Beaujolais and Valois.

At the south end of the Galerie de Valois is **No 177** where, in 1789, Charlotte Corday purchased the knife with which she assassinated Marat in his sulphur bath.

●➡ *Return to the* **Galerie de Montpensier** *on the west side.*

Due to the absence of police, agitators flourished, and on 12 July 1789 Camille Desmoulins, a lawyer and journalist, leapt on to a table outside the Café de Foy and incited the crowd to riot. His speech is regarded as the spark that kindled the French Revolution for, two days later, the mob stormed the Bastille in search of ammunition. The café, which no longer exists, occupied **Nos 57–60** at the north end of the Galerie. Strangely, no plaque marks its position.

●➡ *Continue ahead. R* **Galerie de Beaujolais**.

At **Nos 79–82** is **Le Grand Véfour**, the last of the Palais Royal's luxury restaurants to survive. It is renowned not only for *haute cuisine* but for its history and Restoration period decor. During the Directory period, the restaurant was called the Café de Chartres. Napoléon and Joséphine, Victor Hugo and members of the royal family dined here and some of their favourite seats are still indicated. Recently restored, the exquisite ceiling, painted *c*.1815, is probably the finest to grace any restaurant in the world. Fortunately, it may be glimpsed by non-diners through the large windows.

●➡ *Pass the west façade of the restaurant. R Rue de Beaujolais.*

No 9, which faces Rue Vivienne, was the home of the novelist Colette. A wall plaque commemorates her occupancy.

●➡ *Return westward and continue to Rue de Montpensier L.*

On the corner is the **Théâtre du Palais Royal**. In the 19C, galleries were added to its façade, giving the building an appearance reminiscent of New Orleans.

●➡ *Continue southward.*

Jean Cocteau, the poet and artist, lived at **No 36** until his death.

●➡ *Ascend the steps immediately opposite No 30 Rue de Montpensier and follow the passage (Passage Hulot) to Rue de Richelieu. Immediately L is the Molière fountain.*

Location 3	**FONTAINE MOLIÈRE** *Visconti 1844*
Rue de Richelieu	In the mid-19C, Paris had many more fountains than now. This fanciful example (floodlit at night) commemorates Molière, 1622–73, and bears his statue by **Seurre**. The great playwright died in a

house which formerly stood nearby, at No 40 Rue de
Richelieu.

●● *Proceed northward.*

No 38, **Tachon**, is the outstanding cheese shop of the
business quarter.

●● *First L Rue des Petits Champs. Proceed to Rue Ste
Anne (first L).*

Occupying the south-west corner site is No 45 **Rue
des Petits Champs**. Designed by **Gittard** in 1671, this
mansion, now a bank, was the house of the composer
Lully. Externally, its ground floor has been much
altered.

●● *Follow Rue Ste Anne northward. Second R Rue
Rameau leads to Square Louvois.*

Location 4	**LES QUATRE FONTAINES** *Visconti 1844*
Square Louvois	Designed by **Visconti** at the same time as his Molière fountain, four (quatre) French rivers are allegorically represented.

The square was laid out in 1839 on the site of the opera house where the Duc de Berry was assassinated; the last rites were administered to him at the theatre by the Archbishop of Paris, who is said to have come only on condition that the building, which he considered an unholy place, would be subsequently torn down – it was.

●● *Continue eastward to the **Bibliothèque Nationale** ahead.* |
| Location 5 | **BIBLIOTHÈQUE NATIONALE** |
| 58 Rue de Richelieu

Open Monday–Friday 09.00–20.00. Saturday 09.00–17.30. Closed for two weeks from the Monday following Easter Monday. Admission free. Cabinet de Médailles et des Antiques and temporary exhibitions open Monday–Saturday 13.00–17.00. Admission charge. | Apart from the British Library, the Bibliothèque Nationale is the largest library in Europe and possesses the world's most extensive collection of printed works in the French language. Although two 17C mansions owned by Mazarin form the core of the complex, and the main courtyard is 18C, the majority of the buildings were added in the 19C. Some early interiors survive and the Reading Room of 1868 is exceptional.

History Charles V created the Bibliothèque Royal in 1368 by housing 1,000 volumes in one of the towers of the Old Louvre; these were sold to the Duke of Bedford in 1425, during the English occupation of France, but the collection was dispersed at the end of the Hundred Years War. Louis XII is regarded as the true founder of the present library, as he acquired the books of the Milanese Sforza family, adding them, in his Blois château, to those that he had already inherited from Charles VIII.

In 1547 François I decreed that, henceforth, one copy of every book printed in France should automatically be sent to join the royal collection of almost 2,000 volumes, which were then kept at Fontainebleau. By 1666, more than 200,000 had been acquired and Louis XIV's chief minister, Colbert, moved them to his own mansion in Rue Vivienne. The collection was first opened for public inspection in 1692. Finally, the library was transferred to its present site, where it was combined with Cardinal Mazarin's collection in 1720. |

The Bibliothèque Nationale now comprises all types of printed material, including periodicals, maps, engravings, photographs and musical scores. Original manuscripts, coins, medals and antiques are also incorporated in the collection. Pride of place, however, must be given to the twelve million printed books, which date from the 15C and include two Gutenberg bibles.

In 1985 the Galeries Vivienne and Colbert were restored to provide additional accommodation.

•• *Enter the courtyard (no smoking allowed here or within the buildings).*

In 1731 **Robert de Cotte** remodelled the façades of the 17C Hôtel Mazarin, the Galerie Neuve, added for John Laud, the Scottish banker, in 1719 and part of the Hôtel de Nevers, to form the present Louis XV-style courtyard. The remaining buildings, with the exception of the 17C Hôtel Tubeuf, seen later, are 19C extensions.

•• *Enter the vestibule from the wing R.*

Immediately ahead is the **Salle de Travail** (Reading Room) constructed by **Henri Labrouste** in 1868. This may not be entered without a reader's ticket but is clearly visible behind its glass entrance.

Slender iron columns support the nine majolica domes, which are pierced to provide uniform top-lighting.

•• *Return to the vestibule, turn R and proceed to the room R of the stairs (when open for exhibitions). Continue through this ante-room to the 17C Galerie Mansart.*

This room forms part of a two-storey sculpture gallery, added for Mazarin by **Mansart** in 1645 to link the Hôtel Mazarin with the Hôtel Tubeuf. Mazarin's monogram is above the entrance. The ceiling was painted by **Grimaldi**.

•• *Return to the vestibule. Immediately opposite, proceed through the Administration suite (if convenient) to the Salon d'Honneur.*

The salon's wood panelling is 18C.

Displayed is the original plaster statue of the seated Voltaire, by **Houdon**, 1781.

Voltaire's heart is entombed in the statue's wooden pedestal.

•• *Exit and ascend the stairs to the landing.*

Beyond the security gates lies a suite of rooms forming the **Cabinet des Médailles et des Antiques**. Founded in the 16C, the collection comprises 400,000 coins and medals from many countries, together with antiques. Generally exhibited are the largest antique cameo yet discovered, depicting the *Apotheosis of Germanicus*, and the *Throne of Dagobert* on which the early French kings were crowned at St Denis.

•• *Exit from the museum, descend the first flight of stairs, turn R and ascend to the top floor. Facing the Manuscript Room R is the Galerie Mazarine.*

The **Galerie Mazarine** forms the upper floor of Mansart's two-storey mid-17C gallery and is occasionally open for temporary exhibitions.

The ceiling was painted by **Romanelli**.

●● *Exit from the Bibliothèque Nationale and return to Rue de Richelieu L. First L Rue des Petits Champs. Continue to the courtyard of No 8 Rue des Petits Champs L.*

The courtyard faces the Hôtel Tubeuf, designed by **Le Muet** in 1635.

Now forming part of the Bibliothèque Nationale complex, the hôtel, built for Duvet de Chevry, Inspector of Finance, was acquired in 1643 by Cardinal Mazarin to house his private collection of paintings and *objets d'art*. This was one of the last Paris hôtels to be built of brick and stone.

Originally, the courtyard was enclosed by a wall with a central portal.

The doorway and ground floor windows of the hôtel were subdivided in the 18C.

Internally, some Italian décor survives from Mazarin's occupancy. Maps and plans are now kept within the hôtel, which is not generally open to the public.

●● *First L Rue Vivienne.*

A courtyard L is formed by the north façade of the Hôtel Tubeuf, its link building, the **Galerie Mansart**, also in brick and stone, by **Mansart** 1645, and R, part of the east façade of the Hôtel Mazarin.

●● *Cross the road and enter, at No 6 Rue Vivienne, the **Galerie Vivienne**.*

At **No 37**, A Priori Thé is a famous Paris tea-house, where snacks may be consumed 'al fresco' throughout the year, protected by the gallery's glass roof.

●● *First L Rue des Petits Pères. First L Rue de la Banque.*

On the corner of Galerie Vivienne L is **No 5**, **Le Bougainville** bar. A plaque reveals that the navigator Bougainville died here in 1811. It was he who brought the tropical plant that bears his name to the Mediterranean, where it now grows in such profusion.

●● *Return southward. Third L Rue de La Vrillière. Facing Rue Catinat (first L) is the entrance to the Banque de France.*

Location 6	**BANQUE DE FRANCE** *Mansart 1638*
Rue de La Vrillière	The bank, founded by Napoléon in 1800, was transferred to its present site from Rue d'Aboukir in 1812. Behind the doors, which are usually closed, are the Cour d'Honneur and main building, constructed by **Mansart** in 1638 as the Hôtel de La Vrillière and remodelled by **De Cotte** in 1719. This became the property of the Comte de Toulouse, son of Louis XIV and Madame de Montespan, and was thus known as the Hôtel de Toulouse. In 1792, its then owner, the Princesse de Lamballe, was murdered at La Force prison during the September massacres. Most of the complex is relatively modern.

●● *Follow Rue Catinat to Place des Victoires.*

| Location 7 | **PLACE DES VICTOIRES** |

Maréchal de la Feuillade, the young Dauphine's tutor, developed the Place privately in 1685, thus reviving the capital's century-old tradition of imposing squares, begun by Henri IV.

Hardouin-Mansart laid out the square, but the houses were designed by **Prado**. Originally, the façades were uniform, with arcaded shops on the ground floor, but many were remodelled in the 19C.

Bosio designed the central statue of Louis XIV, the third on the site, for Louis XVIII in 1822. It is regarded by many as the finest equestrian example in Paris. **Desjardins'** original statue, made in 1687 to celebrate the Treaty of Nijmegen, was destroyed at the Revolution.

Bas-reliefs on the pedestal depict the crossing of the Rhine and, on the north-west side, Louis XIV distributing decorations.

●● *Follow Rue Vide Gousset, which leads diagonally north-westward to Place des Petits Pères.*

At **No 10** Place des Petits Pères, the second shop L, **Au Panetier**, is an outstanding bakery. Founded in 1902, the property retains much of its Belle Epoque decor, including a Rococo-style ceiling and colourful tiles, all recently restored. A wide variety of breads are baked over oak-wood by Bernard Lebon in the original brick oven.

●● *Proceed to Notre Dame des Victoires on the north side.*

| Location 8 | **NOTRE DAME DES VICTOIRES** |

Place des Petits Pères

Notre Dame des Victoires is a church to which annual pilgrimages in honour of the Virgin have been made since 1836. The 17C tomb of the composer Lully, and paintings by **Van Loo**, are its chief attractions.

Construction began in 1629 for the '*Petits Pères*', Augustinian monks who walked barefoot. It was designed by **Pierre Le Muet** but completed by **Sylvain Cartaud** in 1740. Louis XIII sponsored the building to honour his pledge that he would erect a church dedicated to the Virgin if he defeated the Huguenots at La Rochelle in 1627. 'des Victoires', added to the dedication, commemorates his victory. At the Revolution, the church was adapted to accommodate the Stock Exchange.

Baroque in style, the south front's upper floor is flanked, unusually, by obelisks.

●● *Enter from the south front.*

Letters and other papers from the church's archives are displayed in glass cases facing the entrance.

At the south end is the exceptional Baroque organ loft, carved in the 18C.

More than 30,000 ex-voto plaques giving thanks to the Virgin for her assistance are fixed to the walls of the church.

In the **west aisle's** second bay, above its north arch, is the tomb of the composer Jean-Baptiste Lully, d.1687. The bronze bust is by **Coysevox** and the marble figures by **Cotton**.

•● *Continue ahead to the **chancel**, at the north end.*

Panelling, added to the chancel in 1688, has been partly gilded.

Seven paintings by **Carle Van Loo**, executed between 1746 and 1755, are fixed to the chancel's walls.

Behind the high altar, the subject is Louis XIII's pledge made at La Rochelle. The remainder depict scenes from the life of St Augustin.

•● *Exit L. Second L Rue du Mail.*

Location 9	**RUE DU MAIL**

No 7 is a 17C mansion that once belonged to Louis XIV's controller of finance, Colbert. The unusual design of the capitals at upper level includes intertwined snakes, Colbert's personal emblem (*coluber* is Latin for snake).

No 37 is the premises of *Le Figaro*, the well-known French daily newspaper.

•● *R Rue Montmartre. First L Rue d'Aboukir. First L Rue Réaumur. Immediately L is M Sentier.*

3

Place de la Concorde, Invalides and Musée d'Orsay

The capital's largest and most splendid square, Place de la Concorde, is visited; here, Louis XVI was guillotined in 1793. This is followed by Napoléon's tomb at Invalides, the great 18C hôtels of Paris's most fashionable quarter and the national collection of Impressionist paintings at the Musée d'Orsay. Visitors may wish to devote half a day each to the Hôtel des Invalides and the Musée d'Orsay as there is so much to see.

Timing: The Orangerie and Rodin museums are closed Tuesday.

The museums of the Légion d'Honneur and d'Orsay are closed Monday.

Only on weekdays may the exteriors of most of the great 18C hôtels of the Faubourg St Germain be viewed, through their open doorways.

Fine weather is essential for the Tuileries Garden and Place de la Concorde. A night visit to the latter is recommended as it is then spectacularly floodlit.

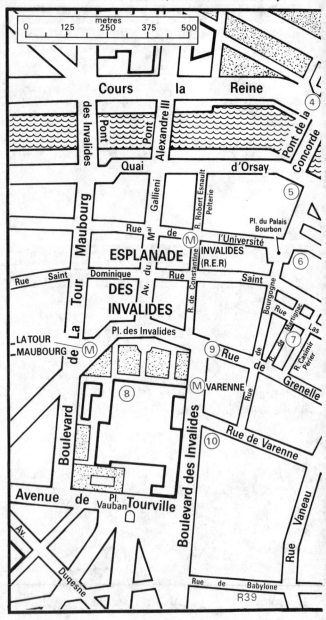

Locations
1 Jardin des Tuileries
2 Place de la Concorde
3 Musée de l'Orangerie
4 Pont de la Concorde
5 Assemblée Nationale
6 Faubourg St Germain
7 Ste Clotilde
8 Hôtel des Invalides
9 Rue de Grenelle
10 Musée Rodin
11 Pentémont
12 Grande Chancellerie de l'Ordre
   Nationale de la Légion
   d'Honneur
13 Musée d'Orsay

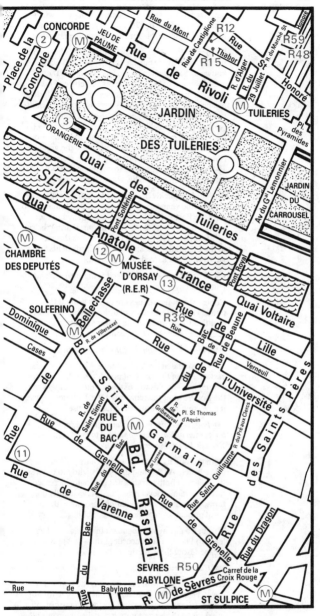

Start *M Tuileries line 1 Pont de Neuilly/Château de Vincennes. Exit from the station and proceed eastward. First R enter the Tuileries Garden.*

Location 1	**JARDIN DES TUILERIES**
Open daily dawn–dusk. Admission free.	The Jardin des Tuileries (Tuileries Garden), of sixty-three acres, is the most popular open space for a fine weather stroll in the centre of Paris. Trees, ponds, fountains and statues – but very little grass – are laid

out, particularly at the east end, in a manner which is typical of the formal, 17C French style. **André Le Nôtre** was responsible for their present appearance.

History In the Middle Ages, much of the site was a rubbish tip that lay outside the city wall in an area known as Sablonnière. Later, its clay led to the establishment of kilns for the manufacture of *tuiles* (tiles), hence the name 'Tuileries' chosen by Marie de Médicis. In 1564 the grounds were laid out east of the newly built Tuileries Palace. The grandfather of Le Nôtre was responsible for the original garden. By the mid-17C the garden had become run down and Louis XIV's minister, Colbert, commissioned the great **Le Nôtre** to begin its rehabilitation. Work, planned in 1649, took several decades to complete, Le Nôtre retaining nothing from his grandfather's period.

The garden quickly became the capital's most fashionable venue for promenading, and remained so until the Palais Royal's garden was opened to the public, shortly before the Revolution. During the riot of 10 August 1792 Louis XVI fled across the garden to the Legislative Assembly. Two-thirds of his Swiss guard were massacred in the garden.

•► *Proceed immediately ahead to the Bassin Rond (Round Pond).*

Copies of antique statues are placed around the pond. The indiscriminate addition of statues, mostly of little artistic value, is the major alteration made to the garden since Le Nôtre completed his work.

•► *Follow the tree-lined central path westward.*

Le Nôtre created the long Grande Allée to form the eastern end of the axis that now leads to the Arc de Triomphe. The axis was extended the other way to the Louvre after the removal of the Tuileries Palace; it now continues westward to La Défense.

•► *Follow the first tarmac path L to the south side of the garden and ascend the steps R to the* **Terrasse du Bord de l'Eau** *(Waterside Terrace).*

Both this and its northern counterpart were created by **Le Nôtre**. As the land dropped slightly to the west, the height of both terraces was gradually increased, thus maintaining level promenades. Evidently this terrace was always a popular playground with the royal princes, even though it was 'public territory'.

Through a passageway beneath this terrace, which leads to Place de la Concorde, Louis-Philippe escaped from the Tuileries Palace in 1848.

•► *Continue westward.*

Running parallel with the terrace is the noticeably lower **Terrasse des Feuillants**, built as a path for horse riding. Its name commemorates the monastery which overlooked the terrace until it was dissolved in 1791.

The **Jeu de Paume**, built in 1861 as a real (royal) tennis court, stands at its west end. *Jeu de paume* literally means 'game played with the palm of the hand', as real tennis originally was. The national collection of Impressionist paintings was long held here but is now located in the Musée d'Orsay.

•► *Continue to the west end of the Terrasse du Bord de l'Eau.*

➡ Alternatively, enter the Musée de l'Orangerie L (location 3).

From the end of the terrace, a close view of a copy of the statue *La Renommie, (Fame on a Winged Horse)*, by **Coysevox**, is gained. The originals of this, and its partner, also by Coysevox, *Mercuré, (Mercury on a Winged Horse)*, came from the grounds of the château at Marly. They were brought here in 1719, initially to decorate a swing bridge, which had been built to cross the moat between the Tuileries Garden and Place de la Concorde in 1716 – until then there had been no direct access from the Place to the garden. When the moat was filled and the bridge demolished, they were transferred to their present positions. In 1987, in order to preserve Coysevox's originals from pollution, the statues were transferred to the Louvre and replaced by copies.

➡ Descend the ramp from the terrace.

Below, flanking the ramps to this and the north terrace, are four of the garden's most outstanding statues. They represent famous rivers and all, except *Nile*, were transferred here from Marly *c.*1720.

On the east side R, from Versailles, is *Nile*, by **Ottone**, 1692.

Facing this L is *Loire et Loiret*, by **Van Cleeve**, 1707.

➡ Proceed towards the ramp to the north terrace.

Immediately L is *La Seine et La Marne*, by **N. Coustou**, 1712.

Facing this R is *Le Tibre*, by **Boudry**, 1689.

➡ Continue northward to the east end of the projecting section of the north terrace.

Immediately behind its east wall stand the ruins of two Renaissance arches from the Tuileries Palace.

*➡ Return southward to the **Bassin Octogonal** (Octagonal Pond) and proceed clockwise.*

Around the pond's east side are four more outstanding statues, which represent the seasons, and are the work of **N. Coustou** and **Van Cleeve**. These statues, the garden's first, were erected here in 1680.

➡ Proceed westward towards Place de la Concorde.

In the wall niche R is a copy of the bust of Le Nôtre, 1613–1700, by **Coysevox**. The original is in St Roch church, where he is buried.

A tablet in the wall niche on the south side, immediately opposite, commemorates the first gas balloon ascent, made from the garden by Charles and Robert in December 1783.

➡ Exit through the gates ahead to the Place de la Concorde. Turn R and follow the pedestrian crossing to the foot of the obelisk on the central island and proceed to the obelisk.

Location 2	**PLACE DE LA CONCORDE**

Very much the heart of modern Paris, the Place de la Concorde incorporates an obelisk, fountains and pavilions; on its perimeter are trees and two Classical hôtels. It was here that Louis XVI and, later, his arch-enemy Robespierre, were guillotined.

History Following the Treaty of Aix la Chapelle in 1748, many French cities celebrated by constructing squares and erecting statues in honour of Louis XV. The city of Paris held an architectural competition to design this 21-acre square, to be built on what was then open country, and more than fifty architects took part, including Servandoni and Soufflot. Eventually, the octagonal design of the royal architect, **Jacques-Ange Gabriel**, was selected; the square was first named Place Louis XV.

A firework display was held in 1770 to celebrate the marriage of the Dauphin (later Louis XVI) and Marie-Antoinette. The crowd that poured into the square was too great, panic ensued and 133 were crushed to death in the ditch that then surrounded the Place – an ominous precursor of the carnage that would mark the last years of Louis XVI's reign.

In 1792, the name of the square was changed to Place de la Révolution and in October that year a guillotine was erected here for the first time; it was brought from the Place du Carrousel, a simple matter as the instrument had a wheeled base. The first victims, however, were not aristocrats, but robbers who had attempted to steal the crown jewels.

Louis XVI was guillotined in the Place on Sunday 21 January 1793, entering on foot from the Rue Royale but the Terror did not really begin until May that year: by the time it ended 1,119 had been executed in this square alone; guillotines were also set up at Place de la Bastille where 73 died and the Place de la Nation where 1,306 lost their lives. Apart from the King, eminent victims to die here include Charlotte Corday (17 July 1793), Marie-Antoinette (16 October 1793), the Girondins (31 October 1793) Philippe Egalité (6 November 1793), Madame Roland (10 November 1793), Danton (5 April 1794) and Robespierre (28 July 1794). When the Terror ended in 1795, the square was given its present name. It was briefly renamed Place Louis XVI in 1823.

The opening of the Pont de la Concorde in 1790, followed by Napoleonic developments, greatly altered the perspectives from the Place, but the 19C alterations made for Louis-Philippe by **Hittorff** are responsible for much of the square's present detail.

Obelisk and fountains When the square was conceived in 1748, the Paris Prévôt des Marchands (merchants' provost) commmissioned a bronze equestrian statue of the 'well-beloved' (Louis XV) from **Bouchardon**. This was completed by **Pigalle** and erected, where the obelisk now stands, in 1763. Revolutionaries toppled the statue in 1792 and replaced it with a figure representing 'Liberty'. It is alleged that this inspired Madame Roland's lines that eventually sent her to the guillotine, 'O Liberty, what crimes are committed in your name!'

The obelisk, which replaced 'Liberty' in 1836, was made in the 13C BC and is the oldest monument in Paris. It comprises a monolithic block of granite from Aswan, Egypt, and originally stood in the Temple of Thebes, where the obelisk appears to have served as an astronomical instrument, measuring the sun's shadow. Like London's Cleopatra's Needle, which is 6 feet 6 inches shorter, the obelisk was presented by Mohammed Ali, Viceroy of Egypt, in 1829.

Hieroglyphics on this, as on most Egyptian obelisks, glorify the conceited Rameses II.

The 19C pedestal, of Breton granite, depicts how the obelisk was lowered, transported and re-erected.

Both fountains, 19C additions by **Hittorff**, also for Louis-Philippe, are based on those in St Peter's piazza, Rome. They represent inland navigation (north side) and maritime navigation (south side).

●● *Face the Champs Elysées to observe the elements that surround the Place as described.*

Perimeter Originally, **Gabriel** surrounded the Place de la Concorde with a balustrade and a dry moat, broken only to permit the entrance of thoroughfares (which have since increased in number) and by four pairs of guardhouses at the corners. The dry moat was filled for Napoléon III in 1852.

Gabriel's guardhouses, never used as such, were eventually rented privately as pavilions. It was always intended that they should support statues but these were not added until the 19C, several sculptors, including **Pradier** and **Cortot**, being responsible. Each one represents a provincial French city; all were cleaned and restored in 1988.

In the north-west corner the pavilions represent Brest and Rouen.

It was at a point approximately 40 feet from the Brest statue, in the direction of where the obelisk now stands, that the guillotine was erected for Louis XVI's execution.

Flanking the entrance to the Champs Elysées are recently made copies of the *Marly Horses*, by **G. Coustou** which were brought here from the château of Marly in 1794. They depict *Africans mastering the Numibian horses*, and the originals, like the statues flanking the entrance to the Tuileries Garden, were transferred to the Louvre in 1987.

Four Classical buildings stand on the north side.

The most westerly, the **US Embassy**, 1935, replaced the 18C Hôtel Grimod de la Reynière.
Two distinguished mansions flank the Rue Royale: to the west, the Hôtel Crillon and to the east, the Hôtel de la Marine. **Gabriel** designed the matching façades of both, and their combination of grandeur and humanity, rare in Paris, has created what are to many the capital's most attractive domestic buildings in the Classical style. Constructed 1763–72, both are fronted by colonnades, probably influenced by Perrault's work at the Louvre.

Sculptures on the pediments are the work of **M. A. Slodtz** and **G. Coustou**.

Gabriel intended that the two hôtels should be official residences, but he was not responsible for the work behind the façades and they were both, in the event, subdivided.

On the west side, the **Hôtel Crillon** originally provided four separate residences. It now accommodates the luxury-grade Hotel Crillon and the French Automobile Club. Of great historic importance to Americans, it was here that France signed the Treaty of Friendship and Trade with the thirteen independent American states on 6 February 1778, thereby recognizing their independence from Britain. Signatories included Benjamin Franklin.

The eastern block, the **Hôtel de la Marine**, has been the home of France's Naval Ministry since 1789. It was originally the royal furniture store, rather in the manner of an English royal wardrobe, and from this building an unsuccessful attempt was made in 1792 to steal the crown jewels. Also accommodated is the French Environment Ministry.

With these two buildings, **Gabriel** began the creation of the Rue Royale which had been part of his comprehensive plan for the square, as was the Pont de la Concorde, put in hand much later.

East of the Hôtel de la Marine is the **Hôtel de La Vrillière**. Built by **Chalgrin** in the second half of the 18C, its design influenced that of the modern embassy, which it counterbalances.

Talleyrand died in this house in 1838.

➥ Return to the east (Tuileries Garden) side of the square (push the red pedestrian button to halt the traffic). Proceed southward and ascend the steps L, at the corner, returning to the Terrasse du Bord de l'Eau. Ahead, at it west end, is the Orangerie.

Location 3	**MUSÉE DE L'ORANGERIE**
Jardin des Tuileries *Open Wednesday– Monday 09.45– 17.15. Admission charge, half-price Sunday.*	The collection of Impressionist and modern paintings, bequeathed to the city of Paris by Jean Walter and Paul Guillaume, is exhibited here in the building, completed in 1853, that originally housed the palace's orangery. Apart from the Musée d'Orsay this is the most comprehensive display of Impressionists in the capital.

➥ Exit and descend from the terrace to Place de la Concorde L. R Quai des Tuileries; follow the pedestrian crossing to Pont de la Concorde.

Location 4	**PONT DE LA CONCORDE** *Perrouet 1790*

Splendid views are gained from this bridge, the final element in **Gabriel's** Place de la Concorde project. The upper parts are constructed with stones from the Bastille, which, it is said, were re-used so that Parisians might tread on this symbol of royal oppression. However, in 1932 the width of the bridge was doubled and the Bastille stones are not obvious.

➥ Cross the bridge to the Assemblée Nationale directly ahead.

Location 5	**ASSEMBLÉE NATIONALE**
Palais Bourbon 33 Quai d'Orsay *Only the public gallery may be visited and then only during sessions of the Assembly (at varying times*	France is, effectively, governed from here, as this is where the Chambre des Deputés, parliament's Lower House, sits. The Upper House (Sénat) is accommodated separately in the Palais du Luxembourg. Since the terrorist bombings of 1986, the palace has been out of bounds to visitors, apart from the public gallery.

History The site was purchased *c.*1720 by the

usually from 15.00 but not in summer). The Prime Minister answers questions on Wednesday afternoon and queues are then long. Foreign visitors must produce their passports.

Dowager Duchess Louise Françoise de Bourbon, the legitimized daughter of Louis XIV and Madame de Montespan, and she commissioned **Girardini** to build the palace, which was completed in 1728. Louis XV acquired the building in 1756, but sold it nine years later to the Prince de Condé, grandson of the dowager duchess. The prince was in desperate need of suitable accommodation, as his existing residence had to be demolished for the new Théâtre de l'Odéon. He enlarged and embellished the palace from 1777, employing **Lassurance, Gabriel** and **Aubert.**

Revolutionaries decreed that the palace was national property in 1790 and it then accommodated the Council of Five Hundred. The national archives were kept here 1799–1808. At the Restoration, Louis XVIII returned the complex to the Condé family but the state purchased it from them in 1827 and the palace was converted for the Corps Legislative.

Between 1940 and 1944 the German military administration of the Paris region occupied the building as its headquarters.

Exterior Although impressive, the north façade is in fact the rear of the palace. It was remodelled in 1807, in a heavy Greek style, by **Poyet**, for Napoléon, who had commissioned the work to complement the Greek-style Madeleine church, which closed the vista facing it. Louis XV had proposed a similar redesign when he bought the palace but sold the building before work could be put in hand.

The pediment of the great portico, by **Cortot**, 1842, depicts France between Liberty and Order, surrounded by Agriculture, Commerce and Peace.

Flanking the steps are *Minerva*, by **Houdon** and *Themis*, by **Roland**.

Reliefs on the wings are by **Pradier** and **Rude**. Facing the road are statues of Sully, L'Hôpital, D'Aguessau and Colbert.

•• *Enter the public gallery from the small building R. Passports must be presented here.*

The crescent-shaped assembly room was created in 1838. Proceedings are conducted by the President of the Assembly, who faces the deputies (totalling 491). The government of the day occupies the front bench and the political left and right sit to the president's left and right, respectively.

Although other parts of the palace may not be visited, there are no exceptional interiors apart from paintings by **Delacroix** in the library.

•• *Exit, cross to the riverside, and proceed westward.*

Behind trees, immediately west of the palace, is the Hôtel Lassay, built in 1724 for Lesparre de Lassay. This was incorporated in the complex by the Prince de Condé in 1770 and renamed the Petit Bourbon. At the Revolution, it became the Ecole Polytechnique, but Condé returned to live there at the Restoration. It is now the official residence of the President of the National Assembly.

The connecting wing, the Galerie des Fêtes, was constructed in 1848.

Further west is the **Ministère des Affaires Etrangers** (Foreign Affairs), built by **Lacornée** in 1845.

Facing the Ministry building is the monument to President Aristide Briand, d.1932.

•• *Continue ahead (immediately ahead is the Pont Alexandre III). First L Rue Robert Esnault-Pelterie. First L Rue de l'Université. Proceed to Place du Palais Bourbon (passed L is the rear of the Hôtel Lassay).*

The south façade of the palace, viewed through the archway, is the only one by **Girardini** to survive.

Identical mansions in Louis XVI style, begun in 1776, surround the remainder of the Place.

•• *Proceed to the south side of the square and follow Rue de Bourgogne southward. First L Rue St Dominique.*

Location 6	**FAUBOURG ST GERMAIN**

Rue St Dominique marks the entrance to the Faubourg St Germain, with its great 18C mansions, now mostly converted to embassies or government offices. Originally a suburb of St Germain, the town which had evolved around the great abbey, this *faubourg* was open country until the completion of Invalides in 1674 led to its westward extension. This soon became the most fashionable quarter in Paris, the nobility and wealthy merchants moving to it from the Marais and remaining until the Revolution, when many were guillotined and their residences taken.

The area's fortunes revived at the Restoration but the new streets around the Champs Elysées were soon to become the fashionable place to live and gradually the great mansions, most of which were now too large for family occupancy, were converted to offices.

Fortunately, many of the 18C mansions remain, although they can generally be glimpsed only behind their walled courtyards on weekdays when the gates are open for the passage of cars.

•• *Proceed eastward along Rue St Dominique.*

Nos 35–37, now the **Ministère de l'Agriculture**, were built in 1724 as the Hôtel Broglie, alterations being made early in the 19C. The Baroque courtyard can generally be seen.

No 16, now the **Ministère de l'Armée**, was built by **Aubry** *c*.1714 as the Hôtel Bourbon-Busset.

No 14, **Hôtel de Brienne**, also by **Aubry** *c*.1714, was the home of Lucien and later, Laetitia Bonaparte (mother of Napoléon). General de Gaulle's provisional government sat here in 1944–6, immediately after the German retreat, and the Cross of Lorraine on the pediment commemorates this.

•• *First R Rue de Martignac.*

Location 7	**STE CLOTILDE** *F. C. Gau 1856*
Rue Las Cases	Ste Clotilde, regarded by many as the finest Gothic Revival church in Paris, is virtually a mid-13C building, which happened to be built 600 years late. César Franck was organist here for thirty years.
Open daily but closed 14.00–17.00.	

•• *Enter the church.*

Internally, the accurate Gothic detailing continues.

●● *Exit L. Ahead Rue Las Cases. Passed R is the rear of the Hôtel de Broglie. R Rue de Bourgogne. First L Rue St Dominique.*

No 45, **Crédit National**, is a fine example of the Classical style.

No 28, Maison de la Chimie, was built by **Lassurance** in 1708 for Frédéric Maurice de la Tour d'Auvergne, as the Hôtel Rochefoucauld d'Estissac. Its great staircase (Escalier d'Honneur), by **Servandoni**, may be viewed Tuesday–Friday.

Nos 40–51, also now occupied by **Crédit National**, are basically 18C.

No 57 was built as the **Hôtel de Sagan**, by **Brogniart** in 1784, for the Princess of Monaco. The centre of its north façade may be glimpsed through the gates.

●● *Continue ahead to the Esplanade des Invalides. Follow the path to the centre and turn L towards the Hôtel des Invalides.*

| Location 8 | **HÔTEL DES INVALIDES** |

Grounds and courtyards open daily 07.00–19.00 (18.00 in winter).

Admission free.

Musée de l'Armée (Army Museum), which includes the Dôme church, containing Napoléon's tomb. Open daily 10.00–18.00 (closes at 17.00 from October–March). Admission charge for the Musée de l'Armée. Tickets may be used on two consecutive days, but once the Dôme and sections of the museum have been left they may not be re-entered.

Son et Lumière performances in English are held in the Cour d'Honneur daily from late March to mid-October at 22.15 (23.15 early May to mid-August). Admission charge.

Musée d'Histoire Contemporaine (Contemporary

The Hôtel des Invalides, constructed in the 17C as a home and hospital for veteran or disabled soldiers, is the capital's grandest architectural ensemble to have been built in Louis XIV's reign. Resembling a palace rather than a soldiers' home, the hospital was designed by **Libéral Bruant**, although both its churches, St Louis and the Dôme, were added by **Jules Hardouin-Mansart**. Almost one-third of the complex houses the Musée de l'Armée (Army Museum) but the attraction to most visitors is the tomb of Napoléon, whose body was brought here from St Helena in 1840, nineteen years after his death.

History In medieval times it was the responsibility of monasteries to care for elderly and wounded soldiers, but in practice most were left to fend for themselves. Henri IV established a home for them in 1604 and, under Richelieu, the Palais de Bicêtre was adapted as a military hospital. However, these measures proved inadequate and in 1670 François Michel de Louvois, the Under-Secretary for War, who had reorganized the army and was regarded as a benefactor of the common soldier, persuaded Louis XIV to commission a home and hospital expressly for their use; an example shortly to be followed in England by Charles II at Chelsea. Finance was obtained by compulsory contributions for five years from monasteries, serving soldiers and local markets.

A competition to design the complex was won by **Libéral Bruant** who, after the death of **Le Vau** had supervised the building of the Salpetrière, which cared in a similar way for the very poor. A site was chosen on the Plaine de Grenelle, then outside Paris, and, as at Val de Grâce, Madrid's Escorial Palace was the inspiration for the layout of cloistered barracks around a church. Louis XIV laid the cornerstone on 30 November 1671. **Bruant's** design, excluding the churches, was virtually built by 1674 and two years later 6,000 veterans and disabled soldiers moved in, accompanied by priests, doctors

3

History). Open April–July and September 14.00–18.00. October–March 10.00–13.00 and 14.00–17.00.

Musée de l'Ordre de la Libération. Open Tuesday–Sunday 14.00–17.00. Closed August.

Musée des Plans-Reliefs. Open daily April–September 10.00–17.45, October–March 10.00–16.45.

and nursing staff. Almost immediately, Louvois fell out with **Bruant**, and **Hardouin Mansart** was commissioned to build the hospital's two churches, St Louis des Invalides, for the soldiers and a royal church, the Dôme des Invalides.

On 14 July 1789 the first major event of the French Revolution took place here, when rebels stormed the hospital, disarming the sentries and equipping themselves with 28,000 rifles from the stores; they then marched on the Bastille to acquire gunpowder.

In 1840, the remains of Napoléon were brought from St Helena to the Dôme and now lie in its crypt.

Invalides is at present occupied by approximately seventy pensioners, the National Institute, and the Army's Museum and Medical Department.

Exterior Robert de Cotte laid out the esplanade in front of Invalides, 1704–20.

☛ *Proceed ahead to Place des Invalides, facing the hospital's garden, which is bordered by a dry moat.*

Bronze 17C and 18C cannon line the ramparts; the battery, which still fires triumphant salutes, was seized by the occupying Germans in 1940 but returned in 1946.

Bruant's north wing, approximately one-eighth of a mile long, faces the esplanade. Behind it, **Hardouin-Mansart's** dome, completed afterwards, is best appreciated later.

☛ *Proceed ahead through the gateway to the garden.*

In the top section of the façade's portal is an equestrian relief of Louis XIV, supported by *Prudence* and *Justice*; it is a copy by **Pierre Cartellier**, 1815, of the original by **G. Coustou**, 1736, which was damaged in the Revolution.

Seated on plinths, *Mars* and *Mercury*, by **Coustou**, flank the entrance.

Dormer windows are embellished with individually designed surrounds, in the form of military trophies.

The entire range was originally the residence of the governor and his administrators; doctors to the right and orderlies to the left.

☛ *Pass through the archway to the Cour d'Honneur.*

This, the most important of the hospital's fifteen enclosed courtyards, is regarded, apart from Perrault's Louvre colonnade, as the finest example of Classical architecture in Paris. Originally, the east and west ranges provided the soldiers' quarters on the first floor, with kitchen and dining rooms below.

At the corners, the projecting structures are embellished with horses trampling military trophies.

☛ *Follow the east range L to its central pavilion.*

Louvois, who had prompted the King to build the hospital, self-importantly arranged for his personal arms to be carved on sections of the building. Louis XIV promptly removed them, but Louvois nevertheless gained his recognition with a pun: the head of a *loup qui voit* (watching wolf) is incorporated in the design of the fifth attic window south of the east range's central pavilion.

The Musée de l'Armée (Army Museum) is entered from the central pavilions of both the east ranges. Tickets are sold from the west range R and these also give access to the Dôme church (Napoléon's tomb). Or they can be purchased at a ticket office closer to the Dôme, but queues there are always longer.

The central pavilion of the south range ahead, designed by **Bruant**, provides the north front of **St Louis des Invalides**. This was the only part of the 'soldiers' church' that he would build as, almost immediately following its completion, a disagreement with Louvois led to his dismissal and the appointment of **Hardouin-Mansart** as architect for this and the Dôme church. However, it is believed that the new architect made few basic changes to Bruant's original simple design for St Louis's.

Below the pediment stands 'the little corporal', a bronze figure of Napoléon, made by **Seurre** in 1833 to surmount the Vendôme column, where it stood until 1863. It was brought here in 1911.

•● *Enter the church directly below this pediment, by the door L.*

Fitted with a plain barrel-vault the building has nine identical bays.

The high altar is situated at the south end.

Galleries were built at the same level as the hospital's dormitories so that the disabled could reach them more easily.

Most of the captured enemy standards, hanging below the clerestory, were brought from Notre Dame at the Revolution. First hung in both churches, which had been designated Temples of Mars, 1,417 of them were burned by the hospital's governor as the Allies entered Paris in 1814; more were accidentally burned in 1851. Now, all that survive hang in this church, including, at the east end, Nazi swastikas. The church of St Louis is one of the few remaining locations in the world, apart from museums, where this symbol of the Third Reich can still be seen.

Above the north entrance is the organ loft. The 17C instrument was played at the first performance of the Berlioz *Requiem Mass* in 1837; artillery on the esplanade supplemented the orchestra in the church.

This building and the Dôme originally shared a common chancel and a double-fronted altar, but a window has separated them since 1873. Through this can be seen the baldachino of the Dôme's high altar.

Below, in the crypt (generally not open), are buried former hospital governors, together with 19C and 20C marshals and generals.

•● *Exit R and pass the staircase. First R Corridor de Metz, proceed to the end.*

Immediately R, the long east wall of St Louis adjoins the Dôme church.

•● *Proceed ahead to the centre of the walled trench.*

Originally part of Hardouin-Mansart's design, the trench, with its swing bridge, has been restored.

The **Dôme des Invalides** was built as the Eglise Royal

(royal church) for Louis XIV, who considered adopting it as his mausoleum. **Hardouin-Mansart** based the work on drawings by his great-uncle, François Mansart, for a never-to-be-built Bourbon mausoleum, which was to stand in the precincts of St Denis Cathedral. The typically Jesuit building did much to establish the French Classical style in church architecture and many regard it as amongst the greatest works of Louis XIV's reign.

Construction began in 1677, one year after Bruant's services had been dispensed with, but, due to the extravagance of its interior, the Dôme was not consecrated until 1706. When Hardouin-Mansart died two years later it was still not quite finished and his brother-in-law **Robert de Cotte** completed the work.

With the reburial here of Louis XIV's marshal, Turenne, in 1800, the church did, after all, become a mausoleum not for the King but for military heroes – culminating in Napoléon's interment in 1840.

In 1680 a central avenue, the Avenue de Breteuil, was laid out in what was then open countryside, to provide yet another extensive Paris vista.

Exterior The cupola, begun in 1691, is more pointed than most other notable examples; e.g. St Peter's, Rome; St Paul's, London and the Val de Grâce, Paris.

In 1715 the cupola's ribs, the lead trophies between them and the lantern were gilded, a process that was repeated four times, the last being in 1989.

Until the Revolution, twelve statues stood at the first storey's roof level.

The coat of arms on the pediment is by **Coysevox**.

Standing on the lower cornice are figures of the Four Virtues, by **Coysevox**.

In the niches flanking the entrance are statues of L St Louis by **N. Coustou**, after **Girardon**, and R Charlemagne, by **Coysevox**, *c*.1705, after **Martin Desjardins**.

●● *Unless already purchased, proceed L to the low west range (signposted) for tickets to enter both the Dôme and the Musée de l'Armée. Enter the church.*

Internally, the north-orientated Dôme is cold and functional, immediately creating the impression of a pantheon to honour the dead, which of course is what it eventually became. The building is designed to a Greek-cross plan, but with the corners filled by circular chapels which have cupolas painted by **B.** and **L. Boullougne** and **M. Corneille**. Further chapels between them are formed by east and west apses.

●● *Turn L and proceed to the central, apsidal chapel on the west side.*

Immediately L is St Jérôme's Chapel, with carvings by **N. Coustou**. It was here that Napoléon's sarcophagus rested for eleven years while the crypt was under construction. Jérôme Bonaparte, d.1844, lies in the large black sarcophagus; he was the younger brother of Napoléon, who appointed him King of Spain. The ashes of Jérôme's eldest son and his wife's heart repose in this chapel.

The central west chapel accommodates the tomb of

Louis XIV's marshal, Turenne, d.1675. His body was transferred here by Napoléon from the basilica of St Denis, thus beginning the church's conversion to a military pantheon.

Marshal Lyautey, d.1934, lies in the Chapel of St Gregoire R; his tomb was designed by **Albert Laprude** in 1963.

Behind this is the heart tomb of La Tour d'Auvergne, d.1800, 'first grenadier of the Republic'.

•● *Continue clockwise to the central apsidal chapel on the east side.*

Immediately L, in the Chapel of St Ambroise, is the tomb of First World War leader, Marshal Foch, d.1929, by **Landowski**.

The central east chapel contains the monument and heart tomb of Vauban, d.1707, by **Etex**, 1847.

Immediately R, in the Chapel of St Augustin, is the tomb of Joseph Bonaparte, d.1860, by **E. Guillaume**. Joseph, Napoléon's elder brother, became King of Westphalia.

•● *Proceed to the centre of the church to view the interior of the dome.*

The central painting, in need of restoration, by **Charles de la Fosse**, depicts St Louis offering Christ the sword with which he has vanquished his enemies.

Around the inner dome are frescos of the apostles, by **Juvenet**.

Below, medallions, also by **Juvenet**, depict French kings.

The four Evangelists by **De la Fosse**, at lower level, complete the dome's decoration.

Directly beneath the dome, the circular opening in the floor was cut in 1842 when **Visconti** began work on the crypt to accommodate Napoléon's tomb, which can be seen immediately below.

•● *Proceed to the east end of the church.*

Until 1873 the chancel was shared by both churches but they were then separated by the present window.

The high altar, originally double-sided, was altered and enlarged by **Visconti** in 1842. Its present baldachino (canopy) is entirely his work.

Paintings above the sanctuary are by **N. Coypel**.

Facing the screen that divides the two churches are the tombs of Napoléon's close friends: General Bertrand, d.1844, and General Duroc, d.1813.

•● *Descend the steps.*

Flanking the entrance to the crypt are two colossal bronze figures bearing imperial regalia, by **Duret**; one holds the orb, the other the crown and sceptre.

The doors were made from melted-down cannon captured at the battle of Austerlitz.

Above the entrance are inscribed words from Napoléon's will which translate: 'I request that my ashes should lie by the Seine, in the midst of the people of France, that I have loved so dearly.'

Napoléon Bonaparte, who was born at Ajaccio, Corsica, in 1769, died at St Helena in 1821. His **tomb** lies in the centre of the crypt. Louis-Philippe negotiated for seven years with the British Governor of St Helena for Napoléon's body to be transferred from that remote island to Paris. On 8 October 1840 it arrived and the coffin was opened for two minutes.

For a while, the coffin lay beneath the cupola (the floor was not then open), but it was later transferred to St Jérôme's Chapel, where it remained until the crypt was ready to receive it on 3 April 1851.

Napoléon's sarcophagus, carved from red Finnish porphyry, and resting on a pedestal of green Vosges granite, was completed in 1861. His battles are named in the crypt's star-shaped mosaic pavement.

Six coffins, of varying types of wood and metal, successively fit one inside the other encasing the body in the manner of an Egyptian pharaoh. Within, the Emperor's heart, lies at his feet in a silver urn. A very private part of Napoléon's anatomy, however, rests elsewhere. In a glass jar, embalmed in preserving fluid and resembling a pickled walnut, it was auctioned in London during the 1950s.

Twelve colossi by **Pradier**, standing against the columns, represent Napoléon's major campaigns.

●━ *Turn R and follow the ambulatory.*

Bas-reliefs on the circular wall, based on designs by **Simart**, depict Napoléon's civic achievements.

In the south chapel R, the statue of Napoléon in his coronation robes is by **Simart**.

In front of this statue is the tomb slab of Napoléon's only son, Napoléon François, d.1832. He had been appointed King of Rome by his father, but never reached the city, dying at Vienna, aged twenty-one. During the early part of the German occupation of France, Hitler, wishing to gain French co-operation, ordered that the young man's body should be transferred to Paris from the Hapsburg crypt in the Austrian capital. It arrived in Paris on 15 December 1940, the hundredth anniversary of Napoléon's interment at Invalides.

●━ *Exit from the church R and proceed first R to the Corridor de Nîmes, signposted Musée de l'Armée.*

From the central windows R (indicated 'Tombeau de Napoléon à Ste Hélène') Napoléon's tombstone from St Helena can be seen, set in the grass in front of St Louis's church.

●━ *Continue to the Cour d'Honneur and follow the Galerie de l'Occident ahead to its centre. Enter L the west block of the Musée de l'Armée.*

Founded as the artillery museum in 1794, the Musée de l'Armée incorporates collections from the Arsenal, private families (taken at the Revolution) and Napoléon III. It also includes an outstanding collection of arms and armour from the Middle Ages, but of greatest interest to most English-speaking visitors is the memorabilia from the Napoleonic period and both world wars.

This section of the museum displays arms and armour

from the François I and Henri IV periods, plus exhibits from the First and Second World Wars.

Immediately R, the Salle François I, which was a dining-room, preserves its original fresco (restored).

The sword and the brass tomb-plaque of François I are exhibited in the display case against the centre of the wall R.

Opposite is the armour made for Ferdinand I's horse.

On the end wall hangs a painting by **Pierre Dulin** that depicts Invalides under construction.

•• *Return to the entrance hall.*

Jousting armour occupies the **Salle Henri IV**, on the other side of the entrance. The toy-like miniature suits of armour that are displayed were manufacturers' samples produced to obtain orders.

•• *Ascend to the second floor.*

The **Musée de l'Ordre de la Libération** displays items referring to the Second World War, with particular emphasis on the occupation and liberation of France and the Nazi holocaust.

•• *Ascend to the top floor.*

The **Musée des Plans-Reliefs** was founded by Louvois, based on the collection begun by Marshal Vauban, master of fortifications for Louis XIV. Maps, plans and models date from the 17C.

•• *Descend the stairs, exit and proceed ahead to the central pavilion of the courtyard's east range, where the museum continues.*

In the **Salle de Turenne** (R of the entrance) is a 17C model of Invalides.

On the wall L is the famous painting of Napoléon in coronation robes, by **Ingres**, 1806.

•• *Ascend to the second floor, turn R and proceed clockwise.*

Items from the accession of Louis XIII to the end of the Second Republic (1610–1852) are displayed.

Towards the end L are one of Napoléon's greatcoats, his battle-tent furniture and the flag of farewell raised at Fontainebleau on his abdication in 1814.

Napoléon's bedroom at Longwood House, St Helena, is reconstructed; some original furniture includes the camp bed on which he died.

The third floor deals with Napoléon III's reign, culminating in the Franco–Prussian War. In addition, posters, drawings and photographs from both world wars are displayed.

•• *Exit from the Hôtel des Invalides to Place des Invalides, R Rue de Grenelle.*

Location 9	**RUE DE GRENELLE**

Before the Faubourg St Germain was built up, this street led to a game reserve, where hares were hunted in their *garenelle* (little warren) – hence the name adopted for the thoroughfare. Between the late 17C and late 18C more than two hundred mansions were built in the Rue de Grenelle, encouraged by the

completion of the nearby Hôtel des Invalides. Fifty of
them have survived, but few remain as private
homes.

No 142 Now the Swiss embassy; **Delamair** built this
as the **Hôtel de Chanac de Pompadour** in 1750.

No 127 One of the finest Louis XV period
residences, this was built as the **Hôtel du Châtelet** by
Mathurin in 1770, and briefly served as the palace of
the Bishops of Paris.

No 138 Built as the **Hôtel de Noirmontiers**, by **Jean
Courtonne** in 1724; **Lassurance** was responsible for its
internal decoration, ten years later, for Mademoiselle
de Sens. The mansion became the army's staff HQ,
Marshal Foch dying here, 20 March 1929.

*●● First R Rue de Bourgogne. First R Rue de
Varenne. Cross the road to the Musée Rodin.*

Location 10	**MUSÉE RODIN** *Aubert 1730*
Hôtel Biron 77 Rue de Varenne (47 05 01 34) *Open Tuesday– Sunday 10.00– 1800. Closes at 17.00 October– March. Admission charge, half price Sunday.*	Major works of the sculptor **Auguste Rodin** are displayed in this mansion, where he spent his last nine years; they also spread into the garden. The Hôtel Biron, which retains much of its original appearance, is the only great 18C mansion in the Faubourg St Germain that the public may enter.

History Abraham Peyrenc, maître des requêtes, who
had acquired the title 'Sieur de Moras' commissioned
the building from **Gabriel the
Elder**. Peyrenc, a wigmaker, had speculated
successfully in John Law's financial bubble. Six years
later, the Duchesse de Maine, granddaughter of the
Prince de Condé and wife of the son of Louis XIV
and Madame de Montespan, bought the property and
redecorated it in the style of Boffrand. In 1754, the
Duc de Biron, a general who served in the
revolutionary government, acquired the house,
which still bears his name. Biron was guillotined in
1793 and the building then became a dance hall.
During the First Empire it was the residence of the
papal legate, and later, the Russian ambassador.

In 1820 the convent of the Sacré Coeur acquired the
mansion for a girls' boarding school. Unfortunately,
the mother superior, Sophie Barat, was a philistine
and ripped out the exquisite carved panelling, as she
thought it was 'vain'. In spite of this act (not
presumably because of it!), she was canonized in 1925.

Religious communities were dissolved by law in 1904
and the state acquired the property, permitting artists
to use its facilities. Matisse, Isadora Duncan and
Rilke were briefly in occupancy, the latter
introducing Rodin to the house. Rodin was permitted
to occupy the ground floor on condition that he
bequeathed his works to the state and planned the
Rodin Museum. The sculptor (born Paris 1840) lived
here from 1908 until his death in 1917, after which the
museum was established.

Exterior As it was built virtually in the country, on
the very edge of the *faubourg*, space was available to
permit an exceptionally large garden and a spacious
room layout.

To the west is the chapel built for Sophie Barat by
Jean Lisch in 1875.

•• Enter the museum.

Interior Most works are in bronze or in white marble with, for weight reasons, the larger, heavier sculptures occupying the ground floor or garden.

Some of the original carved panelling was repurchased and decorates ground-floor salons on the garden side.

•• Turn L and pass the card shop.

The Kiss and *John the Baptist* are seen immediately.

Rodin's first exhibited work, *The Age of Brass*, 1876, was considered so perfect that the sculptor was accused of producing a cast from life.

•• Ascend the 18C staircase to the first floor.

In addition to Rodin's smaller works and plaster casts, his personal collection of works of art, including paintings by **Monet, Renoir** and **Van Gogh** are displayed.

•• Exit from the house and turn L.

Garden Towards the north-west corner is *The Thinker*.

West of the house is *Balzac*.

•• Proceed to the building's south façade.

Much more Baroque in style, this façade has a *Three Graces* pediment, which was added to the house later in the 18C.

•• Proceed anti-clockwise.

In the north-east corner is the *Porte de l'Enfer* (gateway to hell), followed by the *Burghers of Calais*.

•• Exit from the museum R, rue de Varenne.

No 73, built by **Boffrand** in 1735 for the abbey of St Germain des Prés, was remodelled by **Leboursier** in 1785.

No 69, now a government building, was designed as the **Hôtel de Clermont** by **Leblond** in 1714 and extended in 1775.

No 78, the **Hôtel de Villeroy** of 1724, behind its courtyard, is faced by a 19C building.

No 72 was built in 1700 as the Grand Hôtel de Castries.

No 57, the **Hôtel Matignon**, since 1935 the official residence of the Prime Minister, is one of the faubourg's finest mansions. It was begun in 1721 by **Jean Courtonne** and completed by **Antoine Mazin** for the son of the Marshal of Luxembourg. However, before the building was ready for occupation, it was purchased by the Comte de Thorigny, Jacques Goyon de Matignon, and named after him.

Talleyrand owned the property 1808–11, when it became the residence of Louis-Philippe's sister, Madame Adelaide. From 1888 to 1914 the hôtel was the Austro-Hungarian embassy. In 1935, it accommodated the office of the President of the Conseil d'Etat (Council of State).

There has been much remodelling but internal Rococo work by **Fragonard** and **Huet** survives.

At the rear is the largest private garden in Paris.

●● *Return westward. First R Rue de Bellechasse. Proceed to the Rue de Grenelle corner (first L).*

No 110, now the Ministère de l'Education, was built as the **Hôtel de Rochechouart** by **Mathurin Chapital** in 1778. This is an outstanding example of the Louis XVI style; its massive façade, fronted by the courtyard, can generally be seen.

●● *Continue westward.*

No 166, now the **Mairie of the 7th arrondissement**, was built as the **Hôtel Brissac**, by **Boffrand** and **Leroux** for Marshal de Villars in 1731.

No 101, immediately opposite the Mairie, is the late-Louis XIV **Hôtel de Charolais**, built by **Lassurance** in 1714 for the Marquis de Rothelin. It now accommodates the Ministère de l'Industrie et de Tourisme.

●● *Return eastward to the Pentémont church.*

Location 11	**PENTÉMONT** *D'Ivry 1756*
106 Rue de Grenelle *Open (like most Protestant churches in Paris) for services only.*	The church was built as a convent chapel. Internally, a serene atmosphere prevails but there are no noteworthy features. Grisaille paintings decorate the dome's ceiling.

●● *Exit L, and cross the road.*

No 85, the **Hôtel d'Avaray**, was built by **Leroux** in 1718. Horace Walpole lived here during his term as British Ambassador to France.

No 81, the **Petit Hôtel d'Estrées**, was built in 1709.

No 79 was built by **De Cotte** in 1713 as the **Grand Hôtel d'Estrées** for the Duchesse d'Estrée. The hôtel has been the Russian embassy since the late 19C.

The original mansard roof has been replaced by the present pedimented top storey.

●● *First L Rue de St Simon. Second L Boulevard St Germain. First L Rue St Dominique.*

No 1, built by **Boffrand** *c.*1710 as the **Hôtel Amelot de Gournay**, is fronted by an unusual oval courtyard.

Nos 3 and **5** were built *c.*1710 as the **Hôtel de Tavannes**. Gustav Doré, the artist, lived at No 5 from 1849 until his death in 1883. The fine doorway incorporates a scallop shell emblem.

●● *Immediately cross Rue St Dominique and Boulevard St Germain and proceed northward, following Rue de Villersexel to Rue de l'Université R.*

No 51 was built by **Lassurance** as the **Hôtel de Soyécourt**, commencing in 1707. The doorway to the courtyard is flamboyantly carved with trophies.

●● *Return westward.*

No 78, built in 1687, has been immaculately restored and can generally be viewed through its doorway.

●● *First R Rue de Bellechasse. First L Rue de Lille.*

Location 12	**GRANDE CHANCELLERIE DE L'ORDRE NATIONAL DE LA LÉGION D'HONNEUR**

Hôtel de Salm
64 Rue de Lille

Musée Nationale de la Légion d'Honneur et des Ordres de Chevalerie open Tuesday–Sunday 14.00–17.00. Admission charge.

The present building is a late-19C reproduction of the finest hôtel to be constructed in the reign of Louis XVI. Built as the Hôtel de Salm for the German Prince Frédéric III de Salm-Kyrburg, its extravagance ruined him, and his architect, **Pierre Rousseau**, bought the hôtel, renting it back to his client a year later. Eventually guillotined, the prince ended his life completely penniless. In 1795, the hôtel was offered as a prize in a lottery won by Lieuthrand, an apprentice wigmaker. However, the new owner proved to be no luckier than the first as he was imprisoned for forgery and mysteriously disappeared. Madame de Staël, whose husband was the Swedish ambassador, bought the hôtel in 1799.

Three years later Napoléon created the Ordre de la Légion d'Honneur and the hôtel became its headquarters in 1804. The Communards burnt the building down in 1871 but it was rebuilt as an exact replica in 1878.

The main, south façade, exquisitely restored in 1987, including regilding, faces the Rue de Lille.

On the pediment, the words 'Honneur et Patrie' (honour and country) were first inscribed in 1804, when the building became the Legion's premises.

•• *Continue ahead. First R Rue de Solférino.*

Classical bas-reliefs, in the panels above the ground floor windows, are all that survive from the original building.

•• *First R Quai Anatole France.*

Originally, the palace garden reached to the Seine. Sculptures and reliefs are by **Jean-Guillaume Motte, Boguet** and **Philippe Laurent-Roland**.

•• *First R Rue de Bellechasse (pedestrianized here). Enter the museum.*

The Musée de la Légion d'Honneur et des Ordres de Chevalerie exhibits costumes, decorations, paintings and tapestries connected with France's only Order, which is awarded for twenty years' military or civil service to France.

•• *Exit L Rue de Bellechasse and proceed R to Quai Anatole France to view the north façade of the Musée d'Orsay.*

Location 13	**MUSÉE D'ORSAY**

1 Rue de Bellechasse

Open Tuesday–Saturday 10.00–18.00. Sunday 09.00–18.00. Thursday open until 21.45. Admission charge. (Queues are shortest at lunchtime.)

A grandiose gesture that only the French would contemplate. It is to this 19C railway station, converted at enormous expense, that those wishing to view the national collection of Impressionist and Post-Impressionist paintings must make their pilgrimage. Queues are generally long, both to enter the museum and, once inside, for the woefully inadequate toilet facilities. Strangely, the magnificent Impressionist paintings, all that most visitors wish to see, are on the top floor and there is no mechanical access from the ground to the middle level.

The great **Gare d'Orsay** (station) was built on the site of the Palais d'Orsay by **Victor Laloux** in 1900. It is a steel-framed building, clad with stone to harmonize with the Louvre on the opposite side of the river. Due for demolition in 1971, the structure was saved by the state and listed as a protected building. Conversion to a museum was soon approved and its opening planned for 1981, but this was eventually delayed until December 1986. The architectural competition, held by President Giscard d'Estaing, was won by **Gae Aulenti**.

The river façade, seen from Quai Anatole France, is the most imposing. Allegorical figures and the names of the stations formerly served (at upper level) are exuberantly displayed in the Belle Epoque manner.

•● *Enter the museum from the Rue de Bellechasse esplanade.*

Exhibits have been acquired from various sources, but chiefly the Jeu de Paume, Palais de Jeu de Tokyo and the Louvre. The period covered is the second half of the 19C and the early years of the 20C. It is recommended by the museum that visitors should proceed through the ground floor to the upper level, ending with the middle level. However, more than 5,000 works are displayed, not counting photographs, plans, models etc., and many will prefer to see the Impressionists and Post-Impressionists (upper level) first, before exhaustion sets in.

•● *From the entrance hall turn R, walk up two flights of stairs to the middle level (no lift or escalator connects these floors) and then take the escalator to the upper level.*

Impressionist and Post-Impressionist paintings, followed by the Pont Aven School and the Nabis, are exhibited, basically in chronological order.

•● *At the end turn R and descend by stairs to the middle level.*

Splendid examples of Art-Nouveau furniture and ironwork by **Guimard** are the highlights at this level for most visitors.

•● *Descend by stairs to the ground floor.*

Models of L'Opéra and the original group *Danse* by **Carpeaux**, which originally stood outside it, are exhibited at the east end.

Works by **Bonnard** and **Vuillard** on the south side enliven the display of 19C paintings.

•● *Exit from the museum R to Musée d'Orsay (RER station).*

•● *Alternatively, exit L. Third L Boulevard St Germain. Cross the road to M Solférino.*

4

Eiffel Tower

Virtually the symbol of Paris, the century-old Eiffel Tower still dominates the city and to make the ascent is a must for practically all first-time visitors. A great number of museums are passed on the way to the tower; not all will interest everyone, nor would it be possible to visit all of them on the same day.

Timing: To avoid disappointment, the Eiffel Tower's top stage should be ascended only in fine weather; views are usually clearest two hours before sunset.

Musée d'Art Moderne de la Ville de Paris and Musée de la Mode et du Costume close Monday; other museums close Tuesday.

Les Egouts (sewers) may be visited afternoons Wednesday to Sunday.

4

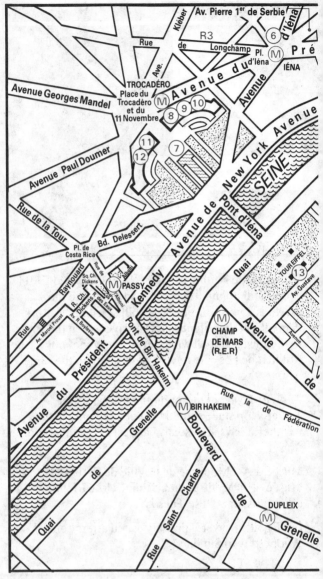

Locations

1 Pont de l'Alma
2 Egouts (sewers)
3 Musée d'Art Moderne de la Ville de Paris
4 Centre National de la Photographie
5 Musée de la Mode et du Costume
6 Musée Guimet
7 Palais de Chaillot

8 Musée National des Monuments Français
9 Musée du Cinéma
10 Théâtre National de Chaillot
11 Musée de l'Homme
12 Musée de la Marine
13 Tour Eiffel
14 Parc du Champ de Mars
15 Ecole Militaire
16 UNESCO

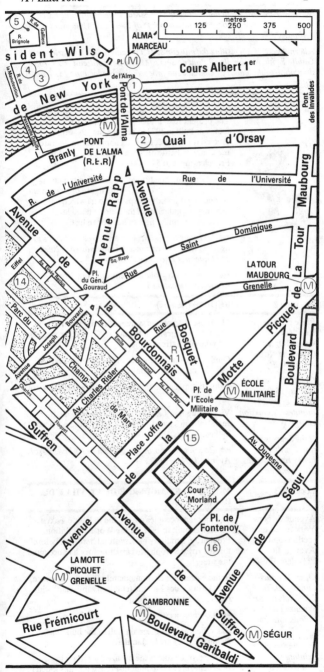

Start *M Alma Marceau line 9 Pont de Sèvres/Mairie de Montreuil. Exit from the station and proceed to the south side of Place de l'Alma and Pont de l'Alma.*

Alternatively, if not visiting the museums, M Trocadéro, line 6 Charles de Gaulle Etoile/Nation; line 9 Pont de Sèvres/Mairie de Montreuil. Exit from the station to the Palais de Chaillot and proceed direct to location 13, Tour Eiffel.

Location 1	**PONT DE L'ALMA**

The present steel bridge, with a clear span of 361 feet, was built in 1972 to replace the 19C original erected for Napoléon III. Its name commemorates the Crimean battle of Alma won by the Anglo-French army in 1854.

Saved from the first bridge, and fixed to the north-east pier, facing upstream, is the figure of a *zouave* (French light infantry corps member) which has long served as an indicator of the Seine's flood level. Three other similar figures have been lost.

●● *If visiting the Egouts (sewers) cross the bridge to its south side. The entrance L is signposted 'Visites Publiques des Egouts de Paris'.*

●● *Alternatively, follow Avenue de New York westward to location 3.*

Location 2	**EGOUTS** (Sewers)

Place de la Résidence Quai d'Orsay (opposite No 93) (47 05 10 29)

Open Wednesday–Sunday 15.00–20.00, every 20 minutes. Admission charge.

If the Seine is in flood or there is heavy rain no visits are permitted.

The present sewerage system of Paris (Egouts) was laid out by **Belgrand** in the mid-19C and corresponds with the city's street plan.

Guided tours of 300 metres of the subterranean galleries are made, lasting one hour.

Exhibition panels in the museum relate the history of the system.

Victor Hugo, in *Les Misérables*, set the scene for Jean Valjean's hazardous escape from the barricade in these sewers.

●● *Return to the north side of Pont de l'Alma. First L Avenue de New York.*

Location 3	**MUSÉE D'ART MODERNE DE LA VILLE DE PARIS**

Avenue de New York (children's section) and 11 Avenue du Président Wilson

Open Tuesday–Sunday 10.00–17.40 (closes 20.30 Wednesday). Admission charge.

NB times may vary for temporary exhibitions.

The museum occupies part of the Palais de Tokyo, which was built in 1937 for the World Exhibition. Previously, a military bakery stood here, but before this the royal Savonnerie carpet factory had occupied the site.

In the eastern block, immediately R, is the entrance to the Musée des Enfants (children's museum) with regularly changing exhibits.

●● *Continue westward.*

Bas-reliefs against the main wall of the building facing the river are by **Janniot**.

On the terrace stands the bronze *La France* by **Bourdelle**, erected to honour French patriots killed in the Second World War.

●● *First R Rue de la Manutention. R Avenue du Président Wilson. The museum is entered R.*

Paintings by the Paris School from the early 20C are exhibited. Those represented include **Derain**, **Dufy**, **Matisse**, **Modigliani**, **Rouault** and **Soutine**. The famous *Dance* by **Matisse** and the world's largest painting – 6,095 square feet, *La Fée de l'électricité* (*The good fairy of electricity*) – by **Dufy**, are on the lower floor.

Temporary exhibitions are frequently held and many items from the permanent collection are not then displayed.

•● *Exit L.*

Location 4

Palais de Tokyo

Open for temporary exhibitions Wednesday– Monday 09.45– 17.15. Admission charge.

CENTRE NATIONAL DE LA PHOTOGRAPHIE

Previously accommodating the national collection of modern art, this is now the most important photographic gallery in Paris.

All exhibitions are temporary as there is no permanent collection.

•● *Exit L. First R Rue Brignole. First R Avenue Pierre 1er de Serbie. Proceed to the corner (first R) of Rue de Galliera.*

Location 5

Palais Galliera, 10 Avenue Pierre 1er de Serbie.

Open Tuesday- Sunday 10.00– 17.40. Admission charge. No flash photography is allowed.

MUSÉE DE LA MODE ET DU COSTUME

Built in 1888 by the Duchesse de Gallieri, wife of a philanthropic financier, the palace is an Italian Renaissance-style building.

The museum displays a selection of outstanding examples of fashions from its vast collection of more than 5,000 outfits, dating from 1735 until the present.

•● *Exit L and continue ahead to Place d'Iéna. Turn R and proceed to the Musée Guimet on the north-west side.*

Location 6

Département des Arts Asiatiques des Musées Nationaux

6 Place d'Iéna

Open Wednesday– Monday 09.45– 17.00. Admission charge. Half-price Sunday.

MUSÉE GUIMET

This museum commemorates Emile Guimet, who founded it at Lyon in 1879 but, since 1945 it has been, technically, the Asian department of the Louvre. Guimet presented his collection of Indian and Far Eastern art to the state in 1888 and it was then transferred to Paris. Additions from the Louvre have greatly increased the number of exhibits, which are displayed on three floors as follows:

Ground floor Nepalese and South-East Asia, including sections from Khmer Buddhist temples.

First floor Indian sub-continent, plus the archaeological collection from Vietnam and China, of Robert Rousset.

Second floor Michael Calmann collection of Chinese porcelain, Buddhist banners discovered in a cave and Japanese dance-masks.

•● *Exit R. Third R Avenue du Président Wilson. Proceed ahead to Place du Trocadéro et du 11 Novembre.*

Facing the Palais de Chaillot is the equestrian statue of First World War leader **Marshal Foch**.

4

Location 7	**PALAIS DE CHAILLOT**

17 Place du
Trocadéro et du 11
Novembre

This exhibition building, designed as two separate
wings, was constructed, like the Palais de Tokyo,
specifically for the World Exhibition of 1937. Four
museums and a theatre now occupy the Palais.

Its hill-top site, the Colline du Chaillot, was
favoured, in the 16C, by Marie de Médicis, who built
a house here that was later to be remodelled for
Anne of Austria. Marshal Bassompierre, a
companion-at-arms of Henri IV, bought the property
but he annoyed the powerful Cardinal Richelieu in
1613 and was sent to the Bastille, not before, it is
said, burning 6,000 love letters. Henrietta of
England, who had married Louis XIV's younger
brother, Philippe d'Orléans, converted the house to a
convent in 1651. Early in the 19C, Napoléon
purchased the convent, intending to build a palace
for his son on its site. The convent was demolished
for the new building, but although **Percier** and
Fontaine designed a great palace which would have
eclipsed Moscow's Kremlin, it was never built.

'Trocadéro', which the area was named in 1827,
commemorates the Spanish fortification near Cadiz
that the French had captured four years earlier. Place
du Trocadéro was laid out in 1858 and its name
extended to 'et du 11 Novembre' to commemorate
Armistice Day.

●● *Enter the east (L) pavilion and proceed diagonally
R.*

Location 8	**MUSÉE NATIONAL DES MONUMENTS FRANÇAIS**

Palais de Chaillot,
17 Place du
Trocadéro et du
11 Novembre

*Open Wednesday–
Monday 09.00–
18.00. Admission
charge.*

Founded in 1879, following a suggestion of the
architect **Viollet-le-Duc**, the museum comprises
plaster casts chiefly made from large, decoratively
carved sections of buildings, and copies of stained
glass and murals. These trace the evolution of French
monumental art from the Romanesque to the
Classical periods. All are full size and closely match
the original colours and textures. Exhibits are
presented on four floors in chronological, regional
and school order, beginning at the ground floor.

●● *From the museum's exit turn immediately R. Turn
R and descend the stairs to the Musée du Cinéma.*

Location 9	**MUSÉE DU CINÉMA**

Palais de Chaillot,
17 Place du
Trocadéro et du
11 Novembre

*Open for guided
tours only,
Wednesday–
Monday 10.00,
11.00, 14.00, 15.00,
16.00. Admission
charge.*

*Film shows
Wednesday–Friday
15.00, 19.00, 21.00.
Saturday and*

A huge collection of memorabilia will delight the
movie buff. On permanent display are Edison's
kinetoscope, models of Eisenstein's sets, and
costumes worn by Greta Garbo and Rudolph
Valentino.

See the daily paper *Le Monde* for the week's
programmes (under *Spectacles*).

*Sunday 15.00,
17.00, 19.00, 21.00.
Admission charge.*

*•● Exit and proceed ahead to the front foyer.
Immediately L is the entrance (one of several) to the
theatre.*

| Location 10 | **THÉÂTRE NATIONAL DE CHAILLOT** |

*Palais de Chaillot,
17 Place du
Trocadéro et du
11 Novembre*

*Information office
(47 27 81 15).*

In 1948, the theatre hosted the third UN General
Assembly, and from 1951–72 the Théâtre National
Populair (TNP) performed here. Up to 1,800 can be
accommodated, surrounded by décor much of which
is the work of **Bonnard**, **Dufy** and **Vuillard.**

*•● Exit from the east pavilion L and proceed to the
west pavilion. (Immediately L is another entrance to
the theatre.) Proceed ahead to the Musée de l'Homme.*

| Location 11 | **MUSÉE DE L'HOMME** |

*Palais de Chaillot,
17 Place du
Trocadéro et du
11 Novembre*

*Open Wednesday–
Monday 09.45–
17.15. Admission
charge.*

This museum of mankind's development represents
an amalgamation of the Galerie d'Anthropologie and
the Musée d'Ethnographie du Trocadéro. Exhibits
from pre-history, Africa and Europe, together with
temporary exhibitions, are on **Floor 1**.

The USSR, Arctic, Near and Far East, Pacific and
America are dealt with on **Floor 2**.

Particularly highly regarded are the Aztec exhibits
from Mexico.

There is also a collection of primitive musical
instruments, recordings of which may be purchased.

*•● Exit from the museum and proceed ahead to the
front foyer. Immediately L is the entrance to the
Musée de la Marine.*

| Location 12 | **MUSÉE DE LA MARINE** |

*Palais de Chaillot,
17 Place du
Trocadéro et du
11 Novembre*

*Open Wednesday–
Monday 10.00–
18.00. Admission
charge.*

While in no way rivalling the scope of London's
National Maritime Museum at Greenwich,
enthusiasts of naval history will discover much of
interest.

Louis XIV's minister, Colbert, instructed that scale
models should be made of all important ships, and
many of these are displayed.

Figures on the *Soleil Royal* were carved by the great
sculptor **Coysevox.**

Napoléon's imperial barge of 1811 is exhibited.

In 1752, the Marquis de Marigny commissioned
paintings of the French ports and these provide an
important topographical record.

Also exhibited are a model of Columbus's *Santa
Maria*, an explanation of how the obelisk was
transported from Egypt to the Place de la Concorde
and *Redoubtable*, an early nuclear submarine.

*•● Exit from the west wing of the Palais R. First R
follow the terrace and descend the steps (either side).*

The terrace formed the entrance to the 1937
exhibition. Forty artists were responsible for the
statues and reliefs.

On the south faces of the pavilions that terminate
each wing of the Palais, the words of the poet Valéry
are inscribed in gold.

◗◖ Pass the pool and cross Pont d'Iéna to the Tour Eiffel. Proceed ahead L to its Pilier Nord (north leg).

Location 13 | **TOUR EIFFEL**

Champs de Mars

Open daily 09.30–24.00. Closes at 23.00 in winter.

The admission fee charged depends on the height of the stage visited and whether lifts are used.

Since it was erected in 1889, the Eiffel Tower has symbolized Paris to the rest of the world. However, when it was projected, many complained that the giant structure would disfigure the capital.

Gustave Eiffel, a structural engineer from Dijon who specialized in suspension bridges, conceived this tower as the centrepiece of the World Fair, which was held on the Champ de Mars in 1889 to mark the centenary of the French Revolution. First projected in 1884, the proposal met with furious opposition; the composer Gounod and writers Zola and de Maupassant were among its chief opponents on artistic grounds; many others feared that the tower would be unstable. Nevertheless, construction began in 1887 and the great tower was ready in time for the opening of the exhibition two years later. By then, admiration of Eiffel's technical achievement had overcome all dissent. Originally called the Tour de Trois Cents Mètres (Tower of 300 metres), at 984 feet high it was the world's tallest man-made structure until the erection of New York's Empire State Building in 1931.

Initially, permission was given for the Eiffel Tower to stand for only twenty years, i.e. until 1909, but in 1904 a radio antenna was installed at the top and the tower's continued existence was assured. Radio and television have been transmitted from here since 1918 and 1957 respectively, the television antenna increasing the structure's height to 1,051 feet.

Eiffel explained that the geometric form of the tower's pig-iron structure was 'primarily determined by mathematical considerations dependent on wind force'. Numerous interesting facts about the Eiffel Tower have been revealed, among them:

- total weight 7,000 tons
- ground pressure only 57 lb per square inch (equivalent to that exerted by an adult seated on a chair)
- in the strongest wind the tower never sways more than 4½ inches from the vertical
- all the girders are hollow
- each of the 12,000 components is replaceable
- there are 2.5 million rivets
- on hot days, metal expansion increases the tower's height by up to 6 inches
- stairways to the top comprise 1,652 steps
- the tower, which is constantly inspected for signs of rust, is completely repainted every seven years, when up to 40 tons of paint are used. It was last painted in 1988.

◗◖ Proceed to the Pilier Nord (north leg).

At the base of this leg, on its south side, is a gilded bust of Eiffel, 1832–1923, by **Antoine Bourdelle**, 1930.

The ascent may be made by lift from here or from the Piliers Ouest (west) and Est (east).

In the Pilier Ouest the lift retains part of its original mechanism of 1899.

From the Pilier Sud (south) access is by steps only
(363 to the first stage). Also from here, on the north
side, is a direct lift to the luxurious Restaurant Jules
Verne on the second stage; this lift is free of charge
for those who have reserved a table.

The **first stage**, at 187 feet, provides good close views
of the surrounding area.

At its lower level is a *restaurant rapide*, Le Parisien.

A section of an original staircase is displayed; all
were replaced in 1983.

Also exhibited is an original lift pump, still in
working order.

The **Belle France Brasserie** stands on the site of the
famous Restaurant Flamande.

•● *Continue by lift or stairs (700 steps) to the next
stage.*

At the **second stage** is the Restaurant Jules Verne
(45 55 61 44).

A buffet nearby serves more economical fare.

•● *Continue, by lift only, to the next stage.*

The platform of the **third stage**, at 899 feet, supports
a pavilion that can accommodate 800 people. From
here, the most 'aerial' views of Paris are obtained. In
perfect conditions locations up to 45 miles distant,
including Chartres Cathedral, are visible.

•● *Ascend the short flight of steps to the open terrace
at the upper level.*

Immediately L, through a window, Eiffel's *salon* may
be viewed. The engineer virtually retired here at the
age of sixty-two to conduct aerodynamic
experiments.

Waxwork figures commemorate Edison's visit to
Eiffel in this room on 10 September 1889.

A model of Edison's phonograph is displayed.

Opposite the stairs, a plaque commemorates the first
radio-telegraphic link between the tower and the
Panthéon, which was achieved by Ducrelet and
Roger in 1898.

Surmounting the tower is a red warning beacon,
which once revolved but is now fixed.

•● *From the foot of the tower proceed south-
eastward, crossing Avenue Gustave Eiffel, to the Parc
du Champ de Mars. Ahead lies the Ecole Militaire.*

Location 14 | **PARC DU CHAMP DE MARS**

Originally laid out in 1767, on what had been market
gardens, to provide the parade ground of the Ecole
Militaire, the park owes its present appearance to the
work of **C. J. Formigé**, 1908–28.

The Champ de Mars was opened to the public in
1780 and from here the first scientifically designed
balloon was released by Charles in 1783; it
descended forty-five minutes later, near Le Bourget
and was attacked by local peasants who thought it
was a monster. The following year, Blanchard made
his epic balloon flight from the Champ de Mars to

Billancourt. On 14 July 1790 Bastille Day was commemorated on the parade ground by the Festival of Federation. A crowd of 300,000 observed an open air Mass, during which Louis XVI, Talleyrand and Lafayette swore their oath of loyalty to the republic.

By 1794, the state officially rejected Christianity, although its leaders still believed in an all-powerful force and the immortality of the soul. Led by Robespierre, a procession marched from the Tuileries Palace to the Champ de Mars as part of the Festival of the Supreme Being.

During the Second Empire, a racecourse was laid out; five World Exhibitions have taken place on the site.

In 1889 the city of Paris exchanged, with the Ecole Militaire, land at Issy le Moulineaux for the Champs de Mars, and the latter's function as a parade ground ended.

●● *Continue ahead to the first major thoroughfare, Avenue Joseph Bouvard, which leads L to Place du Général Gouraud. Follow Avenue Rapp which runs diagonally ahead L. First R Square Rapp.*

Built by **Jules Lavirotte** in 1899, **No 3** in the far corner L, is reminiscent of the Modernist work of Gaudí in Barcelona.

●● *Return to Avenue Rapp R.*

No 29, also by **Lavirotte**, was built in 1901 for the ceramic manufacturer, Alexandre Bigot. Its exuberant entranceway is of particular interest.

●● *Return southward to Place du Général Gouraud. Cross Avenue de la Bourdonnais to Avenue Joseph Bouvard ahead. From the bus stop L take No 87 to the Ecole Militaire (thus saving a tedious ten-minutes walk). From the bus stop follow the north façade of the Ecole Militaire to Place Joffre.*

A statue of First World War leader Marshal Joffre, by **Raoul de Sarte**, 1939, faces the academy.

Location 15	**ÉCOLE MILITAIRE**

Place Joffre

For permission to enter the complex, write well in advance to Le Général Commandant Militaire, Ecole Militaire, 13 Place Joffre.

Even though less ambitious than originally envisaged, this great military academy is one of the outstanding architectural groups of Louis XV's reign. It was here that Napoléon received his training to become an officer.

History In 1751 Louis XV gave Paris-Duverney, an entrepreneur who supplied equipment to the army, permission to found a military academy. It is said that the King's favourite, Madame de Pompadour, had been instrumental in persuading Louis that his reign should be commemorated by a foundation to rival his predecessor's Hôtel des Invalides.

However, the King would not provide finance and money was eventually obtained by levying a tax on playing-cards. Members of aristocratic families, who lacked funds, were to be trained here for three years to become officers; barracks being provided to accommodate up to 500. A site was chosen, near Invalides, on the same Plaine de Grenelles, and **Jacques Ange Gabriel** was commissioned to design the complex.

The Ecole Militaire became a higher officers' school for the élite in 1777, and Napoléon 'passed out' here to become a lieutenant in the artillery. Aged fifteen, he had come from Brienne Academy, wanting at the time to be a sailor. Few know that the future Emperor of France actually wrote to Portsmouth with a view to joining the British navy. It seems that he was turned down, a decision that proved to be one of the most momentous in European history. In 1787, the academy was dissolved by Louis XVI and became a depot and barracks for the Swiss Guard, who remained here until suppressed at the Revolution. The National Guard took over the buildings in 1848. Thirty years later, the Ecole Supérieure de Guerre occupied the complex and French and Allied officers have been trained here ever since.

The north façade of the Ecole Militaire is the most important, and regarded as one of the finest examples of 18C architecture in Paris. Its central range incorporates the first-floor guardroom, the Salon des Maréchaux (Marshals' Salon) now the commander's quarters, and R the Chapelle St Louis.

Completed in 1773, the pedimented central pavilion, reminiscent of a château, is surmounted by a square cupola.

Its portico is supported by eight gigantic columns.

Above are four figures; that of Victory L was modelled on Louis XV and is the only statue of that monarch to have survived the Revolution.

Pediments of the two lower side wings, added by **Brougniart** in 1782, are decorated with trophies.

North and south wings are 19C extensions.

●▬ Return northward to the corner gateway at No 1 Avenue de la Motte-Picquet, the only entrance to the complex. If permission to view the interior has been obtained proceed to the gatehouse.

●▬ Alternatively, proceed to the rear of the complex as described later.

Visitors may be shown the Chapelle St Louis, the main staircase and the Cour d'Honneur.

Wrought-iron railings, designed by **Gabriel**, separate the Cour d' Honneur from the Cour Morland.

Louis XV laid the foundation stone of the rather plain **Chapelle St Louis** in 1769. It was here that Napoléon was confirmed.

●▬ Exit from the complex R to Place de l'Ecole Militaire. First R Avenue Duquesne. First R Avenue de Lowendal. Proceed to the railings of the Ecole Militaire R.

Those who have not entered the complex may view from here the Cour Morland and behind it the Cour d'Honneur.

●▬ Proceed to the south side of Place de Fontenoy, occupied by the curved façade of the UNESCO building.

4

Location 16   **UNESCO**

7 Place de
Fontenoy

*Open daily 09.30–
12.30 and 14.00–
18.00. Admission
free.*

Opened in 1958, the headquarters of the United
Nations Educational, Scientific and Cultural
Organization (UNESCO), was designed by three
architects: **Marcel Breuer, Pier Nervi** and **Bernard
Zehrfuss.**

A curved Y shape was chosen for the secretariat's
building and a separate conference hall has since
been linked with its south end.

The blue UN flag flies at the entrance.

•• Continue southward along Avenue de Lowendal.

Flags of all member countries are passed L.

*•• First L Avenue de Suffren. Proceed to the central
gateway of the UNESCO complex.*

Sculptures include:
Silhouette at Rest, a reclining figure by **Henry Moore**
Relief by **Hans Arp**
Black mobile by **Calder**.

•• Continue ahead to M Ségur.

Itinerary 5

5

Arc de Triomphe/Champs Elysées/Bois de
Boulogne

The world's most famous thoroughfare and
triumphal archway are visited, and the most
appealing section of the Bois de Boulogne
described.

Timing: Fine weather is preferable for the Champs
Elysées and essential for the Bois de Boulogne.

5

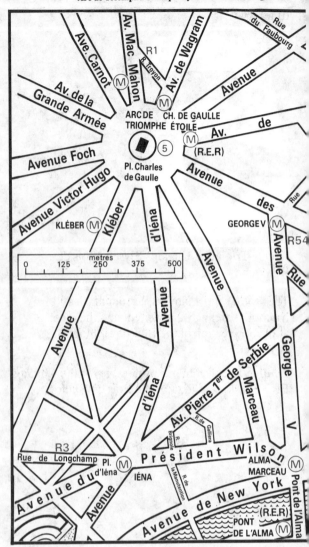

Locations

1 Petit Palais
2 Pont Alexandre III
3 Grand Palais
4 Avenue des Champs Elysées
5 Arc de Triomphe

(For locations 6–10 see map on page 88.)

Start *M Champs Elysées Clémenceau, line 1 Pont de Neuilly/Château de Vincennes, line 8 Balard/Créteil-Préfecture. Leave the station by the Petit Palais exit. Proceed ahead to the Petit Palais which is entered from Avenue Winston Churchill.*

Location 1	**PETIT PALAIS** *Girault 1900*

Avenue Winston Churchill

Musée des Beaux Arts de la Ville de Paris open Tuesday–Sunday 10.00–17.40. Admission charge, free Sunday. Times, etc. may vary for temporary exhibitions.

Both the Petit Palais and the Grand Palais occupy the site of the immense Palais de l'Industrie, an iron and glass structure, designed by **Jean Viel**, which had stood here since 1855. It was demolished in 1897 for the construction of the present buildings.

Commissioned for the World Fair of 1900, the Petit Palais has a Classical façade with an Ionic colonnade which is punctuated by a monumental Renaissance-style portal.

●● *Enter the museum.*

Most exhibits were bequeathed privately. Ranging from antiquities to the 20C, highlights include paintings by the Impressionists and Post-Impressionists.

●● *Exit L and proceed to Pont Alexandre III.*

Location 2	**PONT ALEXANDRE III** *1900*

Epitomizing the Belle Epoque, the exuberantly decorated bridge was constructed as part of the 1900 World Fair and named to commemorate the tsar who negotiated the Franco/Russian alliance of 1892. The foundation stone was laid jointly by Tsar Alexander's son and successor, Tsar Nicholas II, and President Félix Faure, in 1896.

The steel structure spans the Seine with one arch.

Gilded, winged horses on high plinths flank both ends of the bridge.

●● *Approach the north-west corner.*

Crouching beside the boy riding a fish is an extremely life-like crab. For almost a century, children have patted it and held the boy's fingers, which is why they are so shiny.

In the centre of the bridge, facing downstream R, is the allegorical figure of Neva, the river on which stands Leningrad.

This is balanced on the upstream side by a similar figure representing the Seine.

●● *Return to Avenue Winston Churchill. On the west side, facing the Petit Palais, is the Grand Palais.*

Location 3	**GRAND PALAIS** *Girault 1900*

Avenue Winston Churchill

Open for temporary exhibitions and the Palais de la Découverte (at the west end) Tuesday– Sunday 10.00– 18.00. Admission charge. (Some exhibitions are entered from the north side.)

Like the Petit Palais, the Grand Palais was constructed for the 1900 World Fair, but this building is more reminiscent, externally, of the heavier Louis XVI style. An iron framework, clad with stone, has a flat, glass dome (not visible from close quarters).

The south wing L forms part of the University of Paris.

A fanciful Ionic colonnade fronts the east façade. Behind this, a mosaic frieze traces the history of art.

•● *Enter from the colonnade.*

Internally, much of the detail is Art Nouveau although the building has been modernized to provide 54,000 square feet of exhibition space.

From the vestibule, the inside of the dome can be glimpsed but is mostly hidden by a fabric covering to the exhibition stands.

Iron staircases and galleries are exceptionally delicate.

•● *Exit L. First L Avenue du Général Eisenhower.*

Facing the north façade, in Square Jean Perrin, is the nymph fountain by **Raoul Laroche.**

A second entrance to the Grand Palais, from the north side, is frequently used for temporary exhibitions.

From this square, the flat glass dome comes into view.

•● *First L Avenue Franklin D. Roosevelt.*

The west section of the building accommodates the **Palais de la Découverte**.

•● *Enter from the lofty portico.*

The exuberantly decorated circular foyer, in modern Rococo style, is exceptional and may be viewed even if not visiting the exhibition.

Founded in 1937, as a museum of science and discovery, the Palais houses a Planetarium, together with both temporary and permanent displays.

•● *Exit R and proceed to Rond Point des Champs Elysées L.*

Location 4	**AVENUE DES CHAMPS ÉLYSÉES**

Running diagonally north-westward from Place de la Concorde to the Arc de Triomphe, this is probably the world's best-known thoroughfare. Undoubtedly, much of its fame depends on its great length – almost two miles – and width of 232 feet – combined with the superb end vistas provided by the Arc de Triomphe and the Place de la Concorde's obelisk.

History For most of its existence, the Champs Elysées (Elysian Fields) has had a rural aspect. Laid out on swampy ground by **Le Nôtre** in 1667, the unpaved track was lined with double rows of elm trees and first named the Grand Cours; it was renamed Champs Elysées in 1709. The Duc d'Antin extended the avenue to the Chaillot Mound, where the Arc de Triomphe now stands, in 1772. Even by the end of the 18C, only six private hôtels had been built along it, but by 1828 speculative building was well under way. During the Second Empire, amusement halls proliferated.

The Avenue today The Champs Elysées has now acquired three distinct identities. Between the Rond Point and Place de la Concorde, the avenue is bordered with wooded parkland, interspersed with the occasional small theatre and restaurant. Westward, towards the Arc de Triomphe, the south side accommodates many travel offices and other commercial premises. The north side is where the shops, mainly clothing boutiques, cafés and places of entertainment are concentrated and is of greater interest to most visitors.

•► *Proceed westward, remaining on the south side, to No 25.*

Fronted by a Bureau de Change, this mid-19C hôtel is the last privately occupied mansion to remain on the avenue. It was built for the Polish La Paiva, who married a Prussian count and became famous for her supper parties. The hôtel's original onyx staircase survives.

•► *Cross the avenue (with great care) to No 44, the Café la Colisée, opposite.*

This café's name commemorates one of the avenue's earliest buildings that stood on the site, La Colisée theatre, constructed in 1770 with a capacity of 40,000.

•► *Proceed westward, remaining on the north side.*

No 68 is the headquarters of **Guerlain**.

No 74, **Galerie du Claridge**, is lined with luxury clothing boutiques, including Lanvin. In the centre of the atrium is a unique glass timepiece which always attracts spectators.

No 116b is the entrance to **Le Lido** (43 63 11 61), still, after almost half a century, the capital's top night-spot. Specializing in the world's most elaborate cabaret sets, as backgrounds for the Bluebell girls, Le Lido is open to diners from 20.00 and for the revue only, at 22.15 and 0.30, when champagne is obligatory.

•► *Cross to the south side of the avenue.*

No 127 is the **Office de Tourisme** de Paris (47 23 61 72).

No 133, **Drugstore Elysées**, France's first drugstore, was very *à la mode* when it opened in the 1960s.

•► *Return to the north side of the avenue, from where the Arc de Triomphe may be approached by an underground passageway.*

Location 5	**ARC DE TRIOMPHE** *Chalgrin*
Place Charles de Gaulle *Viewing platform and museum open daily 10.00–18.00. Closes at 17.30 October–March.*	The Arc de Triomphe, the world's most famous triumphal archway, at 164 feet high, is the largest ever erected. It was commissioned by Napoléon in 1806 to commemorate the victorious campaigns of his 'glorious army', and the elderly **Jean François Chalgrin** won the architectural competition. **History** Initially, the arch was to be built where the

Admission charge (same price for steps or lift).

Bastille had stood, but it was eventually decided that the Place d'Étoile would provide a more imposing site. Work began in 1808 and a wall and two elegant toll pavilions by **Ledoux**, which stood on the east side of the Place, had to be demolished. The arch was built on a lawn in the centre. Foundation problems slowed progress, however, and after two years, when Napoléon's second Empress, Marie-Louise, made her triumphal entry into Paris along the Champs Elysées, the structure was only a few feet high. A dummy arch, painted on canvas supported by scaffolding, was therefore erected. Work on the arch, halted following Napoléon's downfall in 1815, was resumed in 1832 and completed structurally for Louis-Philippe four years later – a total construction period of twenty-three years. Sculptural embellishments, most of which formed a later phase, refer to the French Revolution, as well as Napoleonic triumphs.

In 1840, the chariot bearing Napoléon's remains brought back from St Helena, where he had died nineteen years earlier, passed through the arch and down the Champs Elysées witnessed by 100,000 spectators, many of them in tears. Since then, important processions have invariably followed the same route. The coffin of Victor Hugo lay in state beneath the arch on 1 June 1885, before being transferred to the Panthéon.

Chalgrin's design is not strictly Classical, there being no columns or Orders. It was obviously inspired by the arches of St Denis and St Martin, erected in Louis XIV's reign.

Against the arm R, on its plinth, stands the structure's finest carving *Rising of the People in 1792, summoned by the Genius of War*, often referred to as 'La Marseillaise', by **Rude**. Originally, **Rude** was to have been responsible for all the sculptural work, but his rivals (and inferiors) **Etex** and **Cortot** intrigued against him and the work was shared among many sculptors.

The upper storey of this and the other sides are decorated with circular shields, on which are inscribed the names of thirty-two victorious battles.

It was proposed by **Rude** that a huge, allegorical figure of France bearing a sword and torch, accompanied by a lion, should surmount the arch, but this was eventually vetoed. Later, a model of a quadriga was placed on the arch as an experiment; however, it was never implemented and the top of the archway remains unadorned.

•• *Enter the main arch (facing east/west).*

Names of 152 battles are inscribed on the inward-facing sections of the piers.

•• *Proceed to the south arch (facing Avenue Kléber).*

On this, and the corresponding north arch, the piers and walls are inscribed with the names of officers from the Revolution and First Empire periods. Those who were killed, or seriously wounded, are underlined.

A floor plaque, dated 4 September 1870,

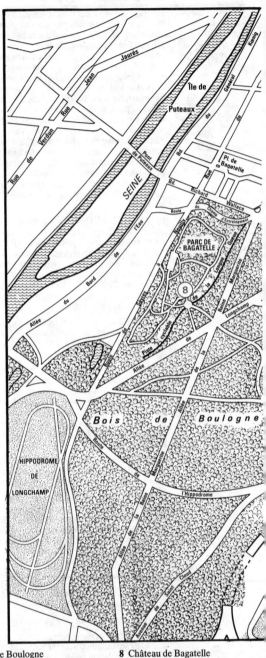

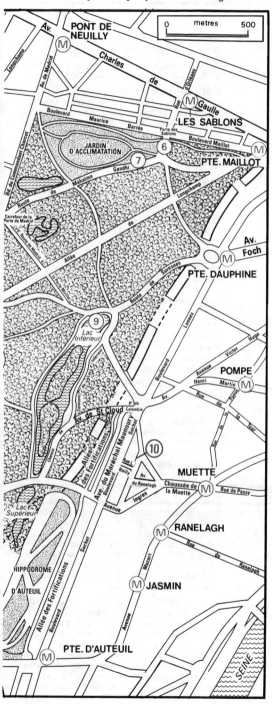

commemorates the proclamation of the Third Republic.

In the centre, set in the pavement, is Napoléon's bronze eagle emblem.

On the north side, a floor plaque records the return of Alsace and Lorraine to France in 1918.

Between the two eastern piers, an inscribed slab marks the tomb of the Unknown Soldier, buried here 11 November 1920 to represent all Frenchmen killed in the First World War. Members of the old soldiers' associations first lit the flame on 11 November 1923, and it is rekindled in a brief ceremony every evening at 18.30. France's annual remembrance service is held here 11 November, a national holiday.

At the foot of the tomb slab lies a bronze plaque, in the form of the shoulder flash of the Allied Expeditionary Force that freed Paris 25 August 1944.

The viewing platform and museum are approached from the north-east pier by stairs, or from the north-west pier by lift.

The symmetrical pattern made by the twelve avenues which lead from the Place below can best be appreciated from the platform. Originally, the Place Charles de Gaulle was named the Place d'Etoile (star) because of the shape of the square, from which only five thoroughfares formerly radiated.

Displays describe the construction of the arch and the ceremonies that it has witnessed. Mementoes of Napoléon and of the First World War are also exhibited and there is a continuous audio-visual presentation in English.

•● *Return to the pedestrian subway but turn L and proceed to the western exit Avenue de la Grande Armée. Take any westbound bus to Les Sablons.*

•● *Alternatively, proceed ahead to M Argentine and train to M les Sablons, direction Pont de Neuilly. At Les Sablons station, exit and cross to the south side of Avenue Charles de Gaulle L. First R Rue d'Orléans leads to Boulevard des Sablons and the Bois de Boulogne.*

Location 6	**BOIS DE BOULOGNE**

Once the hunting forest of the Valois kings, the Bois de Boulogne (Boulogne wood), with more than 2,000 acres of public open space, is similar in size to London's Richmond Park. It incorporates lakes, two racecourses (Longchamps for flat-racing, Auteuil for jumping) and a museum of rural crafts, but much of it is still heavily wooded with oak trees, some of which are several hundred years old.

The area received its present name early in the 14C, when woodcutters erected a chapel named after the church of Notre Dame at Boulogne, to which they had recently made a pilgrimage. In the mid-16C, the forest was enclosed. Louis XIV laid out the long straight *allées* that survive today and also, later in his reign, gave the public access once more. During the Revolution many trees were cut down to supply firewood, and more were lost after the battle of Waterloo, when English and Russian troops camped in the forest. The park's present appearance owes much to Haussmann, who formed the lakes, imitating the Romantic style of the Serpentine in London's Hyde Park, and created the racecourse at Longchamps in the south-west corner. At the same time, the great wall which bounded its east side was demolished.

•● *Immediately R of the Carrefour des Sablons is the entrance to the* **Jardin d'Acclimatation***.*

Open Wednesday–Monday 09.00–18.30 (18.00 in winter). Admission charge.

The garden is primarily aimed at children, and incorporates a small zoo, workshop, dolls' house and miniature car track.

•● *Exit R first R Route du Mahatma Gandhi.*

Location 7	**MUSÉE NATIONAL DES ARTS ET TRADITIONS POPULAIRES**

6 Route du Mahatma Gandhi

Open Wednesday–Monday 09.45–17.15. Admission charge, half-price Sunday.

The museum, with more than 5,000 exhibits, describes day-to-day life in France before the Industrial Revolution. Agricultural equipment and implements used for cottage industries are displayed, many in room settings. There are also examples of crafts, costumes, toys and games; folklore is explained.

•● *Exit from the museum R and follow Route du Mahatma Gandhi westward to Carrefour de la Porte de Madrid. Second R Route de Champ d'Entraînement. Proceed to No 4, the first house R, which is partly hidden by trees and a high fence.*

De Gaulle lived here, 1944–5, following the liberation of Paris, and in 1953, the Duke and Duchess of Windsor leased the palatial house from the city of Paris. Elizabeth II visited her uncle (formerly Edward VIII) here in 1972, shortly before his death; the Duchess died in an upstairs bedroom in 1986. Most possessions were then sold, but the house has since been leased to Mohamed el Fayed, the Egyptian owner of the Paris Ritz Hotel and London's Harrods store, and most of the furniture has been returned.

•● *Return eastward. First R follow the Piste cycliste de la Longue Queue to the entrance to Bagatelle R.*

Location 8	**CHÂTEAU DE BAGATELLE**

Route de Sèvres à Neuilly

Open daily. Admission charge. Tours of the château April–September, Saturday and Sunday 14.00–16.30 Admission charge.

Temporary exhibitions are occasionally held in the château.

Bagatelle's enclosed gardens are at their best when the famous irises bloom in the south-west corner in May and the roses, also at the south end, and the water lilies, in the north-west corner, in June.

The Comte d'Artois (the future Charles X) purchased a dilapidated mansion on the site in 1775 and wagered his sister-in-law Marie-Antoinette that he would rebuild it in three months. He won his bet easily as work was completed in 64 days, to the designs of **Belanger**, who reused the existing foundations. The English Hertford family acquired the property in the 19C and it became the residence of Sir Richard Wallace, natural son of the fourth Marquess. Wallace presented the rose garden to the city, but the family's outstanding collection of art treasures was transferred to Hertford House,

London, where, since 1897, it has been exhibited to the public as the Wallace Collection. The City of Paris purchased the château in 1905.

From the Bagatelle exit follow Route des Lacs à Bagatelle ahead. Continue to Lac Inférieur, keeping to the north side of Racing Club de France.

Alternatively, to shorten the route, return to Carrefour de la Porte de Madrid. Second L Boulevard Richard Wallace. Third R Rue de Longchamps. First R Place de Bagatelle. Return by bus 43 to central Paris.

Location 9 | **LAC INFÉRIEUR**

This lake, by far the largest in the Bois de Boulogne, provides its most picturesque element and is delightful on a fine day.

Proceed clockwise following the lakeside.

Rowing boats may be hired in the north-east corner (deposit required). From the centre of the east side a ferry operates to the two islands that are linked by a bridge.

Continue to the south end of the lake, where it is separated from Lac Supérieur by Carrefour des Cascades. First L Route des Lacs à Passy leads to Avenue Ingres. First L Avenue Raphaël. Proceed ahead to rue Louis Boilly.

Location 10 | **MUSÉE MARMOTTAN**

2 Rue Louis Boilly

Open Tuesday–Sunday 10.00–17.30. Admission charge.

This museum houses the world's largest collection of works by the Impressionist painter, Claude Monet.

Paul Marmottan, an art historian, bequeathed his house and collection of Renaissance and First Empire works to the Academy of Fine Arts in 1932. In 1950 Donop de Mouchy donated his paintings by **Claude Monet** which, in 1971, were supplemented by sixty-five further Monets, given by the painter's son Michel.

First Empire furniture and paintings on the ground floor are followed by Renaissance works, which include a room of outstanding illuminated manuscripts.

Descend to the Salle Monet.

This subterranean gallery was excavated specifically for the Monet paintings.

Eight works by other Impressionists displayed first, include paintings by **Renoir**, **Pissarro** and **Sisley.** The Monet collection is dominated by examples from his monumental water-lilies series executed at Giverny. Unfortunately, the same painter's historically important *Impression, soleil levant* (*Impression, sunrise*), which gave the movement its name, was amongst several paintings recently stolen from the museum.

Further Monets are exhibited on the first floor of the house.

Exit L. First R Avenue Raphaël. First L Avenue de Ranelagh leads to Chausée de la Muette and M Muette.

6

Montmartre

Due to the many painters who work in the colourful Place du Tertre, Montmartre is still regarded as bohemian and artistic. However, the last of the great avant-garde artists left the quarter at the outbreak of the First World War, just four years after the completion of its best-known building, the Sacré Coeur. In spite of the commercialism, charm still prevails, particularly on the north-facing hillside slopes, which are ignored by most tourists and where tree-lined 'village' alleyways are reminiscent of London's Hampstead.

Timing: Any day is suitable, but the Musée de Montmartre is closed in the morning and on Monday.

Locations
1 St Jean l'Evangéliste
2 Chapelle des Auxiliatrices
3 Place du Tertre
4 St Pierre de Montmartre
5 La Butte de Montmartre

6 Sacré Coeur
7 Musée de Montmartre
8 Moulin de la Galette
9 Cimetière de Montmartre
10 Boulevard de Clichy
11 Moulin Rouge

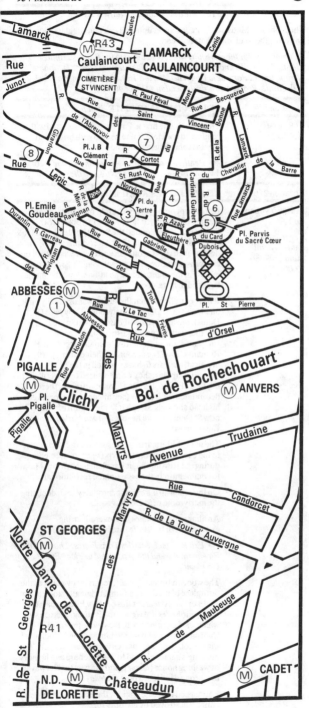

Start *M Abbesses, line 12 Porte de la Chapelle/Mairie d'Issy.*

The Abbesses Métro station's entrance, unusually, retains its glass roof. Exit and cross the road immediately ahead.

Alternatively, for those wishing to proceed direct to the Butte (summit of Montmartre's hill) and the Sacré Coeur, M Pigalle, line 2 Porte Dauphine/ Nation, line 12 Porte de la Chapelle/Mairie d'Issy. Bus 64 from Place Pigalle to the Butte. Proceed directly to location 4, Place du Tertre.

Location 1	ST JEAN L'EVANGÉLISTE *Baudot*
17 Rue des Abbesses	This church, the first in Paris to be constructed with a reinforced concrete frame, is clad with bricks and there is some unusual mosaic work.

 Return towards Abbesses station. Second R Rue Yvonne Le Tac. Proceed to No 11 on the south side R.

Location 2	CHAPELLE DES AUXILIATRICES

11 Rue Yvonne Le Tac

Crypt open Saturday and Sunday 09.00– 19.00.

In the crypt of the earlier church, built over the ancient shrine of St Denis, St Ignatius de Loyola and St François Xavier founded the Society of Jesus and took their first Jesuit vows in 1534. Everything was destroyed at the Revolution and the precise site of the church is unknown. The present building was erected in 1887 in the approximate position where the shrine is believed to have stood.

It has been alleged that the shrine was originally built on the site of St Denis's martyrdom. Dionysius (St Denis), the first bishop of Paris, was martyred, together with his priest Rusticus and deacon Eleutheris, during an anti-Christian purge by the Romans *c*.250. The account of their deaths, partly mythical, appears to have evolved in the 8C. According to this, they were tortured over a grill on the Ile de la Cité, taken to Montmartre and there decapitated. St Denis is then alleged to have picked up his head and walked with it to the suburb of what is now St Denis, where he fell, and was buried by a Christian woman.

The name Montmartre is presumed to be a reference to the execution of the martyrs (*martyres*); briefly, during the Revolution, it was changed to Mont Marat, to commemorate the assassinated revolutionary.

On the rear wall is a carving, probably 13C, depicting the martyrdom of St Denis.

An altar and side tables, discovered during excavations of the Butte, are believed to be 7C.

 Exit R. First L Rue des Trois Frères. Third R Rue Ravignan. Ascend the steps ahead to Place Emile Goudeau.

The wooden Bateau Lavoir, regarded by many as the birthplace of modern painting, originally stood at **No 13**. In the early years of this century Picasso painted *Les Demoiselles d'Avignon* in his studio there, a work which was instrumental in the development of Cubism. Others who joined him included Modigliani, Max Jacob, Braque, Juan Gris and Van Dongen. The building's name referred to its earlier use as a laundry or washing house (*lavoir*), and the way that it swayed in a strong wind like a boat (*bateau*) at sea.

Earmarked for preservation, the Bateau Lavoir was entirely destroyed by fire in 1970.

●● Ahead Rue Ravignan. First L Rue de la Mire leads up the steps to Place Jean-Baptiste Clément. Ahead Rue Lepic continues uphill R to join Rue Norvins.

At the intersection ahead of Rue Norvins, Rue des Saules and Rue St Rustique, Utrillo painted what is probably the best-known view of Montmartre; surprisingly little has changed.

●● Follow Rue Norvins ahead to Place du Tertre.

Location 3	**PLACE DU TERTRE**

Montmartre was still *c.*1871 a cheap but difficult to reach village and much favoured by young avant-garde artists, led by the composer Berlioz. However, at the outbreak of the First World War, most of them migrated to Montparnasse which became, briefly, the bohemia of Paris. Now, the Place du Tertre, Montmartre's tourist centre, is the haunt of commercial painters, who will sell their Paris views or paint the portrait of anyone with the time and money to spare.

Immediately R, in the north-west corner, **No 21**, now a tourist office, was the House of Free Commerce, founded in 1920 by Jules Dépaquit.

A plaque on its wall commemorates the world's first petrol-driven car, which was built in Montmartre by Louis Renault, who completed it 24 December 1898.

●● Proceed clockwise round the square.

In the south-east corner, **No 3**, **Maison Poulbot**, became in 1790 Montmartre's first *mairie*.

●● Continue eastward from the north side of the square, following Rue Norvins. Ahead lies St Pierre de Montmartre.

Location 4	**ST PIERRE DE MONTMARTRE**
Rue du Mont Cenis	Due to its relatively modern exterior, St Pierre (Peter), the parish church of Montmartre, is unjustly neglected by most visitors. In fact, the interior, one of the oldest in Paris, is of much greater interest than that of its more famous neighbour, the Sacré Coeur.

History A church, dedicated to St Denis, was built in the 7C on the foundations of a Roman temple which lay just north of St Pierre. The present building was begun in 1143 as the church of a Benedictine nunnery, the Abbaye de Montmartre. A fire badly damaged many of the monastic buildings in 1559, and in 1680 the abbey vacated its premises, moving down the hill; the entire church was then made available to the parish. This is now all that remains of the ancient abbey. It is believed that Dante was a parishioner of St Pierre during part of his sojourn in Paris.

Exterior The west front of the church was remodelled in the 18C, and the aisles and transepts were rebuilt between 1838 and 1905.

Its porch, built *c.*1683 to replace the 12C original, was kept when the west façade was remodelled.

The three bronze doors were designed by **T. Gismondi** in 1980.

●● Enter the church from the west front.

Interior Flanking the central portal are two monolithic stone columns, much worn. They are believed to have been taken from the nearby Merovingian church of St Denis, built in the 7C and, possibly, their shafts originated from the Roman temple previously on its site. Their marble capitals appear to have been carved between the reigns of Clovis and Dagobert I.

The base of the southern column is probably original.

Three elements – a gallery, a triforium and a clerestory – make up the walls of the **nave**. These lean outward, probably due to the strain placed on them by an earlier vault that collapsed in 1180 and was replaced by a wooden ceiling, which remained until the present vault was built in 1470.

The **north aisle** was entirely rebuilt in 1876 but not vaulted until 1905.

Stained glass in the aisle's windows (also in the apse and south aisle) was designed by **Max Ingrand** in 1953.

A high wall once stood at the east end of the nave's third bay, dividing the parish section of the church from the monastic section.

The fourth bay of the nave is noticeably different from the others, as its arches are Romanesque rather than pointed. This indicates that there was a reasonably lengthy interval before work began on the three most westerly bays, which are entirely Gothic.

An upright tombstone, in the fourth bay of the north aisle, L of the door, commemorates the founder of Montmartre's abbey, Queen Adelaide of Savoy, consort of Louis VI Le Gros (the Fat). The Queen died there in 1134.

•● *Proceed to the north transept.*

When the **north transept** was rebuilt in 1905, its vault of 1470 was re-used.

•● *Continue to the chancel.*

The **chancel**'s Romanesque cross-rib vault was built in the first half of the 12C, thus making it the oldest in Paris. It is noticeably lower than those in the rest of the church.

The two arches of the chancel are the oldest examples of the pointed Gothic style to survive in the capital (St Denis lies technically outside Paris).

Both columns of the most easterly arch, which are bound for support, are similar to those already seen flanking the entrance; they are also believed to be 7C.

The north and south chapels were rebuilt in 1905 but retain their vaults of 1502.

•● *Proceed to the* **south aisle**.

Standing in the southern chapel is the Renaissance font, made in 1537; it is similar to St Sulpice's and one of the oldest in Paris to survive.

The **south transept**, rebuilt in 1874, also retains its vault of 1470.

Rebuilt in 1838, the south aisle was vaulted in 1905.

● Exit from the church. First L Rue St Eleuthère. First L Rue Azaïs. First L Rue du Cardinal Guibert.

St Pierre's Gothic-style apse, and Romanesque-style tower, although 19C work, are attractive features. From the roof of an earlier tower a telegraph station operated between Paris and Lille, 1794–1844.

● Return southward to Place du Parvis du Sacré Coeur.

Location 5	**LA BUTTE DE MONTMARTRE**

In Montmartre, the Butte (hillock) refers to the summit, which is 423 feet above sea level. It was an important religious centre long before the advent of Christianity. Due to its strategic position, La Butte has witnessed several important military events. Henri de Navarre occupied it in 1589. Napoléon fought his last battle against the Allies here in 1814, before expulsion to Elba. The Communard uprising began on the Butte.

● Remain on the esplanade to view the south façade of Sacré Coeur.

Location 6	**SACRÉ COEUR** *Abadie 1873–1910*

Place du Parvis du Sacré Coeur

Dome ascent and crypt open April–September 09.15–19.00. At other times dependent on the weather. If doubtful telephone 42 51 17 02. May–October, 9.00–13.00 and 13.30–18.30; November–April, 9.00–12.30 and 13.30–17.00. Admission charge to each.

This whiter-than-white domed church, apparently floating above the rooftops of Paris, has become, for all its architectural mediocrity, one of the capital's best-loved symbols.

History Following the defeat of France by the Prussians in 1871 and the suppression of the Paris Commune, a Catholic movement evolved demanding that a church should be built on the Butte de Montmartre, the highest point in Paris, dedicated to the Sacré Coeur (Sacred Heart of Christ). It was believed that the French had lost the war due to their wickedness and that the erection of such a church would expiate their sins. **Paul Abadie** was commissioned to design the building and funds were sought from public subscription. Three million contributed and in 1873 plans were approved by the National Assembly. Unfortunately, the ground proved to be porous and extensive excavations were necessary. When **Abadie** died in 1884, only the foundations had been laid; however, work continued, accurately following his design, which was based on the Byzantine Romanesque style of the 12C St Front in Perigueux, a church that the architect had restored prior to gaining the Sacré Coeur commission. Nevertheless, another thirty-five years passed before the church was consecrated in 1919.

Exterior Practically all detailing is in the Romanesque style.

On the parapet of the south façade's vestibule stand equestrian figures of St Louis and Joan of Arc, by **Lefèbvre**, 1927.

Reliefs above the façade's two side windows depict *Christ and the Samaritan Woman*, by **A. d'Houdain**, and *Mary at the House of Simon*, by **L. Noël**.

The statue of Christ, beneath the pediment, is by **Michel**.

Two of the vestibule's columns bear south-facing

plaques which record Pope John Paul's attendance at prayer here in 1980 and the first service held at the Sacré Coeur in 1885, long before the building was finished.

◖ Enter the church, generally by the door R.

Interior The high altar stands at the north end.

Immediately on entering, the darkness of the interior presents a startling contrast to the external brightness of the sunlit stonework.

Abadie's Greek Cross plan is apparent.

The original stained glass in the church, shattered during the German retreat from Paris in 1944, has been replaced.

*◖ Proceed to the **chancel**.*

The vault's mosaic was designed by **Luc Olivier Merson**.
Joan of Arc, one of many figures, is depicted kneeling at Christ's feet.

◖ Return to the south door; R of this is the entrance to the stairs to the dome and the crypt.

Views of the interior of the Sacré Coeur from the **dome's gallery** are probably of greater interest than those over Paris, which add little to what has already been seen from outside the church. Ninety-four steps lead to the lantern.

*◖ Descend and proceed to the **crypt**.*

The Sacré Coeur's treasures are displayed and an audio-visual display relates the history of the building.

◖ Exit R. First R Rue de Cardinal Guibert passes the west façade of the church, which continues the Romanesque style.

At the north end stands the campanile, added by **Lucien Magne** in 1904. Its bell, 'Savoyard', at eighteen tons one of the world's heaviest, was presented by the Savoy diocese and cast at Annecy in 1895.

◖ Exit from the church R. First R Rue du Chevalier de la Barre. First L Rue de la Bonne.

From this street, the view southward of the Sacré Coeur is dominated by its tower rather than its dome. Relatively few tourists venture this side of the church and a more peaceful atmosphere prevails.

◖ L Rue St Vincent. At the crossroad with Rue du Mont Cenis continue ahead following Rue St Vincent.

Immediately L are the grounds of the Musée de Montmartre; but there is no longer an entrance from here.

Immediately past the steps L is the **Vigne de Montmartre**, Paris's only vineyard, which can be viewed through the railings but not entered.

Ahead, the westward view from the crossroad with Rue des Saules is one of Montmartre's most picturesque.

North of Rue St Vincent's continuation lies the **Cimetière St Vincent**, where Maurice Utrillo, the painter of Montmartre, is buried. He lived until 1956 but only his earlier works are regarded as exceptional.

●● First L Rue des Saules. First L Rue Cortot.

Location 7	**MUSÉE DE MONTMARTRE**

12 Rue Cortot

*Open Tuesday–
Saturday 14.30–
18.00 and Sunday
11.00–18.00*

The quarter's ephemera, and specimens of Montmartre porcelain, manufactured 1767–99, are exhibited. Painters Renoir, Utrillo and Dufy lived in this 17C house at various times.

●● Exit R. Ahead Rue de l'Abreuvoir. First L Rue Girardon. Second R Rue Lepic. Immediately R is what was once the Moulin de la Galette.

Location 8	**MOULIN DE LA GALETTE**

83 Rue Lepic

Now an Italian restaurant, Restaurant du Graziano, the former Moulin de la Galette, surmounted by its windmill, was a popular open-air dance hall in the late 19C. Renoir's painting of its vivacious night life has immortalized the Moulin's name. The Debray family, who ran the ballroom, had owned the wood-built structure since 1640, acquiring its windmill from Rue des Moulins in 1668; much rebuilding has since taken place.

●● Return to the Rue Girardon junction and continue westward following Rue Lepic.

Théo Van Gogh owned **No 54**, his brother Vincent staying here with him 1886–8 (see the plaque).

●● First R Rue Joseph de Maistre. Second L Rue Caulaincourt. After the large junction the road passes over part of the Cimetière de Montmartre. Descend the steps L to Avenue Rachel. Enter the cemetery L.

Location 9	**CIMETIÈRE DE MONTMARTRE**

20 Avenue Rachel

Open until 17.30.

The cemetery, laid out in 1795, is, apart from Père Lachaise, the best known in Paris. Buried here are the composers Berlioz, Delibes and Offenbach; novelists Dumas, Stendhal and Zola; painters Degas and Fragonard; the ballet dancer Nijinsky and the actor/playwright Sacha Guitry.

●● Exit from the cemetery and follow Avenue Rachel southward to Boulevard de Clichy.

Location 10	**BOULEVARD DE CLICHY**

Having left Montmartre's cemetery, the land of the dead, the visitor is now very much in the land of the living. Boulevard de Clichy, with its cinemas, sex shops, 'live' shows and fast-food outlets, is a concentrated version of London's Soho. North Africans have virtually taken over, and kebab stalls are everywhere. It cannot, however, be claimed that charm and quality are the hallmarks of much of this vulgar, honky-tonk land.

●● Continue eastward to Place Blanche.

6

Location 11   **MOULIN ROUGE**

82 Boulevard de
Clichy (40 06 09 19)

*Open for dinner
20.00.
Performances 22.00
and 24.00.*

Opened in 1889, the Moulin Rouge (Red Mill) was
where Toulouse-Lautrec sketched many of his
famous studies of cabaret artistes including Jane
Avril, La Goulque, Yvete Guilbert and Valentin le
Désossé. The Moulin Rouge, reminiscent of the Lido
on the Champs Elysées, is under the same
management. Although the sets here may be less
spectacular, the quality of the choreography,
including the invariable can-can finale, certainly
compensate.

• *Continue eastward to Place Pigalle and M Pigalle.*

The name of the Place commemorates the sculptor
and painter Jean-Baptiste Pigalle.

La Madeleine and the great shops

La Madeleine not only refers to the huge Neo-Classical church of Ste Marie Madeleine but also the area that surrounds it, which includes Rue du Faubourg St Honoré, one of the world's most famous streets for *haute couture*. A great number of luxury shops are passed on this route and even the hardiest window-gazer may well prefer to make several visits, rather than attempt to see everything in one day.

Timing: Many of the smaller shops close on Monday, and some on Saturday afternoon.

The Cernuschi and Nissin de Camondo museums close Monday and the latter also closes on Tuesday and 12.00–14.00.

Locations
1 Parc Monceau
2 Musée Cernuschi
3 Musée Nissim de Camondo
4 Musée Jacquemart-André
5 St Philippe du Roule
6 Rue du Faubourg St Honoré
7 Palais de l'Elysée
8 British Embassy

9 Cité Berryer
10 Place de la Madeleine
11 Ste Marie Madeleine
12 Boulevard de la Madeleine
13 Rue Vignon
14 Chapelle Expiatoire
15 Boulevard Haussmann
16 Lycée Condorcet
17 Rue Edouard VII

Start *M Monceau, line 2, Porte Dauphine/Nation. Exit towards Parc Monceau.*

Alternatively, if not visiting the park or museums, M St Philippe du Roule, line 9 Port de Sèvres/Marie de Montreuil. Exit and proceed to St Philippe du Roule church, location 5.

Location 1   **PARC MONCEAU**

Due to its miniature scale and picturesque layout,
this has been called the St James's Park of Paris,
but it is smaller, there are amusements for
children (roundabouts, pony-rides), architectural
follies, and one of the best surviving examples of a
Ledoux pavilion. Laid out by **Carmontel** for
Philippe Egalité in 1778, the park's name
commemorates the vanished village of Monceau.
Picturesque ruins survive, but there were
originally more, and the park was first known as
the Folies de Chartres.

Ahead, the late-18C Rotonde de Chartres was built
by **Ledoux** as a toll-house. Its design is based on

Bramante's Tampietto. Formerly serving as the park gatekeeper's lodge, it has now been converted to public toilets. The toll-houses were inserted where roads pierced the Paris wall, as collection points for the taxes imposed on all goods entering the capital.

Claude Ledoux designed all the toll-houses in the style of antique temples; there were forty-five varieties and no adjacent buildings were alike. Parisians despised the tax, which is now regarded as one cause of the Revolution, and the Paris wall was breached two days before the storming of the Bastille.

Every toll-house, each a splendid example of Neo-Classical architecture, survived until 1859 when the city limits were extended, thereby making them superfluous. Only three others now remain, Rotonde de la Villette, Barrière de l'Enfer (Place Denfert-Rochereau) and Barrière du Trône (Place de la Nation).

●● *Enter the park. First L follow the path to the pond and the Corinthian colonnade, which curves around the east side.*

It has been alleged that the colonnade formed part of the projected mausoleum of Henri II and Catherine de Médicis at St Denis, but some dispute this.

●● *Continue ahead along the path behind the colonnade, passing the ruined arch. First L the main path, Allée de la Comtesse de Ségur, leads to the exit at Avenue Velasquez. Proceed to the first house R.*

Location 2	MUSÉE CERNUSCHI
7 Avenue Velasquez	Cernuschi, a banker, died in 1896 and left the house and his collection to the city.
Open Tuesday–Sunday 10.00–17.40. Admission charge, free Sunday (except for special exhibitions).	Ancient examples of Chinese art dating from the Neolithic period are exhibited. Outstanding are the 5C stone *bodhisattva* and the 8C T'ang dynasty silk panel, depicting horses and grooms.

●● *Exit R. First R Boulevard Malesherbes. First R Rue de Monceau.*

Location 3	MUSÉE NISSIM DE CAMONDO
63 Rue de Monceau	This annexe to the Musée des Arts Décoratifs displays 18C French furniture and *objets d'art*, in Louis XVI-style settings. The house was built in 1911 for Count Moise de Camondo, and in 1936 he presented it to the city, together with its contents, in memory of his son Nissim, killed in the First World War. Although the house is relatively modern, the visitor gains a good impression of 18C life, many rooms being fitted with period panelling and carpets, several from the Aubusson and Savonnerie works. Of particular interest are pieces of furniture by the great **Riesener**, the tapestry series *Fables de la Fontaine* and a service of Sèvres porcelain, each piece of which is painted with a different bird.
Open Wednesday–Sunday 10.00–12.00 and 14.00–17.00. Admission charge.	

●● *Return to the entrance.*

Immediately L, a wall plaque commemorates the last members of the Camondo family, all of whom were exterminated at Auschwitz.

●● *Exit R and proceed ahead to Place de Rio de*

Janeiro. *Continue following Rue de Monceau, which stretches directly ahead. Second R Rue de Courcelles.*

On the Place du Pérou corner, **No 48, Galerie C.T.**, dealers in Asian arts, possesses unusually fat, pagoda-style eaves.

•• Return southward following Rue de Courcelles. Second L Boulevard Haussmann. Proceed to No 158 and enter the courtyard. Ascend the ramp ahead.

Location 4	**MUSÉE JACQUEMART-ANDRÉ**
158 Boulevard Haussmann *Open Wednesday–Monday 13.00–18.00. Closed August. Admission charge.*	Sponsored by the Armand Hammer foundation, old-master works, representing most European schools, are displayed. The château was built *c.*1870 for Edouard André. **Ground floor** French paintings and sculptures from the Louis XV period and works by **Rembrandt**, **Canaletto**, **Reynolds** and **Murillo** are displayed. Some ceilings are decorated with **Tiepolo** frescos. **First floor** Italian Renaissance and the Venetian School. Outstanding is *St George Slaying the Dragon*, by **Uccello.** *•• Exit R. Third R Rue du Faubourg St Honoré.* *•• Alternatively, if not wishing to visit the western end of the Rue du Faubourg St Honoré, exit R. First L Rue de Courcelles. Second R Avenue Myron T. Herrick. First L Rue du Faubourg St Honoré, proceed to location 5, St Philippe du Roule.* **No 208**, much remodelled, was built as the **Hôpital Beaujon** in 1748. *•• Continue westward to the western, i.e. second, junction with Rue Berryer.* **No 11 Rue Berryer** was built by **Visconti** in the 18C as the Hôtel Pontalba. It now houses the **Foundation Salomon de Rothschild**, and temporary exhibitions are held from time to time. President Paul Doumer was assassinated here in 1932. *•• Chocolate-lovers should continue westward, crossing Avenue Hoche and following the last stretch of Rue du Faubourg St Honoré.* **No 225, La Maison du Chocolat**, is where Robert Linxe makes and sells his world-famous, slightly bitter chocolates and chocolate cakes, generally rated the finest in Paris. By selecting a small quantity, one participates in the St Honoré luxury without vast expenditure, and passes, with a diminished sense of deprivation, the tempting establishments that follow. Make sure that the selection includes Linxe's exquisite *framboise* (raspberry cream). *•• Return eastward to St Philippe du Roule.*
Location 5	**ST PHILIPPE DU ROULE** *Chalgrin 1784*
154 Rue du Faubourg St Honoré Place Chassaigne Goyon	Roule was an ancient village of which nothing survives. This entirely Classical church which stands on the site of its predecessor, was designed as a Roman, early-Christian basilica, a style popular in Paris in the late 18C and early 19C. *•• Enter from the south front.*

Ionic columns, sensitively designed, entirely surround the internal space, in which the high altar is centrally positioned.

A stone vault was planned, but funds never became available and the original wooden ceiling remains.

The Classical pulpit is exceptional.

●● *Proceed to the chancel at the north end.*

Chapels were added by **Etienne Godde** in 1858.

●● *Exit L Rue du Faubourg St Honoré.*

Location 6	**RUE DU FAUBOURG ST HONORÉ**

Regarded by many as the most luxurious street in the world, practically all the great names in Paris fashion are represented. Comparisons with London's Bond Street are inevitable, particularly for the eastern stretch between the Elysée Palace and Rue Royale, but here the emphasis is more on ladies' fashions and there are no covered arcades.

Laid out in the 13C, the street was first named Chemin du Roule. St Honoré was a 6C bishop of Amiens and when the parish church was dedicated to him, the names of the *faubourg* (quarter) and its main street were changed. 'St Honoré' survived, even though the church was later rededicated to St Philippe. Many of the shop window displays are works of art, which will be admired even if there is no intention of making a purchase. The north (sunny) side of the street has most shops. Apart from the Elysée Palace and British Embassy, both on the south side, there is little of outstanding architectural interest.

No 101, **Dalloyau Gavillon**, founded in 1802, is one of the capital's great *pâtisseries*. Here, in 1955, the now ubiquitous chocolate/coffee gâteau known as an Opéra was created. Coffee macaroons, Caprice (pear) and Mogador (chocolate sponge-cake/mousse) are the specialities. Chocolates are also exceptional.

●● *Third L Avenue Matignon.*

●● *Alternatively, continue eastward.*

Passed R are the offices of *Le Figaro*, the daily Paris newspaper.

●● *Continue southward, First R Rue Rabelais.*

No 2 Le Jockey is the most exclusive club in the world. Founded in 1834 in the Boulevard des Capucines, by the English Lord Henry Seymour, whose intention was to improve the standard of French racehorses, the club was one of the capital's great attractions for Edward VII. Membership is difficult to obtain as an ancient pedigree is demanded and at least a hundred existing members must give their approval. The Duke of Edinburgh is one of the few foreigners to have been admitted. However, Le Jockey now has an affiliation with White's Club in London.

●● *Return to Rue du Faubourg St Honoré R and cross the road.*

110–112, Hotel Bristol. One of the capital's few remaining ultra-luxurious hotels, the Bristol boasts –

unique in central Paris – a heated, rooftop swimming pool with an outdoor sunbathing terrace. Furnishings throughout are antique or reproduction. In summer, meals are served in the hotel's highly regarded restaurant **Le Bristol** (42 66 91 45), under an awning in front of a vast garden, which has been laid out on the roof of the hotel's car park.

•• *Continue eastward. Second R Avenue de Marigny.*

No 27, **Pierre Cardin**.

Opposite, facing Place Beauvau (created in 1836), behind partly gilded wrought-iron gates, the **Ministère de l'Intérieur** has occupied its greatly expanded 18C mansion since 1861.

•• *Continue eastward. Immediately R, on the Avenue de Martigny corner, is the Palais de l'Elysée. NB for security reasons, no pedestrians may pass the Palais on this side of the road.*

Location 7	**PALAIS DE L'ÉLYSÉE** *Molet 1717*

55–7 Rue du Faubourg St Honoré

Since 1873 the Elysée Palace has been the official residence of the president of the republic, but only since the change to presidential government, forced through by de Gaulle in 1958, has L'Elysée become effectively the decision-making centre of French policies. No part is open to the public, but its courtyard façade may be viewed from the opposite side of the road.

History It is difficult to believe now, but when built, as the Hôtel d'Evreux, for Henri de la Tour d'Auvergne, Comte d'Evreux, this was a dilapidated quarter. By repute, Evreux was extremely mean, and the Regent, to cure him of this trait, insisted on visiting the count. To receive his exalted guest suitably, Evreux had to spend a great deal of money on the mansion and thus transformed it into a sumptuous palace. However, the strain of parting with all that money was too much, and poor Evreux died, an imbecile, three years later.

Madame de Pompadour, Louis XV's despised mistress, bought the property in 1750 and commissioned **Boucher**, **Verberk** and **Van Loo** to decorate its interior. In addition, the grounds, much of which had been given to Evreux by the Regent, were extended southward to the gardens of the Champs Elysées. Although their love affair had long ended, Madame de Pompadour bequeathed the estate to Louis XV. The King, however, never stayed here and the house was occupied by foreign ambassadors. When Louis XVI inherited the property, he presented it to his cousin Bathilde d'Orléans, who gave the palace its present name.

At the Revolution, the building became a restaurant/ night club and a funfair was held in its garden.

Murat, husband of Napoléon's sister Caroline, purchased the estate in 1805, but on becoming King of Naples gave it to Napoléon, whose first consort Joséphine occasionally stayed here. Napoléon signed his second abdication in the Elysée Palace on 22 June 1815, following his defeat at Waterloo.

The future Napoléon III, when Louis-Napoléon,

lived here from 1848 until he moved to the Tuileries Palace, on becoming emperor following his *coup d'état* in 1851.

Visiting royalty who have stayed in the palace from time to time include Queen Victoria, for the World Fair of 1855, and Elizabeth II in 1957.

De Gaulle thoroughly disliked the palace, although he, like each succeeding president, has left his mark. Pompidou introduced modern works of art, but Giscard d'Estaing promptly replaced them with Louis XVI antiques, even though he used only the presidential office. It was Pompidou also who commissioned 'Studio Jupiter', the anti-nuclear fallout shelter beneath the building, from where France's nuclear defence system is controlled. Mitterrand, a modernist, introduced sculptures by **Picasso**, **Giacometti**, etc. in the garden and put the decor of his private suite in the hands of contemporary artists, including the French '*enfant terrible*', **Philippe Starck**.

In spite of all these changes, the Salon Doré, decorated for the Empress Eugénie by **Louis Godon** in 1861, and now the presidential office, has survived unaltered.

Trophies flanking the entrance arch refer to Evreux's military status as a colonel-general in the cavalry.

The 'Elysée army', effectively the president's bodyguard, is stationed in the east wing.

•• *Continue eastward to the British Embassy, also on the south side of the road.*

Passed (**No. 41**) is the residence of the US ambassador.

Location 8	**BRITISH EMBASSY** *Mazin 1723*

35–59 Rue du Faubourg St Honoré

Napoléon's second sister, Pauline Bonaparte, bought the property – built as the Hôtel de Charost – in 1803 and some of her furniture remains, including her outstanding Empire-period bed, now placed at the disposal of British ambassadors. Following Napoléon's first exile in 1814, Wellington, then a general, purchased the house from her and moved in within a week. He related in a letter his amusement on discovering that, like the Elysée Palace, his garden ran down to the 'Elysian Fields'.

The embassy's dining room was originally a Protestant chapel and here, in 1833, the composer Berlioz married Harriet Smithson; Liszt was in attendance as best man. The novelist Thackeray was also married here three years later.

Above the gates are carved the royal arms of the United Kingdom.

Unless the gates are opened to admit vehicles, little of the building can be seen.

•• *Continue eastward.*

Adjoining the embassy, **No 33** was the birthplace, in 1874, of the novelist Somerset Maugham.

From here eastward are concentrated the fashion shops, including: **No 46**, **Courrèges**; **No 38**, **Yves St Laurent**; **No 29**, **Pierre Cardin** and **Lancôme**;

No 25, **Pierre Balmain**; No 30, **Guy Laroche**; No 23,
Ted Lapidus and **Cartier**; No 28, **Hermés**,
consistently judged to be one of the world's finest
window displays (all fourteen of them); **No 19**, **Karl
Lagerfeld**; **No 15**, and **No 22** opposite, **Lanvin** (No 13
does not exist, as the superstitious Empress Eugénie
suppressed it); **No 2**, **Gucci**; **No 1**, **Jacques Heim**.

*First L Rue Royale (see page 142 for its south
section). First L Cité Berryer (entered from No 25 Rue
Royale).*

Location 9   CITÉ BERRYER

The Cité Berryer market transferred to Place de la
Madeleine in 1987 and the much needed
refurbishment of this attractive thoroughfare,
virtually a wide, elongated courtyard, began. Bars
and restaurants predominate, with the emphasis, in
summer, on alfresco eating.

*Return to Rue Royale L and continue to Place de
la Madeleine.*

Location 10   PLACE DE LA MADELEINE

A 'foodies' paradise, no other gastronomic centre in
the world approaches this extraordinary square.
Caviar, truffles, champagne, foie gras, rare fruits and
cheeses, all are to be found in Place de la Madeleine's
luxurious shops. A visit on an empty stomach is not
recommended as the suffering will be intolerable.

On the Rue Royale corner L, is **No 27 Cerrutti 1881**,
the fashionable men's clothing store.

Boulevard Malesherbes runs diagonally north-
westward (first L).

Closing the vista can be seen the undistinguished
church of **St Augustin**, designed by **Baltard** (architect
of the demolished Les Halles market buildings) in
1860. It was the first French church to be built with an
iron structure.

Proceed clockwise around Place de la Madeleine.

No 17, Caviar Kaspa Not only does this
establishment sell various types of caviar and smoked
fish, but many of its products may be sampled in the
first-floor restaurant.

No 17, Créplet Brussol A vast range of cheeses, all of
which are finally matured in the cellars below, has
made this one of the capital's great *fromageries*.

No 19, La Maison de la Truffe Although preserved
truffles are always in stock, only during autumn and
winter are they available fresh. In late October the
white variety from Italy, the most aromatic and the
most expensive, begins to arrive. This is followed, in
late November, by the black Périgord truffles.

Cross Rue Tronchet.

No 21, Hédiard Hédiard sells a range of foods,
specializing in exotic fresh fruits, house-brand
confectionery, preserves of all types, spices, teas and
coffee beans.

No 26, Fauchon Possibly the world's finest luxury
food store, Fauchon occupies two buildings in the

north-east corner of the Place, separated by the Rue de Sèze.

In the north shop, first seen, the windows are virtually exhibitions of the pastrycook's and confectioner's arts. Inside is the famous café (standing only) where gateaux, ice cream, etc. may be enjoyed (pay first before collecting the items required).

Fauchon's shop on the east side of the Place is larger and offers thousands of goods, including prepared take-away luxury dishes. The range of *charcuterie* is particularly staggering.

•• *Continue southward to the Rue Royale corner (second L).*

No 2, Ralph Lauren, the men's outfitter, now occupies this building, which for many years was the Paris headquarters of Thomas Cook, the international travel agents. Formerly, its ground floor housed the Café Durand, where Zola drafted his 'J'Accuse' letter, published in Clemenceau's journal *L'Aurore*, which accused the army of concealing evidence in the Dreyfus case; Zola was subsequently found guilty of libel.

•• *Proceed to Ste Marie Madeleine in the centre of the Place.*

Immediately east of the church is a flower market.

The old Cité Berryer market is now held in the Place de la Madeleine Tuesday and Thursday.

Location 11	STE MARIE MADELEINE
Place de la Madeleine	Dedicated to St Mary Magdalene, 'La Madeleine' was initially designed as a Classical temple to honour Napoléon's victorious army, and a vengeful, almost pagan force prevails.

History The foundation stone of a domed, Baroque church, virtually a copy of the Panthéon, then under construction, was laid in 1764, but its architect, **Constant d'Ivry**, died in 1777 and **Couture** took over. Work ceased at the Revolution, with the south portico still unfinished, and the building became successively a stock exchange, parliament house, library and a bank. In 1806 Napoléon commissioned **Pierre Vignon** to replace the building with a hall of fame for his victorious army, and the existing structure was demolished. Work recommenced, seemingly inspired by the Roman Maison Carrée at Nîmes. In the event, however, the Arc de Triomphe took over the planned function of the building, and it was decided that it should revert, as originally intended, to a church. The interior, therefore, was redesigned, work continuing at the Restoration, when Louis XVIII decreed that 'La Madeleine' would serve as an act of expiation for the guillotining of Louis XVI and Marie-Antoinette. However, in 1837, prior to its completion, there was a proposal that Paris's first railway terminal should be sited here and the church narrowly escaped demolition. A new architect, **Jean-Jacques Hure**, took over and the building was finally consecrated and dedicated by Louis-Philippe to St Mary Magdalene in 1842.

Exterior The building is entirely surrounded by a

gigantic Corinthian colonnade resting on an 11-foot-high base, the south side of which provides the entry steps. Statues of the thirty-four saints, that occupy niches in the walls, were added later in the 19C.

The pediment's *Last Judgement* relief, carved by **Philippe Lemaire** 1833, has been heavily restored. It depicts a far from emaciated Christ.

Below is inscribed '*Rendue à sa destination primitive en 1816*' (Returned to its original purpose in 1816).

The bronze doors, illustrating the Ten Commandments, were designed by **Triquetti**, best known in England for his work at Windsor Castle's Albert Memorial Chapel.

•● Enter the church.

Interior La Madeleine is windowless and the gloom, combined with a liberal application of marble, evokes a mausoleum.

Standing in the first chapel on the west side is a marble group, *Baptism of Christ*, by **Rude**.

Sculptures and decoration throughout are entirely 19C.

Three saucer domes, providing some natural light, lead the visitor to the apse at the north end.

Paintings of the apostles by **Pradier**, **Rude** and **Foyatier** decorate the wall behind the sanctuary's arcade.

The apse's ceiling fresco, by **Ziegler**, depicts Christ giving his blessing. Historical figures in the painting include Constantine the Great and Joan of Arc.

At the base, Napoléon receives the imperial crown from Pope Pius VII.

The marble altarpiece, depicting Mary's Assumption, is by **Carlo Marochetti**, 1837.

The most southerly chapel on the east side accommodates a marble group, *Marriage of the Virgin*, by **Pradier**.

•● Exit L, cross to the east side of the Place, and follow Boulevard de la Madeleine, which runs diagonally north-eastward.

Location 12	**BOULEVARD DE LA MADELEINE**

This is the most westerly of the Grands Boulevards, created 1670–1705. They were built between the Porte St Denis and the Bastille, on part of the site of the 200-foot-wide rampart (*boulevard*), surrounding the Paris wall, which extended in a semi-circle between what are now the Place de la Concorde and the Place de la Bastille. Following his victories in Germany and Holland, Louis XIV decided that the city's defences were no longer necessary and, apart from fragments of the wall, everything was demolished. Originally known as the 'Boulevard des Maréchaux' or, more simply, 'The Boulevard', stretches of varying length have since been given separate, identifying names: Madeleine, Capucines, Italiens, Montmartre, Poisonnière, Bonne Nouvelle, Saint Denis, Saint Martin, Temple, Filles de Calvaire and Beaumarchais. They are not to be confused with

Haussmann's boulevards, which were laid out from the mid-19C in a far more regulated way.

Nos 17–25, Aux Trois Quartiers The name of this department store, the most luxurious in Paris, commemorates a play that was popular in the 19C. Goods are of high quality, with ladies' gloves (ground floor) and linens (third floor) being particularly highly regarded.

No 15 This building (formerly No 11) was, in the 19C, the confectioner's, 'A la Marquise de Sévigné', where Marie Duplessis died in 1847. She was the prototype of Alexandre Dumas the younger's *La Dame aux Camélias* and Marguerite, in Verdi's *La Traviata*.

●● *Return westward. First R Rue Vignon.*

Location 13	**RUE VIGNON**

Rue Vignon, an attractive street, includes several speciality food shops.

No 18, Tanrade, founded in 1820. The Tanrade family, which still owns the premises, moved here just after the First World War. Their fresh *marrons glacés*, available only in winter, hand-made preserves and bitter chocolate are world-famous. The shop's Art-Deco furnishings are original and beautifully maintained.

No 21, La Ferme St Hubert Expertly kept cheeses, at a reasonable price for the Madeleine area, are beautifully displayed.

No 24, La Maison du Miel Honey and honey derivatives have been sold here by the Galland family since 1908. Much of the honey comes from their own French beehives, with each new season's produce available from late summer.

●● *Continue to the end of Rue Vignon. R Rue Tronchet. First L Rue des Mathurins. Second R Rue Pasquier. Immediately L is Square Louis XVI.*

Location 14	**CHAPELLE EXPIATOIRE** *Percier* and *Fontaine* 1826

Square Louis XVI

Open daily 10.00–17.45. Closes 17.00 October–March. Admission charge.

Built on the site of the cemetery where the decapitated bodies of Louis XVI and Marie-Antoinette lay for twenty-one years, this chapel was commissioned by the late King's brother, Louis XVIII, as an act of French expiation for their execution.

The cemetery, then attached to the convent of Ste Marie Madeleine, was opened in 1722. Buried here were the bodies of the 133 crushed to death during the fireworks display given to celebrate the marriage of Louis XVI and Marie-Antoinette in 1770, the Swiss Guards killed defending the Tuileries Palace in 1779 and the 1,119 guillotined in the Place de la Concorde between 26 August 1792 and 24 March 1794. In 1797, the cemetery was abandoned and sold to a royalist lawyer who lived nearby and had noted exactly where the most illustrious victims were buried. All the bodies were removed in 1815, most being transferred to the catacombs; those of Louis XVI and Marie-Antoinette, however, were removed to the crypt of St Denis Cathedral.

● *Purchase tickets R of the entrance, proceed through the double doors and pass through the garden (the stones on either side are not tombs but symbolic).*

On either side of the steps are buried Charlotte Corday, Marat's assassin, and Philippe Egalité.

● *Enter the chapel.*

Immediate L is the memorial to Marie-Antoinette, by **Cortot.** She is shown supported by an allegorical figure of Religion, the face of which was modelled on Louis XVI's sister, Madame Elisabeth, who was guillotined later. Below are inscribed the words of Marie-Antoinette's last letter, written to Madame Elisabeth on the day of her execution, 16 October 1793.

Louis XVI's memorial, by **Bosio**, shows the King being conducted to heaven by an angel in the form of his confessor, the abbot Henry Essex Edgworth, who was by his side at the guillotine, 21 January 1793. Beneath is inscribed the King's moving will, in which he forgives his persecutors.

Above the door, the bas-relief, by **Gerard**, depicts the transfer of the royal remains to St Denis on 21 January 1815, the twenty-second anniversary of the King's execution.

In the crypt, an altar marks the spot where Louis XVI's body had been buried.

● *Exit L. First R Boulevard Haussmann.*

Location 15 | **BOULEVARD HAUSSMANN**

The name of this long thoroughfare commemorates Baron Georges-Eugène Haussmann, a Protestant of Alsatian descent, who was Napoléon III's city planner extraordinaire. Haussmann, trained as a lawyer, was appointed Prefect of the Seine, aged forty-four. He rebuilt approximately a third of the capital between 1852–70, and the ancient warrens, mainly of three-storey houses occupied by the poor, were replaced by wide, straight avenues, lined with seven-storey terraces of apartments, which only the *bourgeoisie* could afford; the artisan class was thereby effectively banished to the suburbs. It has been suggested that the Emperor commissioned the new boulevards to allow his troops to move speedily against insurgents, but this is disputed.

Unfortunately, Haussmann was not a preservationist and much fine and historic architecture was lost, particularly on the Ile de la Cité, where practically all the medieval streets were replaced. The incorruptible Haussmann even demolished his own birthplace in Rue du Faubourg du Roule. Most visitors to Paris find little of interest within 'Haussmannized' areas. Sadly, the planning supremo had no great architect at his command and the terraces are monotonously repetitive.

● *Continue eastward to the Rue Tronchet intersection and cross to Au Printemps store on the north side.*

No 64, Au Printemps Apart from its vast ground-floor perfumery, this old-established department store has now allocated its entire **Le Printemps de la Maison** building to household items.

→ Proceed to the next block.

Known as **Le Printemps de la Mode**, the second building concentrates on fashions; men's on the ground floor.

→ Continue eastward.

→ Alternatively, proceed between the two sections of Au Printemps and follow Rue de Caumartin northward to location 15, Lycée Condorcet.

No 40, **Galeries Lafayette** Again spread over two buildings, Galeries Lafayette is slightly more luxurious, practically all the fashionable brand names being represented. Evocative of the Belle Epoque, its second building consists of pretty galleries built around a circular glass-domed atrium.

→ Directly opposite is Marks and Spencer.

No 35, **Marks and Spencer** The famous British chain store's Paris outlet attracts French shoppers with its reasonable prices; clothing quality is significantly higher than in England. English-style bacon and cheeses (rather too well-refrigerated) are the great attraction for expatriates and anglophiles.

→ Exit L. Third R Rue de Caumartin.

Location 16	**LYCÉE CONDORCET** *Brongniart 1783*

Rue de Caumartin

It seems incongruous that this outstandingly calm structure should be sited in the pedestrianized Rue de Caumartin, an amusing but brash thoroughfare, reminiscent of London's Carnaby Street.

Certainly one of the finest Neo-Classical buildings in Paris, the Lycée's powerful, beautifully proportioned façade might have been lifted from Florence. It was built, just before the Revolution, as a Capuchin convent.

→ Return southward and cross Boulevard Haussmann to Rue de Caumartin's southern continuation. Second L Rue Boudreau. First R proceed to Square de l'Opéra Louis Jouvet (passing R Théâtre Athénée). Continue to Rue Edouard VII and Place Edouard VII.

Location 17	**RUE ÉDOUARD VII**

Fortunate indeed is England's Edward VII to be commemorated by this street and its Place, which form the centrepiece of a delightful, village-style succession of small squares linked by curved archways and colonnades.

Edward was a great francophile and the street was named as a tribute to the King, following his visit to Paris in 1910.

His equestrian monument, by **Landowski**, is the only public statue of an Englishman in the city.

→ Continue ahead to Boulevard des Capucines R, which leads to Boulevard de la Madeleine and M Madeleine.

Les Halles Forum and the Pompidou Centre

The sunken shopping complex developed on the old Les Halles market site and the nearby Pompidou Centre are, apart from the Bastille Opera House, the only completely new public developments of importance in the centre of Paris to have been built since the Second World War. In spite of conservationists' regrets, they have given a lift to what had become lifeless areas. Four ancient churches are passed on route.

Timing: St Germain l'Auxerrois is closed 12.00–14.00.

The Musée National d'Art Moderne is closed Tuesday.

Brancusi's Studio is open Saturday and Monday, and Thursday afternoons.

Apart from Sunday services, St Leu-St Gilles is closed in the morning.

8

Locations
1 Mairie of the 1st
  Arrondissement
2 St Germain l'Auxerrois
3 Oratoire du Louvre
4 Galerie Véro Dodat
5 Bourse du Commerce
6 St Eustache
7 Forum des Halles
8 Fontaine des Innocents
9 Rue des Innocents
10 Rue de la Ferronnerie
11 St Merri
12 Centre Georges Pompidou
13 L'Atelier Brancusi
14 'Le Défenseur des Temps' Clock
15 St Leu-St Gilles
16 Tour de Jean Sans Peur

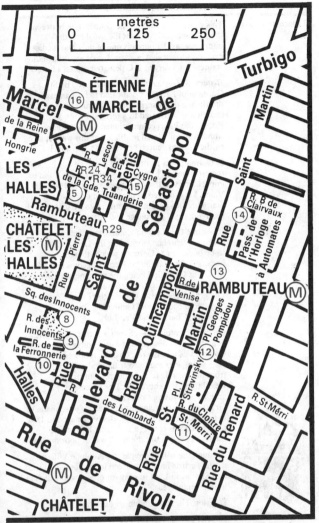

Start *M Louvre, line 1 Pont de Neuilly/Château de Vincennes. Exit and proceed southward, passing the east façade of the Louvre.*

Location 1	**MAIRIE OF THE 1ST ARRONDISSEMENT** *Hittorff 1857*
Place du Louvre	As it is attached to St Germain l'Auxerrois by an arch, many wrongly believe that the 19C mairie's bell tower is part of the medieval church. The Gothic-Revival-style tower houses bells that play music by Couperin daily at 13.00. •• *Proceed beneath the bell tower's arch to the courtyard to view the north façade of St Germain l'Auxerrois.*

Location 2	**ST GERMAIN L'AUXERROIS**

2 Place du Louvre

This church was built in the Gothic style between the 13C and 16C, without the usual lengthy intermissions. Its porch is one of only two medieval examples to survive in Paris. Inside are outstanding statues and a carved 17C pew, the capital's finest.

History St Germain was founded *c.*560 by St Germain of Paris and dedicated to his namesake, the Bishop of Auxerre, d.448. Rebuilt in the 8C, the church was converted to a fortress by the Vikings. Robert the Pious commissioned a new building, which was completed by 1025, but this was replaced by the present church between the 13C and 16C.

St Germain was incorporated in the city of Paris by the erection of Philippe-Auguste's 12C wall and its importance was thereby increased. In the 14C, the Valois kings moved to the Louvre opposite and St Germain thus became the sovereign's parish church, receiving royal patronage and gifts.

It became the custom for important designers and architects who had worked on the Louvre extensions to be buried in St Germain which, therefore, became known as the 'St Denis of genius and talent' (St Denis Cathedral being the royal necropolis). Amongst the artists interred were Le Vau, Lemercier, De Cotte, Gabriel the Elder, Soufflot, Coysevox, Nicolas and Guillaume Coustou, Boucher, Chardin and Van Loo.

On two occasions, the church was threatened with demolition for new road construction but reprieved. Colbert was initially responsible, followed by Napoléon, who wanted a triumphal way created from the Bastille to the Louvre. During the Revolution, the church became successively a granary, a printing works and a Temple of Gratitude. Renaissance-style changes were made to the chancel in the mid-18C. Badly damaged in 1831, the church was restored by **Viollet-le-Duc** and **Lassus**, 1838–55, but the work was of poor quality.

Through the will of the painter Adolphe Willette, d.1926, artists have assembled in the church on the first Sunday in Lent to pray for others who will die in the coming year.

Exterior The nave and inner aisles are 14C.

Gaussel added transepts, outer aisles and chapels to both the north and south sides in 1439.

•• *Return to Place du Louvre L and proceed to the west front.*

Completed in 1439, the porch, which is the most outstanding feature of the church, was designed in the Burgundian fashion by **Gaussel**; this and the Sainte Chapelle's porch are the only medieval examples in Paris to survive. The large statues, however, are modern.

Rooms above the outer bays originally stored St Germain's archives and treasures.

•• *Enter the porch.*

Star vaults are fitted to the three central bays.

The outer bays have simple cross-vaults; their large

bosses are carved to depict L the *Nativity* and R the *Last Supper*.

Although made *c.*1220, the central portal was heavily restored in the 19C when all the large figures were added; unfortunately, the tympanum and central pier were removed in the 18C to accommodate processions.

Flanking portals are early 16C and in the Renaissance style. Unusually, both have double apexes, which appear to indicate a change of design after work had begun.

•● *Enter the church by its north portal and proceed to the centre of the nave's west end.*

Interior The rather sombre, late-Gothic **nave** is rib-vaulted and flanked by double aisles. Its 14C stained glass was replaced by the present grisaille work in 1728 to increase natural light.

Above the west entrance is the restored organ, by **Clicquot**, 1771; this came from the Sainte Chapelle.

St Germain's most important furnishing, the '*Banc Royal*' (royal pew), occupies the fourth bay of the inner north aisle. This large pew was designed by **Le Brun** and carved by **François Mercier** in 1682; even the 'fabric' of its canopy being made of wood. Although primarily intended for the churchwardens' use, it is believed that the king and members of the royal family sat here when attending services.

•● *Proceed to the Chapelle de Notre Dame de Compassion, which faces the rear of the Banc Royal.*

A carved 15C French triptych, restored in 1988, may be illuminated by pressing the adjacent switch.

Both windows of the **transept** are filled with 15C stained glass. Side windows are of 16C Renaissance stained glass.

•● *Proceed to the* **crossing**'s *north-east pier.*

Against the pier, facing west, is a 15C painted wooden figure of St Germain.

Renaissance adaptations were made to the **chancel** in the mid-18C, the most grievous loss being its rood screen, carved by **Goujon**; fortunately, some of the screen's reliefs survive in the Louvre. The chancel's low, wrought-iron screen that replaced this was made by **Pierre Damiez** in 1748.

Fluting and garlanded capitals were added to the chancel's columns in 1745.

•● *Follow the* **outer north ambulatory** *to its east end, where three chapels stand in line.*

In the most northerly are two statues from the Rostaing family tomb, made in 1582 and 1645.

Beneath the next chapel's altar lies a figure of Christ, part of a pietà made by **Jean Soulas** in 1505.

•● *Proceed past the last east chapel to the first south chapel.*

In this chapel are 17C marble statues of two French chancellors: Etienne d'Aligré, d.1635, and his son, d.1677, both by **Laurent Magnier.**

•● Continue to the inner bay that precedes the south transept.

This bay is 11C and forms the base of the south clock tower. Three of the arches remain round-headed in Romanesque style, although much restored.

Behind, standing above the outer bay's flamboyant doorway, is a late-15C polychrome figure of the Virgin. Against the crossing's south-east pier, facing west, stands a 15C wooden effigy of St Vincent.

The 13C **Saint Sacrement** chapel of four bays, which stretches along the entire south side of the nave, is divided from the outer south aisle by a 19C wooden screen.

•● Proceed to its most westerly bay, enter the chapel and return eastward.

A 15C statue of St Mary of Egypt, in the second bay from the west, originally stood outside the church, forming part of the main portal.

Against the next bay's east wall is a 15C wooden crucifixion scene.

A 14C stone Virgin, of the Champagne school, stands in the chapel's east bay, forming part of the altar's reredos.

*•● Return to the west end of the **nave**.*

Against the nave's west wall, immediately south of the central doors, stands a 13C figure of St Germain, carved in stone by a member of the Paris School.

•● Exit L. First L Rue des Prêtres St Germain l'Auxerrois.

Unusual gargoyles decorate the south façade of the church.

As on the north side, the nave and inner aisle are 14C, the outer aisle, chapels and transept being added by **Gaussel** in 1439.

The south transept's rose window is in the late-Gothic Flamboyant style.

•● Continue eastward.

Although the bell tower's 11C base survives, as seen internally, the remainder has been rebuilt.

At midnight on 23 August 1572 the former bell of St Germain was rung from here to give, unwittingly, the signal to begin the St Bartholomew's Day massacre of Protestant Huguenots, many of whom had been invited to Paris to celebrate the marriage between the Protestant Henri de Navarre (later Henri IV) and Marguerite de Valois. It is believed that the slaughter was planned by Charles IX, Catherine de Médicis, Cardinal Duc de Guise and the future Henri III. During the three-day massacre, approximately 8,000 victims were slaughtered throughout France. Henri de Navarre, however, renounced Protestantism in front of the King and was spared.

•● At the east end of the church, cross the road ahead and proceed R towards Place de l'Ecole. Turn right to view the east end of the church.

The chancel, together with its inner ambulatory, was completed by c.1220, but its outer ambulatory and chapels were added three hundred years later, in Renaissance style.

The tiled pyramids above the chapels were built to accommodate the bones from tombs in the old cloister.

Flying buttresses support the chancel's apse.

•● *Follow Rue de l'Arbre Sec, which passes the east end of the chancel.*

An unusual frieze above the windows, consisting of sections of fishes (carp), decorates the central east chapel, which was presented by the Tonson family.

When the gate to the elementary school on the north side is open, a view of the north façade of much of the church can be gained.

In the apse's most westerly bay is an outstanding Renaissance doorway.

•● *Continue ahead following Rue de l'Arbre Sec.*

The name of Rue de l'Arbre Sec (dry tree) commemorates the gallows that once stood at its north end, near the Rue St Honoré junction.

•● *First L Rue de Rivoli, proceed to Rue de l'Oratoire (third R) but continue just past the corner.*

Facing Rue de Rivoli, in front of the apse of the Oratoire church, is the monument to Admiral de Coligny, 1517–72, the Huguenot leader, who lived nearby and become the first victim of the St Bartholomew's Day massacre.

•● *Return to Rue de l'Oratoire, first L. First L Rue St Honoré.*

Location 3	**ORATOIRE DU LOUVRE** *C. Métezeau and Lemercier 1630*
145 Rue St Honoré *A Protestant church, therefore open only for services.*	This church, which was commissioned by Cardinal Betulle for his Oratorian congregation, witnessed the funeral services of Louis XIII and his consort, Anne of Austria. At the Revolution, the Oratorians were suppressed and the building became an arms depot, and later a storehouse for the opera. Napoléon gave the church to the Calvinists in 1811 and it has remained Protestant ever since. The north portal was added in 1845. •● *Enter from this portal.* A balustrade runs around most of this serenely Classical, centrally orientated church. •● *Exit L. First R Rue Jean-Jacques Rousseau. Second L Galerie Véro Dodat.*
Location 4	**GALERIE VÉRO DODAT** *1822*
	An early Parisian example of an enclosed shopping arcade, the Galerie Véro Dodat is the capital's prettiest, but in need of restoration. Originally created by two pork butchers, it soon became fashionable and rentals were high. Gas-lighting was an added attraction. The gallery retains delicate window and door surrounds of brass, and the ceiling combines glass and painted panels.

◗◖ Return to Rue Jean-Jacques Rousseau L. First R Rue Adolphe Jullien. Ahead Rue de Viarmes and the Bourse du Commerce.

Location 5	**BOURSE DU COMMERCE**

Rue de Viarmes

Built as the Corn Exchange in 1767 and now the only survivor of the old Les Halles complex, this circular structure was remodelled by **Blondel** in 1888. Its immediate predecessor had also been a corn exchange, but formerly the site had been occupied by the Hôtel de La Reine, later Hôtel de Soissons, built for the ex-Queen Catherine de Médicis by **Delorme** and **Bullant** in 1572. After her death in 1589, the building became a brothel; it was demolished in 1748.

◗◖ Turn R and follow Rue de Viarmes.

Facing the Porte du Louvre entrance to the Forum des Halles, and attached to the wall of the Bourse, is a fluted column, the only remnant of Catherine's hôtel. It is believed that this may have been part of an observation tower used by her astrologer Ruggieri.

The monogram CH (Catherine and her late husband Henri II) survives, although faded, at upper level.

Internally, the central gallery accommodates brokers who deal in food commodities.

◗◖ Continue anti-clockwise around the Bourse. First R Rue Clémence Royer. R Rue Rambuteau.

Rue Rambuteau is renowned for its many restaurants, which bravely survived the many years of excavating *'le grand trou'* (great hole) for the replacement of the old Les Halles market with the present forum.

◗◖ Continue ahead. First L Rue du Jour.

Location 6	**ST EUSTACHE**

Rue du Jour

Guided tours daily (French only) at 13.00.

Apart from its Classical west front, St Eustache, the parish church of Les Halles, is the prime example in Paris of the French Renaissance at its most ornate. The outstanding 17C tomb of Colbert and some fine paintings, including a work by **Rubens**, ornament the interior.

History A small chapel on the site, dedicated to St Agnes, is recorded in 1214; it primarily served workers in the surrounding Les Halles market. Soon this building was rededicated to St Eustache. As Les Halles market grew, the need for a larger church became apparent; François I provided a generous donation towards it and the foundation stone was laid in 1532.

The architect is unknown, but it has been suggested that **Lemercier** was responsible. Due to financial problems, the church could not be consecrated until 1637 and even then the west front was unfinished. In 1793, during the Revolution, a riotous Festival of Reason took place at St Eustache, and two years later the building became a Temple of Agriculture. A fire in 1844 led to comprehensive restoration by **Baltard**.

The church has a strong tradition of choral and organ music: Bizet's *Te Deum* was premièred here in 1855 and Liszt's *Messe Solennelle* in 1866. Concerts are still held, those on Christmas Eve and St Cecilia's Day being particularly noteworthy. Three parishioners baptized in the church were later to become world-famous, but under other names: Armand de Plessis (Cardinal Richelieu) in 1585, Jean-Baptiste Poquelin (Molière) in 1622, and Antoinette Poisson (Madame de Pompadour) in 1721. Louis XIV made his first communion in this church, La Fontaine was buried here and Mirabeau lay in state at St Eustache in 1791, prior to the transfer of his body to the Panthéon. The composer Lully married here in 1662.

Exterior By the middle of the 18C, the Renaissance west front, still unfinished, was replaced with a completely new façade. This was built in Classical style by **Hardouin-Mansart**. However, it was also doomed to remain unfinished, the planned south turret never being built.

•● *Continue along Rue Rambuteau to Place René Cassin and follow Allée St John Perse R a short distance southward, to view the south façade of the church.*

The nave was completed in 1637.

The façade of the south transept was ready *c.*1640. Its twin turrets accommodate staircases.

Fixed to the apex of the transept's gable is the emblem of St Eustache – a stag's head with a cross.

Coved niches on either side of the doorway were originally occupied by statues, but these were lost in the Revolution; figures carved on the shafts of the arch and the centre column are modern.

Various Classical motifs mark the earliest application in Paris of North Italian Renaissance ornamentation.

Behind the transept, rising from the crossing, is the bell tower; its spire was removed in the 19C when the tower was used as a semaphore station.

•● *Return to Rue Rambuteau R and proceed eastward.*

The chancel was completed in 1630.

Above the circular Lady Chapel, which protrudes eastward from the apse, the small bell tower, built in 1640, was restored in 1875.

•● *First L Rue Montmartre.*

Houses cling to the north side of the church, thus inhibiting views of the façade.

•● *First L Impasse St Eustache. Proceed to the end of this cul-de-sac to view the north transept.*

The Renaissance façade of the north transept, reminiscent of its southern counterpart, was also completed *c.*1640.

•● *Return to Rue Montmartre.*

Facing Impasse St Eustache is **Passage de la Reine de Hongrie.**

A market stall-holder in the passage petitioned Marie-Antoinette, who after they had met remarked that she resembled the Queen of Hungary. Both the stall-holder and the passage were henceforth known

as the Reine de Hongrie. During the Revolution the
luckless lady was judged to be a royalist and
guillotined.

●● *Continue northward. First L Rue du Jour.*

From the Rue du Jour, a picturesque view is obtained
of the upper part of St Eustache's north façade
towering above the houses.

No 4, for long the Paris town house of Royaumont
Abbey, was also the residence of Montmorency
Bouteville, executed by Richelieu for duelling. The
house has been much remodelled but its
entranceway, although dilapidated, is original.

●● *Continue ahead to the west front of the church and
enter by the south door.*

Interior Immediately L of the entrance, fixed to the
west side of the south aisle's north pier, is a large
medallion and a fulsome tribute to François de
Chevert, d.1769.

●● *Proceed to the west end of the **nave**.*

By repute, the plan of St Eustache was modelled on
Notre Dame's and it matches the cathedral's
dimensions, except in length. Immediately, the great
height of the church compared with its width is
apparent, very much a Gothic rather than a
Renaissance characteristic.

As the arches of the arcades are so high, there is
space only for an unusually shallow gallery above.

The floor of the church was once paved with
tombstones, including those of Colbert, Rameau and
Admiral de Tourville, who defeated the combined
English and Dutch fleets off Beachy Head in 1690.

At the west end of the nave, on the north side, is the
organ by **Ducroquet**, with its case designed by **Baltard**
in 1854.

●● *Proceed towards the **north aisle**.*

On the tympanum of the nave's west door is the 17C
painting of St Eustache's martyrdom, by **Simon
Vouet.** Allegedly, the saint and his family were forced
into a hollow bronze bull which was then made white
hot.

In the second chapel is a copy of *The Adoration of the
Magi* by **Rubens.**

●● *Proceed to the centre of the nave.*

Facing the pulpit is the outstanding churchwardens'
pew by **Le Pautre** and **Cartaud.** It was presented by
the Regent, Philippe d'Orléans, *c.*1720.

●● *Return to the **north aisle**.*

A model in the fourth chapel depicts the relocation of
the Les Halles market to Rungis in 1969.

Relics of St Eustache and his martyred companions
are kept in the next chapel.

●● *Proceed to the crossing.*

The extravagant vault of the **chancel** is embellished
with pendants.

Choir stalls came from the convent of Picpus.

●● *Proceed to the **north ambulatory**'s second chapel (Ste Geneviève).*

The 16C painting, *Tobias and the Angel*, is by **Santo di Tito.**

Two bays further north, in the Chapelle de Ste Marie Madeleine, a 17C painting by **Manetti** depicts the saint's ecstasy.

An early **Rubens**, *Pilgrims at Emmaus*, in the next chapel, below R, was painted *c.*1611.

The tomb of Louis XIV's controller of finance, Colbert, d.1683, by **Le Brun**, dominates the next chapel. Made 1685–7, it is regarded as an outstanding example of 17C French sculpture. Figures of *Colbert* and *Abundance* are by **Coysevox**; that of *Fidelity* is by **Tuby**. Colbert's funeral service was held in the church at night because it was feared that his unpopularity, due to the restrictions on grain exports that he had introduced, might lead to an attack on the cortège.

At the east end of the church is the semi-circular **Chapelle St Sacrement**.

Frescos, by **Couture**, are 19C.

Surmounting the altar is a *Virgin and Child*, by **Pigalle**.

Stained-glass windows, based on cartoons by **Philippe de Champaigne**, are by **Soulignac**, 1631.

●● *Follow the **south ambulatory**.*

Murals in the fourth south ambulatory chapel, at window level, are by **Antoine Ricard**, 1633.

The late-17C pietà, in the sixth chapel (Ste Agnes), was painted by **Luca Giordano**.

A late-14C statue of St John the Baptist stands in the **south transept**, on the column between the two doors.

The third south aisle chapel, known as the musicians' chapel, is dedicated to Ste Cécile (Cecilia), the patron saint of music.

The composer Jean Philippe Rameau, d.1764, played the organ at St Eustache and is buried in the church. He is commemorated in this chapel by a bust against the west wall and, beside it, a wall plaque of 1835.

The composer Franz Liszt assisted at Mass in the church in 1866 and 1886; his wooden bust, against the chapel's east pillar, is modern.

At the east end of the chapel's south wall, a plaque commemorates Mozart's mother, who was buried at St Eustache in 1778.

●● *Exit from the church ahead and enter the Porte du Jour of the Forum des Halles.*

Location 7	**FORUM DES HALLES**
Vidéothèque de Paris. Open Tuesday–Sunday 12.30–23.00. Saturday 10.00–23.00. The	This sunken, multi-level shopping centre is the focal point of the redeveloped 53-acre site formerly occupied by the market buildings of Les Halles. Incorporated are a swimming pool, billiards hall, gymnasium, the **'Grande Epoque'** waxworks museum (annexe of the Musée Grevin) and a holographic

admission charge permits two hours viewing.

Musée Grevin (Grande Epoque). Open Monday–Saturday 10.30–18.45, Sunday 13.00–19.15. Admission charge.

Musée de Holographie. Open Tuesday–Saturday 10.00–19.00. Sunday 13.00–19.15. Admission charge.

exhibition. Opened in 1988 at 2 Grande Galerie – reached from Porte Saint Eustache – is **Vidéothèque de Paris**, where thirty screens are available to view historic films relating to Paris, dating from 1910.

The famous Les Halles food market had stood on the site since the 11C but, as at London's Covent Garden, modern traffic congestion became intolerable and the market was transferred to Rungis, near Orly Airport, in 1969. Unfortunately, whereas Covent Garden's historic, iron-framed buildings were retained, similar examples at Les Halles, mostly built in the mid-19C by **Baltard**, were demolished; many regret their loss. However, it was decided that Paris needed a 'lung' in what was a congested area, and a sunken development, mostly covered at ground level with gardens and tree-lined walkways, was commissioned. Landscaping was finished in 1988 and already the flower beds and the newly revealed view of St Eustache present a pleasing aspect.

Many visitors will make several visits to the Forum, exploring the upper gardens in addition to the shopping levels. The following brief tour is suggested for an initial visit.

•● *Descend by escalator from Porte du Jour.*

Immediately L is the billiards hall.

Ahead L is a display of tropical greenery.

•● *Continue ahead descending two further flights of steps.*

The **Piscine Suzanne Berlioux**, immediately L, is an Olympic-size public swimming pool.

•● *Continue ahead, following the Grande Galerie.*

At Place Carrée are situated Métro and RER stations (Châtelet Les Halles).

•● *Continue ahead.*

The sunken square is the only part of the development to be open to the sky.

•● *Continue ahead and ascend the escalator to the Porte Lescot exit. Ascend to Level 1, the Grand Balcon, (east side). Turn R and proceed to No 55* **Musée Grévin (Grande Epoque)** *in the south-east corner.*

This is a new annexe of the Musée Grévin waxworks museum, long established in Boulevard Montmartre (see page 152). Its theme, 'Voyage à la Grande Epoque', deals with the period 1885–1900, regarded nostalgically as Paris's Belle Epoque. Modern techniques are incorporated and many scenes animated.

•● *Exit L and continue clockwise.*

At **No 21** Grand Balcon is the **Musée de Holographie**.

•● *Exit from the Forum des Halles at Porte Lescot R and proceed to Square des Innocents ahead. In the centre stands the fountain, approached from its north side.*

Location 8	**FONTAINE DES INNOCENTS** *Lescot 1549*
Square des Innocents	Designed by **Lescot**, with reliefs by **Goujon**, the masters responsible for the earliest part of the

Louvre's Cour Carrée, this Renaissance fountain, although much altered, is the finest in Paris.

Henri II commissioned the structure, which originally backed on to a wall of the 12C Church of the Innocents facing Rue St Denis. After the church was demolished and its cemetery abandoned in 1788 the fountain was moved to its present position.

Originally, the fountain's base had vertical sides from which spouts provided water. In 1865 **Gabriel Davioud** created the present stepped base and water cascades down it from the basin fountain which he erected.

Davioud also added the cupola surmounting the structure.

Before these alterations were made, a balustrade had fronted each archway, which, prior to the Revolution, provided a good viewpoint from where the nobility could observe the processions when the sovereign entered Paris via the Rue St Denis. Below the balustrades were reliefs by **Goujon**, since removed to the Louvre.

Figures of naiads, carved between the twin pilasters, by **Goujon**, survive on this and the east and west sides.

Above them, the monogram H commemorates Henri II, who commissioned the fountain.

•● *Proceed to the south side (facing Rue des Innocents).*

When built, the fountain was only three-sided. However, because the structure was moved to its present free-standing position *c.*1788 a new side was required; it was designed by **Pajou**, with figures, in imitation of **Goujon's** style, by **Houdon.**

•● *Proceed southward to the arches between Nos 11 and 13 Rue des Innocents.*

Location 9	**RUE DES INNOCENTS**

The Innocents church faced Rue St Denis, giving its name to the street that ran to its south and also, later, the present square. West of the church stretched the Cimetière des Innocents, the most important burial ground in Paris. Shortly before the Revolution, the cemetery was pronounced a health hazard and, in 1785, the bones were removed to the Catacombes, and the present Square des Innocents was laid out.

No 11, on the south side of the street, retains traces of the arches from the old cemetery's galleries; once they were painted to depict the *danse macabre*.

•● *Proceed through the arches. L Rue de la Ferronnerie.*

Location 10	**RUE DE LA FERRONNERIE**

Friday 14 May 1610 was a warm, sunny day and the fifty-six-year-old Henri IV, on his way to visit Sully, his first minister, commanded that the leather hood to his coach should be lowered. In the morning the King's son, the Duc de Vendôme, had warned him of a prediction by La Brosse, the astrologer, that he would die that day, but Henri, who was not a

superstitious man, took no notice. Although greatly respected, several attempts had already been made on the King's life and as the open coach squeezed through the narrow Rue de la Ferronnerie, a lunatic schoolmaster from Angoulême, named Ravaillac, who believed that the King planned to murder the pope, stabbed him twice and Henri died shortly after being taken back to the Louvre.

The assassination took place outside No 11, on the south side, and it is alleged that the shop that then stood there bore a sign of a crowned heart pierced by an arrow. Soothsayers also commented on the many recurrences of the number 14 in the King's life; they included: the date of his murder and the number of letters in his name, Henri de Bourbon.

The north side of the street is occupied by an early, partly restored apartment block, almost 400 feet long, built in 1669.

•● *Continue eastward. Second R Boulevard de Sébastopol. First L Rue des Lombards (named after the Italian bankers from Lombardy who lived there). Second L Rue St Martin.*

Location 11	**ST MERRI** *16C*
78 Rue St Martin	Constructed in the first half of the 16C, St Merri's is an extremely late example of a church built entirely in the Flamboyant Gothic style. Most of its stained glass is original. Alterations and additions in the mid-18C include outstanding Baroque carving by the **Slodtz** brothers. Paintings by **Vouet**, **Van Loo** and **Coypel** are displayed.

History St Merri stands on the spot where Medericus (St Merri), abbot of St Martin's, in Autun, died in 700. An early church or chapel was built and dedicated to the saint, possibly in the 9C, when Medericus became patron saint of the capital's Right Bank. A large building replaced this in the 13C, but the present St Merri was constructed 1500–58, a remarkably short time for an important Paris church. This speed was made possible chiefly because of the financial support received from the wealthy Lombard moneylenders who lived in the parish. Surprisingly, for such a late date, the Flamboyant Gothic style was used throughout, with no hint of Renaissance detailing.

In the mid-18C, the chancel was given Classical embellishments and a Saint Sacrement chapel was added to the south-west, supervised by **Boffrand**; the **Slodtz** brothers were responsible for much of the Baroque detail.

At the Revolution, the building became a Temple of Commerce and later, a hospital. Parishioners have included the Englishman, Edmund Rich, who was to become archbishop of Canterbury in the 13C, and Boccaccio, author of *The Decameron*.

Exterior The west front, completed in 1526, faces Rue St Martin, an important Roman road.

Its 16C stiff-leaf frieze survives, but the original statues ornamenting the portal were destroyed by revolutionary iconoclasts; their replacements were made in 1812.

The north-west belfry houses the oldest bell in Paris. Cast in 1331, this miraculously escaped melting down at the Revolution.

The south-west tower's upper storey was lost in a fire and never replaced.

Part of a chapel from the earlier church was incorporated in the present building and its original 13C window, in the south-west bay, R of the main façade, faces Rue St Martin.

Buildings cluster around the south side.

•● *Follow Rue du Cloître St Merri to view the 16C north façade.*

The name of this street commemorates the cloister that stood on its site from the 15C and where the canons lived. It was near here that a young boy, waving a tricolour, was shot dead in June 1832. Victor Hugo, in *Les Misérables*, based the death of Gavroche on this incident.

Unusually, construction of St Merri's began at the west end and proceeded eastward. From this narrow street, only a restricted view of the north aisle and north transept, completed in 1526, can be gained.

•● *First L Place Igor Stravinsky. Proceed towards the central lake.*

From the lake can be gained the best view of St Merri's chancel and its chapels, all completed by 1558. As at Notre Dame, St Merri's chancel is as long as its nave and, due to this, the church became known as 'Notre Dame la Petite' (the small).

•● *Return to the west front and enter the church.*

Interior Although the nave has only one north aisle, it incorporates a wide outer south aisle.

Above the west door is the much-restored organ on which Saint-Saëns once played; its case and loft are original.

Large windows provide good illumination, a rare advantage in a Parisian Gothic church.

Much stained glass survives in the church from the early 16C and early 17C. Particularly outstanding are the earliest fragments, in the first three bays of the nave.

•● *Proceed to the **north aisle**.*

The baptistery occupies the north-west bay.

In the floor of the chapel that follows, at its west end, is a 15C tomb slab engraved with a figure.

A marble 18C pietà stands in the next chapel.

The staircase in the chapel two bays further east leads to the **crypt**, where small exhibitions are occasionally held (admission free).

On the crypt's west wall are two grotesque-head corbels.

Capitals and bosses have stiff-leaf decoration.

The tombstone of Guillaume le Sueur, d.1530, stands against the west wall.

•● *Ascend the stairs and proceed to the north side of the nave.*

The pulpit was carved by the **Slodtz** brothers *c.*1760.

● *Return to the north aisle and continue eastward to the north transept.*

The transept was completed in 1526, at the same time as the nave's west front. As with most French transepts, there is no outward projection.

Some 16C glass survives in both transepts, attributed to **Pinaigrier.**

Against the north transept's east wall is the painting of St Merri releasing prisoners, by **Simon Vouet**, 1644. St Merri, by tradition, often pleaded successfully for the release of captives.

Ribs form petal shapes on the crossing's vault.

● *Proceed eastward.*

The **chancel**, completed in 1558, and the last part of the church to be finished, was altered for Louis XV in 1752 by **Boffrand**, who faced most of the surfaces with marble; a 16C rood screen was removed in the process. Most detailing was executed by the **Slodtz** brothers.

The high altar's marble crucifix was made by **P. Dubois.**

Above, the gilded *Glory* was made by **M. A. Slodtz** in 1758.

As in the transepts, the stained glass, fitted *c.*1540, is believed to be by **Pinaigrier.**

● *Follow the ambulatory to its south side.*

A 17C painting on wood, in the south ambulatory's second chapel from the east, depicts St Peter's crucifixion.

● *Continue westward towards the south transept.*

Against the crossing's south-east pillar, facing west, is a painting, *The Blue Virgin* by **Van Loo**, 1765.

Completed, like the north transept, in 1526, the **south transept**'s glass is also original and attributed to **Pinaigrier.**

● *Proceed to the south aisle's first chapel.*

Standing against the east pier, facing north, is a late-15C baptismal font.

● *Continue ahead to the large Saint Sacrement Chapel, which projects southward.*

This Baroque chapel, with its three shallow domes, was added by **Boffrand** in 1745. Decoration, by the **Slodtz** brothers, includes two outstanding bas-reliefs carved by **P. A. Slodtz** at upper level on the east and west walls.

On the south wall, above the altar, is the painting *Pilgrims at Emmaus* by **Coypel.**

Enclosing the 13C south-west chapel is a 16C carved Renaissance screen, brought here from the ancient chapel of the Judge Consuls when it was demolished.

● *Exit. L. First R Rue des Lombards. First R Rue Quincampoix.*

Passed R **Nos 10–14** have exceptional Rococo keystones above their doors and windows.

No 12 is entirely rusticated.

●▪ Continue ahead.

At **No 43**, John Law began his dubious activities in 1717. Law, the son of a Scottish goldsmith, killed a rival in a duel and had to flee the British Isles. His financial acumen was soon appreciated by the Regent, Philippe d'Orléans, and he was appointed Comptroller General, becoming responsible for the introduction of banknotes as a replacement for gold and silver coins. In 1717, Law was granted a twenty-five-year trading monopoly in the French-controlled American state of Louisiana and set up his Compagnie des Indes Occidentales to manage it. The following year he founded the city of New Orleans, naming it in honour of the Regent, his patron. Law persuaded the public that Louisiana, then yellow-fever-ridden swampland, had a rich potential, and soon shares in his company were in such demand that barriers had to be fitted at the ends of the street to control would-be investors. After one year the bubble burst, Law was forced to resign and fled to Italy.

●▪ Continue northward. First R Rue de Venise leads to Place Georges Pompidou. Proceed ahead to the Centre Georges Pompidou.

Location 12

CENTRE GEORGES POMPIDOU
Rogers/Piano 1977

Place Georges
Pompidou

*Centre open
Wednesday–
Monday 12.00–
22.00. Admission to
the Centre is free.*

*Musée National
d'Art Moderne
(fourth floor) and
Galerie
Contemporaine
(first floor) times as
for the centre except
that they open 10.00
Saturday and
Sunday. Admission
charge, free
Sunday.*

*No smoking is
allowed in the
Centre.*

The Pompidou Centre (Centre National d'Art et de Culture Georges Pompidou), which occupies much of the area known as Beaubourg, was completed in 1977 and is one of Europe's major High-Tech structures. Although the building accommodates a public library and an industrial design centre, of greatest interest to most visitors is the National Museum of Modern Art, and the outstanding views from the Centre's top floor.

Beaubourg, originally a separate village, became part of Paris in the 12C when it was enclosed by Philippe Auguste's new wall. In recent years, the area decayed, many houses being demolished in 1936, and when it was decided to redevelop Les Halles, Beaubourg was incorporated in the scheme. In 1969 President Pompidou decided to commission a multi-purpose cultural centre that would demonstrate links between the arts and everyday activities. An international design competition was won by the Englishman **Richard Rogers** and his Italian collaborator **Renzo Piano.** Almost one million square feet of floor space is provided and over six million people visit the centre each year.

Built in High-Tech style between 1972 and 1977 the structure is entirely supported by its external walls, thus permitting almost 90,000 square feet of uninterrupted space per floor.

From the piazza, which fronts the building, performers entertain onlookers in a manner reminiscent of London's Covent Garden.

●▪ Proceed R towards the south end, enter the Centre and turn L.

Immediately ahead is part of the **Bibliothèque Publique d'Information** (public reading library), which occupies three levels of the building. French and foreign publications may be studied here but not removed.

•• Proceed to the north-west corner and ascend by escalator or lift to the fourth floor (immediately L of the escalator is a lift for the handicapped).

Musée National d'Art Moderne This museum, in which the great modern masters, from the Fauves to the present time, are represented, was transferred to the Centre from the Palais de Tokyo in 1977. A free plan is provided.

Retain the entry ticket if later intending to visit the Brancusi Studio museum in the piazza.

This is a rare example, in Paris, of a national museum where all the exhibits can be seen in one visit without undue exhaustion. On entering the museum, works by **Matisse** lie ahead; the visitor then turns R to view the Fauves and more work by **Matisse** and **Bonnard.**

•• Return northward, remaining on the east side of the central aisle.

The Cubists – **Picasso**, **Braque**, etc. – are followed by Abstract and Expressionist works, basically in chronological order.

•• Descend, from within the museum, to the third floor.

Works by contemporary artists, shown in the **Galeries Contemporaines**, are changed several times during the year.

*•• Exit and proceed to the **Salle d'Art Graphique**, also on the fourth floor. Ascend to the fifth floor.*

The best views from the Centre are gained from the fifth floor's Grande Galerie, which is uncovered at its south end.

•• Proceed clockwise around the gallery

A café with an open-air terrace, and a temporary exhibition area (admission charge – theme changes four times a year) occupy this floor.

•• Descend and exit from the Centre.

Between the Centre and St Merri church (approached from beside the fountain in Place Igor Stravinsky) is the **Institut de Recherche et de Coordination Acoustique/Musique**. Here musicians learn how modern technology can be applied to music; its studio is not open to the general public.

•• Proceed to the north-west section of the forecourt's upper level. L'Atelier (studio) Brancusi is housed in the double-gabled prefabricated building.

Location 13	**L'ATELIER BRANCUSI**
Place Georges Pompidou	Sculptures by the Romanian **Constantin Brancusi** are displayed in a reconstruction of his studio.
Open Monday and Thursday 12.30–18.00, and Saturday 10.30–18.00. Admission by the ticket purchased for the Musée National	*•• Immediately north of the Brancusi studio, Passage de l'Horloge d'Automates leads to Rue Bernard de Clairvaux. Turn R.*

*d'Art Moderne
(ring the bell to gain
entry).*

Location 14	**'LE DÉFENSEUR DES TEMPS' CLOCK**
Rue Bernard de Clairvaux	This animated public clock, of brass and steel, was made by **Jacques Monestier**, who took five years to assemble it. A plaque commemorates the unveiling by Jacques Chirac in 1979. On the hour, the 'defender of time' fights with the dragon, but at 12.00 and 18.00 he also has to contend with the crab and the bird.

•● Return to Rue Rambuteau R. Fourth R Rue St Denis.

Location 15	**ST LEU-ST GILLES**
92 Rue St Denis	This church combines a 16C Gothic nave with an early-17C Classical chancel. Some 16C sculptures are displayed.

*Open Sunday
10.00–12.30,
Monday 17.00–
22.00, Tuesday–
Thursday 13.00–
22.00, Friday and
Saturday 13.00–
23.00.*

A chapel on the site, erected in 1235, became too small and was rebuilt, with an aisleless nave, in 1319. Further rebuilding took place in the 16C and this time, a south aisle and transept were included. The chancel and its ambulatory were reconstructed by 1611 and only then was parish church status gained. In 1858 the Boulevard de Sébastopol was laid out, necessitating the curtailment and rebuilding of the east end. The double dedication is to Lupus, Bishop of Sens (St Leu) and Giles Aegidius (St Gilles) a hermit who lived in Provence.

Parts of the west front's portal survive from the original chapel of 1235.

•● Enter the church.

The low nave is a late example of the Gothic style. In contrast, the chancel is high and Renaissance.

Beneath the chancel lies a **crypt**, created in 1780 by **Charles de Wailly**, for the Order of the Knights of the Holy Sepulchre. The verger will show this when convenient; it is approached from the north ambulatory behind the high altar.

An entombed Christ, carved in the 16C, is displayed within the crypt.

A vaulted chapel leads to the **Sacristie des Messes**, at the west end of the south ambulatory. Its altar's 15C retable came from the Church of the Innocents.

*•● Proceed to the **south aisle**'s second chapel from the west.*

The marble group of the Virgin as a child, with her mother St Anne, was made by **Jean Bullant** for the Ecouen Palace in 1510.

•● Exit R Rue St Denis. Second L Rue Etienne Marcel. Cross the road and continue westward. The Tour de Jean Sans Peur is situated just before Rue Française, overlooking the playground.

Location 16	**TOUR DE JEAN SANS PEUR** *1408*
20 Rue Etienne Marcel	A rare Paris example of a Gothic domestic building, this tower is all that survives of the Hôtel d'Artois.

Jean Sans Peur (without fear) ordered the assassination of the Duc d'Orléans and added this square, stone-built tower as a defence measure against reprisals. When built, it backed on to the city wall.

👣 *Return eastward to M Etienne Marcel.*

L'Opéra

L'Opéra, the world's largest and most glamorous theatre, is approached via Rue de Rivoli and Rue St Honoré, two luxury streets with the emphasis, in the latter, on food. At the other end of the entertainment scale, the 'naughty' Folies Bergère is passed.

Timing: The Musée Grévin and Musée des Arts Décoratifs are open in the afternoon but the latter shuts Monday and Tuesday.

9

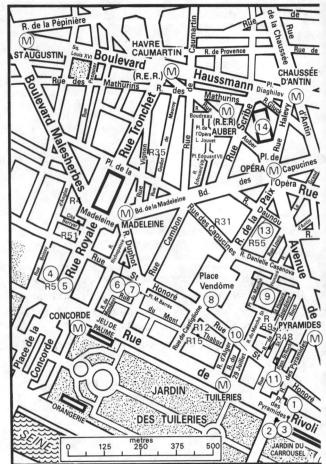

Locations

1 Place des Pyramides
2 Musée des Arts Décoratifs
3 Rue de Rivoli
4 Maxim's
5 Rue Royale
6 Robespierre's House
7 Eglise Polonaise
8 Place Vendôme
9 Rue du Marché St Honoré
10 Rue St Honoré
11 St Roch
12 Avenue de l'Opéra
13 Harry's New York Bar
14 L'Opéra
15 Opéra Comique
16 Le Nouveau Drouot
17 Folies Bergère
18 St Eugène-Ste Cécile
19 Musée Grévin
20 Bourse des Valeurs

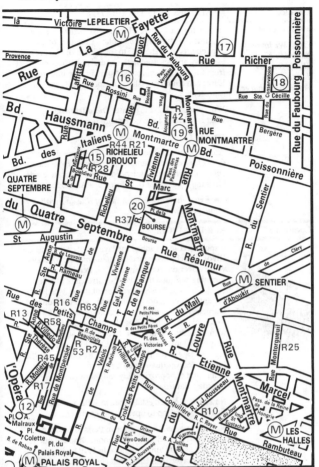

Start M *Palais Royal, line 1 Pont de Neuilly/Château de Vincennes. Exit and proceed southward. At Rue de Rivoli (skirting the Louvre) turn R.*

Location 1	**PLACE DES PYRAMIDES**

Originally, this was called the Place de Rivoli.

In its centre, the gilded bronze equestrian statue of Jeanne d'Arc was made by **Daniel Frémiet** in the 19C. St Joan is still revered by many, and pilgrimages are made to this statue from all parts of France.

•● *Cross immediately to the south side of Rue de Rivoli, turn L and proceed to the Musée des Arts Décoratifs.*

Location 2	**MUSÉE DES ARTS DÉCORATIFS**

107 Rue de Rivoli

*Open Wednesday–
Saturday 12.30–
18.00; Sunday
11.00–18.00.
Admission charge.*

Occupying the Louvre's Pavillon Marsan (see page 35), this eclectic museum displays examples of the applied arts from the 13C to the 20C. Exhibits are everyday articles used in the home and office, ranging from toys to furnishings. Not only France but other European countries, Islam and the Orient, are represented.

Works donated by the painter **Dubuffet** make up what is virtually a separate exhibition.

← *Exit L.*

Adjacent, at 109 Rue de Rivoli, the **Musée des Arts de la Mode** exhibits samples of costumes from the 16C to the present, influenced by the decorative arts. Opening times as for the Musée des Arts Décoratifs.

← *Exit, return to the north side of Rue de Rivoli, turn L and proceed westward.*

Location 3	**RUE DE RIVOLI**

Napoléon commissioned the laying out of the Rue de Rivoli, which was named to commemorate his Italian victory over the Austrians in 1797. **Percier** and **Fontaine** designed the mile-long stretch of arcaded blocks in 1802. The construction of these, which face the entire north sides of the Louvre and the Tuileries Garden, was begun in 1811, but took forty-five years to complete. Each block is identical in appearance, with three storeys above a shopping arcade, broken only by the intersecting streets. The long, arcaded section, east of the Place du Palais Royal, houses the **Louvre des Antiquaires**, a three-storey antique emporium of approximately 250 shops (open Tuesday–Saturday).

No 224, **Galignani**, established in 1802, was the first English bookshop to open on the continent.

No 225, **Angélina**, is *the* place in Paris to take tea, particularly on a Sunday afternoon, although queues then are usually long. Founded in 1910 by René Rumpelmayer, Angélina's hot chocolate, made from ground bars of solid chocolate and served with whipped cream, is rated the best in Paris.

← *At No 228 cross directly to the south side of the Rue de Rivoli.*

A plaque on a pier between the Tuileries Garden railings marks the site of the Salle de Manège, the former riding school of the Tuileries Palace. The revolutionary government's Assemblée Constituante sat there from 1789 until it was succeeded, three years later, by the Assemblée Legislative and from 1792–3 by the Convention Nationale, organizers of 'the Terror'. Louis XVI was tried and sentenced to death in the building.

← *Return immediately to the north side of Rue de Rivoli.*

Nos 228–232, **Hotel Meurice** One of the great old-established luxury hotels of Paris, the Meurice accommodated Alfonso XIII of Spain (suite 108) during his exile. Throughout the Second World War, von Choltitz, the German commander of Paris, appropriated the building for his headquarters and gave himself up to the Allies here on 25 August 1944. It was von Choltitz who disregarded Hitler's orders to blow up the capital's bridges and major buildings as General Leclerc's divisions approached.

Visitors may view the public ground-floor rooms, some of which, particularly the restaurant and Salon Tuileries, have been exquisitely restored, incorporating gilded Rococo-style work.

•• *Proceed to the opposite corner of Rue de Castiglione.*

No 3, Hotel Intercontinental Another luxury hotel, the Intercontinental retains seven beautifully restored lounges, designed by **Garnier**, the architect of L'Opéra.

•• *Continue westward along Rue de Rivoli to the next corner with Rue Cambon (second R).*

No 2 is the premises of **Lanvin**.

No 248, W. H. Smith Established in Paris in 1903, this is a member of the famous English chain of shops that specializes in the sale of periodicals and books. Smith's is the best-known English language bookshop in France, but also, in its cosy, first-floor restaurant, a genuine English breakfast (10.00–12.00) and afternoon tea are served weekdays. Grocery products favoured by anglophiles, such as tea, biscuits, baked beans and breakfast cereals may be purchased to take away.

•• *Continue ahead. Third R Rue Royale. Cross the road.*

Flanking the street and facing Place de la Concorde are, on the east side, the Hôtel de la Marine (Hôtel de la Vrillière) and, on the west side, the Hôtel Crillon (see page 54).

A plaque in French and English, beneath the arcade of the Hôtel Crillon, seen through the iron gate at the corner, commemorates France's recognition of the independence from Britain of thirteen American states, by the Treaty of Friendship, Commerce and Alliance, signed at this hôtel, 6 February 1778. France was the first country formally to recognize their independence.

Below this, a further plaque commemorates Chateaubriand's occupancy 1805–07.

Location 4	**MAXIM'S**
3 Rue Royale	Immortalized by Franz Lehàr in *The Merry Widow*, and featured in many films, Maxim's is still the world's most famous restaurant.

It was opened in 1893, in what had been an ice-cream parlour, by Maxime Gaillard, who spent a fortune on its redecoration; the restaurant was called Maxim's, its proprietor's Christian name being anglicized for the benefit of English-speaking customers. After a slow start Maxim's became popular, but Gaillard died within two years, leaving the business to his head waiter and chef.

Around the turn of the century Maxim's became famous for its beautiful ladies, the '*Grandes Cocottes*', who would arrive around midnight, dressed to kill. This was the restaurant's heyday, when Europe's nobility would almost fight for a table; regulars included the future Edward VII of England, Kaiser Wilhelm II of Germany and the Grand Duke Peter of Russia.

Miraculously, the original Art-Nouveau décor has survived, much of it evidently being acquired from an exhibition c.1900. The corner table, number 16, is the most prestigious and difficult to secure. Formerly it was Edward VII's table, later being favoured by the Duke and Duchess of Windsor and, more recently, Aristotle Onassis accompanied by Maria Callas.

Pierre Cardin, the couturier, acquired Maxim's in 1981 and commissioned the redecoration of the first-floor bar to match the Art-Nouveau style of the restaurant. The bar, but not the restaurant, may be visited by non-diners.

•● *Cross to the east side of the Rue Royale and continue northward.*

Location 5	**RUE ROYALE**

The southern section of the street, from Rue de Rivoli to Rue St Honoré, was built with uniform façades designed by **Gabriel**. Construction began in the 18C, but was not completed until the 19C.
No 6, Fred Top-brand watches, jewellery and leather goods have been sold here since 1936. Madame de Staël lived in the building in 1816.

No 8 This was the residence of the street's architect, **Jean-Ange Gabriel.**

No 10, Lachaume Widely regarded as the top florist in Paris, Lachaume's sensational displays, in an Italian Baroque setting, bring a breath of spring to the capital throughout the year.

The north section of the Rue Royale is described on page 111.

•● *First R Rue St Honoré. Cross to the north side.*

Location 6	**ROBESPIERRE'S HOUSE**

400 Rue St Honoré — A plaque, R of the doorway of No 398, records that the revolutionary leader Maximilien de Robespierre, for ever associated with 'the Terror', lived in the house in the rear courtyard from 17 July 1791 until his arrest, 27 July 1794.

•● *Proceed through the archway to the small, dark courtyard.*

Robespierre lodged in the first floor of the house immediately ahead, above what is now the bar/restaurant **Le Robespierre**. Even though Robespierre was the supreme egalitarian, his accommodation appears to have been surprisingly modest for the most powerful man in France.

•● *Return to Rue St Honoré L. First R Place Maurice Barrès.*

Location 7	**ÉGLISE POLONAISE** *Errard 1676*

Place Maurice Barrès — This, the capital's Polish church since 1850, was built as Notre Dame de l'Assomption to serve the Haudriettes convent, that had moved here in 1632

from its original site beside the Hôtel de Ville. The convent had been founded by Cardinal de Rochefoucauld to provide lodgings for poor widows; abandoned wives and women wishing to do penance were accommodated later.

The large cupola of the church appears to be squashing the structure below, thus earning for it the appellation '*le sot dôme*' (ridiculous dome). It was patterned on Sta Maria dell'Assunzione in Arricia, Italy, that **Bellini** had just completed. **Charles Errard**, the architect of the church, served as the first director of the Académie de France in Rome and was much influenced by current Italian Baroque work. The portico was inspired by the Roman Pantheon.

•● *Enter the church.*

Internally, the entirely circular building is lit only by an inadequate clerestory.

Immediately north of the entrance is a Polish 'Solidarity' banner.

Marbled plaster walls, as in many Roman churches, are divided into eight bays by gilded Corinthian pilasters.

On the north wall, the upper painting is the *Adoration of the Magi* by **Van Loo**.

The cupola's painting, the *Assumption of Mary*, is by **De La Fosse**.

•● *Exit R Rue St Honoré. Second L Place Vendôme. Proceed ahead.*

Location 8 | **PLACE VENDÔME** *Hardouin-Mansart 1698–1720*

The late-17C Place Vendôme has fortunately resisted alteration, and its harmonious façades of hard-wearing limestone present the most elegant domestic development in Paris.

Louis XIV's Comptroller of Finance, Colbert, opposed the speculative plan to develop this square by **Hardouin-Mansart** and five financiers, but following his death in 1683, the King purchased the site and commissioned the scheme. However, war in 1688 delayed the start for ten years. Originally, the Place was to be rectangular, incorporating libraries and academies, but in the event an octagonal shape was adopted and the buildings were entirely residential. Only the façades were designed by **Hardouin-Mansart**, other architects being responsible for the remainder; when built, the houses could be entered only from the rear. The square was first called Place des Conquêtes in honour of Louis XIV's victories. Its present name commemorates the mansion that had stood on the site belonging to César, Duc de Vendôme, the son of Henri IV and his mistress, Gabrielle d'Estrées.

An equestrian statue of Louis XIV, by **Girardon**, already stood in the centre by 1699 and this survived until the Revolution.

The 144-foot-high column, first known as the Colonne d'Austerlitz, was erected by Napoléon in 1806 to commemorate his victories of the preceding year, and the battle of Austerlitz. It is enclosed with bronze taken from 1,200 Russian and Austrian cannon, captured during that battle. Reliefs, by **Bergeret**, depict Napoléon's engineering feats – building bridges, crossing mountains, etc.

At first, a statue of Napoléon in Roman dress, by **Chaudet**, surmounted the column. Royalists replaced this, in 1814, with a large fleur-de-lys, but Louis-Philippe erected a new statue of Napoléon in 1833. This statue, now known as the 'little corporal', was transferred to the Invalides in 1911, where it remains. It was replaced by the present statue of Napoléon, a copy of Claudet's original, by **Augustin Dumont**. Communards, led by the painter Gustave Courbet, toppled the statue in 1871, but it survived and three years later Courbet was forced to pay for its re-erection, a financial burden that ruined him.

•● *Proceed anti-clockwise, following the east side of the square.*

Apart from **No 6**, **Georgio Armani**, the menswear shop, this side of the square is dominated by famous jewellers: **No 12**, **Chaumont**, where Frédéric Chopin, the composer, died 17 October 1849; **No 20**, **Mauboussin**; **Nos 22–24**, **Van Cleef and Arples**; **No 26**, **Boucheron**.

•● *Cross to the square's north-west range, where more world-famous jewellers have their premises.*

No 23, **Cartier**, was, in the 18C, the residence of the Scottish financier John Law, who also owned Nos 5, 22 and 26 as investments.

No 21, **Schiaparelli**.

Nos 15–17, the **Ritz Hotel**, is rated amongst the world's most luxurious hotels. The building, renovated at great expense in 1986, was previously the home of Armand Louis de Contaut Biron, Duke of Lauzun and Biron, 1747–93. The Duke fought for the Americans in the War of Independence.

Nos 11–13, **Ministère de Justice** The ministry has been accommodated here since 1815.

•● *Return eastward. First L follow the road (that becomes Rue de la Paix) and cross to No 28 Place Vendôme.*

No 28, **Charvet**, is the country's most fashionable shirt-maker, ranking with similar establishments in London's Jermyn Street.

•● *Continue ahead. First R Rue Danielle Casanova. Second L Rue d'Antin.*

At **No 3**, once the Mairie of the 2nd arrondissement but now the Banque de Paris et des Pays Bas, Napoléon married Joséphine in 1796.

•● *Return southward and continue directly ahead following Rue du Marché St Honoré.*

Location 9	**RUE DU MARCHÉ ST HONORÉ**

Restaurants, shops and bars line this intimate, village-like street and the Place du Marché St Honoré which bisects it.

A Jacobin monastery occupied much of the area until

the Revolution, but a street market was established here in 1810.

• *Proceed clockwise around the Place.*

Unfortunately, the Place du Marché St Honoré was spoiled when the authorities constructed, in its centre, what is probably the most hideous modern development in central Paris, a multi-storey car park that appears to have strayed from East Berlin.

No 20, Potron et Fils Poissonnerie, in the south-east corner, is a large, wet-fish shop, rare in the city centre.

• *First L Rue du Marché St Honoré continues southward.*

No 9, Mon Victor, sells the finest poultry and game in Paris.

• *Second L Rue St Honoré.*

Location 10	**RUE ST HONORÉ**

Since the 12C the Rue St Honoré has functioned as the 'high street' of the Right Bank. It is narrower than its western extension, the Rue du Faubourg St Honoré, and the emphasis here is on food rather than clothing. The most fashionable shops are to be found between Rue Royale and Avenue de l'Opéra.

No 211, St James and Albany Hotel, now apartments, was the Noailles family mansion.

• *Continue eastward to St Roch church.*

Location 11	**ST ROCH**
296 Rue St Honoré	Visitors to St Roch find the interior particularly appealing due to its numerous monuments and works of art. The majority have been acquired from other demolished buildings and are a rare find in a Paris church, most of which lost their treasures at the Revolution.

History The Faubourg St Honoré became a parish in 1633 to serve part of the congregation of St Germain l'Auxerrois. A westward migration of the nobility to the area had taken place and the population was growing rapidly. **Lemercier** designed the church, and its foundation stone was laid by Louis XIV in 1653. Money ran out in 1660, however, and work was suspended with only the chancel, transepts and one bay of the nave completed. A lottery held in 1701 provided more finance but, instead of completing the nave, a Lady Chapel and, behind it, a Holy Communion Chapel, were added at the east end. However, in 1719, John Law, recently converted to Catholicism, donated sufficient money for the nave and vaulting to be completed. The building was consecrated in 1740.

A hillock was removed by Haussmann in the mid-19C when the Avenue de l'Opéra was laid out. Prior to this, the church was approached by descending seven steps – now it is necessary to ascend twelve.

Exterior The south façade, designed in Jesuit style by **Robert de Cotte**, was built by his son **Jules-Robert**. Sculptures originally decorated the building externally and internally, making St Roch the most splendid Baroque church in Paris; most of these, however, were destroyed at the Revolution.

Bullet holes in the west side of the façade, now patched up, were made by Napoléon's troops (he was then a general) on 5 October 1795, when firing against royalists threatening the Convention sitting in the nearby Tuileries Palace.

● Follow the Passage St Roch, which runs R along the east side of the building and continue towards the north end of the church.

The circular, domed Lady Chapel was built by **Hardouin-Mansart** in 1719. A 19C oratory projects from this but is not visible externally. These additions increased the length of St Roch to 410 feet, 16 feet shorter than Notre Dame.

● Return to the south façade and enter the church.

Interior Due to the rising ground it was simpler to orientate the church north/south.

Much of the original carving in the church was by **René Charpentier**, a student of Girardon, but little of his work has survived, and most of St Roch's internal detailing, particularly inside the chapels, is 19C.

Above the main doorway is the original organ made by **Lescot** and **Cliquot** in 1765; its case is in the Rococo style.

*● Proceed to the **west aisle**.*

Immediately L in the first bay stands the marble font, made in 1845.

In the next chapel, the *Baptism of Christ* group was carved by **Lemoyne** in 1731.

The monument to Pierre Mignard, d.1695, follows. It was designed by **Lemoyne** in 1774; the moving figure of Mignard's daughter, Catherine, Comtesse de Feuguières, kneels beside his bust, the work of **Girardon**.

The Chapelle des Déportés, which follows, commemorates victims of Hitler's concentration camps.

● Proceed to the centre of the nave.

The pulpit's unusually ornate sounding board, by **Simon Challe**, 1758, is carved in imitation of fabric. Its gilded figure represents truth exposing error.

*● Continue to the **crossing**.*

The shallow dome is painted with a *Baptism of Christ*, by **Roger**, 1864.

Stretching eastward from the crossing are the chancel, ambulatory and two chapels, each receiving varying gradations of natural light, which create a theatrical effect typical of the Baroque style.

*● Proceed L to the **west transept**.*

Both transepts were redesigned internally by **Etienne Louis Boullée** in the mid-18C.

Against the first north arch of the ambulatory is the bust of Le Nôtre, by **Coysevox**, 1707, commemorating the great landscape gardener who is buried below it.

*● Follow the ambulatory northward towards the domed **Lady Chapel** behind the chancel.*

Facing south, on the Lady Chapel's south-west pier L, is the painting, *Resurrection of the widow of Naïm's son*, a 17C work by **Le Sueur**.

● Enter the chapel.

The dome of **Hardouin-Mansart**'s Lady Chapel is painted with *The Triumph of the Virgin*, by **J.-B. Pierre**, 1756.

Above the altar is a carved *Nativity* by **François** and **Michel Angier**, 1669, brought from the church of Val-de-Grâce.

● Proceed behind the Lady Chapel.

The small Chapelle de l'Adoration was added for Holy Communion in 1706.

*● Follow the **east ambulatory** southward.*

Against the north-east pier of the crossing, facing south, is the statue of St Roch, by **Lejeune**, 1745.

In the east aisle's third chapel south of the transept is the tomb of Duc Charles de Créqui, a governor of Paris, d.1687, by **Coysevox**.

Against the north wall of the next chapel south is the statue of Cardinal Guillaume Dubois, the Regent's first minister, by **Coustou**, 1725.

The monument to the astronomer, Maupertuis, d.1759, by **d'Huez**, stands against the east wall.

In the most southerly chapel stands the tomb of Henri de Lorraine, Comte d'Harcourt, d.1666, by **Renard**.

The bust of François de Boune de Créquy, Duc de Lesdiguières, d.1687, is R of this.

● Exit L and follow Rue St Honoré eastward.

No 256, **Verlet**, is the best-known coffee shop in Paris and there is a wide selection of beans for purchase.

No 163, on the south side of Place André Malraux, marks the approximate position of the Porte St Honoré, a moated gateway in Charles V's wall. To the north of this, on 8 September 1429, Joan of Arc attacked the English who, although defeated at Orléans, still occupied the capital under the leadership of Henry VI's Regent, the Duke of Bedford. Joan was wounded in the arm by an arrow and her troops retreated, thus ending the 'Maid's' only Paris offensive.

● Proceed north-westward following Avenue de l'Opéra.

Location 12	**AVENUE DE L'OPÉRA**

Haussmann laid out the avenue 1854–79, starting at both ends and working toward the centre. It is now dominated by the travel industry.

● Proceed northward to the Rue des Pyramides junction (second L).

At this point stood a hillock, the Butte St Roch, from where Joan of Arc attacked the St Honoré gateway. The mound, then the centre of a poor area, was reduced in height in 1615, but not entirely removed until the avenue was laid out.

Probably the shop of greatest interest to English-speaking visitors is at **No 37**, **Brentano's**, which, behind its gleaming brass frontage, holds a large stock of English and American books.

•► *Second L Rue Daunou.*

Location 13	**HARRY'S NEW YORK BAR**
5 Rue Daunou	Opened in 1911 by Tod Sloane, an American jockey, this is the world's original Harry's Bar. Sloane removed the counter and mahogany panelling from his New York premises and shipped it here, where it remains. Originally called the New York Bar, its first barman, a Scot, Harry MacElhone, bought the premises in 1923 adding his own name as a prefix. During the 1920s and 1930s Harry's Bar became the 'in place' for American visitors and expatriates, Hemingway and Scott Fitzgerald being *habitués*. Harry's son Andy and grandson Duncan have continued the MacElhone family patronage.

The ground-floor bar is decorated with English public-school shields, commissioned in the late 1920s, and US college pennants, acquired *c.*1940. It was here, in 1925, that barman 'Pete' Petiot invented the Bloody Mary cocktail. On American election nights, when by tradition the customers' straw vote predicts, usually correctly, the outcome, Rue Daunou often has to be closed to control the crowds.

•► *Exit L. Second R Boulevard des Capucines. Proceed to Place de L'Opéra. Cross to the central island.*

Location 14	**L'OPÉRA** *Garnier 1875*
Place de L'Opéra	L'Opéra, still the largest theatre in the world (118,400 square feet), is the Second Empire's most important building and virtually its symbol. It now stages ballet rather than opera. Designed in Neo-Baroque style, the exuberantly decorated façade dominates the commercial centre of Paris. A splendid new opera house, first mooted in 1820, was incorporated in the plan for Haussmann's redevelopment of the important business centre of Paris for Napoléon III in 1858. The first Paris opera house, reconstructed on the Left Bank, had opened in 1669 under the direction of the composer Lully, and there were many successors. However, the present building was envisaged as a far more ambitious project than any of its predecessors. **Charles Garnier**, then virtually unknown, won the public architectural competition between 170 contestants, by a unanimous vote, with a design inspired by the Neo-Baroque opera house of Victor Louis at Bordeaux. Construction began in 1861 and although the Franco-Prussian war of 1870 briefly interrupted progress, Président MacMahon opened the building on 5 January 1875.

In addition, of course, to performances the opera house is open daily 11.00–17.00. The auditorium may also be seen 13.00–14.00 if there is no rehearsal in progress.

Admission charge includes the small museum.

In 1990, the Opéra de la Bastille took over the operatic function of L'Opéra (Palais Garnier), leaving this building to concentrate on ballet.

The cupola, with its gilded lantern, rises above the auditorium.

Behind, surmounting the gable front of the stage, is a statue of Apollo with a gilded lyre, by **Millet**.

The steel framework of the building is concealed by a plethora of materials.

•● Proceed to the steps in front of the building.

Groups of statues flank the ground floor's west and east arches, representing, from L to R, *Poetry*, *Music*, *Dance* and *Drama*. *Dance*, by **Jean Baptiste Carpeaux**, is so highly regarded that the opriginal sculpture was transferred to the Louvre and is now exhibited in the Musée D'Orsay; the present statue is a replica.

Medallions, on the spandrels of the arcade's central arches, portray famous composers.

Busts above the gallery, also of composers, were later gilded.

The galleries' columns are reminiscent of the Louvre colonnade. Inscribed above them are the words 'Académie Nationale de Musique'.

•● Turn L. First R Rue Auber and first R Rue Scribe skirt the west side of L'Opéra.

Protruding from the auditorium is the curved **Pavillon de l'Empereur**, which now accommodates the library. Its double ramp was built to give direct access by carriage to the emperor's box in the dress circle.

Facing the street is the gilded monument to the building's architect Charles Garnier, 1825–98; its bust is by **Carpeaux**, 1903.

•● Continue clockwise around L'Opéra. Rue Scribe leads to Place Diaghilev, at the rear of the building. First R Rue Gluck.

The Pavillon des Abonnées, protruding from the east side of L'Opéra, provides a covered approach for subscribers.

•● First R Rue Halévy. Continue to the main façade and enter the building.

Garnier not only designed L'Opéra, but meticulously directed its embellishments, dictating their subject matter to the many painters and sculptors involved. Marbles from all the quarries in France contribute to the polychromatic effect.

*•● Proceed through the entrance hall and ascend the **great staircase**.*

Above, the ceiling is painted by **Pils** and **Clairin**.

Each of the white marble steps is 32 feet wide. The balustrade's hand-rail was made from Algerian onyx.

On the first floor is the **avant foyer** (front foyer) with its Venetian mosaic arch to the staircase.

•● Proceed ahead.

The **grand foyer** (great foyer) is decorated with frescos by **Baudry**, set among extravagant gold-leaf decoration.

At the east end of this foyer L is the Rotonde de la Lune (moon rotunda).

At the west end R, is the Rotonde du Soleil (sun rotunda).

The colonnaded loggia, overlooking Avenue de l'Opéra, is not open.

→ Return to the staircase and pass its east side R.

Ahead R is the **Rotonde du Glacier**. Its walls are lined with tapestries by **Mazerolles**; the ceiling is painted by **Clairin**.

*→ Proceed to the box on the east side (its door will be ajar if open) from which the **Salle** (auditorium) may be viewed when not in use.*

Although the entire opera house covers almost three acres, its auditorium can seat only 2,158, compared, for example, with Milan's La Scala which holds 3,600. This is because the two foyers and grand staircase combined were allocated almost the same dimensions as the auditorium. There are five tiers of loggias.

The great chandelier weighs six tons.

Originally, a fresco by **Lenepveu** decorated the cupola's ceiling, but this was covered in 1964 by the present **Chagall** painting, on a false ceiling, of scenes from operas and ballets. While undoubtedly an admirable work, not everyone believes that it is quite in tune with the opulent Second Empire surroundings; 'a flute where trumpets are needed,' complained the late Ian Nairn.

Stretching back 120 feet, the immense stage has accommodated 450 performers.

→ Exit from the box R and proceed ahead to the museum on the west side of the building.

The small **Musée de l'Opéra** exhibits paintings and manuscript scores.

→ Exit to Place de l'Opéra and proceed ahead. First L follow Boulevard des Capucines which, at Rue de la Chaussée d'Antin (first L), becomes Boulevard des Italiens. Continue ahead to Rue Laffitte (fourth L).

Looking northward from the Rue Laffitte junction, a surreal view is obtained of the Sacré Coeur, apparently floating above the façade of Notre Dame de Lorette.

→ Cross to the south side of Boulevard des Italiens. First R Rue de Marivaux. First L Place Boïeldieu.

Location 15	**OPÉRA COMIQUE**
Place Boïeldieu	The Opéra Comique (Salle Favart) provides a further auditorium for the National Opera House company. On its site, in 1783, the Duc de Choiseul built a theatre in the grounds of his house. Its company began with French works but soon turned to Italian opera and became known as 'the Italians'. Eventually the name was also applied to the boulevard which ran in front of it. The present 19C building was set back one block to face away from the noisy thoroughfare.

→ Return to Boulevard des Italiens and cross to its north side R. At the junction, cross to the north side of Boulevard Haussmann. Second L Rue Drouot.

No 6, a tiny Classical building, marks the entrance to

the courtyard of an hôtel that was built as a private mansion in 1748 but now serves as an annexe to the 9th arrondissement's mairie. Occasionally, exhibitions (always free) are held.

● Continue ahead to the Rue Rossini corner (first L).

Location 16	**LE NOUVEAU DROUOT**

Rue Drouot

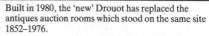

Built in 1980, the 'new' Drouot has replaced the antiques auction rooms which stood on the same site 1852–1976.

Incorporated on the south (Rue Rossini) façade is ironwork from the earlier building.

Items displayed on the basement and first floor are auctioned on the ground floor; watch the television screens for details.

● Return to Boulevard Montmartre L. First L Passage Jouffroy.

Immediately ahead is the enclosed façade of the 19C Hotel Chopin, reminiscent of a provincial station's hotel.

The frontage of its ground floor is embellished with gleaming mahogany.

● At the north end of the passage continue ahead following Passage Verdeau (shuts Sunday and at dusk). L Rue du Faubourg Montmartre. Proceed to the corner shop.

No 35, A la Mère de Famille This exceptional grocery, founded in 1768, sells just about everything sweet, but specializes in home-made preserves.

● Follow Rue Richer, which faces the shop. Continue half-way down where, on the north side, is the Folies Bergère.

Location 17	**FOLIES BERGÈRE**

32 Rue Richer
(42 46 77 11)

Open Tuesday–Sunday.

Probably the world's most famous saucy cabaret, the Folies Bergère gained its name from the nearby Rue Bergère, where it began as a music hall. Strip-tease was introduced in 1894. Shows, changed at regular intervals, last for approximately three hours and comprise an almost non-stop succession of thematic scenes featuring long-legged girls, only a few of whom are fully dressed. Unlike the Lido, meals are not served (there is of course the famous bar).

● Exit L. Second R Rue du Conservatoire. First L Rue Ste Cécile.

Location 18	**ST EUGÈNE-STE CÉCILE** *Boileau 1854*

Rue Ste Cécile

Open Monday–Saturday 09.00–12.30 and 15.00–19.00. Sunday 15.00–19.00.

Very High Gothic in style, this mid-19C church is to Paris what All Saints, Margaret Street, is to London.

● If it is a weekday, return to Rue du Conservatoire and enter the church at No 4 (just push the door to open; the handle does not turn). On Sunday afternoons enter from Rue Ste Cécile.

Excellent ironwork is a feature of the church, with slender piers and delicate balconies on three sides. Decoratively, the building depends on simple paintwork enlivened by gilding and, above all, stained glass. Nowhere in Paris is modern stained glass used to greater effect, the unusually dense colours skilfully providing resonance while avoiding gaudiness.

A spiky pulpit and retable to the altar are in the Gothic Revival tradition reminiscent of **Pugin**.

●● *Exit L Rue du Conservatoire. First R Rue Bergère, L Rue du Faubourg Montmartre. First R Boulevard Montmartre.*

Location 19	**MUSÉE GRÉVIN**

10 Boulevard Montmartre (47 79 85 05)

Open daily April–August and school holidays 10.00–19.00. Other periods 13.00–19.00. Admission charge.

This waxworks exhibition, the Paris version of Madame Tussaud's, was founded by Grévin, a caricaturist, in 1882.

Understandably, most personalities depicted are French and as none is identified it is essential to purchase a programme.

The interior of the Grand Hall is an original example of Belle Epoque decoration.

International celebrities are followed by historical (French) tableaux.

Cinema favourites include Marilyn Monroe, with that famous skirt held in suspension by a permanent draught.

●● *Exit R. First L* **Passage des Panoramas**.

No 57, **L'Arbre à Canelle** café, retains its wooden front, delicately carved in Belle Epoque style.

No 47, **Stern Graveur**, supplier of engraved cards, remains little altered.

No 49, **Lingerie 49**, possesses much original work.

●● *Continue to the end of the passage. R Rue St Marc. Second L Rue Vivienne. Continue ahead to Place de la Bourse.*

Location 20	**BOURSE DES VALEURS** *Brongniart* and *Labarre 1826*

Place de la Bourse

Visitors' gallery open Monday–Friday 11.00–13.00. Admission free.

The Bourse des Valeurs is the Paris Stock Exchange. John Law, the Scottish speculator, operated the first Paris Bourse through his bank in 1717 but it was officially founded in 1724. During the Revolution the Bourse was housed in the church of Notre Dame des Victoires; however, the need for specifically designed accommodation soon became apparent. Napoléon commissioned the present building on ground formerly belonging to the Dominican Order of the Daughters of St Thomas, and work began in 1808.

Surrounded by a Corinthian colonnade, the design of the exterior was inspired by the Temple of Vespasian, Rome.

North and south wings were added in 1907.

●● *Proceed to the south façade of the Bourse. Follow Rue Réaumur eastward, passing the Rue Montmartre junction (third L).*

No 124, **France Cables et Radio** The rust-coloured ironwork of this important Art-Nouveau building is riveted in the manner of a vast Meccano toy. It was built by **George Chedanne** in 1903.

●● *Continue eastward to M Sentier.*

10

Hôtel de Ville and Ile St Louis

Paris's Renaissance-style Hôtel de Ville (City Hall) is visited, and an excursion made to the edge of the historic Marais. The 17C hôtels of the tranquil Ile St Louis are seen, although only one may be entered.

Timing: Fine weather is essential as few buildings are open to the public.

Arrangements must be made in advance (telephone) to visit the Hôtel de Ville's state rooms.

St Gervais-St Protais and St Louis en l'Ile churches are closed Monday; the latter is also shut 12.00–15.00.

The Hôtel de Lauzun is open only from mid-April to mid-September, Saturday and Sunday (free Sunday).

The Bibliothèque de l'Arsenal is open Wednesday at 14.30.

Locations

1 Place du Châtelet	8 Pont Marie
2 Tour St Jacques	9 Hôtel de Lauzun
3 Place de l'Hôtel de Ville	10 Quai d'Anjou
4 Hôtel de Ville	11 Quai de Béthune
5 St Gervais-St Protais	12 Rue St Louis en l'Ile
6 Mémorial des Martyrs de la Déportation	13 Berthillon
	14 St Louis en l'Ile
7 Ile St Louis	15 Hôtel Fleubet
	16 Bibliothèque de l'Arsenal

Start *M Châtelet, line 1 Pont de Neuilly/Château de Vincennes; line 4 Porte d'Orléans/Porte de Clignancourt; line 7 La Courneuve/Villejuif; line 11 Mairie des Lilas/Châtelet. Exit and proceed to the centre of Place du Châtelet.*

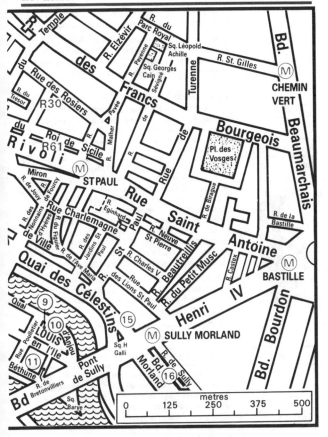

Châtelet Métro station, the largest in the world, actually links four separate stations. When possible, it should be avoided for line changes, as great stretches of subterranean corridors must generally be traversed.

Location 1	PLACE DU CHÂTELET

The name of this large square commemorates the barbican fortress that stood here, until the Revolution, as a gateway guarding the Pont au Change. It has been the headquarters of the Provost of Paris and the Guild Notaries.

No 12 Avenue Victoria, the **Chambre des Notaires** (on the square's north side), displays two ground-floor plaques, that on the east side bearing a much faded plan of the Châtelet, that on the west side a commemorative inscription.

Both theatres in the square were built by **Davioud** in 1862. On the east side is the Théâtre de la Ville.

On the west side is the Théâtre du Châtelet, now the Théâtre Musical de Paris. Apart from the Palais de Congrès and the Bastille Opéra this theatre possesses the capital's largest auditorium. It was here, in 1871, that the Communards were court-martialled.

In the centre of the square stands the Fontaine du Châtelet. Originally known as the Fontaine de la Victoire, it was erected in 1808 to commemorate Napoléon's victories. Additions were made to it in 1858.

•● *Proceed to the north side of Place du Châtelet. R Avenue Victoria (the name commemorates the British queen). First L Boulevard de Sébastopol. First R Rue de Rivoli. On the corner R is the Tour St Jacques.*

Location 2	**TOUR ST JACQUES** *1508–22*
Rue de Rivoli	

This 175-foot-high tower, in Flamboyant Gothic style, is all that survives of the 16C St Jacques la Boucherie church, the body of which was demolished in 1789. During the Middle Ages, an early predecessor of that building marked the starting point for pilgrimages to the shrine of St Jacques (James) at Compostela in Spain; there is a commemorative plaque at the tower's base, on the north side. Shortly after the demolition of the rest of the church, the structure was used as a shot tower.

It is believed that Blaise Pascal carried out experiments to measure air pressure from the tower in 1648, and a 19C statue of him, by **Cavelier**, stands between the arches.

•● *Continue eastward following Rue de Rivoli to Place de l'Hôtel de Ville.*

Location 3	**PLACE DE L'HÔTEL DE VILLE**

Until 1832, the square was called Place de Grève, because it then adjoined the river's foreshore (*grève*). Jobless workers gathered here, hence the expression still in use, *faire grève*, which originally meant unemployed but now means on strike. The public also rallied in the square to protest against autocracy, usually the king's.

From 1310, the Place de Grève was the chief site in Paris for public executions, and although the Place de la Concorde became more important when its guillotine was set up in 1793, executions continued here until 1830. Hanging, axing, guillotining – and worse – took place. Notable executions included:

1572 Huguenot leaders, following the St Bartholomew's Day massacre of their Protestant supporters.
1574 The Comte de Montgomery, who, fifteen years earlier, had fatally wounded Henri II during a tournament and fled to England. Returning to France in support of a Huguenot revolt, he was captured and beheaded.
1610 François Ravaillac, for the assassination of Henri IV.
1617 Eléanor Galligaï, foster-sister and confidant of Marie de Médicis, for sorcery; ordered by Louis XIII, the latter's suspicious son.
1795 Fouquier-Tinville, chief prosecutor during 'the Terror'.
1820 Louvel, assassin of the Duc de Berry.

•● *Proceed to the west façade of the Hôtel de Ville.*

10

| Location 4 | **HÔTEL DE VILLE** *Ballu* and *Deperthes* 1873–82 |

Place de l'Hôtel de Ville

Open Monday at 10.30, admission free. Temporary exhibitions (from the east side in Rue de Lobau). Open Tuesday–Sunday 10.00–19.00. Admission free.

This 19C Renaissance-style building is the City Hall of Paris and the official residence of its mayor. From here, the capital is administered, and state receptions are held within its Grande Salle des Fêtes.

History The administration of the capital assembled initially in the Parlouer aux Bourgeois, and later in the Grand Châtelet. Finally, in 1357, it was transferred to its present site on which stood the Maison aux Piliers (pillared house). When, in the 16C, this building became dilapidated, François I commissioned its replacement from the Italian Renaissance architect **Domenico da Cortona** (Il Boccador), who had already worked at the royal châteaux of Blois and Chambord on the Loire. Work began in 1532 and its central range and south pavilion were completed by 1551; the north pavilion, however, was not begun until 1606. Nevertheless, Cortona's plans were adhered to throughout and the Hôtel de Ville was finished by 1628.

On 17 July 1789, just three days after the fall of the Bastille, Louis XVI was brought in procession to the Hôtel de Ville from Versailles and, standing on the balcony, he donned the revolutionary cockade, which had been designed by Lafayette as a tricolor in red and blue, representing Paris, and white, the royal house of Bourbon.

Robespierre, architect of 'the Terror' was denounced by the Convention and placed under house arrest 27 July 1794. However, he was smuggled out to take refuge amongst his supporters in the Hôtel de Ville. A document calling the workers to arms in his support was drawn up by the Commune, but Robespierre, incorruptible to the last, got as far as signing it 'Ro' but then stopped, as he believed that the document was in breach of the law! Almost immediately, members of the Convention burst in, and Robespierre's jaw was smashed by a musket shot. He was dragged to the Tuileries Palace, and later, by tradition, to a prison cell in the Conciergerie. On the following day, Robespierre was guillotined in Place de la Concorde thereby ending 'the Terror'.

Napoléon introduced a new system of administering the capital in 1805, giving real power to a Prefect of the Seine, who also supervised the police. The Hôtel de Ville became the Prefect's official residence, and an additional wing was added to accommodate him. Henceforth, until 1977, Paris only briefly had a mayor (1848 and 1870–71).

In March 1871, following the humiliating defeat of France by Prussia, the angry Parisians forcibly replaced the government with the Paris Commune, and the Hôtel de Ville became its headquarters. Two months later, the uprising collapsed and the Hôtel de Ville was destroyed by fire. It is believed that the Communards, who were undoubtedly responsible for burning other public buildings such as the Tuileries Palace and the Conciergerie, were the arsonists, but there was no proof. The flames spread so quickly that 600 of their own supporters were trapped inside and perished.

Work began on the Hôtel de Ville's replacement two years later and the building, virtually a replica of its predecessor, was finished by 1882.

The appearance of the Hôtel de Ville has changed little but, in 1977, Paris, for long 'a capital without a head', was given a mayor once more. Each of the capital's twenty arrondissements has a mairie annexe responsible to the mayor of Paris.

Exterior The present building, designed by **Ballu** and **Deperthes**, 1873–82, is a reasonably accurate copy of its predecessor, of which the central section with its twin flanking pavilions was the 16C work of **Domenico da Cortona**. The remainder were additions of 1803 and 1841, built in similar style.

One hundred and thirty-six 19C statues of celebrities, mostly French statesmen, decorate the façades.

Flanking the main entrances are short ornate lamp standards, decorated with putti.

➡ Follow Rue de Rivoli eastward, passing the north façade of the building. First R Rue de Lobau. Proceed to the north entrance to view the interior.

Rooms shown to visitors accommodate civic receptions; the order in which they are seen may vary. Numerous late-19C artists were involved in decorating the interior, which is basically Belle Epoque with a Renaissance influence.

Salon Historique decorated by **Jean-Paul Laurens**.

Salon des Arcades ceiling by **Bonnat**.

Salon des Saisons the *Summer* and *Winter* paintings by **Puvis de Chavannes** are the most important in the hôtel.

Escalier d'Honneur Plans of the grand staircase of the old Tuileries Palace, by **Philibert d'Orme**, were discovered and used as the model for the Hôtel de Ville's.

Grand Salle des Fêtes Influenced by the Hall of Mirrors at Versailles, this was originally the ballroom but now accommodates receptions for heads of state, who have included Elizabeth II.

➡ Exit R and proceed to the south entrance, which leads to the exhibition gallery.

Free, temporary exhibitions are held, generally of major works by international artists.

*➡ Exit R Rue de Lobau. First R Quai de l'Hôtel de Ville. Proceed to the garden's central statue of Etienne Marcel, by **Idrac** and **Marqueste** c.1880.*

Etienne Marcel was an early revolutionary, who attempted to replace royal with parliamentary authority.

In view of his conspiracy with the English it may seem surprising that Marcel has been officially commemorated, but the bronze equestrian statue was erected in gratitude to him for presenting the provost of Paris with his Maison des Piliers in 1357 to serve as the municipal headquarters. The house stood on the site of the central section of the present Hôtel de Ville, facing the Place.

•• *Return to Rue de Lobau. First R Place St Gervais. The historic district of the Marais has now been entered.*

| Location 5 | **ST GERVAIS-ST PROTAIS** |

Place St Gervais

Open Tuesday–Sunday.

This otherwise Gothic building possesses a Classical west front, which marks the earliest adoption of that style in a French church. Within are mid-16C choir stalls with carved misericords, rare in the capital, together with the oldest organ in Paris.

History A basilica is believed to have stood here in the 6C but the earliest documented church was built 1212–1420. Although rebuilding began in 1491 in the Flamboyant Gothic style, it was completed in the Classical style with the west front in 1621. The parish was wealthy, as many of the Right Bank's merchants, particularly those in the wine trade, favoured the quarter. During the Revolution, the building became a Temple of Youth and was notorious for its orgies.

The west front is of major architectural importance as, for the first time, the Classical style was employed in a French church. It was built 1616–21 by **Clément Métezeau the Younger**, possibly to designs by **Salomon de Brosse**; three Classical Orders – Doric, Ionic and Corinthian – are superimposed. The design of this building proved to be influential and many Classical churches followed in the capital.

The wooden doors were carved by **Du Hancy**.

•• *Follow Rue François Miron north of the church and proceed eastward.*

Most of the north façade is hidden by a block of apartments, **Nos 2–14**, constructed in 1734, an early purpose-built example in Paris. The rental produced supplemented the income of the church.

A plaque, L of the first door, '*Ici vécurent les Couperins*' records that the Couperin family of musicians lived here.

•• *First R Rue des Barres.*

Exterior From the central iron gate R a partial view can be gained of the cloister and old churchyard (not open).

•• *Continue ahead.*

On the corner of Rue Grenier sur l'Eau, **No 12 Rue des Barres**, built in 1540, retains exposed timbers on its north side, a rare Paris example.

•• *Continue ahead to the small square that faces the east end of the church.*

From this point the most picturesque view of the church is gained.

The high apse with its massive buttresses was completed in 1540.

•• *Continue ahead. First R Rue de L'Hôtel de Ville. R Rue de Brosse. Enter the church.*

Interior The **nave** was built 1560–1620.

A star-vault forms the roof of the nave and chancel; the aisles are cross-rib vaulted.

At the west end, on its carved Renaissance loft,

stands the oldest organ in Paris, made in 1601 and
enlarged in the 18C. Eight successive members of the
Couperin family were organists here between 1656
and 1826, all of them playing on this instrument.

•➡ *Follow the* **north aisle**.

Standing against the east wall of the baptistery, which
occupies the first north chapel, is a wooden model of
the west front of the church, by **Du Hancy**.

In the third north chapel, against the east wall, stands
a 13C altar; its retable depicts the death of the Virgin.

•➡ *Proceed to the* **crossing**.

Against the crossing's north-east pillar, facing west,
the stone Virgin and Child was carved in the second
half of the 14C.

The **transept** was completed in 1578.

On the north transept's west wall, at wainscot level, is
a 16C Flemish Crucifixion scene, painted on wood.

•➡ *Proceed to the* **chancel**.

Stained-glass windows in the chancel are 16C.

Apart from the first seven upper stalls and the first
front stalls (from the west) on each side, which are
17C, the choir stalls were carved *c.*1545.

Many of their exceptional misericords, now fixed,
depict contemporary trades.

Flanking the high altar are early-17C wooden statues
of St Gervais and St Protais by **Bourdin Michel**.

The altar's six candle-holders were designed by
Soufflot, originally for the abbey church of Ste
Geneviève.

Dominating the **Lady Chapel** which was built at the
east end of the church 1517–40, is the 5-foot-diameter
keystone, dated 1540, which forms the centrepiece of
the gilded vault.

Some of this chapel's stained glass is 16C.

Monuments on the south wall of the adjoining south-
east chapel R, commemorate, from east to west:
Marguerite de Luxembourg, d.1670; René Poitier,
d.1670; Louis Poitier, d.1613.

The tomb monument, angled to the west,
commemorates Michel le Tellier, d.1685, minister of
state to Louis XIV.

•➡ *Exit from the church R. First R Rue François
Miron. Second L Rue du Pont Louis-Philippe. First R
Rue de Rivoli.*

Famed for its virgin olive oil, **A l'Olivier** at **No 23** has
recently moved to these premises from the Ile St
Louis. In addition to selling all types of natural oils,
products derived from them are also available,
including soaps and mustards. Flavoured vinegars and
fresh olives from Provence are additional specialities.

•➡ *Return to Rue du Pont Louis-Philippe L, continue
ahead and cross Pont Louis-Philippe (rebuilt in 1862)
to the Ile St Louis. Ahead, Rue Jean du Bellay leads to
Pont St Louis. Cross to Quai de l'Archevêché. First L
Square de l'Ile de France. Proceed to the Mémorial de
la Déportation in the garden.*

•➡ Alternatively, if not visiting the memorial, after crossing Pont Louis-Philippe, first L Quai de Bourbon.

Location 6	**MÉMORIAL DES MARTYRS DE LA DÉPORTATION** *G. H. Pingusson 1963*

Square de l'Ile de France

Open daily 10.00–12.00 and 14.00–18.30. Closes 17.00 in winter.
Admission free.

This concrete memorial commemorates the 200,000 victims who were deported from France in 1940 to be exterminated in the Nazi concentration camps. It was dedicated by President de Gaulle in 1962.

•➡ Descend the steps on either side to the subterranean chamber.

A small flame burns continuously from the circular brass plaque in the centre of the floor.

Beyond the symbolic iron bars ahead lies the body of an unknown deportee.

Appropriate quotations from writers, including Jean Paul Sartre, are inscribed on the walls. Sculptures are by **Desserprit**.

•➡ Return via Pont St Louis and Rue Jean du Bellay to the north side of the Ile St Louis. R Quay de Bourbon.

Location 7	**ÎLE ST LOUIS**

A wistful tranquillity, plus the city's finest ice-cream emporium, are the great touristic attractions of this 17C island.

The Ile St Louis originated as a single island, but it was subdivided in 1360 to improve the city's defences. One islet was called Ile aux Vaches, and the other Ile Notre Dame. Both were owned by the chapter of Notre Dame, and the former gained its name from the canons' cows (vaches) that grazed it. Popular with bathers and fishermen, the flat breezy islets also proved ideal for washerwomen, who found them ideal for drying clothes.

In 1614, Louis XIII commissioned **Christophe Marie** to reunite the islets and link them with the mainland, but although some buildings were constructed by 1618, the important mansions were not begun until 1638, due to procrastinating objections to the entire development by Notre Dame's chapter. By 1662, the island had already become popular as an annexe to the fashionable Marais, but it was adopted mainly by the wealthy bourgeoisie, rather than the nobility. The riverside hôtels, unusually for Paris at the time, overlook the Seine rather than enclosed courtyards. Several buildings were designed by **Le Vau** and are contemporary with the same architect's extensions to the Louvre's Court Carrée. Unfortunately, only one mansion, the Hôtel Lauzun, is open to the public.

All the hôtels referred to, except the Hôtel Chénizot, were built in the 17C. For reasons of economy, the streets that link the quays were laid out in a regular grid pattern.

*•➡ Continue eastward, to the **Rue Le Regrattier** junction (first R).*

Above the street sign, its old name, Rue de la Femme Sans Teste (headless woman) may be seen. In a niche above the sign the partial figure of a woman, rather more than headless, also survives.

•➡ *Continue following Rue de Bourdon.*

No 19 This large, important mansion unusually possesses three pediments. Parliamentarians once met here.

No 15 Built as the **Hôtel Le Charron**, its courtyard is sometimes open.

No 11 A plaque marks the occupancy of the painter Philippe de Champaigne in 1643.

No 1 Au Franc Pinot, an old-established bar/restaurant, was still a private house in the late 18C, when Cécile Renaud, the owner's daughter, unsuccessfully attempted to assassinate the revolutionary leader Robespierre: she was guillotined.

•➡ *Immediately L is the Pont Marie.*

Location 8	**PONT MARIE**

The name of this bridge, one of the most graceful in Paris, honours not the Virgin Mary, as many believe, but its builder, Christophe Marie, who was responsible for creating the Ile St Louis by reuniting the two islets and linking them to the Right and Left Banks with bridges. All this work was executed at his own expense in exchange for the right to sell the land to developers. The construction of the first bridge, 1614–34, marked the completion of the scheme's initial stage; however, this collapsed on the opening day and twenty were drowned. For a long time, the bridge was lined on both sides with tall, narrow houses, but what remained of them was finally demolished for road widening in 1769. Prone to accidents, the Pont Marie has been rebuilt many times.

•➡ *Continue eastward following Quai d'Anjou.*

No 39, Théâtre de L'Ile St Louis, situated at the end of the courtyard, stages revues.

No 27 The Marquise de Lambert held her literary salons in this mansion.

•➡ *Continue ahead passing Rue Poulletier (first R).*

It was along the route of Rue Poulletier that the island was formerly divided.

Location 9	**HÔTEL DE LAUZUN** *Le Vau (?) 1657*

17, Quai d'Anjou

Open mid-April–mid-September Saturday and Sunday 10.00–17.40. Admission charge (but included in the Saturday admission charge for the Musée Carnavelet and vice versa (see page 198). Free Sunday.

A rare example in Paris of a furnished 17C mansion that is open to the public (albeit on a limited scale), the Hôtel de Lauzun retains many of its exquisite frescos.

Charles Gruyn des Bordes, Commissioner-General for the light cavalry, built this hôtel which, following his death in 1681, was acquired by the French commander at the Battle of the Boyne, Antonin, Duc de Lauzun. The Duke, who only stayed three years, apparently moved here to escape the clutches of his wife, the by then very corpulent Grande Mademoiselle, niece of Louis XIV. Famous residents later include Baudelaire (1843–44), Rilke, the English painter Walter Sickert and Wagner. The City of Paris acquired the property in 1928.

The façade is rather plain as it never received all the proposed embellishments. However, gilded rainpipes, decorated with dolphins at the lower string-course level, are a spectacular feature. The building was not given its present name until 1850, when the plaque, complete with misspelling, was fixed to the wall.

●● *Proceed through the courtyard and enter the hôtel R. Ascend the stairs to the first floor.*

All the main rooms are at upper-floor level, due to risk of the Seine flooding. Although built in Louis XIV's reign, the decoration of the house, which includes work by **Patel** and **Bourdon**, is in an earlier style.

Sedan chairs stand on both landings.

The first-floor salon retains its painted beams.

Painted panels decorate the ante-room.

●● *Ascend to the upper floor.*

This, the 'bel étage', retains the finest rooms in the house, exquisite examples of French Baroque work.

The Music Room, with its gilded musicians' gallery, is outstanding, A reception was held here for Elizabeth II in 1957.

This is followed by the **bedroom** and the **boudoir**.

●● *Exit R and continue eastward.*

Location 10	**QUAI D'ANJOU**

Heavy traffic rather spoils the charm of this otherwise attractive quay, thoroughfares on the other side of the island being more peaceful.

No 15 A plaque records that this hôtel was built for Nicolas Lambert de Thorigny, probably by **Le Vau**, in 1645.

No 9 Honoré Daumier, the artist, lived in this house 1846–63.

No 7 was built for Jacques Brébart in 1642.

No 5 The Petit Hôtel de Marigny was built in 1640 for the Marquise de Marigny.

No 3 Le Vau designed this hôtel, in 1640, to serve as his own residence.

●● *Second R Boulevard Henri IV.*

Immediately L of **Square Barye**, the formal gardens are a remnant of the terraced grounds of the Hôtel Bretonvilliers.

●● *First R Quai de Béthune.*

| Location 11 | **QUAI DE BÉTHUNE** |

At Le Vau's suggestion, all the houses on the Ile St Louis that overlooked the river were given balconies and this quay was first called the Quai des Balcons.

No 18, Hôtel de Comans d'Astry, was built in 1647 for the Controller of Finance. Armand, Duc de Richelieu, the great-nephew of the cardinal, lived here 1728–88.

No 20 Built by **Le Vau**.

No 22, Hôtel Lefebvre de la Malmaison, was built in 1645. During the 19C it was the home of Baudelaire.

●● *Continue westward following the Quai d'Orléans.*

This sunny, tree-lined quay offers famous views of Notre Dame from its west end.

●● *Continue around the island clockwise to the iron-built Pont St Louis (first L). First R Rue St Louis en l'Ile.*

| Location 12 | **RUE ST LOUIS EN L'ÎLE** |

With its lively shops and restaurants and, in its centre, the island's only church, this thoroughfare serves as the 'high street' of Ile St Louis.

No 51 Built as the Hôtel Chénizot in 1730, the building served as the Archbishop's residence in the mid 19C. Earlier, at the start of the Revolution, it had been the home of Thérèse Cabarrus, Marquise de Fontenay. Attempting to flee the country, she was imprisoned at Bordeaux, but released to become the mistress of the province's despot Tallien. On returning to Paris, she became the most famous courtesan of the period, giving birth to eleven illegitimate children. In between, she took part in carnivals and parades, extravagantly dressed as allegorical figures.

A doorway, decorated with griffins, leads to an open courtyard.

Above the portal, Baroque plasterwork incorporates two further griffins which support the main balcony.

●● *Continue eastward, passing Rue Budé (first R) and Rue des Deux Ponts (second L).*

| Location 13 | **BERTHILLON** |

31 Rue St Louis en l'Ile

Closed Monday, Tuesday and late July to early September.

For many ice-cream lovers a visit to Berthillon alone makes their trip to Paris worthwhile. Although self-indulgently closed Monday and Tuesday and between late July and early September, Berthillon's ice-creams and sorbets are now franchised to other establishments on the island and can be obtained every day, albeit at a slightly higher price. Look for the sign 'Glaces Berthillon'.

There is generally a lengthy queue here and the young ladies who serve the ice-creams through the open window have been known to show impatience with the indecisive. A triple cornet is the best buy and the fresh fruit and chocolate flavours are sensational.

There is a small ground-floor parlour.

●● *Continue eastward to the island's church.*

| Location 14 | **ST LOUIS EN L'ÎLE** |

21 Rue St Louis en l'Ile

Open Tuesday–Sunday 09.00–12.00 and 15.00–19.00. Concerts are frequently held.

St Louis's 17C interior, one of the richest in Paris, combines a wide variety of expensive materials, many of which are sumptuously gilded.

The church was begun by **Le Vau** in 1664 and completed by **Jacques Doncet** in 1726.

Externally, the tower, with its spire curiously pierced by round holes, was built in 1765 to replace the original, which had been destroyed by lightning.

An unusual iron clock is fixed to the tower's north face.

•• *Enter the church. On occasions, only the Rue Poulletier (first R) entrance is open.*

Much of the carving within is the work of **Jean-Baptiste de Champaigne**, d.1681, who is buried in the church.

Against the **north aisle**'s fourth outer pier is a plaque, presented to the church by the people of St Louis, Missouri, August 1926, to record the naming of their city after its patron saint.

Outstanding Nottingham alabasters, from the same series as St Leu-St Gilles, form the reredoses of the altars in both transepts and of the high altar.

•• *Exit from the church R and continue eastward following Rue St Louis en l'Ile.*

No 12 Philippe Le Bon discovered the principles of gas lighting at this house in 1799.

Nos 7–9 Between these buildings is the archway of the first mansion to be built on the Ile St Louis, the Hôtel de Bretonvilliers.

No 2, Hôtel Lambert, **Le Vau**, 1642. Although this is the finest mansion on the island, little of it can be seen externally, and the interior is never open to the public. The hôtel's name commemorates its first owner, the wealthy Lambert de Thorigny, who died in 1644, only two years after the building had been completed. Voltaire is reputed to have visited the mansion, the house of his mistress the Marquise de Châtelet. From 1842, it was for many years the property of the Polish Czartoryski family, who entertained Chopin and Delacroix within. The hotel's labyrinth of cellars served as a hideout for Allied airmen who parachuted over France during the Second World War.

Many famous artists have worked on the hôtel's interiors, including **Le Brun** and **Eustache Le Sueur**.

•• *Continue ahead to the Pont de Sully L (completed in 1876) and cross the river. Immediately L is **Square Henri Galli**.*

In 1899, foundation stones of the Bastille's Tour de la Liberté were excavated to the north and brought to this garden. The square occupies what was originally the western tip of the Ile des Louviers, which was not joined to the mainland until 1843, when Boulevard Morland was laid out along its northern edge.

•• *Proceed to the north side of the square.*

10

Hôtel de Ville and Ile St Louis / 166

Location 15

HÔTEL FLEUBET (ÉCOLE MASSILLON)
Hardouin-Mansart 1681

2 bis Quai des
Célestins

In 1857, it was decided to embellish this 17C hôtel, now a school, with Renaissance-style decoration. Although 'over the top', it is hard to condemn the exuberant figures, fruit and trophies, which produce a comic-opera effect.

The mansion was originally built for Gaspard Fleubet, chancellor of Marie-Thérèse.

A 19C extension on the corner is similarly embellished, possibly by the same hand.

●● *Return eastward. Cross Boulevard Henri IV to Place du Père Teilhard de Chardin. Proceed to the south-west façade of l'Arsenal, which faces Boulevard Morland ahead R.*

Location 16

BIBLIOTHÈQUE DE L'ARSENAL

1 Rue de Sully

*Open Wednesday
14.30–16.00 (closed
1–15 September).
Admission free.*

Sumptuous decor from the 17C and 18C may be admired in the Salon de Musique and the apartment of the Duchesse de la Meilleraie.

Henri I founded the Royal Arsenal in 1549 for the manufacture of armaments. Louis XIII disbanded it, and the building was remodelled and extended by **Boffrand** for conversion to a court of law *c.*1723; Fouquet was tried there for embezzlement.

In 1797, the library was brought here; it is public and comprises over a million volumes plus manuscripts and prints. The library's theatre history section possesses an almost complete collection of French dramas, and the illustrated manuscripts are outstanding. Documents concerning the 'man in the iron mask' and the 'affair of the diamond necklace' are of great historic interest. Particularly valuable are the *Book of Hours* belonging to St Louis, and Charles V's bible.

Boffrand designed two main façades, facing Rue de Sully to the north and Boulevard Morland to the south.

On the balustrades of the latter, at roof level, are guns firing bursts of flame, all in stone.

●● *Enter the building from its north-west end facing Place du Père Teilhard de Chardin, and ascend to the first floor. Proceed to the enquiry counter R and await the guide.*

Rooms are viewed in varying order.

The **Salon de Musique**, designed by **Boffrand**, preserves outstanding woodwork from the Louis XV period.

Shown also are the **bedroom** and **cabinet** once occupied by the Duchesse de la Meilleraie. Sumptuously decorated, these two relatively small rooms are panelled, painted and gilded. Due to their low height, they provide a rare opportunity to inspect painted ceilings by **Vouet** at close quarters.

●● *Exit from the library. Ahead M Sully Morland.*

11

South Marais

The ancient Marais quarter evolved from its south-east corner, where two royal palaces, followed by Place des Vosges, were built, and this is where the route begins. Apart from a section around Rue du Temple, all the locations covered lie south of Rue des Francs Bourgeois. A great number of important hôtels are passed but, unlike North Marais (Itinerary 12), few are open to the public.

Timing: Fine weather is essential, due to the limited access to interiors.

The Maison de Victor Hugo is closed Monday.

Guided tours of the Hôtel de Sully (in French only) are given Sunday at 15.00.

Churches are open only for services, but the medieval cloister of Billettes church may generally be visited July–September.

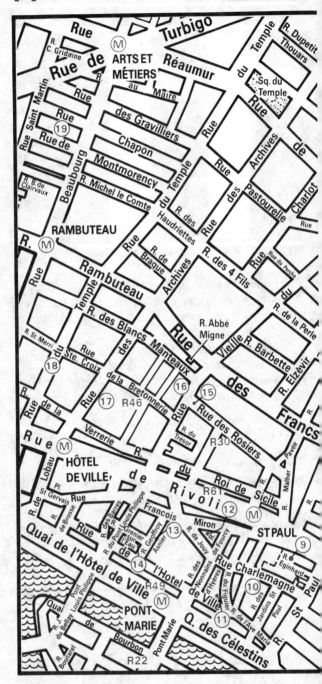

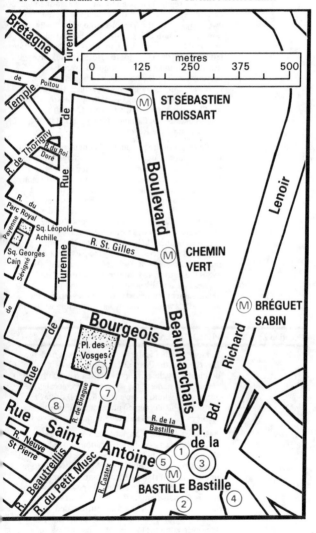

Start M Bastille, line 1 Pont de Neuilly/Château de Vincennes; line 8 Balard/Créteil-Préfecture; line 5, Bobigny-Préfecture/Place d'Italie. Exit and proceed to the Rue St Antoine junction on the west side. Unless visiting L'Opéra de la Bastille remain here to view all the elements of the Place as described and the commencement of Rue St Antoine (Location 5).

Location 1	**THE MARAIS**

The Marais district, in the shape of a triangle, comprises 300 acres, with the points of the triangle marked by Place de la République, the Hôtel de Ville and Place de la Bastille.

Until drained in the 13C, a great marsh (*marais*), which was regularly flooded by the Seine, formed the eastern part of the Right Bank. Much of the land was owned by the Knights Templar, who were chiefly responsible for draining it; the rich alluvial soil provided fertile arable land. In the 14C, Charles V left his Palais de la Cité for the Hôtel St Paul, near the Bastille, and a few manor houses were then commissioned by the nobility. The hôtels de Sens, Carnavelet and Lamoignon were built in the 16C, but it was not until the laying out of the Place Royal, now the Place des Vosges, early in the 17C, that the Marais became the fashionable quarter that it remained until the Revolution.

In the First Empire period, the Faubourg St Germain took over as the area of Paris favoured by aristocrats. In the Marais, tradesmen replaced the nobility and the decline of the quarter set in. It was not until many of the great mansions appeared to be beyond salvation that the rehabilitation of the area began, in the late 1960s. By then, soaring property values in Paris had at last made restoration work a viable proposition, which was further encouraged by generous financial help from both national and municipal resources, following the passing of the preservationist law of André Malraux in 1961. By the 1980s the unexpected miracle had occurred: the Marais had actually been saved! Without its abandonment for almost two centuries most of the great hôtels would certainly have been remodelled or lost.

Location 2	**PLACE DE LA BASTILLE**

For long a rather featureless square, apart from the July column, the Place de la Bastille is now dominated by the new opera house on its south-east corner. The name of the square commemorates the great east bastion, in the city wall, the Bastille St Antoine, which occupied much of the area from medieval times until the Revolution.

Bastille St Antoine Charles V developed the Bastille in 1370 from an existing fortification, not only to strengthen the city's eastern defences, but also to protect his recently built Hôtel St Paul, which stood immediately west of it. When completed, in 1385, the structure comprised an oblong-shaped keep, with high walls punctuated by eight towers of the same height. All was castellated and surrounded by a moat. In spite of its impregnable appearance, six of the seven attempts to overcome the fortress succeeded. Not until the 17C did the Bastille acquire its now renowned status as a prison when, under

Richelieu, those who had displeased Louis XIII were held within its walls by a *lettre de cachet* (an arbitrary order bearing the king's seal). Those guilty of serious criminal acts against the state were sent generally to Vincennes, and imprisonment in the Bastille was not regarded as a disgrace; in any case only fifty could be accommodated at a time. Captives were allowed to furnish their rooms, keep a servant, and entertain mistresses; Cardinal Rohan is reported to have given a dinner party for twenty guests during his internment there. The Bastille was also used to store books that were regarded as offensive, generally due to their advocation of civil liberty. Famous prisoners included Voltaire (twice), the anonymous 'Man in the Iron Mask', his mask really being of velvet; the Marquis de Sade, who wrote *Justine* during his imprisonment; and the English playwright and architect John Vanbrugh, ostensibly for not possessing a passport.

By 1784, the Bastille was proving too expensive to maintain and as *lettres de cachet* had been abolished that year (they were briefly revived by Napoléon) and there were few prisoners, it was agreed that the building should be demolished apart from one tower, which would be kept to commemorate the fortress. An open square with a statue of Louis XVI was to take its place. However, on 14 July 1789 the Bastille still dominated the eastern perimeter of the Marais and the Paris mob, which had already seized weapons from the Hôtel des Invalides in the morning, marched there to gain possession of the 125 barrels of gunpowder stored within. Several hundred revolutionaries, most of them from the provinces, were opposed by just thirty-two Swiss Guards, supported by eighty-two pensioners. The Marquis de Launay, its governor, invited representatives of the revolutionaries to discuss their demands with him and entertained them to lunch. Not knowing this, and fearing they had been arrested, the mob stormed the Bastille and hacked the governor to pieces. Its seven captives were released, including an English lunatic, Mr Whyte, who could not comprehend why he had been freed and tried to return to his cell.

As the Bastille had been a symbol of royal oppression, the mob decided to demolish it and some of the gunpowder taken was used to blow it up that same evening. Part of the masonry was later used to construct the Pont de la Concorde and eighty-three of its massive blocks of stone were carved into models of the Bastille for distribution amongst provincial towns. Lafayette presented the key of the main gate to George Washington and it is now kept at Mount Vernon, USA. Some of the fortress's cellars are believed to survive below ground.

All of France celebrates 14 July, 'Bastille Day', as the true commencement of the Revolution, and it is a national holiday.

On the south side of Place de la Bastille, Rue de Lyon was laid out in 1847 and Boulevard Henri IV in 1866, events which opened up the square at that end, and greatly altered its appearance.

In the centre of the square stands the July column.

11

Location 3	**COLONNE DE JUILLET**

Place de la Bastille

Confusingly, this bronze monument, the July Column, was not inspired by the French Revolution of July 1789 but by a later revolution of 1830. Soon after the formation of the Place de la Bastille, Napoléon planned, as its centrepiece, a 74-foot-high figure of an elephant that would discharge water through its trunk. A plaster prototype, erected in the square, stayed for many years in a delapidated state, Victor Hugo referring to it in his *Les Misérables*, but the project was abandoned.

In 1830, Charles X disbanded parliament and suspended the freedom of the press, attempting a return to the autocratic rule of the *ancien régime*. New revolutionaries would not accept this and raised barricades; Charles, sensing defeat, fled and was replaced by the 'citizen king' Louis-Philippe d'Orléans, who erected this column to commemorate the event and the establishment of his 'July Monarchy'. The Bourbon rule of France was finally ended, Charles X having 'learned nothing and forgotten nothing'.

In February 1848 Louis-Philippe was himself deposed by the mob, who introduced universal suffrage, resulting in the leadership of Napoleon's nephew, Louis-Napoléon Bonaparte, later to be elected Emperor Napoléon III.

Those who died in the riots of 1830 and 1848 are buried beneath the column and their names are inscribed on its base.

The column's shaft is in three sections, reflecting the three days of the July 1830 revolt.

July is represented by the lion and France by the four cocks.

The figure surmounting the column is known as the 'Spirit of Liberty', although it is in the form of a winged mercury by **Augustin Dumont**.

Cleaning and regilding of the monument was completed in 1989.

●● *The new Opéra de la Bastille overlooks the south-east section of the square, occupying the block between Rue de Charonne and Rue de Lyon (unnecessary to proceed to it unless visiting the buildings).*

Location 4	**OPÉRA DE LA BASTILLE** *Carlos Ott 1989*

Place de la Bastille

Opened to coincide with the bicentenary of the French Revolution, this structure may be compared with the Eiffel Tower, which was erected to mark the centenary of the same event. Unlike the Eiffel Tower, however, the Opéra de la Bastille is not intended to be a temporary feature. The Uruguayan-born Canadian architect **Carlos Ott** won the international competition, held in 1982, and work began two years later.

The Opéra de la Bastille occupies the site of a railway station constructed in 1859 but converted to an exhibition hall in 1970.

Two auditoriums accommodate approximately 2,700 and 1,200. Operas and concerts are performed, but ballet remains at L'Opéra (Salle Garnier).

White marble from Véronne has been used for the floors and stairs, and stone from Valreuil lines the walls.

| Location 5 | **RUE ST ANTOINE** |

Rue St Antoine, the 'high street' of the Marais, has existed since Roman times, originally as a highway raised above the flood level of the marshland. On its south side, near the Bastille, Charles V built his Palais St Pol (Hôtel St Paul) in the late 14C and from then, due to its great width, the street was used for games and jousting tournaments. In 1407, the Crown acquired the Hôtel des Tournelles, which stood on the north side of the street, and the Duke of Bedford lived there while acting as Regent for England's young Henry VI. Later, Charles V moved to this hôtel, becoming the first of seven French kings who would make it their main residence. François I, however, then transferred to the Louvre.

Spectacles continued to be held in the Rue St Antoine during the Renaissance period, including the burning of 'heretics', generally Protestants, following trial at the Inquisition's *auto-da-fé*. In June 1559, Henri II fought in a tournament outside the Hôtel des Tournelles against Gabriel de Lorges, Sire de Montgomery and Captain of the King's Scottish Guards. Montgomery's lance broke and pierced the king's visor, fatally wounding him. Henri's widow, Catherine de Médicis, mad with grief, pressurized her son, now Charles IX, into demolishing the Hôtel des Tournelles. The hapless Montgomery escaped the Queen's likely vengeance, fleeing to England, but returned in 1574 to support the Huguenots. He was captured and beheaded for taking part in the Protestant revolt not, as many believe, for accidentally killing Henri II.

At the Place de la Bastille junction, the great barricade of 1848 was erected, and in 1871 the Communards made their final stand.

•➡ Proceed westward.

No 5, Société Générale This building marks the site of the former entrance to the Bastille's courtyard, through which the revolutionary mob gained access to the fortress.

•➡ Continue westward passing Rue Castex (second L).

At **No 17**, **Temple Ste Marie** was built by Mansart in 1639.

Begun in 1632, this church was built for the Convent of the Visitation. A cloister and domestic buildings stood immediately to the north until the monastery was suppressed in 1790. **François Mansart** adopted a circular shape for the building, the first of this type in Paris.

Buried inside are Henri de Sévigné, killed duelling in 1651, and Nicolas Fouquet, Finance Minister to Louis XIV, d.1680. The Temple church has been Protestant since 1803.

•➡ Continue westward to No 21 and enter the courtyard.

No 21, the **Hôtel de Mayenne**, was built for the Duc de Mayenne in 1612, probably by **Jean Androuet du Cerceau**; its gatehouse was heightened later. This was the first hôtel in the capital to be fronted by a courtyard and backed by a garden, an oft-repeated formula in Paris.

Built of red brick, with stone trims, the mansion is typical of the Henri IV period. It has accommodated the Ecole des Francs Bourgeois since 1843.

•• Exit L. Second R Rue de Birague (originally Rue Royale). Immediately ahead is the Pavillon du Roi, centrepiece of the south range of the Place des Vosges.

•• Proceed through the archway to the centre of the Place des Vosges (Square Louis XIII).

Location 6	**PLACE DES VOSGES**

Under gradual restoration since the 1970s, the Place des Vosges, built in Renaissance style, is once again the capital's showpiece square. Although comprising the finest architectural group in the Marais, the Place is completely different in appearance from the rest of the quarter, not only in its format – there are no other important squares in the Marais – but in the appearance of its arcaded brick façades, surmounted by steeply pitched roofs.

History Henry IV commissioned the Place to be laid out on part of the site of the grounds of the demolished Hôtel des Tournelles c.1604. It is not clear who designed the houses but Sully, the King's minister, appears to have assembled a group of architects that included **Baptiste Androuet du Cerceau, Louis Métezeau** and **Claude Chastillon**. Apart from the King's and Queen's Pavilions, on the south and north sides respectively, all the façades were identical. Initially, the entire south side was earmarked for Henri IV's use and the north side for a silk factory; in the event however, no king ever lived there and the silk factory scheme was soon abandoned in favour of a pavilion intended for Henri's estranged Queen, Marie de Médicis; this, similarly, was never occupied by royalty.

It had always been envisaged that the east and west ranges would be sold as private residences, and allocations to members of the nobility were made in 1605. Construction began in 1607 and, to encourage progress, the King is reported to have visited the site every day until his assassination in 1610.

The Place Royale, as it was first called, was officially opened in 1612 for the three-day Chevaliers de la Gloire (glorious cavalier tournament) as part of the celebrations to mark the double marriages of Louis XIII to Anne of Austria, and Elizabeth, the King's sister, to the future Philip IV of Spain. It was the first public square to be laid out in Paris and quickly became the capital's most fashionable address, paving the way for the popularity of the entire Marais quarter. Its name was changed at the Revolution to Place de l'Indivisibilité and again, by Napoléon, to Place des Vosges, in recognition of the first department of France to pay its taxes.

It was intended that all the houses would be built of brick, with stone trims to the façades, but brick had been rarely used in Paris and its laying took too long for the impatient Henri IV. Only the earliest houses were therefore built of brick, the remainder following in timber-framed construction; the subsequent movement of the timbers has resulted in the displacement that is now apparent.

The plaster façades of the later houses were painted to imitate brickwork, a job executed so well that it is possible to distinguish the imitation from the real thing only at close quarters.

For the first time in Paris, viewing balconies were fitted to the houses, thus making it easier for occupants to observe the games and spectacles that took place in the square from its opening day. Originally, the balconies were built of stone, and balustraded, but none of them has survived; the present wrought-iron versions are replacements from various periods.

•● *Proceed to the central garden.*

Square Louis XIII When opened, the area was gravelled and surrounded by a simple wooden fence. At the residents' expense, iron railings with a splendid, partly gilded gate were erected in 1685 and the area was grassed. All this survived the Revolution, because military equipment was stored in the square and had to be safeguarded, but by 1835 the ironwork had deteriorated and was taken down, including the gate, amidst protests led by the square's most illustrious resident, Victor Hugo. The present wrought ironwork, of vastly inferior craftsmanship, was erected in 1839.

Trees were first planted in 1793, but as they were dying, 186 new lime trees were planted to replace them in 1976. Their existence is controversial because the leaves obscure the outstanding architecture for most of the year.

In 1639, an equestrian statue of Louis XIII was erected in the centre of the square. This was destroyed at the Revolution and in 1811 a central fountain was erected in its place. The present statue of Louis XIII, by **Dupay**, 1829, is not highly regarded.

Fountains were added at the corners of the square in 1816; they were restored in 1989 and water flows from them once more.

Houses in the Place Vendôme can be clearly observed only from the side of the roadway adjacent to the railings. Due partly to changes in ownership throughout the years, the numbering is not always original, one number in some cases now applying to more than a single four-bay unit. Few houses now remain unrestored, the state having subsidized the cost of work on the façades and roofs by 70 per cent.

•● *Return towards the Pavillon du Roi and proceed clockwise around the Place.*

No 1, Pavillon du Roi When completed, the pavilion proved to be too small for the new king's use and royalty never lived here. Instead, it was occupied by his concierge until 1666. From then, the property was leased and now, like most in the Place, has been divided into flats. Both this and its neighbour, No 1bis, are built of brick.

No 1bis, Hôtel de Coulanges The Marquise de Sévigné was born here in 1624.

Above the central, first floor window is a bust of Henri IV, added long after the building's completion.

Its main balcony, of 1655, is one of the oldest in Paris.

No 3, Hôtel d'Estrades, completed in 1613, stands on the site of the Hôtel des Tournelles stables. 'Brickwork' is imitation.

•• *Follow the west range of the Place.*

No 9, Hôtel des Chaulnes Completed by 1607, Louis XIII is reputed to have stayed here during the square's opening ceremony.

•• *Enter the courtyard if the door is open.*

In 1655 **François Mansart** added a dining room and an oratory to the wing L and extended the wing R back to the Rue de Turenne.

No 11 Marion Delorme, the famous courtesan, whose lovers are reputed to have included Louis XIII and Richelieu, lived here 1639–48. Almost uniquely, she would not accept money for her favours, only gifts. In 1650, during the Fronde, Mazarin ordered her arrest and she allegedly committed suicide, aged thirty-seven. Some, however, maintained that she escaped to Scotland, returning to Paris in her old age.

No 13, Hôtel d'Antoine de Rochebaron Princesse Anne Chabot de Rohan, one of Louis XIV's last mistresses, lived here in the early 18C. Later, the King presented her with the Hôtel de Soubise.

•• *Proceed ahead to the north-west range.*

No 21 Shortly before his assassination, Henri IV presented this house to Richelieu, but it is not clear whether the Cardinal ever lived here. By 1626, the Place des Vosges had become notorious for its duelling and many aristocrats were being killed; Richelieu therefore decided to ban it. However, in rash defiance of his order, four duelled directly outside this house on 22 June 1627. François de Montmorency-Bouteville and his second, the Comte de Chapelle, were caught and executed.

No 23, Hôtel de Marie-Charlotte de Balzac d'Entragues The wooden door is original.

No 27, Pavillon de la Reine Built, as an afterthought, for Henri IV's queen, Marie de Médicis, the pavilion was never occupied by royalty. Above the arch, on the Place façade, is the sun emblem of the Médicis family.

Parades would exit from the square through here to the Rue de Béarn.

•• *Continue eastward.*

Between **Nos 24** and **22** a house originally closed the square, but this was demolished in 1819 to provide access to the Rue du Pas de la Mule.

•• *Follow the east range.*

No 20 The Marquise de Rambouillet founded Paris salons here in the reign of Louis XIII. Her aim was to foster battles of wits rather than swords. Writers mixed with aristocrats and the excesses of the prevailing 'macho' society gradually dissolved into the affectations of the *'précieuses'* (precious people).

No 14, Hôtel de Villedeuil The Abbé de la Rivière, who owned this house in the 17C, was a close friend of the Duc d'Orléans, acting as tutor to his children. He was later appointed Duke and Bishop of Langres. Another occupant was the chief rabbi of France, who lived in that half of the building overlooking the Place. A plaque below the first floor's fifth window records the hôtel's name.

●● *Proceed to the south range. Its first building, No 6, is now the Maison de Victor Hugo museum.*

Location 7	**MAISON DE VICTOR HUGO**

6 Place des Vosges

Open Tuesday–Sunday 10.00–17.40. Admission charge but free Sunday.

Victor Hugo rented the first floor (referred to by the French as second floor) as an apartment, 1832–48, and among other work, wrote some chapters of *Les Misérables* during his stay.

The entire house has accommodated the museum since 1903.

Maréchal de Levardin was the mansion's first owner, but it later became the residence of Princesse Anne de Montbazon. At the age of twelve she married her cousin, the Prince de Guéménée, and throughout her life had numerous lovers, many of them ending as victims of the guillotine. Her salons were devoted to 'women's lib' and the establishment of standards for the French language. She became the most famous *'précieuse'* of the many who held court in the Place des Vosges.

●● *Enter the house.*

Memorabilia of all kinds connected with Hugo are spread over three floors and the stairway. Rooms on the upper two floors, not open to the public, are reserved for the library.

On the stairway are displayed Hugo's robe of the Académie Française, to which he was elected at the early age of thirty-nine.

The second floor (first floor in English terminology) reproduces the Salle à Manger Chinoise (Chinese dining room) from Hugo's Guernsey villa where he fled during his opposition to Louis Napoléon. Most of the oriental style carving was executed by Hugo himself.

Hugo had fifteen residences during his lifetime, dying in Avenue d'Eylan (since renamed Avenue Victor Hugo); his bedroom from there, which is reproduced, includes the bed in which he died.

Studies and the bust of Hugo by **Rodin** are displayed.

Most of the rather gloomy paintings on view are by Hugo – who also dabbled in many of the plastic arts.

This is the only mansion in the Place des Vosges open to the public, and views above the trees from its upper windows give a unique appreciation of the architecture of the Place.

●● *Exit L and return via first L the Pavillon du Roi and Rue de Birague to Rue St Antoine R. Cross the road.*

No 53 Poissonnerie de la Bastille Bussons's fish shop retains Art-Nouveau ceramic wall tiles.

Some of the best food shops in the Marais are located in this section of Rue St Antoine.

• Cross to the north side of Rue St Antoine and continue westward.

Location 8 — **HÔTEL DE SULLY** *1630*

Caisse Nationale
des Monuments
Historiques et des
Sites
62 Rue St Antoine

*Temporary
architectural
exhibitions open
daily 10.00–18.00.
Generally an
admission charge
but sometimes free.
Guided tour of the
bel étage rooms (in
French only)
Sunday,
Wednesday and
Saturday 15.00.
Admission charge.*

This is regarded as the finest surviving private hôtel to have been built in the reign of Louis XIII. It is now the headquarters of the country's Historic Monuments Commission.

History Designed in 1624, traditionally by **Jean Androuet du Cerceau**, who envisaged a building of rose brick with stone trims, typical of the period, the hôtel was eventually constructed entirely of stone. It was commissioned by Petit Thomas, a gambler, who lost everything in 1624 and had to sell the mansion. It was then purchased by Sully, the seventy-five-year-old former minister of Henri IV, for his retirement.

Exterior Pavilions flank the portal.

• Enter the courtyard.

Richly decorated wings are, unusually, the same height as the main range. Reminiscent of the Musée Carnavalet, reliefs flanking the three central bays represent the seasons and the elements – from L to R around the courtyard: air, fire, autumn, winter, earth and water. The latter is reputed to have inspired the 19C painting, *La Source* by **Ingres**.

The arcaded section R, on the east side, was originally the coach-house.

• Proceed through the central arch to the rear courtyard.

Temporary exhibitions on French architectural themes are held in the wing L.

The two allegorical figures, spring and summer, that decorate the south façade, were added in matching style *c*.1650.

Closing the north side is a garden pavilion, the **Hôtel Petit Sully**, which was completed in 1628 before the main hôtel was finished. Originally open, its arcade, which fronted an orangery, has since been filled.

• Assemble in the main courtyard for a tour of the interior (these take forty-five minutes and a good knowledge of French is desirable).

Interior First-floor (*bel étage*) rooms, which retain a Renaissance influence, are visited together with the sumptuous double staircase.

Many of the rooms are panelled and hung with tapestries, and there are good examples of painted ceiling beams.

• Exit to Rue St Antoine R. Cross the road and proceed westward, passing (first L) Rue St Paul.

Location 9 — **ST PAUL-ST LOUIS** *Martellange/Durrand 1641*

99 Rue St Antoine

This was the first major 17C church in Paris to abandon the Gothic style completely.

History The Jesuits had to evacuate their original, late-16C chapel when they were expelled from France by Henri IV, 1695–1703. Louis XIV, however, supported the Jesuits, who had been joined by Richelieu, his first minister. The King gave the land for a new church, which was initially dedicated to St Louis only. The dedication to St Paul was added much later, as a tribute to the church of St Paul des Champs, which had stood nearby until demolished at the Revolution. **Etienne Martellange** provided the first plans for the building, based on the design of the Jesuits' mother church, Il Gesù, in Rome.

The cornerstone was laid by Louis XIII in 1627 and work proceeded quickly, but after two years **François Durrand** took over, becoming responsible for the crossing and the chancel, together with the entire vault. Cardinal Richelieu consecrated the church in the presence of the royal family in 1641, and conducted its first Mass. When the Marais evolved as the most fashionable quarter in Paris, this became the favoured church of society. Among its musical directors were the composers Charpentier and Rameau.

Buried within are Bishop Hüet, d.1721 and Louis Bourdalone, d.1704, who Madame de Sévigné claimed 'preached like an angel'.

Exterior St Paul–St Louis is typical of the Jesuit style, based on churches built in Rome during the 16C. The cupola, one of the earliest to be constructed in Paris, is concealed from external view at close quarters

Richelieu was mainly responsible for financing the north façade, begun in 1634.

At the apex of its upper pediment, the arms of France and Navarre commemorate their alliance. The arms of Richelieu, originally carved on the curved pediment above the portal, were removed at the Revolution. At the same time, Christ's monogram was replaced by the Baroque 'sun' clock, salvaged from St Paul des Champs.

➭ Enter the church, usually from the north front's west door.

The high altar stands at the south end.

Interior Charles Turnel created the Baroque internal decoration, again in the style of Il Gesù, Rome.

Until the Revolution, monuments filled the chapels, and the mummified hearts of Louis XIII and Louis XIV were kept in the chancel. The hearts were then purchased by the painter Saint Martin, who ground them into his oil paint: evidently they imparted a marvellous sheen. Not all of Louis XIV's heart was used, and Saint Martin presented what remained to Louis XVIII for interment at St Denis.

Flanking the central north doorway are twin holy-water 'shell' stoups given, surprisingly, by Victor Hugo, whose opinion of the Catholic church was highly critical.

➭ Proceed to the crossing.

The spandrels beneath the cupola are carved with reliefs depicting the four Evangelists.

In the east transept L, the painting *St Louis receiving the crown of thorns from Christ* is by the school of **Vouet**.

Opposite, *Christ in the Garden of Gethsemane* was painted by **Delacroix** in 1827.

➡ *Proceed eastward through the arch to the* **Chapelle de Notre Dame des Sept Douleurs.**

The much restored marble *La Vierge de Pitié (Virgin of Sorrow)* by **Germain Pilon**, 1586, is regarded as a masterpiece. It was originally made for the Valois chapel at St Denis.

➡ *Exit from the church L. Immediately L follow the passageway at No 101 (not open weekends or school holidays) through Lycée Charlemagne to the courtyard at the rear of the church. Ascend the stairs in the east range to the top-floor* **bibliothèque** *(open Monday, Thursday and Friday).*

➡ *Alternatively, when the passage is closed, exit from St Paul–St Louis R. First R Rue St Paul. Third R Rue Charlemagne. Third L Rue des Jardins St Paul (location 11).*

The Lycée Charlemagne's library was once the apartment of Père Lachaise, after whom the famous cemetery is named (see page 290).

➡ *Return to the courtyard. Ascend the steps L to the second courtyard. Exit through the archway L. L Rue Charlemagne. First R Rue des Jardins St Paul.*

Location 10 | **RUE DES JARDINS ST PAUL**

Overlooking the school playground, on the west side of the street, is the largest remaining section of Philippe Auguste's 12C wall.

In addition to ramparts, part of the Tour Barbeau, a postern gateway, survives.

Rabelais died in a house in this street, since demolished, in 1563.

On the east side of the street are various entrances, some beamed, to Village St Paul, a rehabilitated quarter of linked courtyards, providing apartments, restaurants and boutiques.

➡ *Continue southward. First R Rue de l'Ave Maria. Immediately ahead lies the Hôtel de Sens.*

Location 11 | **HÔTEL DE SENS** *c.1476*

1 Rue du Figuier

Bibliothèque Forney open Tuesday–Friday 13.30–20.30; Saturday 10.00– 20.00. Admission free.

Of the many important private medieval houses in Paris only four have survived, either in their entirety or in part. The late-15C Hôtel de Sens is one of the most picturesque, although poor 19C restoration has robbed it of much of its authenticity, particularly internally.

In 1475 Tristan Salazar, the archbishop of Sens, commissioned this building as a town house for himself and his successors. Until 1622 Paris remained a bishopric, responsible to the archbishop of Sens, who regularly visited the capital. The mansion became a centre for intrigues during the Catholic League period of the 16C.

Following her exile in the Auvergne, Queen Margot,

first consort of Henri IV, and now very corpulent, came to live here in 1605 at the age of fifty-two. Her preference was for very young men, and a succession of 'toy boys' stayed with her at the hôtel. In 1606, Vermont, a jealous ex-lover, assassinated Saint-Julien, Margot's young page and current favourite, at her carriage door and the ex-Queen, furious with grief, insisted on his execution: he was beheaded in front of her, probably in the hôtel's courtyard, two days later. Almost immediately, Margot left the Hôtel de Sens for good.

In 1760, the mansion became the office of the Paris–Lyons stage coach company. Evidently the journey was so hazardous that passengers made their wills before departure. The hôtel was eventually purchased and restored by the City of Paris in 1911.

Exterior It is now easy to view the exterior of the building, but originally, medieval houses clustered against its walls. Although only pre-dating the Hôtel de Cluny by a decade, the Hôtel de Sens is much more severe, its high, turreted walls presenting a fortress-like appearance.

The gateway retains the original rounded corner turrets; its Flamboyant dormer window is surmounted by stone finials. Unfortunately, the carved tympana of both portals have been lost.

➡ *Proceed to the courtyard.*

The massive, square tower encloses a spiral staircase.

A turret and dormer windows with finials ornament the main façade, which is reminiscent of a Loire château.

Its northern section R has been almost completely restored.

Within the west range, the entire first floor accommodates the Bibliothèque Forney, installed here in 1962 as a reference library specializing in decorative and fine arts.

➡ *Enter the building and ascend the stairs to the library.*

Although most of the room has been rebuilt, outstanding crisp carving survives on the original doorway and balcony, both in Flamboyant style.

➡ *Exit R and follow Rue de l'Hôtel de Ville westward. Pass Rue des Nonnains d'Hyères (first R).*

Immediately R is the garden front of the Hôtel d'Aumont (location 13) remodelled and enlarged by **Mansart** in 1656.

Balconies on this façade incorporate the monogram AD of the builder's son, Duc Antoine d'Aumont.

The garden was laid out originally by **Le Nôtre** in formal style.

➡ *Return to Rue des Nonnains d'Hyères, first L. First L Rue de Jouy.*

On the north-west corner of Rue de Jouy and Rue de Fourcy a man pouring wine (?) from a jug is carved in a niche; probably 17C work.

No 7, Hôtel d'Aumont, was designed by **Le Vau** in 1648 but remodelled by **Mansart** in 1656.

•● *Return eastward. First L Rue de Fourcy. R Rue St Antoine.*

No 133 was the house of Voltaire's sister, Madame de Dompierre.

Its balcony is supported by hideous dragons – very obviously females of the species.

•● *Cross Rue St Antoine and Rue de Rivoli and follow, immediately ahead L, Rue Pavée.*

No 10, a synagogue, was designed by **Hector Guimard** in 1913. **Guimard** is, of course, famed for his Métro entrances, but completed other Art-Nouveau work in Paris, mostly in the 16th arrondissement.

•● *Return to the south side of Rue St Antoine R, which becomes **Rue François Miron**.*

Renamed in the early 17C to commemorate a local magistrate, who was appointed provost of Paris by Henri IV, this street retains some of the oldest properties in the city.

Location 12	**HÔTEL DE BEAUVAIS** *Antoine le Pautre 1660*

68 Rue François Miron

The hôtel was closed in 1987, pending restoration.

Due to its restricted site the layout of the Hôtel de Beauvais is unique amongst 17C examples.

The mansion was built for Catherine Henriette Bellier – known, for self-evident reasons, as 'one-eyed Kate' – wife of Pierre de Beauvais. She served as a lady-in-waiting to Anne of Austria and bravely aided the sixteen-year-old Louis XIV during the Fronde uprising; for this, she and her husband were ennobled. Previously, the 13C town house of the abbots of Châalis had occupied the irregularly shaped site.

Lack of space dictated that, unusually for a 17C Parisian mansion, the main range would directly front the street. Before despoliation at the Revolution, its façade was much more ornate, earning the approval of the Italian, Bernini, who disliked the simplicity of most contemporary French architecture.

The first-floor balcony was erected for viewing processions and from here, Anne of Austria, accompanied by Cardinal Mazarin and Henrietta Maria, watched her son Louis XIV re-enter Paris in 1660 with his consort Marie-Thérèse.

Shops have always occupied the ground floor.

In 1763 the seven-year-old Wolfgang Amadeus Mozart, together with his father and sister, were guests of the Bavarian ambassador and occupied rooms on the second floor.

After restoration, the hôtel will almost certainly be reopened for public viewing.

The vestibule, within a Doric rotunda, accommodates an outstanding staircase, with a balustrade that is carved of stone, unusual in the Marais; its design, the work of **Martin Desjardins**, incorporates sphinxes, serpents and putti.

Gothic cellars with a 13C ribbed vault survive from the earlier house of the abbots of Châalis.

The courtyard, immediately behind the main range,

disguises the irregular shape of the site with its symmetry. A chapel, servants' quarters and stables were built to the south and west, with a terraced garden laid out on their roofs. Decorative rams' heads (*belier*) are a pun on Catherine Bellier's name.

•● *Continue westward. Second L Rue Geoffroy l'Asnier.*

Location 13	**HÔTEL DE CHÂLONS-LUXEMBOURG** *1615*

No 26 Rue Geoffroy l'Asnier

Built of brick and stone, the hôtel awaits restoration. It was commissioned by Antoine Le Fèvre de la Broderie, Henri IV's ambassador to England.

The gateway, one of the finest in the Marais, is surmounted by a massive pediment, carved with a lion's head.

A plaque commemorates the two consecutive names of the hôtel: Châlons in 1625 and Luxembourg in 1659.

•● *Cross the road.*

Location 14	**MÉMORIAL DU MARTYR JUIF INCONNU** *Goldberg, Arretche* and *Persitz 1956*

17 Rue Geoffroy l'Asnier

Museum open daily 10.00–12.00 and 14.00–17.00 but 14.00–17.00 only Saturday and Sunday September– June. Admission charge.

The memorial is dedicated to Parisian Jews who died in the holocaust.

•● *Enter from the side gate of No 17 (past the grille). Press the bell for admission.*

A torch burns perpetually in the crypt.

On the upper floors a museum exhibits documents and photographs connected with Nazi atrocities.

•● *Exit L and return to Rue François Miron L.*

Nos 44–46, restored in 1989, were once the town house of the abbots of Ourscamp sur Oise; Gothic cellars have been discovered.

No 42, **Hôtel de la Barre-de-Carron**, was built by **Pierre de Vigny** in 1772.

No 13, **Maison à l'enseigne du Mouton** (now the Relais de Varsouvie) dates from the second half of the 14C. External exposed beams and small timber windows make this one of the most picturesque houses in Paris.

No 11, **Maison à l'enseigne du Faucheur**, is similar to, and probably contemporary with, No 13.

•● *First R Rue du Pont Louis-Philippe. Cross Rue de Rivoli and continue ahead following Rue Vieille du Temple. Fourth R Rue des Rosiers.*

Location 15	**RUE DES ROSIERS**

Many of the most important Jewish food stores in Paris are to be found in this picturesque street, '*cacher*' denoting that the produce sold is kosher.

As in England, Jewish immigration to France began on a large scale toward the end of the 19C, due to East European pogroms. Many who had settled in Paris fled the German occupation forces in 1940, but 73,000 of them were sent to the concentration camps.

A large number of Algerians emigrated here when the French left their country, and this area of Paris is

now a combination of Jewish and Muslim people who
live together in apparent amity.

No 27, Finkelsteijn (closed Wednesday), is renowned
for its vatrouchka (cheese cake) sold hot in the
morning.

No 7, Jo Goldenberg, remains the best known Jewish
delicatessen in the capital (there is also a restaurant).

Beneath the street sign, facing Rue des Rosiers, a
plaque commemorates six people killed at
Goldenberg's, by a terrorist bomb, 9 August 1982.

• Return to Rue Vieille du Temple R.

Many of the bars and discos in this section of the
street cater for members of the gay community.

*• Proceed northward and cross to the west side of
the road.*

Location 16	**HÔTEL DES AMBASSADEURS DE HOLLANDE** *Cottard 1660*

47 Rue Vieille du
Temple

Most of the ancient hôtels in Rue Vieille du Temple
are obscured by walls with impenetrable-looking
doors that are normally shut. Here also, the door will
probably be closed, but apart from weekends, it may
be opened by ringing the bell.

An alternative name for the mansion is Hôtel Amelot
de Bisseuil.

The late-14C hôtel of the Maréchal de Rieux stood
on the site of the present building and in front of it, in
1407, an assassin, hired by the Duc de Bourgogne,
murdered the Duc d'Orléans. The hotel, remodelled
in 1483, was completely rebuilt, following the
Baroque style, in 1660, this time with its entrance
facing Rue Vieille du Temple instead of, as formerly,
Rue des Blancs Manteaux.

From 1720–27 the mansion was occupied by the
Dutch embassy's chaplain, and Protestant services,
proscribed elsewhere in France, were held in its
chapel. Madame de Staël was baptized there in 1766
and Benjamin Franklin's daughter married in the
chapel. Beaumarchais wrote the librettos for *The
Marriage of Figaro* and *The Barber of Seville* while
living in the hôtel. When the American War of
Independence began, the building became a store for
arms that were to be shipped to the rebels.

Carvings on the street side of the portal, depicting a
medallion between two goddesses of fame, are by
Regnaudin.

The door's carving includes a large head of Medusa.

*• Ring the bell to open the door and enter the
courtyard.*

Carvings on the courtyard side of the portal depict an
allegorical river Tiber and the discovery of Romulus
and Remus.

The entire ground floor of the courtyard is rusticated.

Sundials on the walls of both wings are original.

A passage leads to the second courtyard (not open)
which apparently was built instead of laying out a
garden; its appearance is not original.

● Exit L. First L Rue des Blancs Manteaux. Third L Rue des Archives.

No 40, Hôtel de Jacques Coeur, was built in brick and stone for Charles VII's Chancellor of the Exchequer in the mid-15C. It is one of the oldest houses in Paris.

● Continue southward, passing (first L) Rue Ste Croix de la Bretonnerie.

Location 17	**BILLETTES** 1756

22 Rue des Archives

Church: normally open only for services at varying times. Cloister: open for exhibitions June–September. Admission free.

Although the body of the monastic church, built in 1756, is of little interest, it possesses a 15C cloister that is the only medieval example to survive in Paris.

The Billettes Church, together with its cloister, occupies part of the site of the monastery built in the 14C for the Brothers of Charity, who became known as Billettes due to the heraldic insignia (billet) that they wore. Carmelite monks succeeded them and commissioned the present church in 1756; it was adopted by Lutherans in 1812.

● Enter the church.

An unusual feature of this simple, Classical building is its double gallery.

● Exit from the north door to view the cloister.

● Alternatively if the church is closed, as is usual, return northward to No 26 Rue des Archives (the first door R) and enter the cloister from the west side.

Although plain architecturally, and much restored, this is the only medieval cloister to survive in the capital. Built in 1427, each of its four sides remains; they are cross-rib vaulted.

● Exit first L Rue de Ste Croix de la Bretonnerie. First L Rue du Temple.

Location 18	**RUE DU TEMPLE**

An ancient street, that formerly led to the domaine of the Knights Templar; many notable hôtels survive, although most await restoration.

No 24, on the south-east corner with Rue de Ste Croix de la Bretonnerie, possesses an unusual square turret, built as a watch-tower in 1610.

● Proceed northward to No 41 and enter the courtyard.

No 41 Once the Auberge de l'Aigle d'Or (Golden Eagle Tavern), this is the last 17C coaching inn's structure to survive in Paris.

No 71, Hôtel de St Aignan, part restored, was begun by **Le Muet** in 1640 for the Finance Minister Claude Mesmes and completed ten years later.

Doors to the monumental portal are decorated with great heads, the mouths of which enclose the door knockers (now fixed).

➡ *Enter the courtyard.*

Massive Corinthian pilasters surround the courtyard.

No 79, **Hôtel de Montmor**, built in 1623 for Montmor 'the rich', treasurer of Louis XIII, was remodelled in the mid-18C.

➡ *Enter the first courtyard.*

A carved pediment shelters the balcony. The exceptional depth of the hôtel's windows is reminiscent of Amsterdam. However, they are casement in style, the Dutch sash windows never becoming popular in France as they did in England, chiefly due to the French love of balconies.

➡ *Proceed through the passage to the second courtyard.*

An open staircase of wrought iron L is exceptional.

➡ *Exit L and continue northward. Third L Rue Chapon.*

No 13, (the second building only), was formerly the town residence of the Archbishops of Reims.

➡ *Enter the courtyard.*

An open staircase leads from both sides of the courtyard. In the corner is a well.

➡ *Exit L. First L Rue Beaubourg. First R Rue de Montmorency.*

Location 19	**TAVERNE NICOLAS FLAMEL** *1407*

51 Rue de Montmorency. Restaurant reservations 42 72 07 11.

Now a restaurant, this building, one of the oldest in Paris, was constructed of stone blocks for Nicolas Flamel, a wealthy and philanthropic bookseller, to provide a ground-floor shop for himself and free living accommodation above for the poor. Original reliefs of angels, etc., survive, but the inscription on the ground-floor lintel was re-carved in 1900.

➡ *First L Rue St Martin. Fourth L Rue Rambuteau and M Rambuteau.*

12

North Marais

From the capital's two 17C triumphal archways, the visitor is led to the library of St Martin des Champs, one of the country's finest Gothic halls. The Marais is then entered, keeping to its northern section.

Timing: The Conservatoire Nationale's library is closed in the morning Monday to Friday and Sunday afternoon; its museum is closed Monday and in the morning Tuesday to Saturday.

Musée de la Chasse et de la Nature is closed Tuesday and 12.30–13.30.

Musée de la Serrure is closed August, Monday, Tuesday and 12.00–14.00.

Musée Picasso is closed Tuesday.

Musées Carnavalet and Cognacq-Jay close Monday.

Musée Kwok On is closed Saturday and Sunday.

Archives Nationales are closed in the morning and all day on Tuesday.

St Denys du St Sacrement is closed Saturday and Sunday afternoon.

Notre Dame des Blancs Manteaux is closed Sunday and 12.00–16.00 every other day.

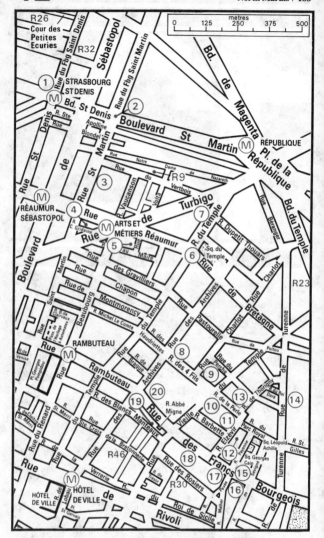

Locations

1 Porte St Denis
2 Porte St Martin
3 Conservatoire National des Arts et Métiers
4 St Nicolas des Champs
5 No 3 Rue Volta
6 Square du Temple
7 Ste Elisabeth
8 Musée de la Chasse et de la Nature
9 Ste Croix–St Jean
10 Hôtel de Rohan
11 Musée de la Serrure
12 Musée Cognacq-Jay
13 Musée Picasso
14 St Denys du St Sacrement
15 Musée Carnavelet
16 Bibliothèque Historique de la Ville de Paris
17 Rue des Francs Bourgeois
18 Musée Kwok On
19 Notre Dame des Blancs Manteaux
20 Archives Nationales

Start M Strasbourg St Denis, line 8 Balard/Créteil-Préfecture; line 9 Pont de Sèvres/Mairie de Montreuil. From the station, take the L exit to Boulevard de Sébastopol R and proceed southward. Second R Rue Blondel.

Rue Blondel and its surrounding streets are a 'red light' district. Ladies of many races are on parade twenty-four hours a day, dressed (to varying degrees) in a titillating manner. Surprisingly, the best display is mid-morning.

•● Continue ahead. R Rue St Denis.

Location 1	**PORTE ST DENIS** François Blondel c.1674

Boulevard St Denis

Straddling Rue du Faubourg St Denis, this archway is, after the Arc de Triomphe, the largest and most impressive in Paris.

It was one of four triumphal arches erected to commemorate Louis XIV's Rhine victories during which forty strongholds were taken in two months. The Porte St Martin also survives nearby, but those of St Antoine and St Honoré no longer exist. All of them occupied the sites of gates in the Charles V defensive perimeter wall, which Louis XIV had demolished as he felt that his victories had made it superfluous.

When built, the arch pierced tree-lined ramparts, later to become part of the Grands Boulevards. Although its design is based on the Arch of Titus in Rome, the 81-foot-high Porte St Denis is much larger. **Blondel**, its designer, insisted that the bas-reliefs should also be in the antique Roman style, and **Girardon** based his designs on Trajan's column and sculptures in the Forum; the **Anguier** brothers originally executed the carvings but they were mostly remodelled in 1887.

For the first time, the name 'Ludovico Magno' (Louis the Great) was publicly displayed to honour Louis XIV.

On the south side, above the arch, the King is depicted crossing the Rhine in 1672.

Allegorical figures, at the base of the obelisks, represent the conquered Netherlands and the Rhine.

•● Proceed to the north side (facing Rue du Faubourg St Denis).

The capture of Maastricht in 1673 is depicted above the arch.

•● Turn L and proceed eastward, following Boulevard St Denis, which becomes Boulevard St Martin.

Location 2	**PORTE ST MARTIN** Pierre Bullet c.1676

Boulevard St Martin

Like the Porte St Denis, this triumphal archway was initially planned in ancient Roman style by **Blondel**; however, it is far less impressive, not only in its scale – just 56 feet high – but also in the quality and extent of its decoration.

Most of the structure's stonework is rusticated.

On the south side, the spandrels are carved with battle scenes depicting the capture of Limburg L and the defeat of the Germans R, by **Legros** and **Le Hongre**.

On the north side (facing Rue du Faubourg St
Martin) the victories featured are L, at Besançon and
R over the Triple Alliance; they are by **Desjardins**
and **Marsy**.

*•• Cross to the south side of Boulevard St Martin.
Ahead Rue St Martin. Fourth L Rue du Vertbois.*

On the south-east corner of Rue St Martin and Rue
du Vertbois, the circular **watch-tower**, built *c.*1273
but re-erected in 1886, formed part of the defensive
wall of the St Martin des Champs priory, now the
Conservatoire National.

Beside this stands the **Fontaine de Vertbois**, erected
in 1712 and restored in 1886.

•• Continue eastward to No 72.

From this point, a section of the **castellated wall** of
the monastery, also built *c.*1275, may be seen
opposite; most of the remainder was demolished in
the 19C.

•• Return to Rue St Martin L. Enter the courtyard L.

Location 3	**CONSERVATOIRE NATIONAL DES ARTS ET MÉTIERS**

292 Rue St Martin

*Bibliothèque
(library) open
Monday–Friday
13.00–19.00;
Saturday 09.00–
19.00; Sunday
09.30–12.00.
Closed August.
(Times may vary
when temporary
exhibitions are
held.) Admission
free. Musée
National des
Techniques et
Métiers open
Tuesday–Saturday
13.00–17.30;
Sunday 10.00–
17.15. Admission
charge, free
Sunday.*

Neglected by most visitors, the Conservatoire
retains, in the former priory's 13C refectory, one of
the finest High-Gothic halls to survive in France. Its
original crisp carving is exceptional. The 11C–13C
priory church of St Martin des Champs, which now
houses the Conservatoire's museum, retains the
capital's oldest example of cross-vaulting and an
extremely early Gothic ambulatory

History A 4C chapel that stood here, dedicated to St
Martin, was destroyed by the Vikings. Henri I
founded the priory of St Martin des Champs on its
site in 1060, but only the heavily restored apse of the
church survives from this period. In 1079, Philippe I
gave the priory to Cluny Abbey. Prior Hugues I
surrounded the complex with a fortified wall *c.*1140,
which was renewed in 1273. The monastic refectory
and part of the church were rebuilt in the 13C, and
the other domestic structures reconstructed in the
first half of the 18C. At the Revolution, the
monastery was dissolved (1790) and since 1798 its
buildings have accommodated the Conservatoire des
Arts et Métiers, founded four years earlier by the
Convention. The 18C buildings were replaced *c.*1890,
but the former church and refectory were spared.

*•• Follow the colonnade R and proceed to the long
Gothic building ahead L.*

This is one of the finest halls in France to survive
from the High-Gothic period and has been described
as the most 'thrilling' architecture in Paris. It is no
longer considered certain, however, that its architect
was **Pierre Montreuil**. Restoration took place in 1845
and 1860.

Windows are double-lancet, and circular with double
quatrefoil tracery.

*•• Enter the building from the second door L at its
west end.*

The vault of the hall is cross-ribbed.

Corbels throughout are carved.

Grisaille glass is 19C.

A central arcade with slender columns divides the hall into two aisles.

Fitted against the east end of the north wall is an exceptionally well-preserved 13C stone pulpit with stiff-leaf decoration.

The pulpit's staircase is pierced with lancets; a maximum of three people at a time are now permitted to ascend.

Modern bookcases, tables and chairs currently occupy most of the area, but originally, long tables and benches ranging along the walls would have furnished the room.

The doorway in the south wall led to the monks' four-sided cloister that ran between the refectory and the church. Its outer side, all that survives of the original cloister, possesses rich 13C carving, again exceptionally well preserved.

•● Exit and return to Rue St Martin L. Continue southward to view the exterior of the former church of St Martin des Champs, on the corner with Rue Réaumur (first L); this now accommodates the museum.

Former church of St Martin des Champs
Rebuilding of the 11C nave took place early in the 13C. It is in the High-Gothic style and pre-dates Montreuil's nave at St Denis.

•● First L Rue Réaumur passes the south façade.

The two-storey tower at the east end of the nave was built *c.*1130 in Romanesque style. Also Romanesque, and built at the same time, the chancel was heavily restored in the 19C and little that is original survives.

•● Return to the west façade and enter the building.

The present king-post roof was added to support the barrel vault in 1885.

Throughout the building the garish decoration is late 19C.

•● Proceed to the east end of the nave and descend the steps ahead.

Immediately above, in the Transitional-style **chancel**, is the earliest cross-rib vaulting in Paris to survive.

Although the double **ambulatory** is an extremely early Gothic example, it is already groin-vaulted.

Capitals are still in the Romanesque style, with a variety of apparently unrestored designs.

The combination of an ancient building and technological exhibits has a surreal effect. An engineer, Vaucanson, founded the museum by bequeathing his collection of tools, machines and instruments to the state in 1783.

Of greatest interest to most visitors are the early forms of transport, including trains, aeroplanes, cars and bicycles, displayed in the **nave**.

•● Proceed north-east of the old church to view the

remainder of the museum, which occupies a further two floors.

Model trains and ancient timepieces are displayed on the ground floor.

●● Exit from the complex L and continue ahead to the west front of St Nicolas des Champs.

Location 4	**ST NICOLAS DES CHAMPS**

259 Rue St Martin

Closed Sunday p.m.

The oft-repeated Paris formula of Flamboyant Gothic, later extended in Renaissance style, is again evident in this church. Its south door, carved by **Colo**, is one of the finest Renaissance examples in the capital. An exceptional Baroque organ case, a 16C triptych and works by outstanding French painters enliven the interior.

History The first church was built here by the Cluniac Priory of St Martin in 1184 for its servants and the local farming community, who were not permitted to worship in the monastic church. 'Des Champs' (in the fields), added to the dedication, refers to the original rural situation of the church. St Nicolas was rebuilt in enlarged form, 1420–80, and an eastward extension, 1541–1615, doubled its size. It is therefore, like so many Paris churches, a combination of the Flamboyant Gothic and Renaissance styles. As the Revolutionary mob entered the church, bent on destruction, the organist, with supreme presence of mind, played the *Marseillaise* and St Nicolas was spared.

Exterior The west front, with its south bell tower, was built entirely in the 15C Flamboyant style.

All the statues were renewed in the 19C but the doors are original.

●● To view the south façade follow Rue Cunin Gridaine.

Two structures, protruding at the west end, are all that remain of the charnel house.

The first seven bays of the nave, with their chapels, survive from the 15C building.

Changes in window design etc. are apparent after passing the sacristy, which protrudes southward. These denote the 16C extension of the nave, with its chapels, by four bays.

The exceptional Renaissance door of the south portal is decorated with bas-reliefs carved by **Colo** in 1581, probably to designs by **Philibert Delorme**.

●● First L Rue de Turbigo.

Although the chancel's most westerly bays were built *c.*1587, its apsidal east end, together with the entire double ambulatory and chapels, were not completed until 1615.

*●● Return to the west front and enter the **vestibule**.*

Interior Seen immediately is the outstanding carved wooden roof of the vestibule which has been extended by partitioning the first two bays of the nave.

*●● Enter the **nave**.*

Immediately above is the loft with its organ, built in 1652 and restored by **Clicquot** in 1777. Its 18C case, surmounted by figures of St Nicolas flanked by two heavenly musicians, is one of the finest Baroque examples in Paris. The instrument was once played by Louis Braille, inventor of the 'touch' alphabet for the blind, who was the church organist for a period in the 19C.

*•● Proceed to the **outer north aisle**.*

At the nave's eighth bay from the west (sixth from the north aisle's partition), changes mark the 16C extension: columns have Doric capitals, windows and arches are rounded and the vault is higher.

*•● Proceed to the **chancel**.*

Fluting was added to the columns as part of the Classical alterations of 1745.

In front of the high altar R stands a large candle-holder, made in the 18C.

The high altar's reredos incorporates two works by **Vouet** painted in 1629. *Apostles at Mary's Tomb* is the main painting; above this is the *Assumption of Mary*.

The four angels surmounting the altar were sculpted by **Sarrazin** in the 17C.

*•● Proceed to the north ambulatory and continue to the **Chapelle St Vincent de Paul**, immediately east of the organ console.*

Within the chapel, an outstanding 16C Flemish triptych depicts Crucifixion scenes.

Ribs of the **ambulatory's** vault meet the shafts of the columns to give the appearance of a palm grove, particularly noticeable as the apse is reached.

The **Chapelle de la Vierge**, at the east end of the church, is decorated, on its north wall, by an *Adoration of the Shepherds*, painted by **C. A. Coypel** in the late 17C.

Against the east wall, the *Virgin and Child* was carved by **N. Delaistre** in 1817, two parishioners being used as models.

•● Continue westward.

On the west wall of the last **south ambulatory** chapel (St Nicolas), the *Baptism of Christ* was painted by **Gaudenzio Ferrari** c.1500. The humanist Guillaume Bude (Budaeus), d.1540, is buried here.

•● Exit L. First L Rue Cunin Gridaine. Cross Rue de Turbigo. Ahead Rue au Maire. Second L Rue Volta.

Location 5	**NO 3 RUE VOLTA** *late 13C(?)*

It is now believed that this timber-framed house was probably built for the Maire of St Martin des Champs in the late 13C and is, therefore, the oldest in Paris.

Originally its street façade was gabled, but this has been replaced since by the sloping roof with dormer windows.

•● Continue northward. First R Rue Réamur leads to Square du Temple ahead.

Location 6	**SQUARE DU TEMPLE**

This square marks the site of the Knights Templar's late-12C stronghold where, from 1792 to 1795, members of the royal family were imprisoned by revolutionaries.

The Order of Knights Templar, founded in 1118 to protect pilgrims to the Holy Land, built their European headquarters here in the late 12C.

The keep of what was virtually the Templars' fortress, became a refuge for fugitives from the king's justice, and those unwilling to pay state taxes. Philippe le Bel would not accept this situation and, with the co-operation of the pope, suppressed the Order in 1307, all Templars in France being arrested in a single day.

Louis XVI and his immediate family were arrested 13 August 1792 and imprisoned in the Tour du Temple, which had been built in 1265 as the keep of the fortress; virtually all the rest of the complex had been demolished. From here, five months later, the King was taken directly to the Place de la Concorde for execution. Marie-Antoinette, and the King's sister Madame Elisabeth, were transferred to the Conciergerie 2 August 1793 where they were imprisoned prior to their execution.

Marie-Antoinette's surviving son, now the titular Louis XVII, had been taken from the Temple on 3 July 1793 to be guarded by a cobbler and never saw his mother again. He was brought back to the Temple the following year and it is believed that a boy, who is known to have died there of tuberculosis on 8 June 1795, was probably the ten-year-old King. Madame Royale, his sister, miraculously survived 'the Terror' and was released from prison, 19 December 1795.

Napoléon demolished the tower in 1808, to prevent it becoming a centre for royalist pilgrimages and the site then became an open-air market for second hand clothes. **Haussmann** laid out the present square in 1857.

• Follow Rue du Temple (which skirts the west side of Square du Temple) northward to Ste Elisabeth, which faces Rue Dupetit Thouars (second R).

Location 7	**STE ÉLISABETH**
195 Rue du Temple	Ste Elisabeth, with its Italian Baroque-style east front, was built as a nuns' church in the 17C. The outstanding late-16C Flemish wood-carving inside, depicting 100 biblical scenes, is amongst the finest of its type in Paris.

The church was built as the chapel of the convent of the Third Order of St Francis, 1628–46. Its predecessor, a temporary building, had been dedicated to Our Lady of Nazareth and St Elisabeth. During the Revolution, the chapel became a flour store, but in 1809 it was reopened for worship, this time as the parish church.

The Baroque east front is a copy of Sta Maria Novella in Florence.

Flanking the clock are the figures of St Elisabeth and St Francis.

Below are mid-19C statues of St Louis and St
Eugénie, the latter being a compliment to Napoléon
III's consort, the Empress Eugénie.

•• *Enter the church and proceed directly ahead to the*
nave.

In the south-east corner of the nave is a painting of
Louis XVI bidding farewell to his family in the Tour
du Temple, prior to his execution.

Fixed to the most westerly pier, facing the high altar,
are the arms of the Knights of St John of Malta, who
inherited much of the Templars' domain.

In 1828, the Rue de Turbigo was laid out west of the
church, necessitating the rebuilding of the chancel,
with its ambulatory, and the nave's south aisle.

•• *Proceed to the most westerly bay of the* **south aisle**.

Above the door is the painting of Georges Girault,
chaplain of the monastic chapel, who, at the
Carmelite convent, became the first victim of the
September massacres of 1792.

•• *Continue ahead to the* **ambulatory**.

Outstanding, late-16C Flemish reliefs, depicting 100
biblical scenes, were fixed as wainscoting to the
ambulatory in 1845. The carved panels were
originally part of the stalls of the abbey church of St
Vaast at Arras. New Testament scenes form the
upper range, Old Testament scenes the lower; each is
identified by a brass plate. An attendant in the
sacristy will illuminate the panels on request.

•• *Follow the* **north aisle** *to its east end*.

The font basin, situated in the most easterly bay, was
made for the church of St Sauveur in 1639.

•• *Exit R. Third L Rue de Bretagne. First R Rue des
Archives. Proceed southward to the junction with Rue
Pastourelle (first L)*.

No 78, Hôtel de Tallard, built by **Pierre Bullet** *c.*1660,
became the residence of Marshal Tallard in 1712, and
then gained its present name. Restored and
converted to apartments in 1987, the hôtel's severely
Classical courtyard can be viewed only when the door
is open; there is a fine staircase by **Bullet** R.

No 76 is the restored **Hôtel Le Pelletier de Souzy**.

No 62 was built as the **Hôtel de Monteglas** in 1709.

Location 8	**MUSÉE DE LA CHASSE ET DE LA NATURE** *Mansart 1651*
Hôtel de Guénégaud 60 Rue des Archives *Open Wednesday–Monday 10.00–12.30 and 13.30–17.30. Admission charge.*	Since 1967 this building, the Hôtel Guénégaud, has accommodated the Museum of Hunting and Nature. Jean François de Guénégaud, Treasurer of France, commissioned the mansion from **François Mansart** in 1651 and it is the only completely preserved Paris hôtel that can definitely be attributed to the great architect. •• *Enter the courtyard (open even if not visiting the museum).* Some remodelling took place in the 18C, including the lowering of the ground-floor windows. •• *Enter the museum.*

12

Outstanding is the original great staircase, preserved from Mansart's interior.

Exhibits include paintings, weapons for hunting and stuffed game. Of particular interest are the portrait of Philippe le Bon in falconer's outfit and *Le Chasse de Diane* by **Brueghel**.

•→ Exit L and proceed to the south corner of the junction with Rue des Haudriettes (first R).

The free-standing **Fontaine des Haudriettes**, designed by **Moreau**, with a naiad by **Mignot**, was built for the Prince de Rohan in 1705 to replace a fountain that had been erected in 1636.

•→ Cross Rue des Archives immediately and follow Rue des 4 Fils, which runs eastward as an extension of Rue des Haudriettes. First L Rue Charlot.

Location 9	**STE CROIX-ST JEAN**

Cathédrale de l'Exerchat Apostolique Arménien Rue Charlot

Apart from services enter from No 13 Rue du Perche.

The church was built in 1624 as the chapel of a Capuchin monastery. Madame de Sévigné attended services here when she lived in the nearby Rue de Thorigny. It is now the Armenian church.

•→ Proceed ahead. First R Continue to No 13 Rue du Perche and request permission to enter the church.

The statue of St Denis R of the high altar was made by the **Marty** brothers in the 17C.

Facing this is the dramatic statue of St Francis of Assisi, carved by **Pilon**.

Gilded panelling in the chancel came from the Billettes church.

•→ Exit R Rue du Perche. First R Rue Vieille du Temple.

Location 10	**HÔTEL DU ROHAN** *Delamair*

87 Rue Vieille du Temple

Open for occasional architectural exhibitions only (usually autumn to mid-winter). Admission charge.

Restored in 1987, this early-18C hôtel forms part of the national archives complex. Now, unfortunately, it may rarely be entered, although the courtyard and exterior can be seen when the gates are open.

History In 1705 Armand Gaston de Rohan, prince bishop of Strasbourg, commissioned this mansion to be built beside the Hôtel de Soubise, recently completed for his parents by **Delamair**. Designed by the same, hitherto unknown architect, the structure is less ambitious, with regular bays presenting a severe exterior.

At the Revolution, the mansion became a powder store and most rooms were spoiled. In 1808 Napoléon converted it into the Imprimerie Nationale (national printing works) a function that it retained until 1925 when the building was partly restored to house the national archives.

•→ Enter the main courtyard and proceed R to the second courtyard.

Immediately R, above the entrance to the former stables, is the famous bas-relief by **Robert Le**

Lorrain, *The watering of the horses of Apollo*, regarded as a masterpiece of 18C sculpture.

⇐ Enter the main building, if open, and proceed to the first floor. It is probable that only enthusiasts of Rococo work will wish to pay the high entry price demanded to enter the exhibitions, which are usually of specialized interest only.

Most interiors have been lost but the **Cabinet des Poinçons** includes a delightful cornice of carved and gilded birds.

Outstanding, however, is the adjoining **Cabinet des Singes** (monkeys' room). Its Rococo panelling, painted in Chinoiserie style by **Christophe Huet** c.1750, depicts monkeys and small boys playing. The boys are meant to be Chinese, but few Europeans had visited China and all that **Huet** knew about them was that their heads were shaven, apart from a pigtail; their features are, therefore, French and they are depicted playing in settings and observed by adults that are entirely French in appearance.

⇐ Exit L. First R Rue de la Perle. Proceed eastward.

Location 11	MUSÉE DE LA SERRURE *Bruant 1685*

Hôtel Libéral Bruant
1 Rue de la Perle

Museum open Tuesday–Saturday (not August) 10.00–12.00 and 14.00–17.00. Admission charge.

Libéral Bruant designed the mansion around a courtyard, for his own occupancy, and apart from the hospitals of Invalides and Salpêtrière, this is the architect's finest work to survive in Paris. It was purchased by Bricard in 1830 to display his comprehensive collection of locks and decorative door hardware. The alternative name of the museum is Musée Bricard.

Busts of four Roman emperors decorate the courtyard façade of the hôtel.

⇐ Enter the building.

Decorative door hardware from Roman times to the present is exhibited.

⇐ Exit R. First R Rue Elzévir.

Location 12	MUSÉE COGNACQ-JAY

8 Rue Elzévir

Open Tuesday–Sunday 10.00–17.40. Admission charge but free Sunday.

Recently transferred here, in the restored Hôtel Donon, the museum is mainly devoted to 18C European paintings and furniture set in rooms fitted with Louis XV and Louis XVI panelling. Additionally, the earliest known **Rembrandt**, *Anesse de Balaam*, and a unique collection of Meissen statuettes are displayed.

⇐ Exit R and continue ahead, following Rue Elzévir to Rue de Thorigny.

Location 13	MUSÉE PICASSO *De Bourges 1659*

Hôtel Salé
5 Rue de Thorigny

Open Thursday–Monday 09.15–17.15; Wednesday 09.45–22.00. Admission charge, half price Sunday.

Picasso's early and late periods are particularly well represented in this large collection, which is beautifully displayed in an outstanding mid-17C hôtel.

The mansion was commissioned in the mid 17C by Pierre Aubert de Fontenay, who became wealthy through his position as collector of the king's salt tax. Salé (salt) therefore became the name given to the hôtel.

Conversion to a museum devoted to the works of Picasso was completed in 1986.

R of the courtyard, the low wing from where tickets are purchased, was built as the coach house; behind this lies a second courtyard.

•• *Enter the main building.*

The great, three-flight staircase is alleged to have inspired that of L'Opéra.

•• *Ascend the stairs and turn R.*

Exhibits were presented to the state by Picasso's heirs in lieu of death duties.

The artist's works are displayed chronologically, most being illuminated by natural light from the large windows.

•• *Exit L. Rue de Thorigny. Second R Rue du Roi. Cross Rue de Turenne ahead to St Denys du St Sacrement.*

Location 14	**ST DENYS DU ST SACREMENT** *Godde 1835*

Rue de Turenne

Open Monday–Friday 09.30–12.00 and 17.00–19.00.

This church was commissioned at the Restoration but took twenty years to complete, in spite of the apt name possessed by its architect.

With its massive Ionic columns, St Denys resembles an ancient Roman basilica.

•• *Enter the church.*

Immediately R, on the west wall of the large chapel, is a *Deposition*, painted by **Delacroix** in 1844.

•• *Exit L and follow Rue de Turenne southward.*

No 66 Within the courtyard, half of the original Hôtel de Turenne survives; it was built in the 17C for the famous marshal's father.

No 60 A brass boar's head on the portal's tympanum recalls that this hôtel, restored in 1988, was built for the Master of the Royal Hunt.

No 58 A stone *Virgin and Child* occupy a Baroque niche.

No 54 Now a school, but built as the **Hôtel de Montrésor** in the 17C, the restored Baroque façade is exceptional.

No 50 The portal retains its keystone and door, carved, unusually, with portrait medallions.

No 41 Incorporated in the façade, at its south end, is the 17C *Joyeuse* (joyful) fountain, by **Durcq**.

No 23, **Hôtel de Villacerf** *c.*1660. Behind rails in the courtyard stands another 17C fountain.

•• *Return northward. First L Rue des Francs Bourgeois. First R Rue de Sévigné.*

Location 15	**MUSÉE CARNAVALET**

Hôtel Carnavalet
23 Rue de Sévigné

Open Tuesday–Sunday 10.00–17.40. NB some rooms are closed

The partly Renaissance exterior of this mansion, with its carvings by **Goujon**, is unique amongst the capital's private hôtels. Since 1989 it has been linked with the Hôtel Le Pelletier de St Fargeau. Exhibits in the Musée Historique de la Ville de Paris relate to the history of Paris up to the early 19C.

*12.00–14.30.
Admission charge
(free Sunday).*

History The first privately owned Renaissance
mansion to be built in Paris, this is the only survivor
from that period in the capital. It was commissioned
in 1554 by the President of Parlement, Jacques de
Ligneris, who had purchased the land from the
convent of Ste Catherine; its design has been
attributed, without evidence, to **Lescot** and **Bullant**
but it seems that **Du Cerceau** supervised the final
stages. A century later, major alterations in the
Classical style were begun by **François Mansart** for
Claude Boislire. The next owner was the widow of
François de Kernevenoch, and it was by a corruption
of her surname that the mansion became known.
Marie de Rabutin, Marquise de Sévigné, leased the
house from 1677 until her death in 1696 and it was
here that she wrote the famous series of 1,500 letters
to her ungracious daughter, Madame de Grignon.
The city of Paris purchased the hôtel in 1866 for the
present museum to portray the history of the capital,
and the property was greatly enlarged by the
construction of three courtyards in its grounds.

Exterior Forming the entrance to the hôtel is the
gateway, built shortly after the mansion itself had
been completed. Its rusticated ground floor is original
but the upper parts were rebuilt in Classical style by
Mansart in 1661.

The entranceway's keystone of a winged abundance
surmounts cherubs and trophies. The figure's base,
originally a globe, was recarved as a carnival mask (in
French '*carnavelet*'), to accord with the name of the
mansion. This and other external carvings are from
the studio of **Jean Goujon**; almost certainly much of
the work is from the master's own hand.

Inset on both sides of the entrance are bas-reliefs of a
lion, also by **Goujon**.

At first floor level, allegorical figures of *Vigilance* and
Force were added by **Gérard Van Obstal** in the 17C.

The central figure, at roof level, is a 19C copy of
Minerva by **Van Obstal**, which had also been added in
the 17C.

Below this, the date 1661 commemorates the
completion of Mansart's alterations to the gatehouse.

Before Mansart's rebuilding, the side wings were not
pedimented.

•• *Pass through the archway.*

Ahead, in the Cour Louis, the bronze statue of Louis
XIV, by **Coysevox**, 1698, is the only statue of the 'Sun
King' in Paris to have survived the Revolution; it was
brought here from the old Hôtel de Ville after the
Commune fire of 1871.

Originally, the mansion consisted of one rectangular
block with side pavilions. When the gatehouse's
wings were added, the pavilions were connected to
them by single-storey arcaded galleries. **Mansart**
added a storey to the galleries and filled in their
arcades.

Decorating the main façade are the original
Renaissance figures depicting the four seasons (L–R
Spring to Winter) by **Goujon**; above them are the
signs of the zodiac.

Also by **Goujon** are the protective spirits bearing torches, carved above the doorway to the stairwell of the L wing.

The wing R has a similar carving above its doorway, but this is a 17C matching pastiche of **Goujon**'s style, by **Van Obstal**.

Similar Goujon pastiche work of the 17C by **Van Obstal** decorates the wings' upper storeys: *Flora*, *Diana*, *Hebe* and *Juno* L, and the *Four Winds* R.

•● *Enter the museum from the courtyard.*

Interior A free leaflet includes room plans and lists the periods that they cover. From this it will be seen that rooms cannot be viewed in numerical order.

The museum, opened in 1880, possesses exhibits covering the capital's history from the earliest times until the 19C. Exhibits displayed at the Carnavalet include topographical drawings and paintings, together with contemporary portraits. In addition, some rooms have been fitted with panelling and furnishings from long-demolished Paris mansions. Temporary exhibitions, often featuring work by modern artists, architects and photographers are held regularly at the museum.

Rooms 8–12, which are in the original hôtel, cover the Renaissance period of the 16C. An outstanding, mid-16C altarpiece, painted with a Last Supper scene, has been assembled beside the entrance to **room 10**.

Behind these rooms is the **Parterre des Drapiers**, one of the three courtyards created in the 19C; much of it came from ancient buildings.

Its west façade was brought from the demolished Bureau des Marchands Drapiers (Fabric dealers' guildhouse), built in 1660; the sculptures have been restored.

Set in the south range, facing Rue des Francs Bourgeois, is the Arc de Nazareth, a 16C archway from the old Rue de Nazareth.

Its reliefs are from the school of **Goujon**.

The iron grille is dated 1889.

Facing this, on the north side of the courtyard, is the central section of the Hôtel des Marets façade, built in 1710.

Displayed on the first floor of the Parterre des Drapiers are exhibits from the reign of Louis XIII and Louis XIV.

In the south-east corner of the **Cour Louis, room No 23** is one of the eight rooms of Madame de Sévigné's former apartment. It is open to the public and contains memorabilia from her period (*frequently closed 12.00–14.30*).

Continue to the French Revolution section, now housed in the adjoining Hôtel Le Pelletier de St Fargeau.

•● *Exit from the museum L Rue de Sévigné.*

Passed L, at **No 29**, is the Rococo portal of the 17C **Hôtel Le Pelletier de St Fargeau** (no entrance from here).

No 52, **Hôtel de Flesselles**, was built by **Pierre Delisle Mansart** for his own occupancy; it has been greatly altered. The mansion is named after a late-18C owner, the last Provost of Paris, who was killed by the revolutionary mob.

•● First L Rue du Parc Royal.

17C hôtels on the north side include:

No 4, **Hôtel de Canillac**, with red brickwork and stone trim.

No 8, **Hôtel Duret de Chevry**, built 1620 for the Treasurer of France.

No 10, **Hôtel de Vigny** Traces of Renaissance brickwork survive in the courtyard.

No 12, **Hôtel de Croisilles**, colourfully restored in 1988.

•● First L Rue Payenne. Pass Square Léopold Achille.

No 13, **Hôtel de Châtillon** From the courtyard its 17C staircase with an iron banister rail may be seen.

No 11, **Institut Tessin**, Centre Culturel Suédois (Swedish Cultural Centre), holds temporary exhibitions of Swedish works. *Open Tuesday–Friday 14.00–18.00, admission free.*

Above the portal is a carved mask.

The wagon roof is allegedly by **Delorme**.

No 5 **François Mansart**, the architect, died in this house in 1666.

•● Continue ahead following Rue Pavée. Immediately L is the Bibliothèque Historique de la Ville de Paris.

Location 16	**BIBLIOTHÈQUE HISTORIQUE DE LA VILLE DE PARIS** *Baptiste du Cerceau (?) c.1611*

Hôtel de Lamoignon
24 Rue Pavée

Open daily 09.30–18.00 (closed first half of August). Admission free.

The mansion was built as the Hôtel d'Angoulême for Diane de France, the legitimized daughter of Henri II and the Duchesse d'Angoulême. Guillaume de Lamoignon, president of the first parlement to sit in Paris, bought the property in 1658 and gave the hôtel its present name. Since 1969, the Hôtel de Lamoignon has accommodated the collection of historic books and manuscripts concerning Paris that was founded in 1763 as the capital's first public library.

Protruding on the Rue Pavée/Rue des Francs Bourgeois corner is a square turret from which all approaches could be viewed. Below it the 'SC' inscription refers to the boundary of Ste Catherine's convent, until the Revolution the largest monastery on the Right Bank.

A similar turret on the south wing was not renewed.

The gateway, facing Rue Pavée, was built in 1708 for the son of Lamoignon.

•● Enter the courtyard.

Attributed to **Baptiste du Cerceau** (son of Jacques Androuet du Cerceau), the hôtel was designed in

1585, although it appears that construction did not begin until twenty-five years later.

This was the first private mansion in Paris to embrace a Colossal Order. Corinthian pilasters front the façade of the main range.

Both end pavilions have rounded pediments, carved identically with hunting themes and crescent moons – the emblem of the goddess Diana the Huntress, an oblique compliment to the first owner of the hôtel, Diane de France.

Extensions were built in 1620 but that on the south side was demolished in 1834; it was rebuilt as a replica in 1968.

•● *Enter the hôtel from the iron-grilled door in the south-east corner. Immediately L is the Reading Room, not open to visitors.*

At its far end, visible from the entrance, is a small section of a beam, painted to depict Diana the Huntress, a further compliment to Diane de France.

•● *Exit from the hôtel R. First L Rue des Francs Bourgeois.*

Location 17	**RUE DES FRANCS BOURGEOIS**

Originally, this thoroughfare, the most important in the Marais, was called Rue des Poulies, referring to the pulleys on the looms of the weavers who inhabited the street. The street's name was changed to Francs Bourgeois (free citizens) in 1334. Free citizens were those permitted to change their residences; the *petit bourgeois* (small traders) were not.

•● *Proceed westward.*

No 31, **Hôtel d'Albret**, was built *c.*1550 for the Duc de Montmorency, Constable of France, and restored in the 18C. Here, in 1669, the widowed Madame Scarron (later to become Marquise de Maintenon) was introduced to Madame Montespan whom she was eventually to replace as Louis XIV's favourite. **François Mansart** remodelled the house *c.*1640 but its present Rococo street façade, rebuilt by **Vautrain** in 1744, was restored in 1988.

No 33 If the doors are open, a fragment of Philippe Auguste's 12C wall can be seen in the courtyard.

No 35, **Hôtel de Guillaume Barbès**, was built *c.*1630.

No 26, the **Hôtel de Sandreville**, was built *c.*1630.

Location 18	**MUSÉE KWOK ON**

41 Rue des Francs Bourgeois.

Open Monday–Friday 10.00–17.30. Admission charge.

This museum of Asian theatre is based on the collection assembled by Kwok On in his Hong Kong residence.

Included are musical instruments, marionettes, porcelain, rare Chinese gramophone records dating from 1920, films, photographs, books and manuscripts.

•● *Exit and cross the road immediately.*

No 30, **Hôtel d'Alméras**, 1598, retains its original gateway flanked by rams' heads.

No 38, **Centre Culturel Suisse** Here stood the Poterne Barbette (small gateway) where, in 1407, Louis d'Orléans, brother of Charles VI, was assassinated on the orders of Jean Sans Peur, Duke of Burgundy.

No 44 was built for Jean de la Balue who had married the widow of Jean Hérouet, secretary of Louis XII. The building retains its corbelled Gothic look-out turret of c.1510 on the Rue Vieille du Temple corner, but it has been heavily restored.

●● *Continue ahead, crossing Rue Vieille du Temple. Proceed first L through the playground to Rue des Blancs Manteaux R.*

| Location 19 | **NOTRE DAME DES BLANCS MANTEAUX** |

Rue des Blancs Manteaux

Open Tuesday–Sunday 10.00–12.00 and 16.00–19.00 (17.00–19.00 July and August).

This late-17C church, with an early-18C south-west front which came from elsewhere, possesses some remarkable wood-carving, including a richly inlaid pulpit.

St Louis founded a monastery for the mendicant Augustinian Order of the Serfs of the Virgin in 1258. Members soon became known as '*blancs manteaux*' (white coats), referring to their habit. Although replaced by the Benedictine Order of St Guillaume, members of which built the present church in 1695, the earlier nickname has been preserved.

The present south-west front was originally built as the main façade of St Eloi by **Sylvan Cartaud** in 1703. However, that church, which stood on the Ile de la Cité, was demolished in 1863 and its façade resited here by **Baltard**.

●● *Enter the church.*

The combined inner door and organ loft, carved in Baroque style, are exceptional.

On the south-east side of the nave is the canopied Flemish pulpit, designed in Rococo style in 1749 and acquired in 1864; its marquetry panels are inlaid with ivory and pewter.

The carved and turned altar rail is one of the best of its type to be found in the capital.

●● *Exit from the north door, if open.*

This doorway was brought from the church of St Bartolémé in the Ile de la Cité. Originally the royal parish church, it was, like St Eloi, demolished by **Haussmann** in 1863.

●● *First L Rue des Francs Bourgeois. Cross the road.*

No 56, **Hôtel de Fontenay**, is early 18C.

No 58 was owned by Louis Le Tonnelier, Baron de Breteuil, a minister of Louis XVI.

No 57 bis Seen through the gate is a circular stone tower from the 12C wall of Philippe Auguste. Only its lower stone section is original.

●● *Cross the road to the Archives Nationales.*

12

Location 20 | **ARCHIVES NATIONALES**

Hôtel de Soubise
60 Rue des Francs
Bourgeois

*Musée d'Histoire de
France – open
Wednesday–
Monday 14.00–
17.00. Admission
charge.*

The national archives of France are housed in the
early-18C Hôtel de Soubise, and the complex that
surrounds it, including the Hôtel de Rohan (location
10). Situated on the first floor of the Hôtel de Soubise,
one of the finest mansions in Paris, is the archives
museum, where many historic documents are
displayed. The rooms incorporate traces of a 14C
chapel and an outstanding Rococo suite designed by
Boffrand.

History The Hôtel de Soubise is an early-18C
remodelling of the Hôtel de Clisson, which had been
built *c.*1375 for Olivier de Clisson, Constable of
France. This was later acquired by the Ducs de Guise,
1553–1696, and renamed Hôtel de Guise. Of the
medieval building, only a gateway and traces of the
chapel survive.

In 1700, Princesse Anne Chabot de Rohan, mistress of
Louis XIV, acquired the property by means of gifts
that the King had bestowed on her, and moved in with
her husband François de Rohan, Duc de Soubise.
Soon, **Pierre Alexis Delamair** was commissioned to
transform the Gothic hôtel in the Classical style and
work was completed by 1709. Delamair had been an
unusual choice for such an important project as he was
then virtually unknown; five years later he also built
the nearby Hôtel de Rohan for the Duke's son.

Few of Delamair's interiors survive, however, as
Prince Hercule-Meriadec, aged sixty, celebrated his
wedding to the nineteen-year-old Marie Sophie de
Courcillon, by commissioning **Boffrand** to remodel
the private apartments in Rococo style, 1712–45.

During the 19C, additional buildings were constructed
in the grounds to provide more accommodation for
the archives, which had been transferred here by
Napoléon in 1808. The nearby Hôtel de Rohan, then
the national printing works, was incorporated in the
complex in 1925.

In the medieval hôtel, Bolingbroke, later Henry IV of
England, gave a farewell banquet before setting out to
wrest the throne from Richard II; Thomas, Duke of
Clarence, resided there during the English occupation
of Paris, 1420–35; François de Guise frequently
entertained his niece, Mary Queen of Scots here; and
the St Bartholomew's Day massacre of Huguenots was
planned in the hôtel in 1572.

At the outbreak of the Revolution, the gunpowder
taken from the Bastille was stored within.

•► Enter the courtyard.

Exterior The courtyard, which is one of the most
impressive domestic examples in Paris, is
exceptionally deep and surrounded by a lavish
Corinthian colonnade. Its horse-shoe pattern follows
the line of a riding school that once stood on part of the
site.

Delamair's façade was built, together with the
courtyard, at the rear of the medieval building,
additional land having been acquired.

A double range of twin columns in the centre is
pedimented to provide an imposing portico.

First-floor allegories of the seasons are copies of the originals by **Robert Le Lorrain**.

Seated on the pediment are allegories of *Magnanimity* and *Magnificence*, also copies of **Le Lorrain**'s originals.

•• *Enter the hall.*

Interior The private apartments of the Prince on the ground floor are not open to the public.

The staircase is 19C.

•• *Ascend to the first floor. Ahead, tickets are purchased for the museum, which includes the private apartments of the princess and remains of the Gothic chapel.*

The museum (**Musée d'Histoire de France**) was opened in 1880. Permanent exhibits, which relate to the city of Paris and the French Revolution, are supplemented by temporary displays.

First entered, the large **Salle des Gardes**, or Grande Antichambre, houses the exhibits relating to Paris. They are in chronological order and each item is numbered. A selection is detailed here.

•• *Proceed to the front block L.*

16 Treaty of Paris 1259 ratified by the seal of England's Henry III.

19 Clément V's papal bull of 1312 transferring the wealth of the Knights Templar to the Knights of St John.

25 Letter from Jeanne d'Arc to the people of Reims. Below this is the only contemporary likeness of the Maid of Orléans to survive. Surprisingly, her hair is long, whereas in films and plays it is customary to portray her with an urchin cut.

•• *Proceed to the front block R.*

37 Edict of Nantes (establishing religious tolerance).

39 Autographed note by Richelieu.

44 Revocation of the Edict of Nantes.

45 Will of Louis XIV.

•• *Proceed to the rear block L.*

56 Will of Napoléon.

•• *Proceed to the rear block R.*

57 Abdication of Charles X.

•• *Proceed to the far end of the room.*

A model of the Bastille stands L.

Chambre de Parade de la Princesse This is the first of the Princesse de Soubise's private rooms, decorated between 1737–9. The princess received her morning visitors in this chamber, which was never a bedroom, and which includes work by most of the great painters employed at the hôtel.

Salon Ovale This is not only the finest room in the building but also one of the most admired 18C rooms in Paris.

Scenes from the *Story of Psyche* are by **Natoire**.

Boffrand painted the ceiling.

La Petite Chambre de la Princesse, originally the princess's bedroom, is decorated by **Boucher**, **Restou** and **Trémolières**.

Both chimneypieces are copies of the originals.

Exhibits relating to the French Revolution are displayed.

Salle du Dais (L of the Salon Ovale) The monogram RS (Rohan/Soubise) is inscribed on the cornice.

●● *Return towards the exit and turn R to the old chapel.*

The **chapel** of the Hôtel de Clisson, built *c.*1375, was remodelled for the Ducs de Guise by **Primaticcio** in the 16C. Three of the windows and some stonework retain Gothic detailing.

●● *Exit from the building to Rue des Francs Bourgeois R. First R Rue des Archives.*

Facing Rue de Braque (first L), at **No 58**, is the Porte de Clisson. This turreted gateway, built in 1380, was retained by **Delamair** when he remodelled the hôtel.

●● *First L Rue de Braque.*

Nos 4–6 were built in 1663 as the **Hôtel Le Lièvre de la Grange**; the mansion's gateway retains its Rococo doors.

No 7 was the residence of Louis XVI's foreign minister, Vergennes, an enthusiastic supporter of American Independence.

●● *First L Rue du Temple. First R Rue Rambuteau. M Rambuteau.*

13

Hôtel des Monnaies and l'Institut de France

The western extremity of the Left Bank and part of
the Faubourg St Germain are visited; many of the
streets passed specialize in antiques. Not to be
missed is the Baroque Fontaine des Quatres Saisons,
the most splendid fountain in Paris.

Timing: Fine weather is essential as few buildings
may be entered.

The Hôtel des Monnaies is open for tours of the
former Mint's workshops Tuesday and Thursday
afternoons.

The Bibliothèque Mazarine (Library of L'Institut de
France) may be visited on weekdays. Proof of
identity must be carried.

13

Locations

1 Hôtel des Monnaies
2 Palais de l'Institut de France
3 Oscar Wilde's Hotel
4 Ecole Nationale Supérieure des Beaux Arts
5 Rue Bonaparte

6 Rue de l'Université
7 St Thomas d'Aquin
8 Fontaine des Quatre Saisons
9 Rue du Bac
10 Au Bon Marché
11 Rue du Cherche Midi

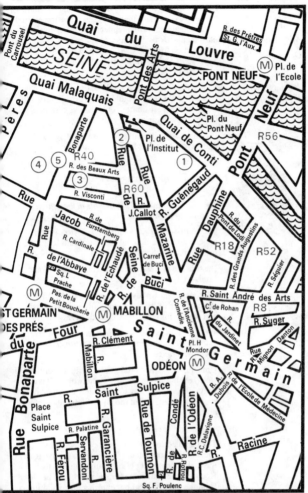

Start M Pont Neuf, line 7, La Courneuve/Villejuif. Exit from the station and cross Pont Neuf. Continue across the Ile de la Cité to the Left Bank. First R Quai de Conti.

Location 1	**HÔTEL DES MONNAIES** *Antoine 1779*
11 Quai de Conti	Built to accommodate the Mint in 1779, commemorative coins, medals and decorations are still produced here, but the standard French coinage is now minted near Bordeaux. Outstanding riverside salons, from the early Louis XVI period, may occasionally be viewed when the museum or temporary exhibitions are open.
Open for guided tours of the mint's workshops in French (duration 45 minutes), Monday and Wednesday 14.15 and 15.00. Closed August. Admission free.	
Musée de la Monnaie et des Médailles usually	**History** The Hôtel Grand Nesle was erected on the site in the 13C. This was rebuilt for Luigi di Gonzaga, Prince de Nevers, in 1572. Apart from the façade of the Petit Hôtel de Conti, added to the complex in 1663, everything was demolished in 1768 to make way for the present buildings.

*open only in April.
Tuesday–Sunday
13.00–18.00.
Admission charge.*

*Occasional
temporary
exhibitions open
Tuesday–Sunday
13.00–18.00.
Admission charge.*

Louis XV decided that the Mint, founded by Charles le Chauve (the Bald) in the 9C, should be transferred here, and an unknown architect, the thirty-five-year-old **Jacques-Denis Antoine** won the public competition for its design. **Antoine** was so appreciative of his own work that he lived here until his death in 1801.

Facing the Quai de Conti, this was the first monumental Classical building in Paris. External decoration is very limited, only the five central bays possessing columns.

Fronting the central attic floor are six allegorical figures by **Le Comte**, **Pigalle** and **Mouchy**.

The central doors bear the monogram of Louis XIV.

Their bronze door knockers are elegantly designed as lions' heads and snakes.

•● *Enter by the door L. Assemble in the courtyard for tours of the mint.*

The courtyard's great south-west portico, which appears to be a triumphal archway, leads to the former mint's workshops.

Busts in the niches depict four kings: Henri II and Louis XIII, XIV and XV.

Visitors are shown several processes in the manufacture of the commemorative coins, medals and decorations that are still made here.

•● *After the tour has been completed, return to the main courtyard and proceed to the north end of the north-west range.*

Unfortunately, the grand salons on the upper floor in which exhibitions are held are rarely open; it is generally possible, however, to view the stone double staircase ahead, one of the finest Classical examples in Paris.

•● *Ascend, if open, to the first floor.*

The panelled rooms that overlook the Seine possess some of the most splendid interiors to survive from the early Louis XVI period. Outstanding is the Rococo **Salle Guillaume Dupré**, which may be viewed from the doorway without entering the exhibition.

•● *Exit L Quai de Conti. Proceed westward to Place de l'Institut, which overlooks the Pont des Arts (first R).*

Location 2	**PALAIS DE L'INSTITUT DE FRANCE** *Le Vau*

23 Quai de Conti

*Bibliothèque
Mazarine open
Monday–Friday
10.00–18.00.
Admission free.
(Visitors must
deposit some item
of identity.)*

*La Coupole (the
dome) may be
viewed internally*

The Institut de France has occupied the complex, which was built in the second half of the 17C, since 1806. The library may generally be entered, but visits to the domed **Salle des Séances Solennelles**, 'La Coupole', are, unfortunately, greatly restricted. Its outstanding tomb monument to Mazarin may, however, be glimpsed through the glass door.

History Part of the site was occupied for centuries by the Petit Nesle, a building that formed a section of the 13C Hôtel Nesle, demolished in the 17C.

As early as 1657, Mazarin considered founding a college for young noblemen from France's recently

*only as part of a
lecture in French.
Saturday and
Sunday 15.00.
Admission charge
(high).
Recommended only
to those fluent in
French and with a
particular interest in
the Institut.*

acquired territories, and three days before he died, in
1661, left an enormous sum for its establishment,
stipulating that he should be buried in the college's
chapel. His successor, Colbert, with the support of
Louis XIV, instigated the project.

The King paid for a quay to be constructed, **Le Vau**
was commissioned to design the college, and work
began in 1662. Although the main buildings were
virtually completed by 1674, it was some years before
the ancillary courtyards were ready to accommodate
the students, and the college eventually opened in
1688. Sixty students were enrolled from Pignerol/
Piedmont, Alsace, Flanders/Artois and Rousillon/
Sardinia; the college soon became unofficially
known, therefore, as the Collège des Quatres
Nations (four nations).

In 1793 Mazarin's foundation was dissolved and the
buildings accommodated, consecutively, a prison, a
civil engineering school and a museum.

The Institut de France was founded by the
Convention in 1795, through the amalgamation of
existing French academies responsible for the arts
and sciences. Napoléon transferred its premises from
the Louvre to the present site in 1806, but only part
of the complex, including the chapel, was allocated
for its use.

Probably the best-known of all the academies
incorporated in the Institut is **l'Académie Française**,
which had been founded by Richelieu in 1635. The
chief task of its members, originally thirteen but now
forty, is to maintain the purity of the French
language; a new word is officially recognized only
when it has been admitted to their *Dictionnaire de
l'Académie*. Members are known as the '*Immortels*'
although, as with many academies of this type,
conservatism has plagued their selection and only a
few have any claim to immortality. Those turned
down have included: Balzac, Beaumarchais,
Descartes, Flaubert, Maupassant, Molière, Pascal,
Proust, Rousseau, and Zola! The academy's patron is
the head of state, who must approve every new
member; most are writers, but representatives of the
church, armed forces and sciences are also eligible, as
are women – but only since 1980.

Exterior **Le Vau** designed the complex to harmonize
with the Louvre's Cour Carrée, across the river,
which he was extending at the time. Its domed chapel
is on the same axis as the central pavilion of the Cour
Carrée's south façade.

A plaque on the face of the east wing commemorates
the Tour de Nesle that stood on its site until
demolished for the construction of the present
building in 1664.

Arcades facing the square originally accommodated
shops, the rents from which helped to support the
college; they have since been filled.

The Jesuit-style chapel was completed in 1674.

Its cupola's ribs are gilded.

The gilded lantern surmounting the cupola was built
to **Le Vau**'s design, but not until 1875.

Dominating the north façade, the portico, with its rich detail, is one of the liveliest in Paris.

Since 1806 the former chapel has served as the ceremonial hall of the Institut.

●● *Pass through the gateway L to the courtyard.*

The old chapel, now the **Salle des Séances Solennelles**, may be entered only as part of the lecture tour.

If not open, the tomb of Mazarin may be viewed through the glass door.

The interior of the chapel, beneath its dome (La Coupole), was adapted by **Antoine Van Doyer** in 1806 to accommodate the Institute's meetings; however, restoration to its original appearance was completed in 1962.

Immediately ahead, the tomb monument to Mazarin was designed by **Hardouin-Mansart** and executed by **Coysevox** and **Tuby** in 1692. It is regarded as one of the most important 17C monuments in France.

The Cardinal lies beneath the monument, his body being transferred here from Vincennes, where he had died in 1684.

●● *Exit ahead to the east range.*

Decorated with pilasters, this range accommodates the **Bibliothèque Mazarine**, a public library since 1643.

●● *Ascend the spiral staircase and press the control button to gain admission; visitors must deposit some form of identity.*

Based on the private collection of Mazarin, the recently restored library, which now contains more than 360,000 items, became, in 1643, the first to be opened to the public.

●● *Exit and proceed westward from Place de l'Institut to Quai Malaquais. First L Rue de Seine. First R Rue des Beaux Arts.*

Location 3	**OSCAR WILDE'S HOTEL**
L'Hôtel 13 Rue des Beaux Arts	A commemorative plaque and medallion, left of the door, record that Oscar Wilde died in this hotel in 1900. Wilde was practically destitute and could not really afford to stay here, writing to a friend: 'I am even dying beyond my means.'

The hotel stands on the site of the 18C Pavillon d'Amour, designed by **Ledoux**; this was demolished in the late 19C for the present building, which in Wilde's time was called the Hotel d'Allemagne. Later renamed the Hotel d'Alsace, when restored in 1968 it acquired its present humble appellation.

●● *Continue westward to the end of the street. First R Rue Bonaparte. Immediately ahead is the courtyard of the Ecole des Beaux Arts.*

Location 4	**ÉCOLE NATIONALE SUPÉRIEURE DES BEAUX ARTS**
14 Rue Bonaparte *Open Monday–* *Friday 08.00–20.00.* *Admission free.*	The main courtyard comprises an early-17C monastic chapel, with outstanding doors by **Goujon**, together with the original school building, one of the finest 19C works in Paris.

History Marie de Médicis built a convent here with a charity hospital attached, c.1603, but in 1606 this was transferred to Rue des Saints Pères. Marguerite de Valois founded, in its place, the Petits Augustins convent, to honour the patriarch Jacob. At the Revolution, Alexandre Lenoir, the painter and art critic, was permitted to store, in the disused monastic buildings, the collection of monumental French art that he had saved from iconoclasts, notably the royal tombs from St Denis. The former convent was opened to the public as a museum in 1795.

In 1858 a new building for the fine arts school replaced the former domestic buildings of the convent, but the original chapel and cloister were retained.

Rioting students caused much damage in 1968 and the famous Beaux Arts Ball has not been held since.

Immediately R, the chapel, built c.1603, possesses, at its east end, the oldest cupola in Paris, only visible internally.

The chapel's three-storey central façade, **Delorme**, 1548, originally fronted Henri II's Château d'Anet.

The door was carved by **Goujon**.

Placed around the courtyard are sections of Gothic and Renaissance structures.

The main range, to the west, designed in Classical style by **Dubon** in 1858 as the fine arts school, is one of the most admired 19C buildings in Paris.

Proceed northward through the arches to the second courtyard.

This, the Cour du Murier (mulberry tree), originally formed the convent's cloister; its decoration is 19C work.

Return to Rue Bonaparte L and cross the road.

Location 5	**RUE BONAPARTE**

Originally called Rue des Petits Augustins, to commemorate Margot's convent, the street was renamed Bonaparte in 1852. Since the Rue Napoléon became the Rue de la Paix, there is surprisingly no longer a street of that name in the capital.

Nos 7–9 were the residence of Monge in 1803 and the birthplace of the father of Impressionism, Edouard Manet, in 1832.

No 1, Joséphine, is renowned for the quality of its antique silverware.

L Quai Malaquais.

No 9, the corner building, was built as the Hôtel Transylvanie in 1628.

Nos 15–17, now part of the Ecole des Beaux Arts, was originally designed, probably by **Mansart**, c.1640 as the Hôtel de Chimay, but remodelled in the 18C for the Duchesse de Bouillon. Henrietta Maria, widow of England's Charles I, lived here in 1662, as, later, did Anatole France.

No 19 was the residence of the writer George Sand.

First L Rue des Saints Pères.

No 5 The painter Manet died here in 1883, surprisingly near to his birthplace.

No 4, Ecole des Langues et Civilisations Orientales (entered from Rue de Lille). This school was founded by the Convention in 1795.

No 28 was designed by **Antoine**, architect of the Hôtel des Monnaies, in 1768. Originally named the Hôtel de Fleury, the building has since 1845 accommodated the Ecole des Ponts et Chausées, a civil engineering school founded in 1747.

No 30, Debauve et Gallais Designed by the imperial architects **Percier** and **Fontaine** this shop is preserved as an historic monument. It is also the oldest *chocolatier* in Paris, being founded in 1818 by a pharmacist Sulpice Gallais, who promoted chocolate for its medicinal qualities.

•• *Return northward. First L Rue de l'Université.*

Location 6	**RUE DE L'UNIVERSITÉ**

Named to commemorate the university's original ownership of much of the surrounding land, the street's greatest mansions are concentrated at this and the west end (see page 66); they are separated by a central stretch which is of little interest.

•• *Continue westward passsing (first L) Rue du Pré aux Clercs.*

No 24, built as the Hôtel de Senneterre, by **Servandoni** in 1728, now accommodates the **Ministère de Commerce**.

No 13, also an 18C building, formerly served as the Venetian embassy.

No 17, the offices of publishers **Editions Gallimard**, was built as the Hôtel Bochart de Saron in 1639.

•• *Second L Rue du Bac.*

No 46, formerly the Hôtel de Boulogne, was built by **Boffrand** in 1742. Chateaubriand lodged here 1815–18. A sumptuous doorway leads to the courtyard.

•• *First L Rue de Gribeauval leads to Place St Thomas d'Aquin.*

Location 7	**ST THOMAS D'AQUIN** *Bullet*

Place St Thomas d'Aquin

Internally, this Baroque church is one of the most theatrical in Paris. A Jesuit-style building, erected for the Dominican Order, St Thomas was begun in 1680.

Its Classical façade, added in 1740, provides superbly appropriate ends of vistas from both Boulevard St Germain and Boulevard Raspail.

•• *Enter the church.*

Nothing interrupts the view from the entrance to the Lady Chapel at the far end, and a very theatrical effect, typical of Baroque architecture, is achieved.

•• *Proceed ahead to the sacristy.*

Panelling is from the Louis XV period.

•• *Continue through the sacristy to the Lady Chapel.*

The ceiling was painted by **Lemoyne** in 1723.

●● Exit ahead Rue St Thomas d'Aquin and Rue de Luynes. Second L Boulevard Raspail. First R Rue de Grenelle.

No 51, Barthélemy, one of the great Paris cheese shops, supplies the Palais de l'Elysée. Although some competitors may keep a greater range, Roland Barthélemy's quality is unbeatable.

Location 8	**FONTAINE DES QUATRE SAISONS** *Bouchardon 1745*

57–59 Rue de Grenelle

An early Parisian example of the Classical style, this unaltered masterpiece is one of the capital's finest Rococo works. The scale and grandeur of its concept in such a relatively narrow street is endearingly quirky.

Turgot, dean of the merchants' guild, commissioned the fountain in 1739 to meet justified complaints that the new and aristocratic Faubourg St Germain lacked an adequate water supply.

Allegorically depicted is the seated city of Paris with the rivers Seine and Marne at her feet.

Representations of the four seasons (quatre saisons), in the form of winged angels, stand on plinths within niches.

●● Continue ahead. First L Rue du Bac.

Location 9	**RUE DU BAC**

Bac (ferry) refers to the ferry service that operated at the north end of this long street until the Pont Royal was built in 1689.

No 85 Originally, the building formed part of the Récollets convent. The triangular pediment, a later addition, and the original curved pediment above it make an unusual combination.

●● Continue to the south-west corner of Rue de Varennne (first R).

No 98 Gilded angels above the door recall that in the early 19C this was the Café des Deux Anges (two angels). Its original fine balconies have survived.

No 102 was built as the Hôtel St Aldegonde early in the 18C.

No 97, formerly the Hôtel de Ségur, built in 1720, was restored in 1988. An original iron staircase survives L of the entrance to the courtyard.

No 110 James McNeill Whistler stayed here in 1892. The painter spent his summers in London and winters in Paris, lodging at various addresses.

Nos 118–120, Hôtel de Clermont Tonnerre
Chateaubriand passed his last years at this address from 1838, writing his famous *Mémoires d'Outre-Tombe (Memories from Beyond the Tomb)* during his stay. He died here 4 July 1848 and is commemorated by a statue in the children's playground opposite.

Both portals and doors are original Rococo work.

No 128, Séminaire des Missions Etrangères (Seminary of Foreign Missions). The seminary was founded by Jean Duval de Clamecy in 1663, to train missionaries for work in Persia.

•▪ Enter the courtyard. Immediately ahead is the chapel.

The original 17C mansion stands south-west of the chapel, behind the iron gate R.

•▪ Continue southward along the Rue du Bac. First L Rue de Sèvres.

Location 10	**AU BON MARCHÉ**
38 Rue de Sèvres	Aristide Boucicaut founded Au Bon Marché, the oldest department store in Paris, in 1852, on the site of an asylum; this shop was rebuilt, in expanded form, on its present site, by **Eiffel** (designer of the Eiffel Tower) and **I.-C. Boileau** in 1876. For more than a century Au Bon Marché has specialized in antiques and oriental rugs.

•▪ Exit R and proceed to the second store, south-west of Rue du Bac.

This building was added in Art-Deco style *c.*1900.

*•▪ Follow Rue de Sèvres north-eastward to Boulevard Raspail (first R) and cross to the **Hôtel Lutetia** at the junction.*

Towards the south end of its west wall, facing Boulevard Raspail, a plaque records that the building was used as a rehabilitation centre in 1945 for French survivors of the Nazi concentration camps.

•▪ Follow Boulevard Raspail southward. First L Place Alphonse Deville. First L Rue du Cherche Midi.

Location 11	**RUE DU CHERCHE MIDI**

Somehow un-Parisian, the delightful north section of this street of 17C and 18C houses retains ancient shop fronts and a gentle curve at its north end, both rare features in the city.

No 23, Jacques Dereux, possesses the best mid-19C shopfront in the street.

No 19 Between the first-floor windows, is a carved figure of an astronomer examining a sundial. Apparently this gave the street its name 'Cherche Midi' (searching for midday).

No 8, Poilâne, is the premises of the world's best-known baker, Lionel Poilâne, who specializes in a sour dough bread. The sign *'Ici Pain Poilâne'* is now a common sight in the capital. Unlike the familiar long *baguettes*, Poilâne's large round loaves have a soft crust, with a slightly sweet flavour; also, unlike *baguettes*, they keep well.

•▪ Continue northward. At the Carrefour de la Croix Rouge, where Rue du Cherche Midi ends, continue directly ahead following Rue du Dragon.

Nos 35–37 display remnants of gables; few others survive in Paris.

•▪ First R Boulevard St Germain. M St Germain des Prés.

14

Luxembourg Palace and St Germain des Prés

The western sector of the Latin Quarter is visited, many of its ancient streets being lined with art galleries, all free of charge. Few open spaces exist on this side of the Left Bank and the Luxembourg Garden provides an important lung.

Timing: Fine weather is essential as only three buildings of importance may be entered: the churches of St Sulpice and St Germain des Prés and the Delacroix Museum (closed Tuesday).

Since the 1986 terrorist bombings, tours of the Luxembourg Palace have been discontinued, but the public gallery remains open when the Senate, parliament's Upper House, is in session.

14

Locations
1 Danton Statue
2 Cour du Commerce
  St André
3 Cour de Rohan
4 Picasso's House
5 No 5 Rue de l'Ecole de
  Médecine
6 Université Pierre et Marie
  Curie
7 Ecole de Médecine
8 Odéon Théâtre National
9 Palais du Luxembourg
10 St Sulpice
11 Boulevard St Germain

For locations 12 to 17, see page 235.

Start *M Odéon, line 4 Porte d'Orléans/Porte de Clignancourt. Exit and proceed westward to Place Henri Mondor.*

Location 1	**DANTON STATUE**

Place Henri
Mondor

DANTON

Georges Jacques Danton, 1739–94, the revolutionary leader, was arrested, on Robespierre's orders, in his house that stood where the statue has since been sited. It is usual to portray Danton in films and on the stage as a handsome young man, rather than the portly reality depicted here.

Not only the house of Danton, but also that of his associate Camille Desmoulins, whence he was dragged to prison, were lost when Haussmann laid out the Boulevard St Germain in the mid-19C.

●● *Cross to the north side of the Boulevard St Germain. Immediately facing Danton's statue is the entrance to the Cour du Commerce St André. Proceed ahead.*

Location 2	**COUR DU COMMERCE ST ANDRÉ**

This picturesque courtyard was opened in 1776 on the site of a tennis court that had stood in the ditch surrounding the Paris wall.

No 8, at its south end, was where Marat, a qualified doctor who had studied at Edinburgh, published his inflammatory *L'Ami du Peuple* (People's Friend). Its demand that 270,000 members of the *ancien régime* should be guillotined led to Marat's assassination by Charlotte Corday.

The **Relais Odéon**, facing No 8, is a brasserie, founded in 1900, which retains Belle Epoque décor.

Parrot's Tavern, opposite, is renowned for its international range of beers.

The last house in the terrace R encloses the basement of a circular tower, one of twenty in Philippe Auguste's 12C wall. The tower originally formed part of an entrance in the wall, known as the Porte de Buci.

●● *First R Cour de Rohan.*

Location 3	**COUR DE ROHAN**

A delightful series of courtyards, neglected by most visitors, gives the impression of a serene country town. Rohan is a corruption of Rouen and refers to the fortified town house of the bishops of Rouen that stood here, within the Paris wall, in the 15C. The 'courtyard' comprises the property's separate courts.

No 9, immediately L, is believed to have been the home of Dr Joseph-Ignace Guillotine, a deputy who invented a machine in 1789 that could perform executions more efficiently and humanely than the hangman. Allegedly, experiments were first carried out in this courtyard in 1792, with sheep acting as the guinea pigs, so to speak. Referred to as Dr Guillotine's 'philanthropic beheading machine', the doctor enthused that victims would feel only 'a slight coolness above the neck'.

●● *Proceed to the second courtyard.*

On the north side L is a creeper-covered house of brick and stone, with a 16C Renaissance façade.

Opposite is the former residence of Diane de Poitiers, mistress of Henri II.

In the south-east corner R, the horse mount is in the form of an iron tripod.

•• *Proceed to the third courtyard.*

An ancient well and pulley survive R.

•• *Return to Cour du Commerce St André R. R Rue St André des Arts. Cross the road.*

No 47, an unrestored 17C hôtel, reminiscent of the Marais, retains its outstanding street façade.

No 45 On the fourth floor lived Billand-Varenne, 'the tiger with the yellow wig', held by many to be more responsible than Robespierre for much of 'the Terror', Marie-Antoinette's execution in particular.

•• *First L Rue des Grand Augustins. Continue to Rue du Pont de Lodi (second L).*

No 8, Relais Louis XIII, occupies a former outbuilding of the 13C convent that stood on the site. No other part of the great complex has survived.

Facing this R is the last Paris home of Picasso.

Location 4	**PICASSO'S HOUSE**
5–7 Rue des Grands Augustins	A plaque records that Pablo Picasso lived in this house from 1936 to 1955, a period that included the German occupation. It was in his great studio here that Picasso painted *Guernica*, a moving protest against the bombing of innocent civilians. Despite Picasso's left-wing views and Hitler's hatred of modern art, for once the Nazis turned a blind eye and he was undisturbed.

The house became known as the Hôtel d'Hercule, due to its frescos and tapestries that depict the labours of Hercules. Louis XII owned the property in the 15C and François I, the 'Renaissance King', lived here as a child.

The hôtel, remodelled in the 17C, is now maintained by the state.

•• *Continue ahead. R Quai des Grands Augustins.*

No 51, Lapérouse Comte de Bruillevert, Louis XIV's Master of Waters and Forests, commissioned this hôtel in the early 18C; it was later purchased by Lefèvre, the King's Master of Beverages, who converted the ground floor to a wine merchant's premises. Famed for its Chablis, and adapted to a restaurant by the new owner Jules Lapérouse, the establishment soon became even more famous for its intimate salons on the first floor, where, because the rooms were technically public, amorous liaisons could take place without committing adultery under contemporary French law. Popular with authors, Lapérouse's clients included Colette, Dumas, Hugo, De Maupassant and Zola. Although its great gastronomic days have passed, the Belle Epoque décor, glimpsed from outside, is exceptional.

•• *Continue eastward. Second R Rue Gît le Coeur.*

14

Second L Rue St André des Arts leads to Place St André des Arts. Turn R and proceed anti-clockwise. Third R Rue Hautefeuille. Proceed to Impasse Hautefeuille (first L).

No 1 **Rue Hautefeuille**, once the town house of the abbots of Fécamp, retains a picturesque 16C turret with an intricately carved corbel and a conical roof.

•• *Continue ahead. Fourth L Rue de l'Ecole de Médecine. Cross the road.*

Location 5	**NO 5 RUE DE L'ÉCOLE DE MÉDECINE**

Now the Institut du Monde Anglophone, this building was designed in 1695 as the Amphithéâtre de St Come, to serve as the lecture hall of the College of Surgeons, founded by St Louis in the 13C.

Although the building is in need of restoration, its tall cupola and sumptuous portal survive.

A plaque, L of the entrance, records that the actress Sarah Bernhardt lived here.

•• *Return westward along Rue de l'Ecole de Médecine.*

Location 6	**UNIVERSITÉ PIERRE ET MARIE CURIE, PARIS VI (CORDELIERS)**

15 Rue de l'Ecole de Médecine

Open daily 10.00–18.00. Courtyard free.

Only a multi-purpose block has survived from the great Franciscan Convent of the Cordeliers; other existing buildings were constructed in the late 19C, specifically for the School of Practical Medicine.

•• *Enter the courtyard and proceed to the free-standing Gothic building in the south-east corner.*

This monastic survivor was built *c*.1370 in Flamboyant Gothic style. Until the 17C, it provided the convent's refectory on the ground floor, the novices' dormitory on the first floor and a granary above.

•• *Return to Rue de l'Ecole de Médecine L and cross the road.*

Location 7	**ÉCOLE DE MÉDECINE** *Jacques Goudain 1776*

University René Descartes Paris V 12 Rue de l'Ecole de Médecine

The school's south façade is judged to be one of the finest Classical examples in Paris.

Louis XV commissioned the building in 1771 to house the Ecole de Médecine, but construction did not begin until three years later. Its site had previously been occupied by the Collège de Bourgogne and the Collège du Prémontrés.

Originally, the complex simply consisted of four wings enclosing a courtyard.

Above the triumphal arch is inscribed 'Université de Paris Faculté de Médecine'. Over this, the relief originally depicted Louis XV but was replaced at the Revolution with the present *Charity*.

In front of its door is a statue of the anatomist Xavier Bichat, d.1802, by **David d'Angers**.

Expansion of the school took place in 1878 and 1900, both wings being designed by **Ginain**.

•• *First L Rue Antoine Dubois. First L Rue Monsieur Le Prince. Ascend the stairs R. Ahead Rue Casimir Delavigne leads to Place de l'Odéon.*

Location 8	**ODÉON THÉÂTRE NATIONAL**
Place de l'Odéon	Resembling an expanded Greek temple the theatre is a typical example of the heavy French Classicism of the late 18C. Now the Paris home of modern drama, it confusingly sports a variety of names, including: Théâtre de France, Odéon Théâtre de l'Europe and Comédie Française. However, it is usually referred to simply as the Odéon.

History The actors of the Comédie Française had been forced to abandon their premises in the Rue de l'Ancienne Comédie in 1770 and Louis XV, a keen theatregoer, decided to provide them with new and permanent accommodation and commissioned a new building; the company was allowed to perform in the Tuileries Palace until this was ready in 1782.

Although the royal architects, **Wailly** and **Peyre**, had supplied plans for a new theatre as early as 1767, the City Architect, **Pierre Moreau**, was appointed to design the building, and construction began in 1774. However, by 1779, progress was proving too slow for the Marquis de Marigny, superintendent of royal buildings, and **Moreau** was replaced by **Wailly** and **Peyre**, much of the theatre's detail being taken from their earlier scheme. The site chosen was the Prince de Condé's family town house, which the King compulsory purchased and demolished in 1773. In 1792, the company divided: republican supporters leaving for what is now the Comédie Française in Rue Richelieu; the royalists remained until they were imprisoned. A new company, concentrating on musical works, was formed in 1797, and the theatre was renamed the Odéon.

Burnt down two years later, the Odéon was rebuilt by **Chalgrin**, few changes being made to its design. It reopened in 1807 but, in 1818, another fire necessitated further rebuilding (the present theatre); and once more the earlier design was followed.

The Marriage of Figaro was previewed here in 1794, its author **Beaumarchais** soon being arrested for its anti-establishment theme. Also previewed here was **Bizet**'s *L'Arlésienne* (in 1872) but the Odéon did not become financially successful until after the Second World War when, under the name Théâtre de France, it specialized in modern drama.

Exterior The Classical portico is an example of the monumental scale favoured in the late 18C.

•• *Follow Rue Rotrou R, passing the west side of the Odéon.*

Ground floor arcades, on both sides of the building, originally accommodated bookshops.

Internally, the auditorium remains one of the finest in Paris. Accommodating 2,000, it was, when built, the city's largest.

The ceiling was repainted, in abstract style, by **André Masson** in 1965.

●● *Continue ahead to Place Paul Claudel. R Rue de Vaugirard. Continue westward to Square François Poulenc, in front of the Luxembourg Palace.*

Location 9

PALAIS DU LUXEMBOURG
Salomon de Brosse 1615–31

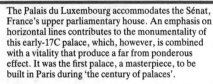

15 Rue de
Vaugirard

Gardens open daily dawn-dusk. Admission free.

Interiors only open the first Sunday in the month as part of a lecture, in French only. (Details from Caisse Nationale des Monuments Historique (48 87 24 14). Admission charge. Sénat public gallery open when in session. Admission free. A passport must be presented.

The Palais du Luxembourg accommodates the Sénat, France's upper parliamentary house. An emphasis on horizontal lines contributes to the monumentality of this early-17C palace, which, however, is combined with a vitality that produce a far from ponderous effect. It was the first palace, a masterpiece, to be built in Paris during 'the century of palaces'.

History Following the assassination of Henri IV in 1610, his widow Marie de Médicis, now acting as Regent for the ten-year-old Louis XIII, acquired estates on the south side of Rue de Vaugirard. Much of the land was purchased from the Carthusian monastery, which lay to the south-west, but the mansion and grounds of François de Luxembourg, who had just died, were added in 1612. Marie wanted to retain her political power and had decided to move to the Left Bank so that she could be near her step-sister Galigaï and friend Concini, both devious intriguers, who had accompanied her from Italy. Marie de Médicis had been born at the Pitti Palace in Florence and commissioned Louis Métezau to build her a similar palace on the site. The architect duly visited Florence in 1611, but on his return found that he had been replaced by **Salomon de Brosse**.

De Brosse persuaded Marie that the Italian Renaissance style would be unsuitable, and his design, with the exception of some Italian detailing, differed little from a château he had already built in the Loire valley. In 1617, Louis XIII, now ruler of France although only sixteen, decided to establish his authority by dealing harshly with those suspected of intriguing against him. His mother, Marie de Médicis, was banished to the royal château at Blois, Concini was murdered and Galigaï executed, as a sorceress, for possessing Hebrew books. Richelieu was confined to the area of his bishopric. Eight years later the King was reconciled with his mother and permitted her to move into the still uncompleted palace, which she named the Palais Médicis. At that time the estate was situated on the edge of Paris, bordering open country. Eventually, the stubborn Marie fell out with Richelieu, also back in the King's favour, and on 10 November 1630 she persuaded Louis XIII to dismiss him; the next day, however, the King changed his mind and the following year, in which the Palais du Luxembourg was at last completed, Richelieu instigated Marie's exile; she died at Cologne in 1642.

Louis XIII outlived his mother by only one year and his younger brother, Gaston d'Orléans, leader of the Fronde, occupied the palace, which then became known as the Palais d'Orléans.

Subsequent residents included Mademoiselle de Montpensier, Louis XIV and other members of the Orléans family.

At the Revolution, the palace became a prison and a court, where those tried included Maréchal de Noailles (aged seventy-nine); Danton, Desmoulins, the painter David, Tom Paine and the Vicomte de Beauharnais, together with his wife Joséphine, later to become Napoléon's consort.

Initially sitting at the Tuileries Palace, the revolutionary government moved in 1794 to the Luxembourg, which was renamed the Palais Directoriale. In 1799, the Consulat sat here, but Napoléon decided to move to the Tuileries in 1800 and the newly created Sénat, the upper house of parliament, took its place. In 1804, the building was altered to accommodate it, by **Chalgrin**.

Notable trials at the palace include those of Maréchal Ney, in 1815, and Louis-Napoléon, later Napoléon III, in 1840. At the Restoration, the complex became the Palais de la Pairie (peerage) but the Sénat returned to the recently extended palace in 1852 and, apart from a brief interruption, sat here until the Germans occupied Paris in 1940, when it became the residence of the Luftwaffe's Field Marshal Sperrle. Since 1958, the complex has once more served as the Palais du Sénat.

Exterior Viewed from Rue de Vaugirard, the palace has changed little, apart from higher roofs, since it was built in the 17C.

The gatehouse wing is heavily rusticated, its first-floor columns' shafts are ringed and their capitals are Tuscan, features copied from the Pitti Palace.

Linking the gatehouse with the end pavilions is an arcade, originally blind but later pierced with windows.

Two-storey wings connect this range with the main building, their upper floors being designed as picture galleries.

In the east wing L the first public picture gallery in Paris opened in 1750; it is now the library's annexe.

A raised marble terrace with a balustrade, approached by semi-circular steps, fronts the main façade of the palace, thus dividing the courtyard. It is a modern reproduction of **de Brosse**'s original, that had been removed by **Chalgrin** c.1800.

•• *Proceed westward following Rue de Vaugirard to No 17 bis.*

Lying back, at the end of the range, is the cloister of the Filles du Calvaire Convent, built by Marie de Médicis in 1631.

In the corner R is its chapel; the queen's monogram and bust are above the entrance.

•• *Continue ahead.*

No 19, the **Musée du Luxembourg**, is open for temporary exhibitions.

•• *First L enter the Jardin du Luxembourg. Follow the first path L.*

Passed L is the **Orangery**, also an exhibitions venue.

•• *Continue ahead.*

Behind trees L is the 18C Petit Luxembourg, which replaced the original built in the early-17C for Comte François de Luxembourg, Duc de Piney. It is strange that the name of an insignificant count was resuscitated for the great palace, the chief reason advocated is simply that 'it sounded well'. Marie de Médicis, wishing to reconcile her differences with Richelieu, presented him with the property c.1635. It is now the official residence of the president of the Sénat. **Boffrand** rebuilt the mansion early in the 18C and some of his internal work, including the staircase, survives.

Immediately L is the fountain commemorating the painter Delacroix, d.1863, by **Dalou**.

•• *Proceed ahead to the south façade of the palace.*

To extend the palace in 1841, **Alphonse de Gisors** brought its entire south façade forward, keeping to the style of **de Brosse**'s 17C work. The latter's original upper floors had been set back, a terrace ran above the ground-floor arcade and a projecting central structure accommodated the Queen's private chapel.

Jardin du Luxembourg The Palais du Luxembourg was the first of the capital's great houses to be built within an extensive private park and the Jardin du Luxembourg now represents by far the largest public open space on the Left Bank, in fine weather acting as a magnet to the local students and children.

Boyceau laid out the garden in formal Renaissance style c.1612, but at the Revolution it became neglected. The garden was later extended southward to the Observatoire, incorporating the grounds of the dissolved Cistercian monastery. In the early 19C, however, the Avenue de l'Observatoire was laid out, and most of this land was lost.

Few of the statues, introduced to the gardens by Louis-Philippe in the 19C, possess great artistic value. Marble figures of French queens and prominent women, all made in the late 19C for the park at Sceaux, decorate the terrace that surrounds the central pond to the south. Included are Marie de Médicis and Mary Stuart, who married François II.

•• *Proceed R to the strip of water on the east side of the palace, leading to the* **Fontaine de Médicis**.

Although the fountain was designed by **de Brosse** in 1624, its figures are later work.

The central **Prometheus** scene, by **Ottin**, was added in 1863.

•• *Proceed to the rear of the fountain.*

This side is decorated with a bas-relief of *Leda and the Swan*, by **Valois**, 1807, transferred here from the Rue du Regard in 1855.

•• *Exit from the garden to Rue Vaugirard L and return to the main courtyard of the palace. If visiting the Public Gallery, or joining a lecture tour, assemble here. Passports will be required.*

•• *Alternatively, continue to Rue de Tournon as described below.*

Public Gallery The Salle des Séances (peers

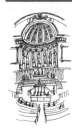

chamber) was created by **Alphonse de Gisors** in 1836 as part of his new south range.

There are 322 senators, each one representing a *département* of France. An electoral college of deputies and counsellors is responsible for their selection; unlike Britain's Upper House, there is no hereditary membership.

Immediately behind the speaker sits the président, flanked by the directeur de service and the secrétaire général. If the French presidency suddenly becomes vacant, the président of the Sénat will act as head of state until a new one has been appointed.

Tour of the palace Since the 1986 terrorist bombings in Paris, visitors have no longer been permitted to view the interiors of the Luxembourg Palace unless they join a specialized lecture tour, which is given once a month. Highlights of the interior, in addition to the Salle des Séances, are as follows.

Grand Staircase Built by **Chalgrin**, its well occupies the upper gallery, which formerly displayed paintings by **Rubens** eulogizing Marie de Médicis and Henri IV.

Salle de Livre d'Or (Golden book room) Originally the audience chamber of Marie de Médicis, it retains some original 17C decoration from her apartment.

Library This was created, on the south wing's first floor, by **de Gisors** in the 19C. Frescos on the Reading Room's dome are by **Delacroix**, 1847.

The library's annexe is decorated with a *Signs of the zodiac* painting by **Jordaens**. It was here, in 1750, that paintings were first exhibited to the public in Paris.

Salle des Conférences Completed in time for the wedding of Napoléon III, the decor of this Neo-Baroque chamber is typical of the heavy ornamentation of the Second Empire.

*Exit from the palace. Immediately ahead, running northward, is **Rue de Tournon**.*

No 27 François I presented this mansion to the royal poet Clément Marot in the 16C.

No 10 Hôtel des Ambassadeurs Until she was murdered on the order of Louis XIII, this was the residence of Concini, his mother's accomplice in intrigue. The King then stayed at the hôtel on occasions. Later it became the home of St François de Sales. From 1730 to 1748 important ambassadors lodged here, hence the building's present name.

No 19 John Paul Jones, the US admiral, died here 18 July 1792. See the plaque L of the door.

No 17 was the residence of actor Gérard Philipe.

No 9 Hôtel de Montmorency, built in the 18C; this was the home of Lamartine.

No 5 Hébert, known as Père (father) Duchesne, lived here. Charles Cros, the poet, accredited with inventing the gramophone, died in the house 9 August 1888. See the first floor plaque.

No 2 Hôtel de Chatillon Balzac lived in this mansion 1827–34; it was built on the site of the ancient town house of the dukes of Savoie. In 1871

Communards broke in and assassinated president Boujean.

●● *First L Rue St Sulpice. First L Rue Garancière.*

No 8, Hôtel de Sourdéac, is a Renaissance mansion, built in 1646 to replace the ancient Hôtel de Garancière. From 1818 to 1849 it was the Mairie of the former 11th arrondissement.

●● *Return northward. First L Rue Palatine. First L* **Rue Servandoni.**

No 12 D'Artagnan, a king's musketeer and the inspiration for the Alexandre Dumas hero, lived in this house when he first came to Paris.

No 14 Exceptional double doors are carved with bas-reliefs. Servandoni R is depicted presenting his proposals for the west façade of St Sulpice.

No 15 Here, Madame Vernet, widow of the artist, hid the writer Condorcet during 'the Terror'. His last work, *Exquisse d'un Tableau Historique des Progrès de l'esprit humain* (*Sketch of the Intellectual Progress of Mankind*), was written here. Condorcet's hideout was eventually discovered and he took poison to escape the guillotine.

●● *Return northward. Second L Rue Palatine leads to Place St Sulpice. Proceed to the central fountain.*

The **Fontaine des Quatre Evèques**, designed by **Visconti** in 1844, incorporates, at its four cardinal points, the figures of leading churchmen who were never (*point*) made cardinals. The fountain is punningly referred to as the Fontaine des Quatre Points Cardinales (fountain of the four cardinal points, or of the four who were never to be cardinals).

Location 10	**ST SULPICE**
Place St Sulpice	St Sulpice is regarded as 'the cathedral' of the fashionable Faubourg St Germain. Probably the most architecturally influential Classical church in Paris, its west façade, in particular, set the style for the capital's monumental 18C buildings. Murals within include work by **Delacroix**.

History Dedicated to Sulpicius, a 6C archbishop of Bourges, the original small church was built in the 12C by the Abbey of St Germain for the peasants in its domain, who, as usual, were not permitted to worship in the monastic church. St Sulpice was rebuilt seven times and traces of the former 16C structure survive in the crypt (not open).

Anne of Austria laid the foundation stone of the present building in 1646 and **Christophe Gamard** was its original architect; however, St Sulpice was to take many years to complete, with five more architects becoming involved. Work began, as usual, at the east end, but was briefly interrupted by the Fronde insurrection in 1648. It resumed a year later with **Le Vau**, who enlarged the building, in charge until his death in 1670, when **Daniel Hard** took over. A lack of funds led to suspension of activities in 1678 with the nave still not begun, and another forty years were to pass before work recommenced, now with **Oppenard** as architect. **Servandoni**'s design was eventually selected for the west façade but some amendments

were subsequently made to it by others.

Exterior Although Oppenard had produced a design for a west façade for St Sulpice c.1720, it was decided to consider others, and an architectural competition was held in 1732; this was won by the Florentine, **Servandoni**, then best known as a stage designer. Work began in 1742, but **Maclaurin** took over three years later and made several amendments.

Due to its composition, this façade of St Sulpice appears to have been influenced by that of London's St Paul's Cathedral. Similarities include two superimposed ranges of columns, short flanking towers and a pediment which, until it was destroyed by lightning, crowned the structure.

A top-floor balustrade replaced the destroyed pediment in 1869.

Balustrades, instead of the planned Renaissance-style pinnacles, surmount the tower.

The north tower was built by **Chalgrin**, who also added the two upper stages to **Maclaurin**'s south tower; work was however halted by the Revolution and never resumed, which is why the south tower is 16 feet shorter and less ornate than its counterpart. Victor Hugo wrote that the towers reminded him of clarinets.

●● *Follow Rue St Sulpice to view the north façade.*

Most of the nave and the Jesuit-style transepts were designed by **Gilles-Marie Oppenard**, who worked on St Sulpice 1718–36.

Gamard, **Le Vau** and **Hard** were responsible for the chancel, with its ambulatory and chapels, all of which were completed by 1675.

Projecting from the east end is the Lady Chapel, where work commenced, but its dome and apsidal form are part of the remodelling by **Charles de Wailly** in 1774.

●● *First R Rue Garancière. First R Rue Palatine.*

●● *Enter the church from the south transept.*

Interior Surprisingly homogeneous, in spite of the long construction period, St Sulpice's interior is spacious and well balanced, with its Greek cross plan being typical of Jesuit churches. Rococo-style decoration throughout was planned by **Oppenard** but little of it was executed.

A copper band runs from the pavement of the south transept to the north transept, indicating the compass position of true north.

●● *Turn L and proceed westward along the **south aisle** to the first chapel L.*

Chapelle St Jean Baptiste Against the west wall is the tomb of Curé Languet de Gergy, d.1750, by **Slodtz**.

Eugéne Delacroix, pre-eminent among the twenty artists who decorated the chapels of this church, was responsible for painting the frescos in the south aisle's most westerly chapel, 1858–61.

●● *Proceed to the west end of the **nave**.*

Against both the nave's second piers from the west,

facing west, are holy-water stoups in the form of
shells. These were given to François I by the
Venetian republic in the 16C and presented to the
church by Louis XV in 1745.

•• Proceed ahead to the pulpit on the south side.

The pulpit was designed by **Charles de Wailly** in 1788.

The west organ loft, best viewed from the centre of
the nave, was built by **Servandoni** in 1750. It houses
one of the world's largest organs, originally made by
Cliquot, but rebuilt in 1861. The case was designed by
Chalgrin in 1776 with figures by **Clodion.**

*•• Proceed to the **north transept**.*

Points marked on the white obelisk, against the north
wall R of the entrance, signify where the sun strikes
from a concealed aperture in the south transept at
midday during the winter. This rather complicated
'timepiece' was designed in 1744.

*•• Proceed to the **Lady Chapel** at the east end.*

St Sulpice's Lady Chapel, designed by **M. A. Slodtz**,
*c.*1775, is one of the finest examples of the Baroque
style in France. Frescos on the walls are by **Van Loo**
and on the dome by **Lemoyne**.

A Virgin and Child by **Pigalle** stands above the altar;
the angels peering from the clouds are by **Mouchy**.

*•• Proceed to the **sacristy**, immediately east of the
south transept.*

The sacristy's wood panelling is exceptional Rococo
work, carved by **Slodtz** to the designs of **Oppenard.** It
is indicative of how the church might have appeared
had Oppenard's complete Rococo proposals been
fully implemented.

*•• Exit from the west door R. L Place St Sulpice.
First R Rue Bonaparte. This section of Rue Bonaparte
is the Left Bank's fashion centre. Passed are: **Yves St
Laurent**, **François Villon** and **Ted Lapidus**. Second L
Boulevard St Germain.*

Location 11	**BOULEVARD ST GERMAIN**

The lively cafés around the church of St Germain des
Prés have long been associated with the artistic and
literary world. Bookshops also abound, encouraged
by the student and tourist markets.

Haussmann thrust this long boulevard eastward from
Pont de la Concorde to Pont de Sully, ruthlessly
destroying the ancient and historic streets that lay in
its path. Work began in the mid-19C and was
completed by 1880. Very soon the cafés and
restaurants just west of St Germain's church became
fashionable, and an artistic quarter developed,
bridging the short period between the popularity of
Montmartre and Montparnasse. In 1940, when the
wartime blackout hindered travelling, this more
centrally placed area took over the 'bohemian'
mantle of Montparnasse and another great period
began, led by Jean-Paul Sartre, whose Existentialist
philosophy was in vogue until the mid-1950s

•• Proceed to Rue de Rennes (first L).

No 149, Drugstore Publicis This, the first of its type

to open in Paris, was the in-place with the younger set throughout the 1960s.

No 151, **Lipp** Both a café and at the rear an Alsatian-style brasserie – a favourite with President Mitterrand.

•• *Cross the boulevard immediately.*

No 172, **Café de Flore** Here the poet Guillaume Apollinaire created his magazine, *Les Soirées de Paris* (Paris evenings), discussing its content with his close friend Picasso at a rear table. In this café also, the philosophy of Existentialism was born, Jean-Paul Sartre and Simone de Beauvoir theorizing for hours. Albert Camus was an occasional visitor, but rarely sat near Sartre, as the two writers detested each other. The café gained its name from a large figure of Flora, goddess of spring, that originally stood at the door but has not survived.

•• *Return eastward.*

No 170, **Les Deux Magots** The birthplace of Surrealism; an outdoor table facing the church is probably the best place from which to study the history and west façade of St Germain des Prés, particularly on a warm sunny day.

When the building was finished in 1873, it was planned that the ground floor would accommodate a novelty shop, and two large wooden figures of *magots* (Chinese mandarins) were brought here to serve as its sign. At the last moment a bar was opened instead, but the name and sign were kept. The original *deux magots* may now be seen internally, beside the central pillar.

•• *Proceed to the west façade of St Germain des Prés.*

Location 12	**ST GERMAIN DES PRÉS**
Place St Germain des Prés	This is the oldest church in Paris, its nave and towers being the only Romanesque structures of major importance to survive in the capital.

History Childebert returned from Saragossa, Spain, in 542 bearing a fragment of the 'True Cross' and 'St Vincent's tunic'. To house these relics he founded an abbey, which was to become by far the richest and most dominant religious establishment in Paris until Notre Dame itself was built. More than 42,000 acres of land, including what are now the whole of the 6th and 7th arrondissements, were presented to the abbey. Its first church, dedicated to Ste Croix (holy cross) and St Vincent, was consecrated in 558 by Germanus, Bishop of Paris who, on his death in 576, was buried in the church. The building was so splendid that it was known as the 'golden basilica', but all that remains of it are some marble shafts which have been re-used in the chancel.

The church was the necropolis of the Merovingian kings for almost a century; Childebert, d.558, and his successors until Dagobert, d.639, being buried in its St Symphorien Chapel. In 754, Germanus was canonized St Germain and it was then decided to rededicate the church to him; the suffix 'des Prés' (in the meadows) is indicative of its rural situation.

In the 9C, the abbey was to suffer four Norman raids

which, from 845–86, led to considerable damage and
the loss of its treasures. Abbot Morard began the
rebuilding of the church in 990, and the towers
remain from this period. By the 11C, the abbey was
one of the most important of those belonging to the
Benedictine Order, which at that time possessed
several thousand monasteries throughout Europe.
The Romanesque nave and transepts were rebuilt in
the second half of the 11C and a new chancel
followed a century later, being contemporary with
Notre Dame. Gothic features were blended with
Romanesque in a Transitional manner.

In the mid-17C, the south transept and south wall of
the nave were rebuilt and the church vaulted. At the
Revolution, the monastery was dissolved and most of
its domestic buildings, apart from the abbot's palace
and some fragments, demolished. The tombs of the
Merovingian kings disappeared and the abbey's
outstanding library was confiscated. Now secularized,
the former abbey church became a saltpetre factory,
1794–5. Major and generally regrettable restoration
of St Germain took place in the 19C, during which
the twin east towers were needlessly truncated. Vivid
internal murals, in appalling taste (only partly
removed), were mostly the work of **Flandrin**.

Exterior St Germain's west tower, *c.*1000, is the
building's oldest structural feature. This has,
however, undergone several changes: its upper stage
dates from the mid-12C when the chancel was rebuilt.

The Romanesque-style bell chamber, constructed in
the 17C, was renovated and given a pointed roof by
Baltard as part of his mid-19C restoration work.

As the portal of the west front had been badly
damaged, an outer porch was added in 1607, creating
a small narthex (ante-chapel). Its wrought-iron door
is modern.

Stretching southward from the outer porch is the
stone-built **presbytery**, constructed in the 18C.

A bust of Jean Habillon, the Benedictine scholar,
d.1707, is in a niche at the south end of its façade.

•➤ *Follow Boulevard St Germain eastward to view
the south façade of the church.*

Adjoining the presbytery, at its east end, is the
Chapelle St Symphorien, rebuilt in the 17C and
recently restored.

•➤ *Continue eastward to the small courtyard.*

In the mid-17C, the south wall of the nave was
rebuilt, together with the south transept, which was
extended westward by a chapel dedicated to St Maur,
now the Chapelle Ste Marguerite.

Attached to the other side of this transept is the
south-east tower. After they had been built, in the
late 10C, St Germain des Prés was known as the
church of the three bell towers. Like its north
counterpart, this tower was truncated *c.*1840.

A blocked, Romanesque window survives on its
south face.

The small Square Destruelles, which lies between the
church and the boulevard, was the monks' burial

233 / Luxembourg Palace and St Germain des Prés

ground. Here, on 3 September 1792, thugs hired by
the revolutionaries, hacked the members of the
establishment to death following their mock trial,
conducted by the notorious Judge Maillard, who
insisted on their immediate execution.

The monks had been incarcerated in the abbey's
prison, which stood on the site of the Hotel Madison
on the opposite side of the boulevard.

Rebuilt in 1163, the chancel is an early example of
the Gothic style, although it retains some
Romanesque features. Its upper section was removed
in the 19C and much detailing was then lost.

The flying buttresses, added *c.*1200, are among the
earliest in France.

Projecting from the east end of the apse is the Lady
Chapel, rebuilt early in the 19C.

• Return to the west front and enter the outer porch.

Interior The portal ahead, carved in the 12C, lost
most of its detail through 17C vandalism. Only the
damaged *Last Supper* lintel indicates its former
splendour.

*• Enter the **vestibule**.*

Dividing the vestibule from the nave is a modern iron
grille, designed by **Raymond Subes**.

*• Enter the **nave**.*

The vault was constructed in 1646.

*• Proceed to the column in the north-west corner of
the **north aisle**.*

The capital of this column is 11C work; gilded copies,
made by **Baltard** in 1848, replaced the others, all
depicting fabulous beasts, which are now in the
Musée de Cluny.

• Proceed eastward through the centre of the nave.

Murals throughout the church, painted 1854–63, are
the work of **Hippolyte Flandrin**, a pupil of Ingres,
who was assisted in his work by other painters,
including his son Paul and Sébastian Cornu. They are
generally regarded as unsympathetic, to say the least,
and appeals to remove them are frequently made, a
situation analogous to that of the Sainte Chapelle.

*• Proceed to the **north aisle**.*

On the wall of the north aisle, facing the pulpit, is the
monument to Flandrin, d.1864; his bust is by **Oudine.**

*• Proceed to the **north transept**.*

Inset in the north wall is the tomb of John Casimir,
d.1672. Casimir had been King of Poland before
becoming abbot of St Germain in 1669. The
monument is by **J. Thibaud** with figures sculpted by
G. Marsy.

*• Proceed to the centre of the **chancel**.*

Although mid-12C, the arches of the arcade are only
pointed around the apse. The others are still round-
headed, columns are rounded and the elements that
make up the walls also remain entirely Romanesque.

All the capitals of the arcade's columns have been renewed.

Above the arcade, the marble shafts of the triforium's short columns came from the 6C church and are a rare surviving example of Merovingian work in Paris. Their capitals and bases are 12C and contemporary with the rebuilding of the chancel.

Originally pointed, the arches of the triforium were flattened *c.*1646 when the clerestory windows were extended downward to increase light.

•● *Proceed to the **north ambulatory**.*

Fortunately, the 19C murals have recently been removed from the walls of the ambulatory which is, therefore, the least altered part of the chancel.

Iron grilles between the ambulatory and the chancel are modern.

•● *Proceed to the ambulatory's first chapel.*

Within this chapel is the tombstone of William Douglas, 10th Earl of Angus, who was killed in 1611, fighting for Henri IV.

The ambulatory's second chapel accommodates the tomb of poet Nicolas Boileau, d.1711; it was transferred here from the Sainte Chapelle.

•● *Proceed to the second apsidal chapel.*

Blind arcading here is a reproduction.

Grisaille paintings in the Lady Chapel, which was rebuilt in enlarged form in 1819, are by **Heim.**

The fourth apsidal chapel retains part of an original 12C blind arcade in Romanesque style.

Both windows contain mid-13C stained glass.

Three tomb headstones are displayed on the south wall of the south ambulatory's first chapel: Descartes, the philosopher, d.1650; Mabillon, d.1707, and Montfaucon, d.1719, both scholar monks of the abbey. Above them is an 18C bust of Mabillon.

Against the south wall of the next chapel is the tomb of Lord James Douglas, d.1645, a Scottish nobleman who fought for Louis XIII; he was the grandson of William Douglas.

•● *Continue westward to the **south transept**.*

The south transept was extended westward and rebuilt in the 17C to form the Chapelle of St Maur; it is now dedicated to Ste Marguerite.

Against its south wall, the large monument commemorates Oliver de Castellane, d.1664, and Louis Castellane, d.1669, both killed in the king's service; the sculptures are by **Girardon**.

The skylit dome of the nave's most easterly chapel was painted with the *Apotheosis of St Maur* by **Restout** in 1776.

•● *Exit from the church R. First R Rue de l'Abbaye. Immediately R Square Laurent Prache.*

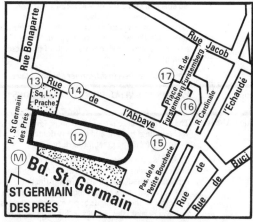

Locations

| Location 13 | **SQUARE LAURENT PRACHE** |

Fragments of St Germain's earlier Lady Chapel, built by **Pierre Montreuil** 1215–55, are displayed. Further remnants are exhibited at the Musée de Cluny.

Stone arches from the monastic Chapter House have been set up against the east wall.

The bronze head of a woman, by **Picasso**, was set up here in 1959 as a monument to the artist's close friend the poet Apollinaire, who died in 1918, aged thirty-eight.

Exit R and cross to the north side of Rue de l'Abbaye.

| Location 14 | **RUE DE L'ABBAYE** |

Following the abbey's dissolution, this street was laid out, immediately north of the church, in 1800 and originally named Rue de la Paix.

Enter the doorway of No 16 (open until 13.30).

Immediately R is part of a large Gothic window with some 13C stonework below it. This is all that survives from the monastic refectory, built by **Montreuil** in 1239. In 1714 the monks constructed a library above it which, during the Revolution, became a gunpowder store. An explosion in 1794 destroyed much of the building, but, surprisingly, most of the manuscripts were saved.

Proceed eastward.

No 13 Remnants of the abbey's main cloister survive. It was built on three floors above an arcade in the 13C and restored in the 17C.

Continue eastward following the north façade of St Germain.

Mostly obscured by later buildings, part of the north transept and the truncated north tower are visible.

Rising behind the modern church offices, at **No 9**, is the chancel, with its flying buttresses.

No 6bis marks the site of **Montreuil's** 13C Lady Chapel. This was badly damaged by the library explosion in 1794 and its remains were demolished in 1800 when the street was constructed. Some stones have been incorporated in the walls of the present building.

•● *Cross the street to the former abbots' palace.*

Location 15	**PALAIS ABBATIAL DE ST GERMAIN DES PRÉS** *1586*
3 Rue de l'Abbaye	The abbots' palace is one of the most important late-16C buildings in Paris and the only domestic building to survive from the great monastery.

Charles de Bourbon, a cardinal and abbot of St Germain des Prés, commissioned this building to replace the medieval palace. He was the uncle of the heir apparent, soon to become Henri IV, and the powerful Catholic League appointed him Charles X in 1589. A year later, however, his nephew, now King, sent him to prison, where he died.

•● *Continue ahead to the Rue Cardinale/Passage de la Petite Boucherie junction.*

When Cardinal Furstemberg laid out Rue Cardinale in 1700 it skirted the monastic tennis court. The street's extension southward, Passage de la Petite Boucherie, now ends at Boulevard St Germain, but before the latter was built many small thoroughfares met at this point. It was then the abbey's place of punishment and a gibbet and pillory stood there permanently; in 1557 two Huguenots were taken to the spot and burnt alive, after having their tongues ripped out. Fortunately, Louis XIII put an end to these macabre activities in 1636.

•● *Continue ahead to (first L) Rue de l'Echaudé.*

The intersection at this point is one of the most picturesque in Paris.

•● *Return westward. First R Rue Cardinale.*

Nos 3–9 are original properties.

•● *L Rue de Furstemberg leads to Place Furstemberg.*

Location 16	**PLACE FURSTEMBERG**

Franz Egon von Furstemberg, Bishop of Strasbourg, supported the French annexation of that city and was appointed a cardinal and abbot of St Germain des Prés. He laid out the square at the south end of the street that now bears his name in 1699. Previously, the area had formed the palace's courtyard.

In the centre of the square are four oriental paulownia trees, which are covered with mauve blossom every spring.

No 4 retains on its south-west corner pillar a sculpted flaming urn, originally part of the entrance arch to the palace's courtyard; the remainder was demolished in 1797.

•● *Cross to the west side of the square and proceed through the courtyard of No 6 to the orange building.*

Location 17   **MUSÉE DELACROIX**

6 Place
Furstemberg

*Open Wednesday–
Monday 09.45–
12.30 and 14.00–
17.15. Admission
charge. Half-price
Sunday.*

The painter Eugène Delacroix lived here from 1857
until his death in 1863. Later, the Impressionist
painter Claude Monet lodged in the house with
Bazille. The building, like its neighbour, No 8, was
converted from a section of the abbey's stables that
stood east and west of the courtyard. Part of
Delacroix's apartment – his bedroom, lounge and a
small library – are shown. Also open are the artist's
studio, which was created in the garden and linked to
the house by an iron staircase. Drawings and sketches
are displayed.

●● *Exit L. First L Rue Furstemberg. L* **Rue Jacob.**

No 7, Galerie Antoinette This was built as the Hôtel
St Paul, in 1640. The seventeen-year-old Racine lived
here with his uncle in 1656.

No 14 A plaque above the door records that Wagner
wrote part of *The Flying Dutchman* here during his
six-month stay, 1841–2.

No 18, Editions Gautier Languereau, possesses
exceptional Art-Deco ironwork, designed in 1928.

No 11, Le Petit Atelier, built in the 15C, now
accommodates an English language school for
children.

Painted rafters on the first floor may be glimpsed
from the street if the room is lit. The house is
occasionally open to visitors, and the exceptional
Louis XIII carved banister may then be seen.

Both this building and its neighbour, **No 13**, possess
good examples of carved keystones above their
doorways.

No 27 The painter Ingres lived here in the 1830s.

●● *Continue ahead. First R Rue Bonaparte.*

Inscribed on the east wall, just before Rue Visconti
(first R), is the original name of the street, Rue des
Petits Augustins, which commemorates the early 17C
monastery.

●● *First R* **Rue Visconti.**

The earlier street name and arrondissement number
survive on the south wall; the thoroughfare was
renamed in 1864 to commemorate the architect.

No 24 A plaque records that Racine spent his last
years here 1692–9.

No 17 Balzac, aged twenty-eight, set up a publishing
house on the ground floor but lost money and had to
sell his printing press. The first work under his own
name, *Les Chouans*, was published from here. The
writer lived on the first floor, later moving to Passy,
where his former rooms are exhibited. An earlier
occupant had been Delacroix, immediately prior to
transferring to Place Furstemberg.

●● *First R Rue de Seine.*

No 36, Chaudin, immediately ahead, and **No 37,
Visconti**, feature works by well-known artists.

●● *Continue southward to Rue de Buci and then
return northward almost to the river.*

•• *Second R Rue Mazarine*.

Nos 10–12 The twenty-one-year-old Molière first
acted at **No 12** which, with the aid of a legacy from his
mother, he built as a theatre in 1643. Stage-struck for
many years, the playwright was able to pursue his
vocation in spite of opposition from his father, who
wanted him to become a lawyer.

Actors lodged next door, at No 10, including
members of the company belonging to Béjart, whose
sister, Armande, was later to marry Molière.

No 28 In this house, in 1822, Jean François
Champollion first deciphered Egyptian hieroglyphics.

No 30 Du Mouriez de Perier, inventor of the water
hose, founded the first Paris fire brigade here in 1722.
De Perier had been a member of the Comédie
Française and once acted as Molière's valet. A
plaque records his death in this house in 1723, but it
does not explain if this was connected in any way with
his other claim to fame, fathering thirty-two children!

No 42 Originally an indoor tennis court, this building
was converted to become the Guénégaud Théâtre,
the first opera in the French language being
performed here in 1671. It was not, however, the
work of the leading French operatic composer Lully
who, being affronted by this supposed snub,
engineered the closure of the company. When
Molière died in 1673, Lully also forced the eviction of
his Comédie Française company from the Palais
Royal. They transferred here and remained until
1689, when the recently opened Collège des Quatre
Nations, disapproving of its proximity, arranged for
their theatre to be closed once more.

At the Carrefour de Buci, with its lively street
market, the thoroughfare becomes **Rue de l'Ancienne
Comédie**.

•• *Continue southward*.

No 14 When the Comédie Française was forced to
leave Rue Mazarine in 1689, they opened here in the
same year with *Phèdre* by **Racine**. Again, the theatre
was built by Molière on a disused tennis court. In
1770, the company once more had to seek new
premises and transferred, under Louis XV's
patronage, to the Tuileries Palace and finally, when it
was completed, the Odéon. Their former occupancy ·
gave this street its present name (see the first-floor
wall plaque).

In the centre of the third floor's façade stands the
figure of *Minerva* by **Le Hongre**.

No 13, Le Procope, founded in 1686 by a Sicilian,
Procopio dei Coltelli, is believed to be the oldest
surviving restaurant in Europe. It soon became a
meeting place for leading writers and politicians;
clients included Napoléon, Victor Hugo, Voltaire,
Oscar Wilde and most of the leaders of the French
Revolution. After being closed for some time, the
restaurant was reopened in 1988, restoration work
sensitively retaining earlier features.

**•• *First L Boulevard St Germain. Cross immediately
to M Odéon on the south side*.**

15

Latin Quarter

The picturesque buildings that form the heart of the
Latin Quarter are the capital's oldest, some of them
retaining cellars dating from the 12C. Visited are the
two most attractive small churches in Paris, St Julien
le Pauvre and St Etienne du Mont, together with the
Panthéon, necropolis of France's illustrious dead.
The Musée de Cluny, the most important medieval
hôtel in the capital, displays works of art from the
Middle Ages and incorporates Roman baths.

Timing: St Julien le Pauvre is closed 13.00–14.30.
St Etienne du Mont, even after restoration, will
probably close Monday and lunchtime.

The mineralogy museum of the Ecole Supérieure
des Mines is closed Sunday and Monday and
mornings Wednesday–Friday.

The Musée de Cluny is closed Tuesday and 12.30–
14.00.

15

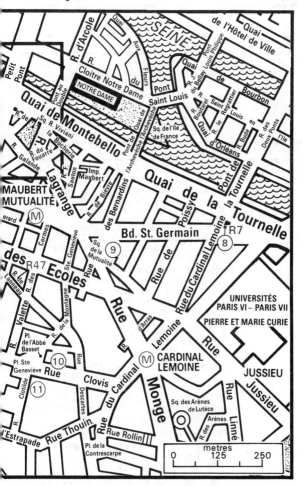

Locations
1 Fontaine St Michel
2 'Little Athens'
3 St Séverin
4 Rue St Jacques
5 Shakespeare and Company
6 St Julien le Pauvre
7 Pont au Double
8 La Tour d'Argent
9 St Nicolas du Chardonnet
10 St Etienne du Mont
11 Lycée Henri IV
12 Panthéon
13 Place du Panthéon
14 Bibliothèque Ste Geneviève
15 Ecole Supérieure des Mines
16 Sorbonne
17 Collège de France
18 Musée de Cluny

Start *M St Michel, line 4, Porte de Clignancourt/Porte d'Orléans. Exit from the station and proceed to the fountain on the south side of Place St Michel.*

Location 1	**FONTAINE ST MICHEL** *Davioud 1860*

Place St Michel — Created in the Second Empire, like the Place itself, this fountain, at the south end, incorporates an inscription (beneath the griffins) commemorating the students' resistance to the German occupying forces as the Allied armies approached Paris in August 1944.

●● *Cross to the east side of Boulevard St Michel L. First R Rue de la Huchette.*

Location 2	**'LITTLE ATHENS'**

Greek restaurants have for long monopolized the warren of ancient streets around St Séverin church. The area, however, retains its picturesque appeal and is extremely lively in the evening, particularly at weekends.

Although, technically, the 'Latin Quarter' covers much of the Left Bank, its heart has always been regarded as the area around the churches of St Séverin and St Julien le Pauvre. Rabelais, in the early 16C, appears to have been the first to coin the name 'Latin' for the quarter, which had previously been known as L'Université – he was referring to the Latin language that was then still used for normal conversation by the university students.

In the mid-19C, Haussmann isolated the quarter by creating the boulevards St Michel and St Germain and widening Rue St Jacques.

Rue de la Huchette was formerly called Rue des Rôtisseurs, the name referring to the roasting of oxen in the thoroughfare during the Middle Ages; it is a strange coincidence that this tradition of spit-roasting here has been renewed, albeit behind the restaurants' windows rather than in the street itself.

Haussmann widened Rue de la Huchette's west entry, which is why some of the houses at this point are 19C; more demolition was planned, but fortunately not executed, and most buildings pre-date the 18C.

●● *Continue ahead following Rue de la Huchette eastward.*

No 23, Théâtre de la Huchette, is the smallest theatre in Paris, accommodating an audience of eighty-five and specializing in the works of Eugène Ionesco.

No 14 The monogram of the builder of this 17C house, DC, is incorporated in its wrought-iron balcony. Painted on the plaster between the first-floor windows at the west end is the letter Y, a complicated pun that indicated a haberdashery.

●● *First L Rue du Chat qui Pêche.*

This street, 6 feet wide, is the narrowest in Paris; its name (fishing cat) refers to an earlier shop sign. Built in the 16C, and then much wider, as No 12 Rue de la Huchette had not yet been constructed, it was formerly called Rue des Etuves (steam baths). Mixed nude bathing was permitted in the establishments and, as can be imagined, there were some 'naughty' goings-on; these eventually led to the baths' closure.

●● *Continue eastward following Rue de la Huchette.*

No 10 In 1795 this was a small hotel where Napoléon, then the equivalent of a Brigadier-General, but soon to gain power, lodged in a back room overlooking the Seine. His next riverside address was to be the Tuileries Palace!

No 4 The façade of this 17C house, remodelled in the 18C, is decorated with masks and its sign '*à la Hure d'Or*' (golden pig's-head), of 1792, is still displayed beneath the third mask.

No 5, Caveau de la Huchette This has long been a popular venue for Traditional Jazz enthusiasts. Its cellars, which are much older than the part-16C superstructure, are alleged to have provided a meeting place for the Knights Templar in the 13C, when a subterranean passageway led to the Petit Châtelet prison nearby.

●● *Return westward. First L Rue Xavier Privas. First L Rue St Séverin.*

Surprisingly, although still narrow, **Rue St Séverin** was evidently widened in 1678.

No 24, immediately L, with its corner rounded-off, retains the old inscription 'Rue Séverin 18', above the present street sign, indicating that the prefix 'St' was removed, as was common during the anti-Christian period of the Revolution; the arrondissement number of 18 is now that of Montmartre.

No 22, with its 8-foot frontage, one of the narrowest in Paris, was the residence of Abbé Prévost, d.1763, author of *Manon Lescaut*.

●● *Return westward and continue ahead. First L **Rue de la Harpe**.*

Only one-third of this street, once the quarter's most important, survives, the remainder being lost in the 19C when Boulevard St Michel was laid out over its southern stretch. In the 10C, synagogues and schools were built in the street for Jews who had moved into the area. Rue de la Harpe has had no fewer than fourteen recorded names, the present appellation referring to a sign depicting David playing the harp, which once stood outside the premises of a harp-maker.

No 35, an elegant 18C hôtel, retains the outline of its *porte cochère* (coach entrance) although this has been filled. Within the courtyard, the staircase R has a fine iron banister.

No 45 is another good examplè of an 18C hôtel.

●● *Return northward. First R Rue de la Parcheminerie. First L Rue des Prêtres St Séverin.*

Location 3	**ST SÉVERIN**
1 Rue des Prêtres St Séverin *Open Monday–Saturday 11.00–19.30. Also Friday and Saturday 21.00–22.30; Sunday 09.00–20.00.*	Parts of St Séverin, the Left Bank students' parish church, survive from the 13C, but its chancel's 15C 'palm tree' ambulatory is the building's most important architectural feature. Attached to the church is a medieval charnel house, unique in Paris. **History** In the 6C the land here was a dry patch surrounded by swamp. Séverin, a hermit renowned for his piety, lived on it and persuaded Cleodald (later St Cloud), the grandson of Clovis, to take holy orders.

15

Shortly after Séverin's death, an oratory was erected to his memory by Childebert I. A chapel and several churches dedicated to St Séverin, replaced this, one being burnt down and another demolished by the Vikings, who were soon to settle in Normandy. St Séverin became, for a while, the necropolis of the Merovingian dynasty.

A new building was established by Henri I in the 11C as the parish church of the Left Bank, and traces of this form the oldest parts of the present structure. From its pulpit, in the 12C, Foulques de Neuilly inspired the Fourth Crusade.

By the early 13C, work had begun on a larger church, parts of which survive in the present St Séverin; however, this and subsequent buildings were never completed in any uniform style, due to long interruptions caused by the lack of finance.

An outer south aisle was added c.1350, but a disastrous fire in the first half of the 15C destroyed it, together with most of the rest of the church. By 1450, the nave and its aisles had been rebuilt and work on a completely new outer north aisle begun. This new aisle and the rebuilt chancel, with its ambulatory, were completed by 1496 and chapels were then added.

The volatile 'Grande Mademoiselle' de Montpensier, cousin of Louis XIV, quarrelled with the curate of St Sulpice in 1681 and transferred her loyalty to St Séverin. At her expense, much unsuitable remodelling of the chancel, in Renaissance style, was put in hand.

In the 19C, the composer Saint-Saëns often played St Séverin's organ at Sunday vespers.

Exterior Although the west front was started as late as c.1212, the Romanesque style was followed to begin with, probably in deference to the earlier building.

Originally, the main entrance to the church was via the north side of the north tower; the present west portal, although also early 13C and Romanesque, was not added until 1839, the year in which St Pierre-aux-Boeufs, from whence it came, was demolished.

Figures in its tympanum are modern.

All detailing above balustrade level changes to Flamboyant Gothic.

Extending southward is the outer south aisle, rebuilt in 1450.

Although the north-west tower's lower stage is early 13C most of the rest of it was rebuilt in 1487.

•➤ *Proceed to the north-west corner of the church. First R Rue St Séverin.*

Serving as the main entry to the church until 1839, the tower's north portal is early 13C, but its tympanum was recarved in 1853.

Standing in a niche at the east end of the outer aisle is a statue of St Séverin. This aisle was added in 1496 and its chapels formed 1498–1520.

•➤ *Continue eastward.*

At the east end of the aisle is the sacristy, added in the 16C and extended eastward in 1646.

First R Rue St Jacques. Cross the road to view the chancel.

The buttressed chancel, wth its chapels and double ambulatory, had been entirely rebuilt by 1495.

Extending southward from the chancel's east end is the circular Communion Chapel, added by **Hardouin-Mansart** in 1673; this is followed by the remains of ossuaries, built *c.*1500, which will be seen more closely later.

First R Rue de la Parcheminerie. First R Rue des Prêtres St Séverin.

The three most westerly bays of the nave are 13C, the remainder were rebuilt in the mid-15C.

Enter R the old graveyard, now a garden, via the gate south of the west end of the outer south aisle.

St Séverin's graveyard had become overcrowded by 1500, and the bones of the occupants were dug up and placed in caskets, which were kept in newly built charnel house ossuaries, now sometimes incorrectly referred to as cloisters.

Enter the church from the west front and proceed to the west end of the nave.

Interior St Séverin's disproportionate width to its height, immediately apparent, evolved because expansion of the building was possible only to the north and south; outer aisles and ambulatories were therefore added.

The first three bays of the **nave**, built early in the 13C in the Flamboyant Gothic style, retain Romanesque elements; their columns are still short and circular and the arches are almost round-headed.

Cloverleaf capitals, half-way up the shafts, are the finest in the church.

Upper windows in the first three bays incorporate late-14C glass, unique in Paris, which depicts the Apostles; this came from the chancel of St Germain des Près. The remainder of the nave's upper windows are 15C. Originally, both the triforia were blind, but glass was inserted on the north side in the 19C.

Fire destroyed the rest of the 13C nave and it was rebuilt in the mid-15C. Again, the Flamboyant style was adopted, but detailing is greatly inferior to the earlier work; for example, the columns have no capitals and the tracery of the triforium is fussy.

Fluting was added to the columns of the rebuilt bays as part of the 17C Renaissance 'improvements' instigated by the 'Grande Mademoiselle'.

The organ's Rococo case was built by **François Dupré** in 1745; figures are by **Jean-François Pichon**.

*Proceed to the **outer north aisle**.*

Flamboyant 15C vaulting to the aisle is exceptional.

Continue to the second north chapel.

The porphyry altar was presented by Madame de Montespan, mistress of Louis XIV.

A 17C painting of St Luke hangs above the altar.

In the next chapel's window the murder of St Thomas

à Becket is depicted; the future archbishop of
Canterbury studied briefly in Paris.

*●● Proceed to the **chancel**.*

Columns around the sanctuary were faced with red
marble and three of the pointed Gothic arches were
rounded; all was the 17C work of **Le Brun**.

The 18C wooden high altar is a composite piece.

*●● Return to the **outer north aisle**.*

Above the first doorway L is a 15C Crucifixion relief.

A 17C painting of St Paul decorates the wall above
the door to the sacristy.

The **double ambulatory**'s late-15C star vault is the
outstanding feature of St Séverin. It is contemporary
with, and reminiscent of, Perpendicular work in
England. Ribs descend to the bases of many of the
columns' shafts giving them their 'palm grove'
appellation. On request, an attendant will illuminate
the area.

*●● Continue to the south-west end of the **chancel's
ambulatory**.*

The first five most easterly columns of the outer south
aisle's arcade are 13C and survived the fire; they
originally formed part of the south wall of the church.

●● Exit R. First R Rue St Séverin.

No 12 possesses an original 17C panelled door.

●● Continue ahead to Rue St Jacques (first R).

Location 4	**RUE ST JACQUES**

Pilgrimages from Paris to the shrine of St Jacques
(James), at Santiago de Compostela in Spain, began
at the Tour St Jacques and then, after crossing the Ile
de la Cité, continued southward along this street,
which received its present name in 1230. Most of Rue
St Jacques was widened by Haussmann, and its
buildings of greatest interest, including Val de Grâce,
lie at the south end (see page 274).

*●● Follow the northern continuation of the street, **Rue
du Petit Pont** L. Proceed ahead to the Rue de la
Bûcherie intersection (first R).*

At its north end, Rue du Petit Pont becomes Place du
Petit Pont and the **Petit Pont** crosses the Seine. The
present bridge, rebuilt in 1853, stands on the site of
the first structure to link the Ile de la Cité with the
mainland. That had been built of wood by the
Romans, and erected here because it was the Seine's
narrowest point.

●● Follow Rue de la Bûcherie eastward.

The small park L was created in the 1920s; it had
once been part of the site of the Petit Châtelet
fortress demolished in 1782.

No 39, Le Petit Châtelet Now a restaurant, this early-
16C timber-framed building previously operated as
an inn of the same name. Its cellars are reputed to be
12C. Until cleared in 1909, hospital buildings stood
between this property and the river.

Location 5	**SHAKESPEARE AND COMPANY**

37 Rue de la Bûcherie

Open daily 12.00–24.00 including Christmas Day!

For long a Paris institution, this shop sells new and second-hand English books, claiming to have the largest second-hand stock on the continent. The name commemorates another bookshop, also called Shakespeare, that stood in the Rue de l'Odéon prior to the Second World War. Its personable owner, George Whitman, a distant relative of the famous American columnist Walter Whitman (see the wall plaque R), hosts Monday poetry readings at 20.00 and Sunday tea parties 16.00–18.00 (by invitation).

High on the wall, east of the roof of No 39, is one of only three open staircases to survive in Paris. In the 17C, it was decreed that henceforth they had to be enclosed.

The front room was created in the original courtyard; stairs lead to smaller rooms and browsers are welcome.

•● *First R Rue St Julien le Pauvre.*

No 14, The Tea Caddy Built as stables for the adjoining house L this tea shop was founded here in 1928 by Miss Kinklin, a retired English lady. She had served as a governess to a member of the Rothschild family for many years and was presented with the property on her retirement. Teas and snacks are still served.

No 16 Dating from the 15C, this house, timber-framed beneath its plaster, became the residence of Isaac Lafférmas, Richelieu's prefect of police and the King's prosecutor, early in the 17C. He added the important stone entrance; its tympanum's carving of Justice holding the scale reflects his legal responsibilities.

Three 14C floors survive below the present ground level, which provided accommodation for the Longport Priory monks from St Julien's. Later they served as a prison, which was disused in the 17C but revived during the Revolution.

•● *Proceed to St Julien le Pauvre.*

Location 6	**ST JULIEN LE PAUVRE**

1 Rue St Julien le Pauvre

Open daily 09.00–13.00 and 14.30–18.30.

This, many people's favourite small Parisian church, is contemporary with Notre Dame, and the oldest surviving example to have been built within the city walls. 'Old Paris' is possibly best represented in the picturesque streets that surround it, and the view of Notre Dame from Square René Viviani, and of St Séverin from Rue Galande, are outstanding.

History St Julien was founded in the late 6C, Bishop Gregory of Tours officiating at Mass in 587. The present church, which was built *c.*1160–*c.*1220, originally belonged to Longport Priory. From 1208, Paris University assembled in St Julien, where its rectors were elected and its teachers biannually reconfirmed the students' rights.

Disturbances in 1524, during which the building was badly damaged by students, led to the ending of the close association between the church and the university, whose members were henceforth barred. Due to this damage, St Julien was forced to close and fell into disrepair. By 1651, with its west end on the point of collapse, a third of the nave was demolished and a new west front built. When Longport Priory was suppressed in 1655 the church became the chapel of the Hôtel-Dieu, the great medieval hospital that stood on the Ile de la Cité, and restoration was put in hand.

Since 1889, St Julien has been a Malachite church and services are held in Greek and Arabic for eastern Catholics. Visitors are welcome to attend Sunday services, which include splendid deep-pitched singing from the male choir.

Exterior The present west front was built in 1651, the 13C nave's original west front and two most westerly bays having been demolished due to their instability.

Sections of colonettes that remain formed part of the original west front's portal.

•● *Enter the courtyard.*

The north aisle's two west bays L were retained and their arches filled to form the sacristy.

Traces of one bay of the gallery, at upper level, survive.

Beside the wall, in the corner, is a Roman paving slab, discovered beneath Rue St Jacques in 1927; originally, it had formed part of the road to Orléans.

•● *Exit from the courtyard L and follow the passage to the wall ahead.*

This fragment of Philippe Auguste's wall incorporates another Roman paving slab.

•● *Follow Square René Viviani to view the north façade of the church.*

The nave and both aisles were completed in the first half of the 13C.

Work began as usual at the east end, but although the chancel was constructed 1160–80, only the east windows are round-headed.

East of the apse, a stone arch marks the site of a medieval well, the water from which allegedly possessed curative properties.

Square René Viviani, a rare Parisian riverside park, was created after the demolition, in 1877, of a three-storey sick bay, built as an extension to the Hôtel-Dieu, which stood across the river.

•● *Return to the west front and enter the church.*

Interior The barrel-vault and clerestory of the **nave** were originally much higher, but the nave's walls were lowered and windows inserted at the former triforium level *c.* 1651.

Arches of the nave's early-13C arcades are round-headed.

The original Gothic vault survives in the **north aisle**.

Fixed to the north wall, in the third bay from the west, is a 13C bas-relief Crucifixion scene, which came from an early chapel of the Hôtel-Dieu.

Although completed by 1180, almost fifty years before the nave's arcades, the arches of the **chancel**'s arcades are already pointed.

The capitals of both columns of the chancel are exceptional examples of Romanesque work. Mythical harpies (rapacious winged women) decorate the famous capital of the south column.

Dominating the interior is the wooden iconostasis of 1901 that screens the **sanctuary**.

The vault of the nave's **south aisle** was rebuilt in the 19C.

Fixed vertically below the aisle's central window is a 15C tombstone.

•● *Exit from the church L to* **Rue Galande** *(first L). Immediately ahead is No 75.*

Originally the Roman road to Lyon, this thoroughfare was named Garlande in 1202 to commemorate an important land-owner; it was later corrupted to its present name.

No 75 possesses exposed timbers. .

•● *Turn L and proceed eastward.*

No 52 is the front part of the building which accommodates the **Caveau des Oubliettes**; photographs are displayed of the medieval cellars which, it is claimed, once formed part of the Petit Châtelet's prison.

No 52 Small carved figures of Quasimodo, Hugo's *Hunchback of Notre Dame*, decorate the upper corners of the second door and windows.

No 65 Built in the 16C, this house has been restored as apartments. Above its door the carved, garlanded head of a woman is original. The gabled roof is one of only thirty to survive in Paris; they were prohibited by law in the 16C due to damp problems caused by the rainwater that collected between them.

No 46, **Auberge des Deux Signes** (inn with two signs) Converted from a coal/firewood merchant's to a restaurant, the owner of this 16C house made a voyage of discovery in 1969. At the rear he uncovered a large 14C window with Flamboyant tracery and a stone vault, which proved to be a remnant of the Chapelle St Blaise, the remainder of which had been demolished in 1770.

An ancient wall was found L of the window.

Below, also at the rear, and approached by a stone spiral staircase, a large 13C vaulted room was discovered which, it is believed, once served as a dormitory for 100 monks from St Julien le Pauvre. If convenient (i.e. outside busy restaurant periods) friendly staff welcome interested visitors.

No 42 Attached to the wall of this house is the oldest 'sign' in Paris. Made in the 13C for insertion above the doorway of St Julien le Pauvre, the bas-relief depicts the saint and his wife ferrying Christ, disguised as a leper, across the river. Its existence at the church is recorded as early as 1380.

•● *First L Rue du Fouarre leads to Rue Lagrange. Ahead Pont au Double.*

The present Pont au Double replaced a 17C structure in 1885. It had been built originally to link the Hôtel-Dieu on the Ile de la Cité with its extensions on the Left Bank. The hospital levied a toll of a *double tournois* coin to cross the bridge, which is how it gained its name. Westward, between the south side of this bridge and the next, Petit Pont, are the famous riverside bookstalls of the **Quai Montebello**.

Stall No 103, just west of Pont au Double, is renowned for its leatherbound volumes, many of which are antique.

•● *Return to Rue Lagrange. First L Rue de la Bûcherie (eastern continuation).*

No 15 The present buildings were begun in 1472 for the Faculty of Medicine.

The circular building L was adapted in 1744 to provide the Amphithéâtre Winslow, a three-storey chamber in which demonstrations were given to medical students.

No 9 The courtyard retains an open staircase, and a blocked well in the corner L.

•● *First R Rue Frédéric Sauton. First L* **Impasse Maubert**.

No 7, Galerie Nostradamus, a stable in the Middle Ages, was restored and remodelled in the late 1960s. Its ancient staircase is enclosed in timber and plaster.

No 8 Probably built in the 15C, this is another rare Paris example of a gabled house.

•● *Return to Rue Frédéric Sauton R.*

No 1 Rue Frédéric Sauton has a small but picturesque inner courtyard of stone and timber.

•● *First R Rue des Grands Degrés leads to Quai de la Tournelle. Proceed to* **Rue de Bièvre** *(first R).*

Barred at both ends and heavily policed, this short street, in spite of appearances, is not out of bounds to pedestrians. The reason for the security is that **No 22** is the private residence of François Mitterrand. Apparently, the President of France still prefers to sleep here rather than at the Elysée Palace. The building is otherwise of no particular interest.

•● *Continue eastward following Quai de la Tournelle to the Rue des Bernardins corner (first R).*

Running northward from the quay along much of the east side of Rue des Bernardins is a covered early-16C arcade, unique in Paris.

No 57 was built in the early-17C as the Hôtel de Nesmond.

No 47, Musée de l'Assistance Publique, occupies the Hôtel Martin, built in 1630. A bayonet forge was established here during the Revolution. *Open Wednesday–Sunday 10.00–17.00 (closed August)*, this museum displays the history of public health care in Paris. (Admission charge.)

•● *Continue eastward to La Tour d'Argent restaurant on the corner of Rue du Cardinal Lemoine (third R).*

● *Alternatively, follow Rue des Bernardins and proceed northward to location 16.*

Location 8	**LA TOUR D'ARGENT**

No 15 Quai de la Tournelle

Founded on the same site in 1582, but rebuilt after its destruction at the Revolution, this is the only long-established great Paris restaurant that is still generally rated to be among the capital's gastronomic leaders (see page 295). It is said that Henri III used a fork for the first time at the establishment's earlier premises and that the same King ennobled the patron for his superb heron pies. La Tour d'Argent is renowned for its pressed duck and the romantic views of Notre Dame from the fourth-floor restaurant's windows.

A **Petit Musée de la Table** is open to clients.

Products used or prepared by the restaurant are sold from the emporium opposite.

● *Exit and follow Quai de Tournelle estward to Pont de Sully (first L).*

Facing the bridge, on the Boulevard St Germain corner, is the **Institut du Monde Arabe**, by **Jean Nouvelle**, 1987. Its museum, approached from Rue des Fosses St Bernard, describes many aspects of Islamic civilization. Open Tuesday-Sunday 13.00–20.00.

● *Exit L Boulevard St Germain. Fourth L Rue des Bernardins.*

Location 9	**ST NICOLAS DU CHARDONNET**

23 Rue des Bernardins

Although St Nicolas was built in the second half of the 17C, its Neo-Classical south front was added as recently as 1930. Internally, the extravagant monuments by **Charles Le Brun** to his mother, and by **Coysevox** to Le Brun are outstanding.

A chapel dedicated to St Bernard stood in the *chardon* (thistle) fields, belonging to the abbey of St Victor; this was rebuilt in 1243 and its dedication changed to St Nicolas. In 1625, a tower was added. The body of the church was reconstructed, in enlarged form, 1656–1709. The chancel, transept and one bay of the nave were built on part of the old graveyard. In 1977, the church witnessed a 'sit-in' by supporters of the traditionalist Archbishop Lefèbvre.

The wooden west door, facing Rue des Bernardins, was designed by **Le Brun**, a parishioner.

Rising from the south-west corner L, is the bell tower of 1625.

● *First L Square de la Mutualité.*

When the south front was rebuilt in 1930, the Neo-Classical style was adopted.

● *Enter the church from its south front.*

The high altar stands at the north end.

Internally, there are paintings by members of the French School, including **Claude**, **Corot** and **Coypel**, and carving and stucco work by **Nicolas Legendre**.

In the south loft, the organ and its case were originally made in 1725 for the Church of the Innocents.

•● *Proceed to the fourth chapel of the **west ambulatory**.*

Chapelle St Charles Against the window stands the monument to Charles Le Brun, d.1690, and his wife, by **Coysevox**.

On the south wall is the monument designed by **Le Brun** for his mother, who is shown emerging in prayer from her coffin to the call of an angel. The work was carved by **Jean-Baptiste Tuby** and **Jean Collignon**.

•● *Proceed to the **east ambulatory**.*

In the second chapel from the south is the monument to Jérôme Bignon, d.1656, by **Anguier** and **Girardon**.

•● *Exit R Square de la Mutualité. First L Rue des Bernardins. First R Rue des Ecoles. First L Rue de la Montaigne Ste Geneviève.*

At the south end of the street Vietnamese restaurants abound; in one of them the young Ho Chi Minh was employed to wash dishes.

•● *Continue up the hill, following the fork R, to Place de l'Abbé Basset which leads to Place Ste Geneviève.*

Location 10	ST ÉTIENNE DU MONT

Place Ste Geneviève

For some years, during extensive restoration, opening hours have been severely restricted; this situation is expected to continue at least until the early 1990s. Even when the work is completed it seems likely that the church will still close at lunchtime and on Mondays.

This early-16C church combines Gothic and Renaissance features in an engaging manner. To many, St Etienne, with its unique rood screen, possesses the most pleasing church interior in Paris.

History This parish church stands in the former grounds of the Abbey of Ste Geneviève, which was founded by Clovis and his consort Clotilde in the 6C.

Initially, local peasants and abbey servants were allowed to worship in the crypt of St Geneviève Abbey's great monastic church, which stood nearby, but in 1211 the abbey provided them with their own building.

By 1492, St Etienne (Stephen) had become too small, due to the expansion of the nearby university, and the present building was commissioned. Work began in the Gothic style, with the chancel and north-west bell tower, but became Renaissance as it progressed. Consecration took place in 1626. At the Revolution, the church became a Temple of Filial Piety and escaped serious damage. Restoration by **Baltard** took place in the mid-19C.

Exterior The ornate west front was designed by **Claude Guérin**, and its cornerstone laid by Marguerite de Valois in 1610; construction took twelve years.

Unusually, three pediments are superimposed, that in the centre being rounded.

All the statues and reliefs are 19C additions or replacements.

Flanking the door are figures of St Etienne L and St Geneviève R.

The north bell tower, completed by *c.*1540, is believed to incorporate stonework from its 13C predecessor.

●● Proceed to Place de l'Abbé Basset to view the north façade.

Exceptionally high aisles were added to the uncompleted nave from 1568.

The north transept was not finished until 1630.

●● Ahead, Rue St Etienne du Mont passes the north side of the church. R Rue Descartes. Proceed to Rue Clovis (first R).

From the junction can be seen a stretch of Philippe Auguste's 12C wall on the south side of Rue Clovis. Originally it was 33 feet high and crenellated.

●● First R Rue Clovis.

Protruding eastward from the apse of the church is the semi-circular Lady Chapel, added in 1660.

Flamboyant Gothic tracery decorates the exterior of the chancel, which was completed by 1540.

●● Return to the west front (passing L the Tour Clovis, described later) and enter the church. NB restoration work may, for some time, necessitate entering St Etienne from Rue Clovis.

Interior Internal cleaning has recently revealed the original pale gold colour of the stonework. The lack of a triforium emphasizes the Renaissance influence in the **nave**. Instead, narrow, double-balustraded galleries that were once hung with tapestries link the pillars.

Most of St Etienne's surviving stained glass was made in the 16C and 17C.

At the west end is the organ case, made by **Jean Buron** in 1632.

Facing the entrance, between the two most westerly piers of the nave, a floor slab bears a Latin inscription '3 January 1857 IN PACE'. This marks the spot and date on which Archbishop Sibour of Paris was stabbed to death by a defrocked priest.

*●● Proceed to the **crossing**.*

The **north transept**'s stained glass comprises reassembled fragments from a *Revelations* window of 1614.

An 18-foot-long keystone, suspended from the crossing, is carved with the Agnus Dei.

Dividing the Gothic chancel from the Renaissance-influenced nave is the *jubé* (rood screen), the only example to survive in Paris. In the Middle Ages every major church had a similar screen, which stood beneath the rood loft. However, as in England, most were demolished because they obscured much of the service from the congregation. St Etienne's *jubé* was due to be removed in 1737 but conservationist parishioners won the day because, as they pointed out, the unusually wide arch already permitted a clear view.

The central, Renaissance section was probably designed by **Antoine Beaucorps** and built 1521–45.

The side doorways, which are more Classical in style,

were added by **Pierre Biard** in 1609. A plaque, L of
the south doorway, refers to this work.

•● *Follow the **north ambulatory**.*

Stained glass in many of the chapels, by **Pinaigrier**,
was made in 1568; it is the oldest in the church.

The **Lady Chapel**, at the east end, is decorated with
paintings by **Largillière**, 1696.

Buried beside the north column is Jean Racine,
d.1699; his tomb was transferred here from Port-
Royal-des-Champs in 1711.

Blaise Pascal, d.1662, is buried beside the south
column.

•● *Proceed to the sacristy, which lies immediately
south of the Lady Chapel, pass the bookstall and
continue to the **charnier** (charnel house).*

This cloister-like gallery, begun in 1605, originally
surrounded a small burial ground that stood east of
the church, and to which, after his fall from favour,
the body of Marat was transferred from the
Panthéon. As the name implies, the gallery may once
have served as a charnel house.

Glazing of the twelve windows was completed in 1609
and most of the stained glass is by **Léonard Gautier**.
Some older fragments, however, are incorporated.

Facing the gallery is the Catechism Chapel, added by
Baltard in 1861.

•● *Return to the **ambulatory** L and proceed to the
second chapel.*

At the Revolution (1793) Ste Geneviève's remains
were burnt in the Place de Grève (now Place de
l'Hôtel de Ville). A small relic was recovered and is
kept in a casket on the south wall. The gilded copper
shrine was made in 1853.

Ste Geneviève died *c*.500 and her tombstone L was
discovered when the remains of the abbey church,
apart from its tower, were demolished in 1803, for
the construction of Rue Clovis.

•● *Proceed to the **south aisle** of the nave and continue
to its second chapel from the east.*

Between this and the next chapel, a plaque
commemorates the Jacobins, preaching friars who
were established in the Rue Jacques in the 13C.

A 17C terracotta *Entombment* scene stands in the
next chapel.

Stained glass of 1586 illustrates the parable of *Those
invited to the feast*.

The pulpit, of 1650, supported by a figure of Samson,
was designed by a **Germain Pilon** who is not to be
confused with the great 16C sculptor of the same
name. Figures were carved by **Claude Lestocart** from
designs by **Laurent de la Hire**.

•● *Exit from the west front L. Cross Rue Clovis to its
south side and enter the courtyard, immediately
ahead, of Lycée Henri IV.*

Location 11	**LYCÉE HENRI IV**

28 Rue Clovis

The courtyard may be entered only during term time. The chapel (former monastic refectory) is open only for lecture tours in French, Sunday at 11.00. Admission charge (relatively high).

The Lycée retains vestiges of the great abbey of Ste Geneviève, which includes the medieval church tower and refectory, together with the 18C cloister.

Clovis and his consort Clotilde founded the abbey c.510, erecting a great basilica in which they were eventually to be buried close to St Geneviève. Dissolved at the Revolution, the abbey's buildings have been occupied by the Lycée since 1789.

The courtyard was formerly the abbey's cloister. Preferring the Classical style, the monastic authorities rebuilt most of the cloister's Gothic buildings, including the library, in 1746.

Retained, however, was the 13C refectory R, with its large quatrefoil windows; this now serves as the Lycée's chapel.

Rising from the north-east corner is the Tour Clovis, all that remains of the great monastic church of Ste Geneviève. This bell tower dates from c.1180, when the 6C church, erected by Clovis, was rebuilt.

It retains an original Romanesque window at lower level.

In addition to the bell tower, the body of the monastic church survived, albeit in a ruinous condition, until 1803, when it was demolished for the construction of Rue Clovis.

•● *Exit from the courtyard L. First L Rue Clotilde.*

Facing the street is the west façade of the 13C refectory.

•● *Proceed clockwise around the Panthéon to its west front, facing Place du Panthéon.*

Location 12	**PANTHÉON** *Soufflot 1759–90*

Place du Panthéon

Open daily April–September 10.00–18.00; October–March 10.00–12.30 and 14.00–17.30.

Admission charge includes access to the crypt and the dome. The ground floor can be viewed only partially until 1991 at the earliest, due to major restoration. For the same reason, the entrance is temporarily at the east end rather than the usual west end.

The Panthéon is no longer a church but a necropolis for France's illustrious dead, although most of the country's military heroes, including Napoléon, lie in the Dôme church at Invalides. Amongst those buried in the crypt are Louis Braille, Victor Hugo, Jean-Jacques Rousseau, Voltaire and Emile Zola.

History In gratitude for his recovery from a serious illness in 1744, Louis XV honoured his pledge to build a new church for the abbey of Ste Geneviève. The architectural competition for it was won by **Jacques-Germain Soufflot**, a close friend of the Marquis de Marigny, superintendent of the royal buildings.

It was decided that the new building would be constructed slightly to the west of the existing church, on the summit of the Mont de Paris (Mont Ste Geneviève), the highest point on the Left Bank and allegedly the Saint's first resting place. The remains of St Geneviève and her gold shrine were to be transferred to the new building. Colleges on the hill were demolished in 1756 and the site prepared. Roman claypits posed a problem for the foundations, but these were completed by 1758 and Louis XV laid the building's cornerstone in 1764. However, in spite of the royal support, more funds were needed and in 1774, with only the portico ready, lotteries were held to provide them.

Soufflot had designed the church to a Greek Cross plan, with a central dome, but like Wren at St Paul's, the architect made repeated amendments to his design as work progressed. In 1781, **Soufflot** died but work continued under the supervision of his pupil, **Rondelet**, and was completed in 1789. However, the revolutionaries dissolved the Augustinian Order, to which the abbey of Ste Geneviève belonged, and the church was closed almost as soon as it had opened. The Marquis de Villette proposed in 1791 that the building should become a necropolis for great Frenchmen, and after the death of Mirabeau that year, the Constituent Assembly put his suggestion into effect. An art critic, Quatramère de Quincy, who named the building '*panthéon français*', was appointed to superintend its adaptation. All Christian references were removed and most windows blocked to provide a more 'appropriate' gloom. Voltaire was the first to be buried in its crypt.

For almost a century, the building's function alternated between that of a church and a secular necropolis, changes which affected its appearance.

Exterior Columns, 72 feet high, support the west front's portico; these are of reinforced concrete, a material that was used here for the first time in Paris. Nowhere better than on the pediment of this portico have the many functional changes of the Panthéon been portrayed.

When completed, in 1790, its bas-relief depicted a cross and angels. Revolutionaries replaced this in 1791 with *France Crowning Virtue and Crushing Despotism* and an inscription, '*Aux grands hommes la Patrie reconnaissante*' (the country remembers its great men) was added.

Napoléon, in 1806, decreed that the building should once more become a church, although its crypt was to continue to serve as a mausoleum.

In 1823, Louis XVIII replaced the dedication with one to St Geneviève and Louis XV.

Louis-Philippe decided in 1831 that the Panthéon should again be a secular necropolis and the pediment gained its present form; the original inscription was restored, and a new bas-relief commissioned from **David d'Angers**.

Next but one to the L of the figure of France stands Mirabeau. Voltaire, turning his head, is seated. Napoléon R leads his troops.

However, in 1851, although the pediment remained unchanged, Louis-Napoléon instructed that the building should be regarded as the national basilica. In 1870, during the Third Republic, it lost this status and in 1871 the building became briefly the headquarters of the Commune. After the burial here of Victor Hugo in 1885 the Panthéon regained its position as the national necropolis.

A huge dome, to rival St Peter's in Rome and St

Paul's in London, had been envisaged but, as was frequently the case in Paris, the scheme was greatly modified. In 1778, work began on the dome's drum; however, one of the columns cracked in 1780 and the supports had to be strengthened. It was hardly surprising, therefore, that the death of **Soufflot** the following year was attributed to stress brought on by his fear that the structure would collapse.

The iron-framed dome has three shells, like that of the Dôme church at Invalides. Surmounting the structure is a cross, which was removed every time the building became secularized.

The main entrance to the Panthéon will revert to the west front when reconstruction work has been completed in the early 1990s.

● Follow Rue Cujas, which skirts the north façade.

The north and south façades of the Panthéon are identical. Originally, tall windows stood between the columns but these were blocked by **De Quincey** in 1791.

At the east end, the vestibule was added in the 19C to provide a sheltered entrance to the crypt, which extends beneath the entire building.

Upper sections of the north and south flanking towers were removed by **De Quincey**.

Some of **Soufflot**'s high windows remain on the east front; originally there were forty-two around the building, but now the Panthéon is lit almost exclusively by skylights.

Enter the Panthéon and descend the steps to the **crypt**.

Interior The body of Voltaire, who had died in 1778, was transferred to the Panthéon in July 1791. He was quickly followed by Mirabeau, a hero of the Revolution, who soon fell into posthumous disgrace when his close connections with the royal family were discovered; his remains were then removed to the cemetery of Ste Catherine. Marat was buried in the Panthéon, following his assassination, but after five months his association with the English was revealed and his remains transferred to the graveyard of St Etienne du Mont.

The Panthéon's sixty tombs are kept in this crypt, occupying chambers which extend from the aisles. Only those of greatest interest are indicated here.

Statues of Voltaire and Rousseau flank the steps.

● Follow the south aisle L.

The best-known are buried as follows:

Voltaire, d.1778, first chamber L.

Soufflot, d. 1781, the Panthéon's architect, second chamber L.

● Continue ahead, ascend the steps and proceed clockwise to the south aisle's continuation.

Victor Hugo, d.1885, third chapel L.

Louis Braille, d.1852, inventor of the reading system for the blind, fourth chapel L.

● *Cross to the north aisle and return eastward.*

Bougainville, d.1811, navigator and discoverer of the tropical plant Bougainvillaea, third chapel L.

● *Return southward.*

Jean-Jacques Rousseau, d.1778, lies in the chamber L, immediately facing Voltaire's tomb.

● *Proceed to the north-east corner of the crypt and ascend the steps to the ground floor of the building (if open).*

The east end can only be viewed from the barrier, while the restoration continues. A marble group, representing The Convention, by **Sicard**, dominates.

Flanking it are statues of Hoche (north side) and Mirabeau (south side).

● *Proceed to the room behind.*

Here is displayed a model of the Panthéon, made by Soufflot's successor, **Rondelet**, which shows the full-height towers as they were originally built.

● *Ascend the next flight of stairs to the chancel's tribune (gallery). Continue to the terrace and the dome. A notice warns of vertigo.*

Throughout the rest of the building, columns, not the external walls, bear the load, and **Soufflot** intended that these should also support the dome. However, **Rondelet** was apprehensive, particularly as one column had already cracked, and substituted piers at the crossing; their heaviness adds a discordant note, in spite of the decorative pilasters.

Paintings on the spandrels of Ste Geneviève's apotheosis were commissioned from **Gros** by Napoléon in 1811.

Foucault gave a public demonstration in 1852 of the earth's rotation, by suspending a pendulum from the centre of the Dome.

● *Further steps lead to the dome's colonnade. Descend to the gallery, which provides a general view eastward.*

In the mid-19C it was decided that the Panthéon should be decorated with murals by **Paul Chenavard** and cartoons were made. However, the work was eventually given to several artists. Only those of **Puvis de Chavannes**, depicting scenes from the life of Ste Geneviève, are of great merit; they are on the south wall of the nave and the north wall of the chancel and may be glimpsed, depending on what parts of the buildings are open.

The monuments, like the paintings, are generally uninspired, the best being those to *Unknown Heroes* and *Unknown Artists*, by **Landowski**, in the south and north transepts respectively.

By the crossing's south-east pier is the monument to Rousseau by **Bartholomé**.

Opposite, by the north-west pier, the monument commemorates Diderot and The Encyclopedists, by **Terroir**.

● *Exit from the Panthéon and return to its west front.*

Location 13	**PLACE DU PANTHÉON** *Soufflot*

Soufflot laid out the semi-circular square and work began in 1771 on the construction of what are now the Universités Paris I, II and V, in the north-west corner; they were later extended westward.

In the south-west corner, matching **Soufflot**'s design of these buildings, is the **Mairie of the 5th arrondissement**, by **Hittorff** *c.*1850. Cleaned and restored in 1987, the building is frequently used for exhibitions, admission always being free.

•• *Proceed to Bibliothèque Ste Geneviève on the north side.*

Location 14	**BIBLIOTHÈQUE STE GENEVIÈVE** *Henri Labrouste 1850*

10 Place du Panthéon

Open Wednesday–Monday 10.00–17.30. Admission free. Occasional tours of the 14C crypt.

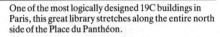

One of the most logically designed 19C buildings in Paris, this great library stretches along the entire north side of the Place du Panthéon.

The Bibliothèque Ste Geneviève's collection originated as the library of Ste Geneviève Abbey. It was built on the site of the Collège du Montaign, which was founded in 1314 and known as the 'Hôtel des Haricots', because haricot beans formed the students' staple diet. Only its crypt survives. Erasmus studied at the college in 1495.

It is clear, externally, that one large room occupies the entire length of the first floor.

Ties, hinting at the iron structure of the building, have been made a design feature in the spandrels, and between the lower windows where they are linked by swags.

Almost six hundred European writers' names are inscribed beneath the upper windows.

•• *Enter the hall.*

Busts of literary giants, including work by **Coysevox**, **Houdon** and **Lemoine**, line the walls.

•• *Ascend to the first floor and enter the* **Reading Room** *R.*

This long, high room, with its slender, iron columns, is particularly well lit from the deep, south-facing windows.

Among the many hundred thousand volumes in its collection are Baudelaire manuscripts and a 12C copy of an English bible.

Visits to the 14C crypt may occasionally be made; ask for details at the information desk.

•• *Exit R. Continue westward. First L Rue St Jacques. First R Rue Soufflot. Third L Boulevard St Michel. Cross to the west side of the boulevard and proceed southward, passing the Luxembourg Garden.*

Location 15	**ÉCOLE SUPÉRIEURE DES MINES**

60 Boulevard St Michel

Museum open Tuesday and Saturday 10.00–

Exhibited in the school's Musée de Mineralogie is one of the world's finest collections of minerals.

The premises, built in the 18C as the Hôtel de Vendôme, were enlarged and partly remodelled *c.*1845. Founded elsewhere in 1783, the mining

15

12.30 and 14.00–17.00; Wednesday–Friday 14.00–17.00. Admission free.

school was transferred here in 1815.

●● *Enter and follow the signs to the museum; ring the bell for entry.*

Precious and non-precious stones in their natural state provide a dazzling display; and examples of unusual rock formations from many countries are also exhibited. Visitors are locked in for security reasons and must contact the staff when wishing to leave.

●● *Exit L Boulevard St Michel. Fifth R Place de la Sorbonne. Ahead is the Sorbonne's chapel.*

Location 16 | **SORBONNE**

Paris Universités III and IV 47 Rue des Ecoles

Courtyards open.

Chapelle de Ste Ursule de la Sorbonne open for temporary exhibitions only or write for appointment. Sunday–Tuesday and Thursday and Friday 09.00–11.30 and 14.00–16.00. Admission charge.

Grand Amphithéâtre open when convenient. Admission free.

Now the home of two Paris universities, the Sorbonne was founded as a theological college by St Louis in the mid-13C. Its 17C chapel, by **Lemercier**, contains the outstanding tomb of Cardinal Richelieu. The remainder of the complex was rebuilt in the late 19C and is of little architectural interest. However, a great mural by **Puvis de Chavannes** decorates the Grand Amphithéâtre.

History Canon Robert de Sorbon (from Sorbon in the Ardennes), chaplain and confessor to St Louis, founded the college which bears his name in 1253. Its object was to train sixteen poor students to become secular priests. Although initially forming only a modest part of the University of Paris, by the late 13C the Sorbonne had become the centre of scholastic theology and was empowered to confer degrees. At the behest of Philippe le Bel, the Sorbonne condemned the Knights Templar, a factor which led to their dissolution in 1312. During the Hundred Years War, the Sorbonne supported the English and the Burgundians, recognizing Henry V as King of France. It condemned Joan of Arc and one of the faculty's advocates, Bishop Pierre Cauchon, was the prosecutor at her trial. In 1469, Louis XI summoned three printers from Germany to set up the first printing press in France at the college.

Until the Revolution all forms of Protestantism were violently opposed and the Sorbonne gave its full support to the St Bartholomew's Day massacre of the Huguenots.

In 1622, Richelieu, a former student, who was soon to become a cardinal and Louis XIII's first minister, was appointed chancellor and he rebuilt most of the complex. The Sorbonne opposed the liberal views of modern philosophers throughout the 18C, gaining much ridicule; it was duly suppressed at the Revolution.

Napoléon re-established the college in 1806 as a state university, its buildings also accommodating the artists whom he transferred from their quarters at the Louvre. From 1821, the administration of Paris University was centred at the Sorbonne, the name of which became synonymous with it.

Wholesale rebuilding of the complex, apart from its chapel, took place in the late 19C, and in 1896 the Sorbonne officially became Paris University, effectively the most important centre for advanced studies in the country. The student uprisings of 1968, which began here and at Nanterre, led to the reform of the French university system. Now, the Sorbonne accommodates the offices of two of the thirteen universities in the Paris region.

Ste Ursule de la Sorbonne From its conception, Richelieu decided that he would be buried here and commissioned **Lemercier**, who had lived in Rome and knew its Jesuit church of Il Gesù, to design the building in similar style. Work began in 1635 and the structure was finished by the time of Richelieu's death in 1642.

Ste Ursule was the first completely Roman-style ecclestiastical building to be constructed in Paris and greatly influenced the 17C Classical churches that were to follow.

Exterior Originally, the pediment was carved with Richelieu's arms, but these were removed at the Revolution and it remains blank.

The Corinthian Order is adopted throughout the building.

•➡ *Follow Rue de la Sorbonne northward and enter the Sorbonne's courtyard R, at No 17.*

The fifteen-step approach to the north portico is reminiscent of Rome's Pantheon.

Above rises the shallow north transept.

The cupola, which many regard as the first true dome to have been built in Paris, is 130 feet high, a dimension that exactly matches the length of the nave.

Circular turrets accommodate stairways.

•➡ *Enter the chapel (if open).*

Interior Temporary exhibitions are held within.

Following the death of **Lemercier** in 1660, the interior was completed by **Charles Le Brun**, but much decorative carving was destroyed at the Revolution, when the church became a Temple of Reason.

Immediately R of the entrance is the tomb of the Duc de Richelieu, d.1822, a descendant of the Cardinal. He was instrumental in the return of the chapel to the faith by Louis XVIII. Now, however, only two services are held each year: 1 October, St Ursula's Feast Day, and 4 December, commemorating Richelieu's death. Some of the cupola's sculptural decoration was restored in the late 19C and its spandrels painted by **Philippe de Champaigne**.

Recently returned to the **chancel** from the south transept is Richelieu's marble tomb, designed by **Le Brun** and carved by **Girardon**. The work was not completed until 1694, fifty-two years after the Cardinal's death.

The Cardinal's dying figure is depicted supported by *Religion*, whilst *Science* grieves at his feet. This monument, one of the finest of its period in France, would undoubtedly have been destroyed by revolutionaries, but Alexandre Lenoir, who had earlier saved the royal tombs at St Denis, threw his body on the work to protect it, receiving a bayonet wound in the process.

Suspended above is Richelieu's hat.

•• *Exit from the north door and return to the Sorbonne's courtyard.*

All the remainder of the courtyard's buildings, which had been reconstructed for Richelieu by **Lemercier**, were rebuilt 1885–1901 in an uninspired manner by **Nénot**. The complex, which continues on the south side of the church, incorporates a multitude of examination halls, laboratories, offices and lecture rooms.

Occupying the east range is the Bibliothèque de la Sorbonne, a library with almost 800,000 volumes.

The courtyard is a meeting place for students and, by tradition, provides what is virtually their sanctuary.

At the north end, beneath the arcade, panels painted by **Weerts** in 1903 illustrate the great Lendit Fair, held throughout the Middle Ages on the Plain of St Denis every 11 June, then an important annual event for Paris students.

•• *Enter the doorway ahead to the corridor. Immediately R is the Grand Amphithéâtre (open if convenient).*

The **Grand Amphithéâtre**, which is the Sorbonne's main lecture hall, can seat 2,700 students. Its famous mural, *Le Bois Sacré* (sacred wood) by **Puvis de Chavannes**, was painted in 1890.

•• *Exit R and follow the corridor to the Rue des Ecoles exit. (NB this exit is closed Sunday and from 13.00 Saturday; a return must then be made to the courtyard, to exit R at Rue de la Sorbonne. First R Rue des Ecoles.)*

•• *Continue eastward along Rue des Ecoles, passing the Sorbonne's north façade, to Place Marcelin Berthelot first R.*

Location 17	**COLLÈGE DE FRANCE** *Chalgrin 1778*
Place Marcelin Berthelot	The independent Collège de France provides public lectures free of charge. Although a Renaissance foundation, its core is a late-15C building, now surrounded by 20C extensions.

François I, inspired by the humanist Guillaume Bude, founded the college in 1530 as a 'republic of scholars'. Its aim was to combat the intolerance and scholasticism then prevailing, particularly at the Sorbonne.

Known as the 'College of Three Languages', the works of Classical authors, until then proscribed due to their paganism, were once again studied from the original Hebrew, Greek and Latin. Henri II, *c.*1550, enlarged the foundation by forming two colleges side by side. On his accession in 1610, Louis XIII replaced them with the Royal College of France and many subjects were added to the curriculum. Rebuilt in 1778, the college survived the Revolution, only the name being changed when it became, as at present, the Collège de France. Famous professors have included the physicists Ampère (electrical amps) and Joliot-Curie (nuclear fission). Since 1852, the college has relied on state sponsorship but retains its independence.

Facing Place Marcelin Berthelot, the core of the building is fronted by a courtyard.

Between the Place and the Rue des Ecoles are gardens. Standing in the garden, to the west R, is a bronze statue of the Italian poet Dante, d.1321, by **Jean-Paul Abe**, 1879.

In front of the courtyard, at the top of the steps, is a statue by **Couvegnes**, 1946, of the 19C physiologist, Claude Bernard, who discovered the function of the pancreas gland at the college in laboratories since demolished.

A marble statue of the Egyptologist Champollion, d.1832, stands within the courtyard.

Ahead, the college's main range, built by **Chalgrin** in 1778, replaced Louis XIII's 17C block. It was extended in 1842 but that section was rebuilt in 1930.

Excavations in 1894 revealed traces of the Greater Baths of Roman Lutetia but nothing now survives *in situ*.

•● *Return westward.*

At the corner, a plaque on the wall of the west wing L commemorates Claude Bernard.

•● *First R Rue St Jacques. First L Rue du Sommerard leads to Place Paul Painlevé.*

Location 18	**MUSÉE DE CLUNY**

6 Place Paul Painlevé

Open Wednesday–Monday 09.45–12.30 and 14.00–17.15. Admission charge. Half price Sunday.

The Musée de Cluny incorporates one of only two complete late-Gothic mansions to survive in the capital, together with extensive *in situ* remains of Roman baths. Exhibits demonstrate the culture of Paris in the Middle Ages. Original 13C statues from the façade of Notre Dame, some discovered only recently, are displayed, together with great medieval tapestries.

History Only two important mansions in Paris have survived from the 15C: the Hôtel de Cluny and the Hôtel de Sens. The Benedictine abbey of Cluny-en-Bourgogne founded a college near the Sorbonne, and in 1340 its abbot, Pierre de Chalas, purchased the Roman baths and surrounding land, and built a town house for himself and his successors. This was rebuilt in 1485, as the present hôtel, by Jacques d'Amboise, Bishop of Clermont and Abbot of Jumièges in Normandy.

Mary Tudor, sister of England's Henry VIII, stayed here briefly while in mourning for her husband Louis XII, and James V of Scotland also resided in the hôtel for a short while. In the 17C it became the residence of the papal nuncio, one of whom was Cardinal Mazarin. The estate was sold at the Revolution and the hôtel became, in turn, the premises of a surgeon, cooper, printer and laundry. Alexandra de Sommerard, an archaeologist, acquired the property in 1833, and when he died in 1842 his house and collection of antiques was purchased by the state. It was opened, together with the Roman baths, in 1844, as a museum of medieval art and culture.

Exterior Ahead, the wall to the courtyard is castellated, a decorative rather than a defensive feature.

The entrances for pedestrians and carriages are original; both are embellished with Flamboyant Gothic decoration.

•● *Enter the courtyard.*

Although late-Gothic, the hôtel exhibits Renaissance influences.

Its crenellations and turrets, as on the courtyard's wall, are purely decorative features.

The Hôtel de Cluny was one of the earliest mansions in Paris to be fronted by a courtyard, with its garden to the rear. Short wings extend southward from both ends of the main range.

Another wing stretches westward at the rear to link with the chapel.

The windows are mullioned.

Gargoyles embellish the roof's frieze.

Above them, the balustrade is Flamboyant.

Dormer windows are decorated with coats of arms.

The west wing L is arcaded.

The polygonal tower, which accommodates a wide spiral staircase, was once used by the navy as an observatory and twenty-one new planets were discovered.

Scallop shells, around the entrance, are the emblem of St James of Compostela, the patron saint of the hôtel's builder, Jacques d'Amboise.

•● *Proceed to the entrance arch in the far right-hand corner.*

Carved above this are the arms of Jacques d'Amboise.

•● *Enter the vestibule.*

Interior Entry tickets and literature are sold, including detailed guides to the museum in English.

Most exhibits, which are displayed throughout the hôtel, are captioned, but not all the rooms display their numbers.

Tapestries and chests, followed by wood carving and Nottingham alabasters, occupy many of the ground-floor rooms.

In the **first room** is the Limoges reliquary of Thomas à Becket *c.*1200.

The **fourth room** retains its original chimneypiece.

Also displayed here is the great Flemish tapestry *La Vie Seigneuriale, c.*1500, valuably depicting contemporary scenes from everyday life in the Loire valley.

Room VIII, entered through the original portal of Ste Geneviève's monastic church, displays original statues from Notre Dame.

The damaged heads of twenty-one kings are the 13C originals from the Galerie des Rois of Notre Dame's west front. These kings of Judah were believed to be French monarchs and 'decapitated' by the Communards. Their heads, all minus noses, were discovered during excavations at the Hôtel Moreau in 1977.

**•• ** *Descend the steps to the Frigidarium.*

The **Thermes Gallo-Romains de Cluny** (Gallo-Roman baths) were built in the early 3C, probably during the reign of Caracula (212–17). Due to their large scale, it has long been thought that the baths formed a public bathing establishment, although some now believe that they belonged to a large private villa. At the end of the 3C the Barbarians sacked the baths, but extensive ruins have survived. Early in the 19C soil was laid over them, and fruit and vegetables were planted. However, the baths were excavated at the Restoration, the Frigidarium being incorporated in the hôtel in 1843, when the building became a museum.

The **Frigidarium** (cold water bath) is by far the best preserved building to survive from the Roman period in France. Its roof, the most extensive Roman example in the country, is groin-vaulted and supported by consoles designed, unusually, as ships' prows; due to this it has been suggested that the baths were built by members of the boatmen's guild.

In the corner, comprising four blocks of stone, is the Roman Jupiter Pillar, the oldest piece of sculpture to have been discovered in Paris. It was a votive-column dedicated by the boatmen's guild to Jupiter, during the reign of Tiberius, 13–47. Also known as the *Pilier des Nautes* (boatmen's pillar), reliefs of pagan gods are carved on the shaft. The column was discovered beneath the choir of Notre Dame during excavations in 1711 and had apparently stood within a Roman temple on the site.

•• ** *Ascend to the* **first floor.

Hanging in the rotunda, facing the stairs, is the museum's most famous series of tapestries, *La Dame et la Licorne* (the lady and the unicorn). Remarkably, the complete set survives; the first five depict the senses but the subject of the sixth is unclear. They are believed to have been made in Brussels *c.*1500 and were discovered in a château near Aubusson in the 19C.

Room XIX displays the famous **Retable de Basle**.

Room XX Built as the abbot's oratory, this chapel possesses the building's only original interior. During the 18C, when the hôtel was owned by a surgeon, it served as an operating theatre.

A high central column supports the Flamboyant star vault.

Niches in the walls originally housed statues of members of the d'Amboise family.

The oriel window is made almost entirely of glass.

An original 15C Flamboyant carved screen to the staircase survives.

Tapestries from Auxerre Cathedral, woven for Bishop Jean Baillet, *c.*1490, decorate the walls of the chapel and the adjoining room. Their twenty-three scenes illustrate the life of St Etienne.

●● *Exit from the museum R, continuing westward following Rue du Sommerard.*

Passed R is the **Caldarium** (steam bath).

Cleaning has recently revealed more clearly the composition of the walls of the Roman baths; string courses of narrow bricks run between the stonework.

●● *First R Boulevard St Michel.*

Immediately R is the **Tepidarium** (warm bath).

Behind this is the exterior of the **Frigidarium**, now incorporated internally in the Musée de Cluny and already described.

●● *First R Boulevard St Germain. Enter the Square de Cluny garden from the corner R.*

A close view of the Roman structures may be gained from this garden, including the **Gymnasium**'s wall, which protrudes northward.

●● *Return to Boulevard St Michel R and proceed ahead to M St Michel.*

16

Montparnasse, Catacombes, and Val de Grâce

An ascent of Europe's highest office block, a descent to the Catacombes and a visit to the two most complete former monasteries in Paris are highlights of this varied route.

Timing: Val de Grâce, the finest Baroque ensemble in Paris, may be entered only Sunday morning and weekday evenings until restoration has been completed.

The Musée de la Poste is closed Sunday.

The Musée Antoine Bourdelle is closed Monday.

It is possible to enter the Observatoire only as part of a guided tour (in French) on the first Saturday in the month, by prior appointment.

The Catacombes are closed Monday, Tuesday–Friday mornings and lunchtime at weekends.

16

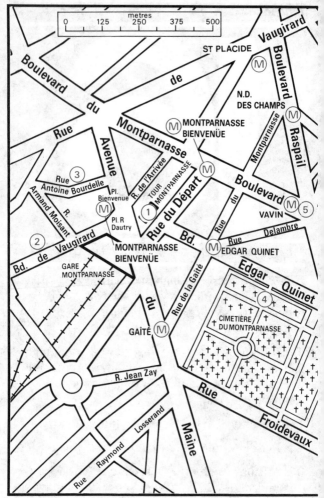

Locations
1 Tour Montparnasse
2 Musée de la Poste
3 Musée Bourdelle
4 Cimetière du Montparnasse
5 Boulevard du Montparnasse
6 Maternité Port Royal

7 Fontaine de l'Observatoire
8 Ney Statue
9 Observatoire de Paris
10 Catacombes
11 Val de Grâce
12 Schola Cantorum
13 St Jacques du Haut-Pas

Start *M Montparnasse Bienvenue, line 4 Porte de Clignacourt/Porte d'Orléans; line 6 Charles de Gaulle Etoile/Nation; line 12 Mairie d'Issy/ Porte de la Chapelle; line 13 Châtillon Montrouge/St Denis Basilique. Exit and proceed to the south side (Gare Montparnasse) of the Tour Montparnasse.*

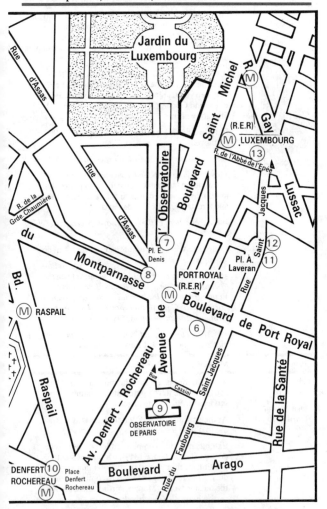

Location 1	**TOUR MONTPARNASSE** *1973*
Place Raoul Dautry	At 656 feet, Europe's tallest office building provides splendid views from its top floor gallery and roof.
Viewing terrace open daily, April–September 09.30–23.30, October–March 10.00–22.00. Admission charge.	

In 1934 it was decided to redevelop to a greater density the Maine/Montparnasse business area, with this high tower block as its centrepiece. Interrupted by the war, the plans were revised in 1958 and work began three years later. A group of French architects was responsible and the building was completed in 1973.

As many feared, the Tour Montparnasse, which possesses few claims to architectural distinction, was

built unduly close to the low-rise city centre, and has proved to be a visual distraction. Shops in the lower levels include branches of C&A and Galeries Lafayette. There is also a sports centre and swimming pool.

A plaque on the **C&A** corner records the 1944 meeting, outside the old Montparnasse Station, between von Choltitz, the German commander of Paris, and General Leclerc, leader of the French liberating army.

Fifty-two floors above accommodate up to 7,000 employees.

•• Ascend to floor 56 by high-speed lift.

This floor is enclosed; a frieze identifies the surrounding landmarks. Distances up to twenty-five miles may be viewed in clear weather. There is a bar and a restaurant, **Le Ciel de Paris**.

•• Ascend steps to the open roof-top terrace (level 59).

From here there is an uninterrupted view, but no amenities.

•• Descend to the ground floor and exit from the tower. Proceed ahead and follow Boulevard de Vaugirard, which leads south-westward, passing the north side of Gare Montparnasse R. Pass the Rue Armand Moisant junction (first R).

•• Alternatively, if not visiting the museums, proceed directly to location 4, Cimetière du Montparnasse.

Location 2	**MUSÉE DE LA POSTE**

32 Boulevard de Vaugirard

Open Monday–Saturday 10.00–17.00.

A delight for philatelists, the museum describes, on five floors, the development of communication services throughout the ages.

At the entrance are 19C letter boxes that visitors may use to obtain the museum's special franking.

Exhibits include a complete collection of French postage stamps (since 1849), a model of stamp-printing machinery and the balloon that was used during the 1870 siege of Paris to communicate with the outside world. Modern sorting and franking methods are also described.

•• Exit L. First L Rue Armand Moisant. First R Rue Antoine Bourdelle.

Location 3	**MUSÉE BOURDELLE**

16 Rue Antoine Bourdelle

Open Tuesday–Sunday 10.00–17.40. Admission charge.

Antoine Bourdelle, 1861–1928, a pupil of Rodin, had a vast output and this house, in which he lived and worked, is now a museum devoted to his sculptures. Bronzes in the garden may be seen through the railings if not entering the exhibition.

Displayed inside are busts of Beethoven, Rodin, Anatole France and Vincent d'Indy.

•• Exit L. First R Avenue du Maine. Proceed via the pedestrian crossing to the east side of the Tour Montparnasse. First R Boulevard Edgar Quinet.

A lively street market operates in the boulevard Wednesday and Saturday.

• Proceed south-eastward to the main entrance of the Cimetière du Montparnasse.

Location 4	**CIMETIÈRE DU MONTPARNASSE**

Boulevard Edgar Quinet

After Père Lachaise, this is the second most famous cemetery in Paris. Its 45 acres were laid out in 1824.

• Follow the path L to the information office (renseignements), which is housed in the third building L.

A free plan is provided and graves of particular interest to the visitor will be indicated. Those buried here include writers Guy de Maupassant and Baudelaire; composers César Franck and Saint-Saëns; artists Fantin-Latour, Houdon and Rude. Dreyfus and the Nazi collaborator Pierre Laval also lie in the cemetery.

• Exit L. Second R Rue du Montparnasse. First R Boulevard du Montparnasse.

Location 5	**BOULEVARD DU MONTPARNASSE**

This boulevard marks the centre of the Montparnasse quarter that took on the bohemian mantle of Montmartre just before the First World War. By the 1930s, however, its great days were already over and it is now the domain of staff from the nearby offices.

No 102, La Coupole, a vast open restaurant, remains one of the capital's most popular brasseries. Much of its mid-1920s decor survives and the chandeliers, red velvet banquettes and paintings on the upper sections of the columns, by **Othon Friesz**, may be glimpsed from the boulevard.

No 108, Le Dôme, is another restaurant surviving from the quarter's great days. Seafood is served, amidst decor by **Slavik**.

• From Le Dôme cross Boulevard de Montparnasse and proceed ahead to the Boulevard Raspail junction.

The **Balzac statue**, by **Rodin**, is inscribed (in French) 'to Balzac to Rodin by their admirers'.

• Cross Boulevard Raspail and follow Boulevard de Montparnasse eastward. Cross to its south side and take bus No 91 eastbound to Observatoire/Port Royal (two stops). From the bus stop continue eastward along Boulevard de Port Royal and enter the gates R of the Maternité Port Royal hospital. Follow the path first L and proceed ahead, passing the chapel, to the east side of the building. Steps R lead to the cloister, indicated by the sign 'Assistante Sociale du Personnel'. Turn R and proceed to the chapel at the cloister's north-east end.

Location 6	**MATERNITÉ PORT ROYAL** *Antoine Lepautre 1646*

121–125 Boulevard de Port Royal

Chapel open Sunday and Monday 10.30.

A little-visited former monastery, the Port Royal's chapel, cloister and chapter house survive. The cloister is probably the best place in Paris to sense the tranquillity of monastic life.

Not established until 1646, this short-lived Cistercian convent was suppressed by Louis XIV in 1664, as it had become a centre of Jansenism. The former monastery was then converted to a prison but became

a maternity hospital in 1814 and has served as such ever since.

Turn R and proceed to the chapel's entrance at the cloister's north-east end.

The **Chapelle du très St Sacrement de Port Royal** was consecrated by the Bishop of Paris in 1648 and soon became an important religious centre.

Philippe de Champaigne, whose daughter joined the convent, painted a series of works for the chapel, some of which are now in the Louvre.

The convent's founder, Angélique Arnauld, lies beneath what had been the nuns' choir.

Proceed clockwise and exit from the cloister beside the staircase (the cloister's north-west door is generally locked) and turn R. Exit from the hospital L. Third R Avenue de l'Observatoire. Continue ahead to the fountain in Place Ernest Denis.

Location 7	**FONTAINE DE L'OBSERVATOIRE** *Davioud 1875*

Place Ernest Denis

One of the city's liveliest fountains, bronze allegories of four continents (the fifth, Oceania, was omitted for the sake of symmetry) are by **Carpeaux**.

Sea horses, fishes and the lugubrious turtle are by **Frémier**.

To the north a distant view of the Luxembourg Palace may be gained.

Cross to the west side of Avenue de l'Observatoire and return southward to the Boulevard du Montparnasse junction (first R).

Location 8	**NEY STATUE** *Rude 1853*

Avenue de l'Observatoire

This statue commemorates Marshal Ney, who fought heroically at Waterloo but was executed nearby, in 1815, for supporting Napoléon throughout his 'hundred days'.

A vigorous figure, in a pose reminiscent of the same sculptor's masterpiece on the Arc de Triomphe, appears to be calling his troops to follow.

Continue southward to the Observatoire de Paris.

Location 9	**OBSERVATOIRE DE PARIS** *Perrault 1672*

61 Avenue de l'Observatoire
(40 51 22 21)

Open every first Saturday in the month for guided tours in French, by appointment only. Closed August. Admission free.

No longer an astronomical observatory, the Observatoire's chief activities are now connected with the International Time Bureau, which has been accommodated here since its formation in 1919.

Colbert commissioned the building for the Académie des Sciences *c.*1666, and four astronomers from the Italian Cassini family were successive directors, from its opening in 1672 until the Revolution. The Paris Meridian of Longitude was calculated here in 1667. Other work of major importance carried out here included the classification of stars by sizes, the measurement of the speed of light, and the preparation of the first map of the moon. The

Observatoire is responsible for setting Co-ordinated Universal Time (UTC), its speaking clock being accurate to one-millionth of a second.

Perrault designed the observatory so that it would be exactly bisected north/south by the Paris Meridian of Longitude, and its walls were built to follow the cardinal points of the compass. Work began in 1667, at the same time as his Louvre Colonnade was being constructed. No iron, for fear of magnetic disorientation, or wood, for fear of fire, was used in its construction.

In front of the north façade is the statue of the astronomer Le Verrier, who discovered the existence of the planet Neptune from here in 1846.

Originally, the building was flat roofed, all domes, and structures in paler stone, being 19C additions.

Both wings were added for Louis-Philippe *c.*1840.

Internal visits are difficult to arrange, particularly for foreigners, but although some astronomical instruments of interest are displayed, the scope of the Paris Observatory is not comparable with that of London's Old Royal Observatory, at Greenwich.

•• *Turn L and follow Rue Cassini eastward. R Rue du Faubourg St Jacques.*

No 38, the **Hôtel Massa**, was originally built in the 18C on the Champs Elysées. It was brought here stone by stone, and re-erected.

•• *First R Boulevard Arago. Continue ahead to Place Denfert Rochereau.*

Place Denfert-Rochereau was originally called Place d'Enfer (hell), but its name was changed in 1879 to commemorate Rochereau, who defended Belfort in the Franco–Prussian war.

The lion in the square refers to the heroic resistance of the Parisians during the Prussian siege of 1870–71.

•• *Proceed to the green pavilion from where the Catacombes are entered.*

Location 10	**CATACOMBES**
Place Denfert-Rochereau *Open Tuesday–Friday 14.00–16.00; Saturday and Sunday 09.00–11.00 and 14.00–16.00. Admission charge.*	A deep spiral staircase must be descended and visits are not recommended for the infirm; torches are no longer necessary. The Catacombes, opened for burials in 1865, contain more than three million skeletons, all neatly arranged in rows as though by the proud owner of a greengrocer's shop. Not surprisingly, with all the bones about, dogs are not permitted. Romans quarried from the Jardin des Plantes region to Porte de Versailles, Montrouge and Gentilly; their passageways became disused and this one, connected with the Montrouge quarry, was reopened in 1785. Its new purpose was to serve as a charnel house, by storing bones excavated from cemeteries in the centre of Paris, which had been closed by government order in 1765 (i.e. prior to the Revolution) due to the danger to public health. During the Second World War this warren of passageways provided the headquarters of the French resistance fighters.

•• Descend the spiral staircase.

Even in dry conditions, the floor is muddy in parts due to condensation. Many passages are followed before the bones are seen, passing, on route, a bath which was used by workers who transported the skeletons.

Bones are identified by the name of the cemetery that they came from and the date of their transfer.

Guillotined victims of the Revolution are seen last, their bones being brought here at the Restoration, mostly from what is now Square Louis XVI.

•• Exit from the Catacombes and proceed north-eastward to Avenue Denfert-Rochereau. Take bus 38 northbound to Observatoire/Port Royal (three stops). From the bus stop continue eastward along Boulevard de Port Royal. Third L Rue St Jacques.

Location 11	**VAL DE GRÂCE**

277 Rue St Jacques

Open Monday–Saturday 10.00–12.00 and 14.00–17.00. Sunday Mass 10.00.

Val de Grâce is a rare Paris example of a complete former monastery. Its centrepiece is a domed, Roman-style church, considered by many to be the finest Baroque building in Paris. The complex has accommodated a military hospital for almost two hundred years.

History Anne of Austria, consort of Louis XIII, purchased a mansion on the site in 1621 for a community of Benedictine nuns from the abbey of Val de Grâce at Bièvre; the abbey itself then transferred here but kept its name. After twenty-three years of marriage, the thirty-seven-year-old Queen was still childless and vowed to build a magnificent church for the nuns if she gave birth. The future 'Sun King', Louis XIV, was born in 1638 and Anne became his Regent on the death of Louis XIII, five years later. She kept her promise to build the new church and Louis XIV, then aged seven, laid its foundation stone in 1645.

Almost as soon as building commenced, Anne dismissed the architect. **Le Mercier** took over, simplified **Hardouin-Mansart**'s west front and redesigned the dome. The Fronde rebellion interrupted work in 1648 and when it was resumed in 1655, Le Mercier had died. **Le Muet** and, later, **Gabriel le Duc** were appointed to complete the scheme.

Anne died in 1666, with the church almost finished, apart from the nave's chapels, and work was suspended the following year; consecration did not take place until 1710, when Louis XIV was seventy-two.

Following the Revolution, the abbey buildings became a military hospital in 1798 and remain so, with the monastic church serving as its chapel. An army medical school was added to the complex in 1850.

Exterior Although **Le Mercier** was responsible for the final appearance of the west front, it is in fact a restrained version of **Hardouin-Mansart**'s original elevation, which had, however, incorporated a frieze between each level, and much heavier volutes; Sta Susanna, Rome, seems to have been its model.

The dome, entirely by **Le Mercier**, is regarded as his greatest work and one of the finest examples in France. Obviously inspired by St Peter's, Rome, it is the most ornate in Paris; **Hardouin-Mansart**'s dome would have had more ribs.

The drum is encircled by a frieze of Bourbon lilies.

Carved on the entrance door of the west front is the gilded monogram AL of Anne of Austria and Louis XIV; this is repeated frequently within the church.

Standing in the north side of the courtyard is a bronze statue of Napoléon's surgeon, Baron Larrey, d.1842, by **David d'Angers**.

➡ Enter the church.

Interior By 1645 **Hardouin-Mansart** had completed the plan of the church and this was followed by his successors. Il Gesù, Rome, and some of Palladio's Italian churches have a similar plan of a short nave and a chancel, with three apses, but this was the first time that it had been adopted in Paris.

Pierre Mignard completed the cupola's mural in 1665; he had studied in Rome and it is typically Roman Baroque in style. The mural's theme is *The Glorification of the Blessed;* and 200 figures, three times life size, are incorporated.

Anne of Austria is depicted, bottom L, presenting a model of the church to God.

Most of the carving in the church also follows the Roman school, with work by the brothers **Michel** and **François Anguier**, **Philippe de Buyster** and **Pierre Sarazin**.

The Baroque baldachino, above the altar, was designed by **Gabriel le Duc**, based on Bernini's work at St Peter's, Rome. Again, however, the conception was **Hardouin-Mansart**'s.

Michel Anguier carved the original nativity scene for the altarpiece, but Napoléon gave this to St Roch, where it remains; the present work is a copy made in 1869. The nativity theme, repeated within the church, is a reference to the greatly desired birth of Louis XIV.

The **Chapelle Ste Anne**, which occupies the north apse and now accommodates the organ, was planned from the outset to be a necropolis for the royal house of Orléans, and from 1662 the hearts of forty-five members of the family were kept here in caskets. Most of the caskets and their contents were destroyed at the Revolution.

The south apse, which forms the **Chapelle St Louis**, was originally the monastic chancel.

➡ Exit from the church L.

An archway first L leads to a courtyard which served as the cloister. Immediately ahead is the former **monastic refectory**, once a museum of military hygiene.

➡ Exit from the cloister R and continue ahead towards the garden.

Immediately R, Gothic ground-floor windows survive from the original mansion purchased by Anne of Austria.

•• Continue ahead.

Anne of Austria frequently stayed in the corner **pavilion**.

Its ringed columns are in the style of Salomon de Brosse.

•• Return to Rue St Jacques and exit from Val de Grâce R.

Location 12	**SCHOLA CANTORUM**

269bis Rue St Jacques

Exceptionally charming ladies are delighted to show visitors around the school premises at most times. Admission free.

Founded in 1640, the English Benedictine Convent of St Edmund survived here until 1818. A Louis XIV salon and staircase, together with the chapel, built in 1674, remain.

Joséphine Beauharnais, later to become Napoléon's consort, was imprisoned on the upper floor for three months during the Revolution.

Three pupils of César Franck established the Schola Cantorum singing school here in 1894 and the chapel has been adapted for musical performances.

Only fragments of the original internal walls can be seen; most of the remainder survives but has been boarded over for acoustic purposes. England's former king, James II, died at St Germain-en-Laye in 1701 and reposed in state in this chapel. His body appears to have remained here, together with those of his daughter Louisa Maria Theresa (1692–1712) and the Duke of Berwick (1670–1734), his son by Arabella Churchill. At the Revolution the coffins were hidden and disappeared, some say to Scotland, but the Catacombes were once directly accessible from the convent and it seems more likely that the remains were transferred there, to escape desecration by anti-royalists.

Displayed in the salon is the Stuart coat of arms.

•• Exit R.

No 269, formerly part of the convent, retains externally the original first-floor entrance to the chapel, now blocked.

•• Continue northward and cross the road.

Location 13	**ST JACQUES DU HAUT-PAS** *1630–88*

252 Rue St Jacques

Open Monday–Thursday 18.15.

This plain, Classical church was favoured by the Jansenists, its patron being the Duchesse de Longueville. Buried within are members of the Italian Cassini family, royal astronomers of the Observatoire.

The carved pulpit is a good Louis XIV example.

•• Exit R. First R Rue de l'Abbé de l'Epée. First R Boulevard St Michel and RER Luxembourg.

Jardin des Plantes/Rue Mouffetard

Remains of the ancient Roman arena of Lutetia are visited, followed by the Jardin des Plantes, which incorporates botanical gardens, a zoo and the Natural History Museum. Rue Mouffetard's 'village' quarter is one of the most picturesque in Paris.

Timing: As few buildings are entered, fine weather is essential.

Most of Rue Mouffetard's food shops close Monday and from 12.00–14.00; Saturday and Sunday mornings are the liveliest time for a visit.

The Gobelins tapestry works may be entered only for guided tours Tuesday, Wednesday and Thursday afternoons.

St Médard church is closed Monday and from 12.30–15.00.

Glasshouses and the galleries of the Natural History Museum (all within the Jardin des Plantes) are closed Tuesday.

17

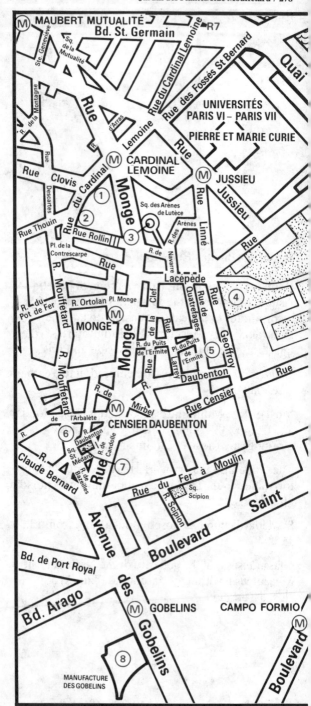

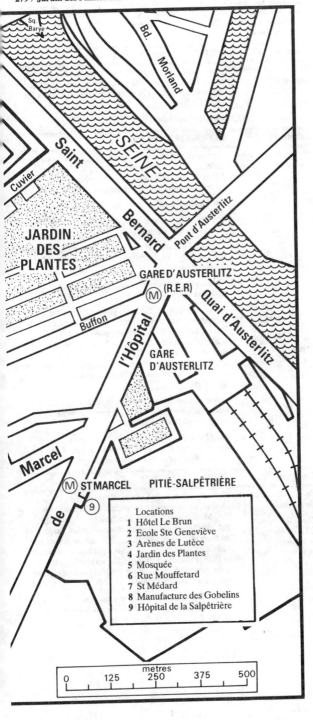

Sq Barye

Bd. Morland

Saint

SEINE

Cuvier

Bernard

Pont d'Austerlitz

JARDIN DES PLANTES

GARE D'AUSTERLITZ

(R.E.R)

Buffon

l'Hôpital

Quai d'Austerlitz

GARE D'AUSTERLITZ

Marcel

de

ST MARCEL

PITIÉ-SALPÊTRIÈRE

Locations
1 Hôtel Le Brun
2 Ecole Ste Geneviève
3 Arènes de Lutèce
4 Jardin des Plantes
5 Mosquée
6 Rue Mouffetard
7 St Médard
8 Manufacture des Gobelins
9 Hôpital de la Salpêtrière

metres
0   125   250   375   500

17

Start *M Cardinal Lemoine, line 10 Boulogne, Porte de St Cloud/Gare d'Orléans, Austerlitz. Exit from the station and follow Rue du Cardinal Lemoine southward.*

Location 1	**HÔTEL LE BRUN** *Boffrand 1700*
49 Rue du Cardinal Lemoine	Restored in 1987, this hôtel was built for Charles Le Brun, the nephew of the great painter and decorator of the same name. The pediment's relief honours the elder Le Brun.

●● *Continue southward.*

Location 2	**ÉCOLE STE GENEVIÈVE**
65 Rue du Cardinal Lemoine	Now a school, the building was originally the Scottish college, which is commemorated by '*Collège des Ecossais*' over the door. The site had belonged to the Roman Catholic church of Scotland since the 14C.

●● *Enter the hall.*

The grand staircase L leads to the chapel, which may be visited only if convenient.

The heart of James II of England once reposed within this severely Classical chapel, but it disappeared at the Revolution.

●● *Exit L and proceed ahead to* **Place de la Contrescarpe**.

This square, one of the most picturesque in the capital, was not created until 1852. The moated Porte Bourdelles, a gateway in Philippe-Auguste's 12C wall, formerly stood to the north-west, just past the intersection with Rue Descartes, and after its demolition the site became a popular area in which to congregate, even though there were then no buildings.

A few *clochards* (mostly now, in reality, homeless alcoholics) are generally in evidence; at weekends street entertainers perform.

●● *First L Rue Rollin. Descend the steps and cross Rue Monge to Rue de Navarre ahead. First L enter the Square des Arènes de Lutèce and proceed ahead.*

Location 3	**ARÈNES DE LUTÈCE**
Square des Arènes de Lutèce *Open daily 10.00–20.30 (closes 17.30 in winter).* *Admission free.*	The only arena from Lutetia, Roman Paris, to survive, its ruins were discovered in 1869, when the Rue Monge was laid out. Much more existed then but, despite protests from conservationists, large sections were demolished for the construction of new buildings. Restoration of what remained took place in 1918. In addition to serving as an arena for the usual bestial 'games' enjoyed in Roman times, plays were also performed; around 10,000 could be seated.

●● *Return to Rue de Navarre L and first R. First L Rue Lacépède. Ahead L is the main entrance to the Jardin des Plantes in Rue Cuvier.*

Location 4 | **JARDIN DES PLANTES**

57 Rue Cuvier

Gardens open daily 09.00–18.00 (closes 17.00 in winter). Admission free.

Ménagerie open daily 09.00–19.00 (closes 17.00 November–April). Admission charge.

Les plus beaux insectes du Monde (The world's most beautiful insects) open Wednesday–Monday 14.00–17.00. Admission charge. Galleries open Wednesday–Monday 10.00–17.00. Admission charge.

Serres Tropicales (Tropical Houses) open Wednesday–Monday 13.00–17.00. Admission charge.

Within the complex are botanical gardens, galleries displaying natural history exhibits and a zoo. London's equivalents, which occupy sites at Kew, South Kensington and Regent's Park respectively, are much more comprehensive and visitors who can readily see them will probably not wish to spend much time or money at the Jardin des Plantes. However, those with specialized interests, or youngsters to amuse, may wish to pay a visit. The grounds, at no cost, provide a pleasant stroll on a sunny day, particularly in May and June, when the display of peonies is exceptional.

History The Jardin des Plantes was founded as the royal herb garden in 1626. Previously this had been situated in the Palais Royal complex on the Ile de la Cité. Herouard and Guy de la Brosse, the royal physicians, were commissioned by Louis XIII to oversee the garden's establishment. Buffon, its curator, extended the garden eastward to the Seine in the 18C, thus creating the 60-acre area that survives to this day. In 1650 the public were admitted for the first time to what was known, until the Revolution, as the *Jardin du Roi* (King's garden).

●● *Enter the garden and take the path first R.*

This path leads to the maze, created on a rubbish heap by the naturalist Daubenton.

The column in the centre marks Daubenton's grave.

●● *Continue eastward.*

The 250–year-old cedar of Lebanon, brought from Kew and planted by Bernard du Jussieu in 1734, was the first tree of its type to be seen in France.

●● *Continue eastward and then follow the path L (Allée des Becquerel). Immediately before the path bears R proceed ahead towards the Rue Jussieu exit.*

A cross-section of a 2,000-year-old sequoia is preserved and tablets are inscribed with the major historical events that occurred as the tree grew.

●● *Continue eastward towards the ménagerie.*

Ménagerie In 1793 the royal zoo at Versailles was closed and its remaining animals brought here. At the same time all circus animals in France were acquired by the state and added to the collection. In 1827 Mohammed Ali of Egypt presented Charles X with a giraffe, the first ever seen in France. Its appearance began the fashion '*à la girafe*' which lasted several years. During the siege of Paris in 1870 most of the animals in the zoo were slaughtered for food. At present, the zoo's comprehensive reptile collection, and the ancillary display of 'the world's most beautiful insects', are exceptional.

Botanical gardens and the major galleries lie south of Allée Cuvier, the main east/west path that bisects the garden.

Between the two south blocks of galleries, towards the west end, is a robinia (*false acacia*) planted in 1636 and believed to be the oldest tree in Paris.

17

At the west end are the **glasshouses** and, behind them, the **zoological gallery**.

●● Exit from the Jardin des Plantes. Directly ahead Rue Lacépède. First L Rue de Quatrefages.

Location 5	MOSQUÉE

2 Rue de Quatrefages

Guided tours Saturday–Thursday 10.00–12.00, 14.00–18.30 (17.30 in winter). Admission charge. Most of the tours are suspended during Muslim festivals. The mosque may usually be viewed unaccompanied 12.00–14.00.

Built 1922–7, the mosque also houses the Islamic Institute for Religious Studies.

●● Enter the building beneath the tower surmounted by a minaret.

The courtyard garden and patio to the south, are in the Hispano/Moorish style. Moorish decor and fine carpets decorate the prayer chamber (remove shoes if entering).

●● Exit, cross to the west side of Rue de Quatrefages and proceed ahead, following the south side of Place du Puits de l'Ermite. First R Rue Larrey. First L Rue du Puits de l'Ermite.

The prison where Madame du Barry and Joséphine Beauharnais, later to become Napoléon's consort, were confined during the Revolution stood in this street, but has since been demolished.

●● Second R Rue Monge. First L Place Monge. Proceed clockwise. Second L Rue Ortolan. First L Rue Mouffetard.

Location 6	**RUE MOUFFETARD**

One of Paris's liveliest streets, the Rue Mouffetard combines restaurants (mainly Greek) and food shops with displays that spill on to the pavements.

In Roman times, this thoroughfare formed part of the great road that led south to Italy via Lyon. It is believed to have gained its name from the *mouffette* (evil smell) of the Bièvre stream that flowed nearby. The Bièvre was used by local tanners, and rotten, unsold vegetables were emptied into it by stallholders in the street. It was partly sunk below ground in 1828 and now runs as an enclosed subterranean sewer.

Standing on Rue Ortolan's south-west corner, outside No 60, is the **Pot de Fer** (iron pot) fountain. First erected in 1627, it was remodelled in 1671. This was one of fourteen fountains supplied by the aqueduct which was created to bring water to Marie de Médicis's Luxembourg Palace.

Along the top runs a frieze of scallop shells and flowers in the Italian style, reminiscent of the Médicis fountain in the Luxembourg Garden.

●● Proceed southward.

No 69, **Le Vieux Chêne** restaurant, displays a carved tree, made from the recovered masthead of a sunken ship. It had advertised an earlier restaurant, Aux Vieux Chêne (old oak tree), which was reputedly cursed.

Most of the food shops are to be found south of Rue de l'Epée du Bois (first L).

No 109 has a particularly outstanding display of fish.

No 3 Rue de l'Arbalète (first L) was the birthplace of the sculptor Auguste Rodin, in 1840.

No 122, between its first-floor windows, possesses the oldest sign in the street. '*À la Bonne Source*' (good spring) publicizing a wine merchant, who operated from the premises in 1592.

No 134, Facchetti, retains its painted façade, the work of the Italian **Aldeari**, a friend of the owner, *c*.1935.

●● *Cross Rue Mouffetard to St Médard.*

| Location 7 | **ST MÉDARD** |

141 Rue Mouffetard

The church is closed Monday; on other days it is closed 12.30–15.00.

St Médard, the parish church of the Rue Mouffetard 'village', was built mainly in the Flamboyant Gothic style but there are Renaissance and Greek Revival elements. In the 18C, its churchyard was the scene of the Jansenist 'miracle' healings, which were followed by the excesses of the hysterical 'convulsionists'.

History Although by repute there was an 8C building on the site, St Médard was first recorded in 1163, when Pope Alexander III attended Mass at the church. It then served a small community living on the banks of the Bièvre stream.

Work began *c*.1550 on rebuilding St Médard's nave, the money for which was provided by the sister of Charles VII's lawyer Reilhac, who had been buried in the church. Fines levied on Huguenots for damage that they caused in 1561 paid for a new, enlarged chancel which was completed, together with chapels, in 1632. Aisles were rebuilt three years later and only then did St Médard achieve parish church status.

Around this time, the church was adopted by the Jansenist sect, followers of Cornelius Jansen, Bishop of Ypres, d.1638. A saintly Jansenist deacon of the church, François de Paris, who died of 'mortification of the flesh' in 1727, asked to be buried in the charnel house, as he considered himself unworthy of burial in St Médard's graveyard. However, the Jansenists venerated him and he was buried in the graveyard with a black marble stone marking his tomb. Sick Jansenists prayed at his grave and miraculous cures were claimed. Young girls, on reaching puberty, were particularly attracted to the shrine, their eccentric behaviour resulting in them being called '*convulsionaires*'. Up to 8,000 are believed to have visited the tomb, eating red-hot coals and demanding to be beaten, crucified and strangled. In 1732, Louis XV put a stop to these antics by locking the graveyard; a satiricist fixed a piece of doggerel to the gate:

'*De par le Roi, défense à Dieu*
De Faire miracle en ce lieu'

(By order of the King, God is forbidden to perform miracles here).

A Lady Chapel was added in the late 18C and various modifications, in the Greek Revival style, were made to the chancel at the same time. St Médard was closed at the Revolution becoming, in 1798, a Temple of Labour.

Victor Hugo, in *Les Misérables*, set the scene for the rediscovery of Jean Valjean by his old enemy, Javert, near St Médard.

Exterior The mid-15C west front retains a Flamboyant window. In the 18C its portal was transferred to the north façade and replaced by the present smaller example.

•• *Enter the garden R and proceed eastward to view the south façade.*

Most of St Médard's old graveyard, which lay south and east of the building, has been replaced by the present garden.

Both aisles were rebuilt in 1665.

Sculptures were added to the flying buttresses in 1902.

A larger chancel, with chapels, was built 1550–1632, the long construction period being due to interruptions commencing in 1586.

The square, steep-roofed Catechism Chapel was added to the south side of the chancel by **Petit-Radel** in 1784.

Concealing the chancel's apse, at the east end, is the Lady Chapel, built on the site of the old charnel house by **Petit-Radel**, *c.*1775.

•• *First L Rue de Candolle. First L Rue Daubenton.*

Two blocked portals are passed.

The west front's original 16C portal is now the entrance to a picturesque alleyway, between Nos 41 and 43 Rue Daubenton. This leads to the north door of the church, which occasionally serves as its only access.

•• *If locked, continue to Rue Mouffetard L and enter St Médard from the west front.*

Interior The original stained glass was destroyed when the Huguenots vandalized the church in 1561; the present glass is modern.

At the west end, the organ, made by **Cliquot** in 1767, has been restored; its case was made by **Pilon** in 1646.

•• *Follow the **north aisle**.*

Although rebuilt in 1665 both aisles retain their 16C vaults; as they acted as buttresses to the nave, they could not be removed with safety.

Many of the vaults in the chapels retain their original carved corbels.

Pillars in the unusually wide **chancel** were fluted as part of the Greek Revival alterations made by **Petit-Radel** *c.*1775.

The chancel's east window was made in 1620.

•• *Proceed to the **north ambulatory**.*

Some columns retain their exuberant Renaissance capitals.

•• *Continue to the south side of the **nave**.*

The pulpit was made *c.*1718.

In the **Chapelle Ste Catherine**, the triptych behind the pulpit is 16C.

•➔ Exit from the west door of St Médard L. Proceed ahead following Rue de Bazeilles, leading to Avenue des Gobelins, and cross immediately to its west side. First L Rue Claude Bernard. Take bus 27 southbound to Manufacture des Gobelins (thus avoiding an uninteresting walk). From the bus stop, which also serves M Gobelins, return northward and enter the Gobelins factory L.

Location 8	**MANUFACTURE DES GOBELINS**

42 Avenue des Gobelins

Open only for guided tours in French, Tuesday, Wednesday and Thursday 14.00– 16.30.

Gobelins tapestries have been made here since the 17C and some of the original buildings survive; the works, however, are 19C. A good knowledge of French is needed to follow the guide's explanation of the different techniques employed and it is possible to observe craftsmen making the tapestries only if the natural light is adequate. Work will be suspended in poor light, as artificial illumination, which changes the appearance of the colours, is not permitted.

Jean Gobelins, a Flemish dyer who in the 15C had settled with others by the Bièvre stream, discovered the secret of making a scarlet dye and founded the family tapestry business, which moved to its present site in 1662. The royal tapestry works was brought from Fontainebleau to Paris by Henri II in the mid-16C and installed here by Henri IV in 1601.

Louis XIV's first minister Colbert added furniture manufacturing in 1667 and formed, under the direction of Le Brun, and later Pierre Mignard, the royal workshops for making the Crown's tapestries and furnishings. Royal carpet manufacture, under the direction of Gobelins since 1662, was brought here from the Savonnerie at Chaillot in 1826. After the Second World War, the manufacture of Beauvais tapestries was also transferred here, the works at Beauvais having been completely destroyed by bombs in 1940. The government owns and runs Gobelins and every item is commissioned for presentation by the state; no private work is undertaken.

•➔ Enter the courtyard.

A statue commemorates the first director of Gobelins, **Charles Le Brun**.

•➔ Continue ahead, enter the works in the corner L and await the guide.

The tour lasts approximately forty-five minutes.

•➔ Exit from Gobelins L. Second R Boulevard St Marcel. Take bus 91 eastbound to La Pitié (two stops) thus, once more, avoiding a monotonous walk.

Location 9	**HÔPITAL DE LA SALPÊTRIÈRE**

47 Boulevard de l'Hôpital

Courtyards and chapel open daily 08.30–18.30. Admission free.

Now part of a massive general hospital complex, most of the 17C buildings of the old Salpêtrière, including the original chapel, survive around its courtyards.

History In 1656 Louis XIV established a hospital for aged and insane women on the site of a saltpetre works founded by his father. It formed part of the

King's Hôpital Général and was soon extended to cater for the rehabilitation of vagrants. There were around 50,000 of them in Paris, and the buildings were extended and redeveloped under the direction of **Le Vau**, 1657–63. In 1684 a women's prison for prostitutes and criminals was incorporated in the complex and it was here that Manon Lescaut was held. The prisoners were given only bread, water and soup and had to sleep on straw. More than 8,000 patients were accommodated in the Salpêtrière, then the world's largest hospital, at the outbreak of the Revolution. Thirty-five captives were murdered there during the September massacres of 1792.

Buildings were added specifically for the treatment of the insane by Viel Saint-Maur in 1789, and in 1795 Philippe Pinel became the first to release such patients from chains.

Between the railway bridge and the hospital's gatehouse stands a statue of Dr Philippe Pinel, d.1826, by **L. Durand**.

●● *Proceed through the gatehouse to the Cour St Louis, laid out as a formal flower garden.*

Although planned by **Le Vau**, the complex, completed in 1663, was developed by **Duval** and **Le Muet**.

The north wing L was begun in 1660, with the help of a donation from Mazarin.

The matching wing, on the south side R, was not built until 1756.

●● *Pass through the central archway to the **Chapelle St Louis**, with its octagonal cupola, immediately ahead.*

Libéral Bruant designed the chapel in 1664 while he was working at Invalides.

●● *Enter from the west end.*

Above the entrance stands the early-18C organ, with its Louis XV-style case.

In the north-west corner is the railed-in 17C font.

Built to a Greek-cross plan, the massive bare interior is divided into eight barn-like areas, each of which was allocated to a specific category of inmate: men, boys, girls, infectious patients, etc. Up to 4,000 at a time could attend Mass in the chapel.

Toward the east end, on the north side, is an iron 17C lectern.

Facing this, to the south, is the unusually plain oak pulpit.

●● *Exit from the north transept and proceed to the inner courtyard.*

From this courtyard a rear view of the complex is obtained.

●● *Turn R and proceed to Cour Lassay, south of the chapel.*

●● *Return to Boulevard de l'Hôpital L and proceed to M St Marcel.*

18

Père Lachaise Cemetery and La Villette

A pilgrimage is made to the world's most famous cemetery, the last resting place of Oscar Wilde, Edith Piaf and Maria Callas. Just a short stroll away is Jacques Mélac, one of the most popular bars in Paris and guaranteed to build up one's spirits before contemplating the hereafter. Ste Marguerite, rarely visited, possesses not only what is claimed to be the grave of the young Louis XVII but also one of the finest Baroque chapels in Paris, painted by the great **Brunetti.** Finally, a tour is made of the capital's new 'park of the future' at La Villette.

Timing: Fine weather is essential for visiting Père Lachaise – a gloomy day should certainly be avoided.

Mélac's bar closes Sunday, Monday and all July.

Ste Marguerite's church closes 12.00–15.00.

All La Villette's attractions are closed Monday, and some do not open in the winter months until the afternoon.

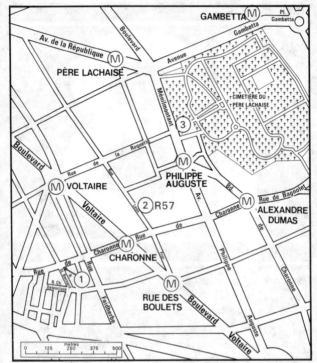

For Location 4 see page 291.

Start *M Fadherbe Chaligny, line 8 Balard/Créteil-Préfecture. Exit from the station R, following Rue St Antoine westward. First R Rue St Bernard.*

Location 1	**STE-MARGUERITE**

36 Rue St Bernard

It is alleged that the ten-year-old Louis XVII, whose parents Louis XVI and Marie Antoinette were guillotined, lies in Ste Marguerite's small graveyard. The Chapelle des Ames is outstandingly decorated by **Brunetti** in the Baroque style.

Ste Marguerite's was built in 1634 for the inhabitants of the Faubourg St Antoine, which had greatly expanded from its parish church of St Paul – St Louis.

The chancel and aisles were extended eastward in 1663 and a Lady Chapel added as a south transept.

Further chapels were added to the north side in the 18C.

•• *Enter the west doorway.*

Flanking the doorway are the two most important paintings in the church.

North side *Massacre of the Innocents* by **Giordano**, late 17C.

South side *Descent from the Cross* by **Salviati**, mid-16C.

In the north aisle's second bay is the tomb of Antoine Fayet, curate of St Paul – St Louis, d.1634, who instigated the building of Ste Marguerite.

Forming the north transept is the **Chapelle Ste Marguerite**, added in 1703.

Attached to its east side is the **Chapelle des Ames** (souls). An attendant will illuminate this on request. **Victor Louis**, architect of the development around the Palais Royal's garden, added this chapel in 1764. Its grisaille decoration, by **Brunetti**, is some of the finest Baroque *trompe-l'œil* work in Paris.

On the east wall, behind the high altar, is a marble pietà. This came from the tomb of the wife of the sculptor Girardon and is the work of two of his pupils.

Request permission to view the small cemetery north of the church.

A simple tombstone is inscribed 'LXVII 1785–1795' implying that it marks the last resting place of Louis XVII, who disappeared while imprisoned in the Temple. As might be expected, the circumstances are swathed in mystery. It is known that a youth died in the Temple, of tuberculosis, on 8 June 1795. Monsieur Bertrand, the cemetery's keeper, who lived nearby, stated that at nightfall on 10 June that year, a cortège arrived at the graveyard of Ste Marguerite from the Temple with a coffin, in which lay the body of a young man; this was then secretly buried in a communal grave. On the following night, Bertrand claims to have reburied the coffin beneath the east pillar of the north transept's doorway. However, nothing was found in this region when excavations took place in 1980.

A further puzzle is that the remains beneath the tombstone appear to be those of a young man of twenty, whereas Louis would have been only ten years old in 1795. Some believe that another child was substituted for Louis XVII in the Temple cell and that, like his sister, the young King was released to live in anonymity.

●● *Exit from the church R. First R Rue de Charonne. Sixth L Rue Léon Frot.*

Location 2	**JACQUES MÉLAC**

42 Rue Léon Frot

Open Tuesday and Thursday 08.30–24.00; Wednesday, Friday and Saturday 08.30–1900. Closed July.

Although situated well away from the city centre (but almost on top of the Charonne Métro station), Jacques Mélac's establishment is a place of pilgrimage for many wine bar enthusiasts, who consider this to be the ultimate of its genre in Paris. Beams, sawdust on the floor and a 'local' ambience, all presided over by the lively and attentive *patron*, who sports one of the finest handlebar moustaches in the capital, create a magical mix akin to that of a good British pub: something that Paris 'pubs', in spite of heavy investment on décor, rarely achieve. Monsieur Mélac is intent on protecting his customers from the horrors of consuming water, and several posters warn of its dangers: 'Fish fornicate in it' (almost *sic*) proclaims one.

Uniquely in Paris, a vine clings to the exterior of the bar, and great merriment ensues when its grapes are harvested each autumn.

●● *Exit L. First L Rue de Charonne. First L Avenue Philippe Auguste leads to Boulevard de Ménilmontant.*

Continue ahead to the entrance to the cemetery second R.

Location 3	CIMETIÈRE DU PÈRE LACHAISE

Boulevard de Mènilmontant

Open daily mid-March–early November 07.30–18.00. Early November–mid March 08.00–17.30.

Many representatives of the arts are buried at Père Lachaise, the world's most famous cemetery. Visitors seek out the tombs of Oscar Wilde, Edith Piaf and, with great difficulty, Sarah Bernhardt. Maria Callas and Simone Signoret, whose remains have been brought here in recent years, are also commemorated.

Père François de la Chaise (1624–1709), confessor of Louis XIV, lived in a house on the site, which had been built in 1626 by the Jesuits. This was rebuilt in 1682, Lachaise contributing to its cost. In 1804 the city of Paris purchased the property and surrounding land for conversion to a cemetery. The remains of La Fontaine and Molière, transferred here later that year, were the first to be interred.

The Paris Communards made their last stand in the cemetery, 27 May 1871, fighting amidst the gravestones. At dawn the following day, 147 of them who had been captured were shot against the wall in the south-east corner (*Mur des Fédérés*) and buried where they fell.

The 116–acre cemetery is the largest and most fashionable in Paris; many of the tombs are dominated by 19C funereal sculpture, little of which is of outstanding artistic interest. Oscar Wilde's tomb, however, is surmounted by a sculpture commissioned from **Epstein**.

A plan of the cemetery may be purchased immediately R of the entrance at Porte du Repos. This indicates the principal points of interest but, in spite of its generous scale, many tombs are difficult to locate. Apart from the names already mentioned, illustrious occupants of Père Lachaise include: **Writers** Apollinaire, Balzac, Beaumarchais, Colette, Gertrude Stein. **Artists** Corot, David, Daumier, Delacroix, Ingres, Modigliani, Seurat. **Dancer** Isadora Duncan.

In the south-west corner, the tomb monument to Abélard and Héloïse was brought here from the abbey at Parnclete, where it had been set up in 1779; the remains of the immortal lovers lie below.

Gothic fragments from the abbey church of Nogent-sur-Seine, rescued by Alexandre Lenoir, form its canopy.

•► *Exit R and proceed ahead to M Père Lachaise. Take line 2 Porte Dauphine to Stalingrad. Take line 7 La Courneuve to Porte de la Villette. Exit L and follow signs to Cité des Sciences et de L'Industrie.*

Location 4	PARC DE LA VILLETTE

30 Avenue Corentin Cariou

La Maison de la Villette. Open Wednesday–Sunday 14.00–19.00. Admission free.

La Villette appeals particularly to children, who represent 70 per cent of the attendance figures. The spherical Géode cinema and the planetarium, both part of la Villette's 'Science City', are the sections of greatest interest to most visitors. Fluency in French is needed to appreciate much of the remainder, although the parkland will undoubtedly prove an attraction when it has matured.

From 1867 to 1974 La Villette was a livestock market

Cité des Sciences et de l'Industrie. Open Tuesday, Thursday and Friday 10.00–18.00; Saturday and Sunday 12.00–20.00; Wednesday 12.00–21.00. Admission charge.

Géode. Film shows Tuesday and Thursday 10.00–18.00; Wednesday, Friday, Saturday and Sunday 10.00–21.00. Admission charge. A combined ticket for entry to the Géode and the Cité des Sciences et de l'Industrie at reduced rate is available here.

and slaughterhouse. Early in the 1960s a vast abattoir was begun, millions of francs being spent on its construction. Deep foundations and a concrete frame were completed, but at this stage it was finally accepted that the advent of refrigerated transport had made the whole project non-viable. The city's greatest white elephant of all time seemed doomed, but to demolish it would have involved more wasted expenditure and an alternative use was sought. In 1970 the City of Paris presented the state with the entire 136-acre site, and festivals and concerts were held in the old cattle market.

Approval was given in 1979 to create a 'park of the future' at La Villette, and four years later **Bernard Tschumi** won the international competition to plan its development.

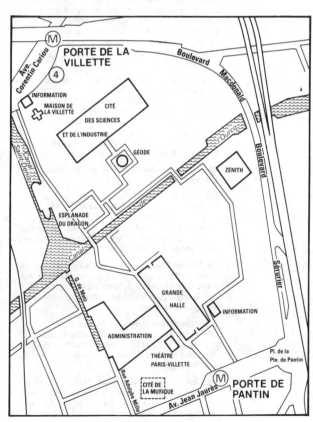

4 Parc de la Villette

La Maison de la Villette The 19C Villette House originally served as a veterinary laboratory and the head office of the meat inspectors.

Temporary exhibitions are held on the ground floor.

The permanent display 'Cent Ans d'Abattoirs' (Hundred years of abattoirs), on the mezzanine floor, traces the history of La Villette.

•— Exit R and follow the esplanade, passing through the Cité des Sciences et de L'Industrie building to the Géode.

At the Géode purchase tickets for the next available performance (see below). Each film show is always full and long delays can occur, particularly during the tourist season, weekends and school holidays. Spend the waiting period viewing the other attractions of the park.

•— Return to the Cité des Sciences et de l'Industrie. Enter the building and ascend to the first floor.

Cité des Sciences et de l'Industrie Visitors expecting to see a futuristic version of London's Science Museum will be disappointed. Non-French-speaking visitors, in particular, will gain an impression of extensive empty areas punctuated with incomprehensible models and film shows. There is, however, a splendid planetarium, but an additional admission charge is levied and, generally, the queue is lengthy.

This seven-and-a-half-acre building began life as the white elephant abattoir that inspired the entire La Villette project. It is four times the size of the Pompidou Centre. **Adrien Fainsilber** was chosen in 1980 to adapt the framework into a 'supermarket of the future' as outlined by President Giscard d'Estaing, with four basic functions of display, documentation, communications and research.

•— Ascend the elevator to the first of the three exhibition levels.

There are four themes: Secrets of the Earth and Universe, Adventure of Life, Evolution of Man's Work, and Communications. Individual highlights are the creation of volcanoes, a model of the nuclear submarine *Nautilus*, the Ariane Rocket, the Aquatic Farm and the Garden of Robots.

The Planetarium (additional admission fee) generally entails a lengthy queue for each performance, given every forty-five minutes, but there is a capacity of 260. Images are received direct from observatories throughout the world.

A documentation centre, **the Mediathèque** (admission free), contains thousands of volumes, periodicals, films and software packs. Videodiscs are presented by robot. Obviously the emphasis is on the French language.

•— Descend to the ground floor. Turn L and exit to the south side of the building. Progress depends on if and at what time the Géode is being visited. However, all further attractions lie to the south of the Géode.

Géode Technically part of the City of Science and

Industry, this spherical cinema is the highlight of La Villette for most visitors.

The 110 foot diameter, spherical cinema, clad with polished steel, was designed by **Fainsilber** and opened in 1985. Inside, the largest hemispheric cinema screen in the world covers 9,000 square feet. It is made of perforated aluminium. Spectators are completely immersed in the image, which is nine times larger than usual, the gauge of the film projected being 70 mm instead of the conventional 35 mm.

➤ *Exit and proceed southward to the canal. Follow the path R and cross by the bridge L. On the south side keep to the upper level and turn L.*

Parkland
The buildings are set in almost 87 acres of parkland, which its planner, **Tschumi**, decided should be a mix of gardens, promenades and follies. Various landscape designers were involved, each having responsibility for an individual sector.

Two canals penetrate the park, and linked galleries, built parallel with them, provide covered walkways.

See the plan of La Villette (page 291) for the position of the remaining sections.

Zénith
Opened in 1984, the building was created for pop and rock concerts. It has a capacity of 6,400.

La Grande Halle
Open Tuesday–Sunday from 10.00.

Built in 1867 as a cattle market, by **Jules de Merindol**, the hall's cast iron and steel structure covers a five-acre site. It has been renovated and enclosed in glass by **Bernard Reicher** and **Philippe Robert** to accommodate trade fairs and large exhibitions.

The building has a capacity of 15,000.

La Cité de la Musique
Christian de Portzamparc was selected as the architect in 1984. Primarily, the 'city' is to serve as the new home of the Conservatoire National Supérieur de Musique, and up-to-date equipment has been installed for teaching music and training musicians.

The concert hall, which seats 800–1,200, accommodates Boulez's Ensemble Intercontemporain.

A new **Gallery of Musical Instruments** displays the Conservatoire's collection of 4,000 items from all periods, previously housed at Rue de Madrid. This will be the first stage of a Centre de l'Instrument de Musique.

A documentation centre is planned for the future.

➤ *Exit from Parc de la Villette and return to M Porte de la Villette.*

Restaurants and Bars

It has been estimated that there are more than 10,000 establishments in Paris where food and drink of some kind are served. The following selection is based on a combination of the author's personal experience and expert advice received. However, it must be emphasized that many other fine restaurants certainly exist, particularly in the middle price ranges, and the visitor will doubtless make his or her own discoveries.

Each establishment is numbered consecutively and these numbers appear on most of the maps throughout this book, with the prefix R for refreshments. Restaurants are shown first, in alphabetical order, but subdivided into groups by price categories, which refer to a three-course evening meal, including an economical wine. It is often possible to eat, at lower cost, a *table d'hôte* lunch even in luxury restaurants. Bars follow, in alphabetical order.

With few exceptions, bars and restaurants close for a few days around Christmas and for approximately four weeks during the holiday period between mid-July and early September. Sunday and Monday are days when many will also close. The situation regarding public holidays varies considerably.

LUXURY RESTAURANTS (OVER 600 FRANCS)

1 Le Bernardin (map page 82) *18 Rue Troyon (43 80 40 61) M Charles de Gaulle Étoile. Closed Sunday, Monday and August.*
The most highly regarded fish restaurant in Paris; there is a branch in New York.
Specialities: sea urchins; Brittany oysters.

2 Le Grand Véfour (map pages 28, 139) *17 Rue de Beaujolais (42 96 56 27) M Palais Royal. Closed Saturday, Sunday and 14 July–20 August.*
One of the world's most beautiful and historic restaurants. See page 41. At lunch, only the *table d'hôte* menu is offered; at dinner, only the *à la carte.* Cuisine is classic with modern touches.
Specialities: turbot; bass; veal kidneys; soufflés.

3 Jamin (map pages 70, 82) *32 Rue de Longchamp (47 27 12 27) M Trocadéro. Closed Saturday, Sunday, July.*
Patron/chef Joël Robuchon is regarded as the most inventive chef in Paris and this is the place to savour modern French cuisine at its finest. Nowhere else have I eaten veal that has such a positive natural taste, is rose pink in colour and yet melt-in-the-mouth tender. Dishes are presented as if they were paintings, and flavours can be subtly unusual, although never worryingly so. Unfortunately, advance bookings can stretch to three months and most visitors to Paris will need to reserve their table long before leaving home. Equally unfortunately, Robuchon's famous 145-franc menu is no more. The seasonal menu (of eight courses, plus an aperitif snack, plus *petits fours*, plus chocolate truffles) is offered at lunch or dinner, and gives an opportunity to taste several Robuchon specialities, particularly his desserts. Many will wish they had brought a 'doggy bag'.
Specialities: ravioli aux langoustines; pineapple tart; potato purée; roast lamb within a salt crust.

4 Lucas-Carton (map pages 105, 138) *9 Place de la Madeleine (42 65 22 90) M Madeleine. Closed Saturday, Sunday, August, 21 December–5 January.*

Renowned chef, Alain Senderens, presides over what is probably the most expensive restaurant in Paris – although a *table d'hôte* menu is offered at lunchtime. The restaurant retains its Belle Epoque décor, based on exquisite Art-Nouveau wood-carving from the master, Majorelle, and is classed as a national monument.

Specialities: duck's liver with celery and apples; pineapple fritters with pina colada.

5 Maxim's (map page 138) *3 Rue Royale (42 65 27 94) M Concorde.*

The most famous restaurant in the world. (See page 141). Original Art-Nouveau décor and atmosphere are all-important, but the food is improving after a bad patch. Reserve at least fourteen days in advance for evenings, and expect to spend at least 1,000 francs per head, which includes dancing. Lunchtime tables are easier to obtain and the cost will be almost halved.

Specialities: sole Albert, vintage champagnes.

6 Taillevent (map page 83) *15 Rue Lamennais (45 61 12 90) M George V. Closed Saturday, Sunday, second week in February, late July–late August.*

For some years, this restaurant has fought a duel with Robuchon's for the accolade of best restaurant in Paris. Taillevent specializes in perfectly cooked established dishes, but with lighter than usual sauces. It is possible to spend only a little more than 500 francs per head *à la carte*. As at Jamin's, long advance booking is necessary.

Specialities: turbot, game, marquise au chocolat.

7 La Tour d'Argent (map pages 241, 278) *15–17 Quai de la Tournelle (43 54 23 31) M Pont Marie. Closed Sunday.*

The oldest established of the great Paris restaurants. (See page 251). La Tour d'Argent, situated on the building's fourth floor, is famous for its romantic views of Notre Dame, its pressed duck, and its high prices. Once, fifteen duck dishes were offered on the menu, but these have been reduced to four. Always on offer is the famous caneton à la Tour d'Argent. This dish, of pressed duck served with a sauce made from its blood, was created by Frédéric, the restaurant's owner during the Third Republic; each one served is given a number, now running into thousands. An economical lunchtime *table d'hôte* menu is offered, but a supplement must be paid if the pressed duck is required (for two people only).

Specialities: salmon; lobster; duck; quenelles; soufflés.

EXPENSIVE RESTAURANTS (300–600 FRANCS)

8 Allard (map pages 209, 240) *41 Rue St André des Arts (43 26 48 23) M St Michel. Closed Saturday, Sunday, August, Christmas week.*

The Allard family no longer own this bistro, one of the best known in Paris, but most of the old favourites have been retained on the menu; alas, however, the incomparable bœuf à la mode is no more. Diners in the cosy, wooden interior face the original zinc bar and open kitchen.

Specialities: escargots; turbot au beurre blanc; caneton aux olives; Burgundies.

9 L'Ami Louis (map page 188) *32 Rue du Vertbois (48 87 77 48)*
M Temple. Closed Monday, Tuesday, second half of July, August.
This is the only Paris bistro where pre-war-style French cooking
can still be found. Sadly, the venerable Antoine Magnin died in
1987, aged 87, but nothing appears to have changed at L'Ami
Louis, including the 'honourably scarred' 1920s decor. Chef Bibi,
Antoine's assistant for many years, meticulously continues to
provide the same enormous escargots, slabs of foie gras and
succulent, buttery roast chicken and game. Helpings are
enormous and the cornucopia of exotic fresh fruits appears to
have been rushed direct from Hédiard's counters in Place de la
Madeleine. Even the coffee is *à la grand-mère*, a Paris rarity. A
week's notice is usually required for an evening reservation, but
lunch can often be booked on the same day.
Specialities: just about everything on the menu.

10 Au Pied de Cochon (map pages 28, 118, 139) *6 Rue Coquillière
(43 36 11 75) M Les Halles. Open 24 hours daily.*
Established before the Second World War as a brasserie to serve
the Les Halles porters, the tradition of opening 24 hours a day has
been maintained since the market's departure. Decoration is
modern, but in a bright, Belle Epoque manner, with mirrors,
painted ceilings and columns. The terrace now overlooks a
pedestrianized street, but for long the brasserie suffered acutely
from the Forum's excavation work.
Specialities: onion soup; grilled pig's trotters with Béarnaise
sauce; apple sorbet with Calvados.

11 Le Bourdonnais (map page 71) *113 Avenue de La Bourdonnais
(47 05 47 96) M Ecole Militaire. Closed Sunday, Monday.*
Modern French cuisine is offered at not too extortionate a price,
and flavours are delicate, often with a Provençal influence. Air-
conditioning is a boon on a hot summer's day.
Specialities: skate; cockle soup; pigeon pie; sweetbreads; all the
desserts.

12 Carré des Feuillants (map pages 49, 138) *14 Rue de Castiglione
(42 86 82 82) M Concorde. Closed Sunday.*
Approached through a courtyard named Espace Castiglione, this
is one of the prettiest of the capital's restaurants. *Table d'hôte*
menus are offered at lunch and dinner.
Specialities: regularly changed, but always including dishes from
the Landes region; fine Armagnacs.

13 Chez Pauline (map page 139) *5 Rue Villedo (42 96 20 70)
M Pyramides. Closed Saturday evening, Sunday, July, Christmas
week.*
A traditional-style bistro, with old spotted mirrors, the emphasis
is on classic French dishes. Rooms are on the ground and first
floors. Service is exceptionally friendly.
Specialities: blanquette de veau; bœuf Bourguignon; calf's head;
rice pudding.

14 Dodin Bouffant (map page 154) *25 Rue Frédéric Sauton
(43 25 25 14) M Maubert Mutualité. Two sessions in the evening.
Closed Saturday, Sunday, 15–31 August, 21 December–5 January.*
One of the city's most reasonably priced *cuisine nouvelle*
restaurants; unusual combinations of food create unfamiliar
flavours, generally successfully. President Mitterrand and Karl
Lagerfeld frequently dine here. Absolutely not to be missed is the

fresh raspberry soufflé, which must be ordered at the same time as the main course.
Specialities: herring marinated with dill; daube of oysters, scallops and pig's trotters in red wine; duck and sweetbreads ragoût; soufflés.

15 Kinaguwa (map pages 49, 138) *9 Rue du Mont Thabor (42 60 65 07) M Tuileries. Closed Sunday, second half of August, 24 December–3 January.*
Rated the best Japanese restaurant in Paris, with some dishes allegedly up to Tokyo standard.
Specialities: sukiyaki, sashimi.

16 Mercure Galant (map pages 28, 139) *15 Rue des Petits Champs (42 97 53 85) M Pyramides. Closed Saturday lunch, Sunday.*
The five-course, *table d'hôte* menu offers some of the best value *haute cuisine* in Paris.
Specialities: foie gras; confits de canard; all desserts, particularly milles feuilles.

17 Pierre Traiteur (map pages 28, 139) *10 Rue de Richelieu (42 96 09 17) M Palais Royal. Closed Saturday, Sunday, August.*
A smart bistro, with long-established popular dishes.
Specialities: mackerel marinated in cider; calves' kidneys with shallots; gratin dauphinois (potatoes cooked with *crème fraîche* and Gruyère cheese).

18 Relais Louis XIII (map pages 2, 209, 240) *1 Rue du Pont de Lodi (43 26 75 96) M St Michel. Closed Sunday, Monday lunch, 1–9 July.*
Exposed beams, bare stonework, this is one of the capital's most picturesque restaurants; all is genuine. A *table d'hôte* lunch is offered.
Specialities: fish and extravagant sauces.

MEDIUM-PRICE RESTAURANTS (100–300 FRANCS)

19 A La Tour de Montlhéry (map pages 28, 118) *5 Rue des Prouvaires (42 36 21 82) M Les Halles. Open 24 hours a day. Closed Saturday, Sunday and mid July–mid August.*
The *patron* – twinkling, bewhiskered Jack (not Jacques) Paul – has British ancestry and is particularly welcoming to English visitors. Jack formerly acted as bodyguard to De Gaulle, and his bistro, in consequence, is a favourite haunt of politicians, such as ex-president Giscard d'Estaing. Great hams are suspended from the beamed ceiling. This is a particularly good place to celebrate the arrival of Beaujolais Nouveau.
Specialities: onglet steak; pigs' trotters.

20 Androuët (map pages 94,105) *41 Rue d'Amsterdam (48 74 26 93) M St Lazare. Closed Sunday.*
A cheese-lover's paradise, Androuët's restaurant, on the first floor, was opened in 1926, above the most famous cheese shop in Paris, founded seventeen years earlier. All main courses incorporate cheese, and an entire meal can be made by selecting from seven cheeseboards. Be warned, however, after ten varieties have been sampled, they all taste the same, ten more and nausea sets in – a bottle of claret is essential as an antidote.
Specialities: Brie de Meaux and the great 'smellies' Epoisses, Livarot, Maroilles and Munster. All cheeses sampled may be purchased from the ground-floor shop – there are five cellars

below, where the largest stock in Paris reaches maturity.

21 Au Duc de Richelieu (map page 139) *110 Rue de Richelieu (42 96 38 38) M Richelieu Drouot. Closed Sunday, August. Service until 05.00.*
The *patron* owns a vineyard in Fleurie and the bistro is *en fête* on the Beaujolais Nouveau arrival day, with Burgundian costumes, music and dancing. A lively bar, separate from the eating area, serves excellent wines by the glass – try the Saint Amour.
Specialities: steaks; Lyonnais dishes.

22 Au Franc Pinot (map pages 154, 168) *1 Quai de Bourbon (43 29 46 98) M Pont Marie. Closed Sunday, Monday.*
An historic, 350-year-old building houses this establishment, which is divided into a ground-floor bar and two beamed restaurant floors below. Bar food includes platters of smoked meats and cheeses. *Table d'hôte* menus are offered.
Specialities: fish; chocolate marquise with chestnut purée.

23 Chez Jenny (map page 188) *39 Boulevard du Temple (42 74 75 75) M République. Service daily until 01.00.*
Many believe that this Alsatian brasserie serves the best choucroute in Paris. Marquetry in the first-floor room, by **Spindler**, is spectacular.
Specialities: choucroute, coq au vin, Alsatian beers and wines.

24 Chez Vong Aux Halles (map page 119) *38 Rue de la Grande Truanderie (42 96 29 89) M Etienne Marcel. Closed Sunday.*
The most celebrated Chinese restaurant in the capital.
Specialities: dim sum; shrimp with lotus leaves; enchanted lamb.

25 L'Escargot Montorgueuil (map page 139) *38 Rue Montorgueuil (42 36 83 51) M Etienne Marcel. Closed Monday lunch, third week in August.*
A huge figure of a snail, above the entrance, emphasizes the name and speciality of this long-established bistro, once the most fashionable in the district. The reception area's ceiling, painted by **Clairin**, was brought here in 1923 from Sarah Bernhardt's dining room. Much of the restaurant's décor was created *c.*1830. There is a *table d'hôte* menu.
Specialities: escargots in many forms, particularly fricassée; caneton à l'orange.

26 Flo (Brasserie) (map page 188) *7 Cour des Petites Ecuries (47 70 13 59) M Château d'Eau. Closed August.*
Always crowded and lively, tables adjoin and this is a splendid place for those on their own, as everybody talks to everyone else. Décor is refurbished, late 19C, with wood panelling and stained-glass skylights. Flo is a member of the chain that includes Julien (No 31) and Le Vaudeville (No 36), where similar food and ambience prevail.
Specialities: foie gras; choucroute.

27 Indra (map pages 83, 104) *10 Rue du Cdt-Rivière (43 59 46 40) M St Philippe du Roule. Closed Saturday lunch and Sunday.*
English visitors in need of a curry 'fix' will find Indra hard to beat. The sauces are particularly delicate, as the French are not too keen on the 'ordeal by fire' varieties so common in England. Most Indian restaurants in Paris offer lassa (one is enough for two people), a refreshing, yoghourt-based drink, which is a much more suitable accompaniment to curry than wine or beer. *Table d'hôte* menus are offered.
Specialities: Punjabi dishes; tandoori fish.

28 Jehlum (map page 139) *30 Rue St Marc (42 96 99 43)*
M Richelieu Drouot. Open daily.
Another Indian restaurant, but less ambitious than Indra.
Specialities: tikka; tandoori.

29 Joe Allen (map page 119) *30 Rue Pierre Lescot (42 36 70 13)*
M Châtelet les Halles. Open daily.
American cuisine and a lively atmosphere prevail. Portions are
very generous. Brunch is served Saturday and Sunday 12.00–
17.00.
Specialities: black bean soup; barbecue ribs; banana pie.

30 Jo Goldenberg (map pages 155, 168, 188) *7 Rue des Rosiers*
(48 87 20 16) M St Paul. Open daily.
The place in Paris for Jewish specialities, although Goldenberg's
small restaurant plays second fiddle to his delicatessen (see
page 184).
Specialities: Israeli foie gras; borscht; smoked fish and meats.

31 John Jameson (map pages 105, 138) *10 Rue des Capucines*
(40 15 00 30) M Opéra or Madeleine. Closed Saturday lunch,
Sunday evening, Monday.
A delightful, 'Dublin Georgian' restaurant has been created
above the Kitty O'Shea bar, in which Irish specialities,
surprisingly still virtually unobtainable in England, may be
sampled. Home-made soda bread (the finest bread that I tasted in
Paris), delectable smoked salmon fron Connemara, and Dublin-
brewed Guinness are a revelation to those unfamiliar with
Ireland. A splendid 'farmhouse' brunch is served on Sunday
at 13.30.
Specialities: as above, plus Irish stew.

32 Julien (map page 188) *16 Rue du Faubourg St Denis*
(47 70 12 06) M Strasbourg St Denis.
Another late-19C brasserie, restored in the same style as
Brasserie Flo (No 26) but even prettier. Food and atmosphere are
similar.
Specialities: saumon en rillettes; cassoulet d'oie; profiteroles au
chocolat.

33 Lipp (Brasserie) (map page 208) *151 Boulevard St Germain.*
No reservations accepted. M St Germain des Prés.
The place to see and be seen – as long as one is seated on the
ground floor. Defined as a brasserie, due to its Alsatian origins
under Monsieur Lippmann, Lipp's is basically a large restaurant
fronted by a small café. Pretty, turn-of-the-century décor features
ceramic tiles illustrating birds and flora. Sadly, the food,
particularly the daily speciality, can be a let-down. I have eaten
better cassoulet from a tin, and the Roquefort can be very rock-
like. Outstanding service.
Specialities: strong Munster cheese (always exceptional);
Fontainebleau à la crème (like a blown-up Petit Suisse, served
with sugar and fresh cream).

34 Pharamond (map page 119) *24 Rue de la Grande Truanderie*
(42 33 06 72) M Etienne Marcel. Closed Sunday, Monday lunch,
July.
Norman specialities are prepared by the patron/chef in this
attractive, 'Belle Epoque' restaurant, with its orange-tree tiles.
Specialities: tripe à la mode de Caen (rated the best in Paris); raie
(skate) au beurre blanc; cider from the Vallée d'Auge.

35 Le Roi du Pot au Feu (map pages 105, 138) *34 Rue Vignon (47 42 37 10) M Madeleine. Open 12.00–21.00. Closed Sunday, July.*
Pot au feu, the chief reason for coming here, is basically a hearty stew, incorporating various cuts of beef, bone marrow and vegetables. It is served first as a bouillon (beef soup) and then followed by the stew itself: ideal on a chilly day. A jolly atmosphere usually develops, partly inspired by the kitsch décor.

36 Tan Dinh (map pages 49, 208) *60 Rue de Verneuil (45 44 04 84) M Solférino. Closed Sunday, second half of August.*
Probably still the best Vietnamese restaurant in Europe, the delicate flavours are completely different from Chinese cuisine. There is a surprisingly good selection of clarets.
Specialities: ravioli filled with smoked goose; lime shrimp.

37 Le Vaudeville (map page 139) *29 Rue Vivienne (42 86 90 11) M Bourse. Open daily until 02.00.*
Originally a theatre, that witnessed the premiere of *La Dame aux Camélias*, by **Dumas**, the Vaudeville's marble and mosaic decor dates from its conversion to a brasserie in 1925.
Specialities: as for Julien (No 32), plus exceptional platters of fruits de mer.

38 Wally (map page 154) *16 Rue le Regrattier (43 25 01 39) M Pont Marie. Closed Saturday lunch, Sunday, Monday lunch, 1–15 January.*
In spite of its European name, Wally's is the best restaurant in Paris from which to be transported to North Africa. One eats basically Moroccan food, in what appears to be a Berber tent. The *table d'hôte* menu permits several dishes to be tasted.
Specialities: tajine; couscous; pstilla (pigeon's meat between leaves of flaky pastry).

INEXPENSIVE RESTAURANTS (BELOW 100 FRANCS)
(NB MANY DO NOT ACCEPT BOOKINGS OR CREDIT CARDS)

39 Au Pied de Fouet (map page 208) *45 Rue de Babylone (47 05 12 27) M Sèvres-Babylone. Open until 21.00. Closed Saturday evening, Sunday.*
A long-established, good-value bistro: arrive early to ensure a table.

40 Beaux Arts (map page 209) *11 Rue Bonaparte (43 26 92 64) M St Germain des Prés. Daily until 10.45.*
Favoured by the Left-Bank students, the lengthy *à la carte* menu includes more exotic dishes than most of the cheaper restaurants. The 48-franc set menu is generally best avoided.

41 Casa Miguel (map page 95) *48 Rue St Georges, M St Georges. Lunch 12.00–13.00, dinner 19.00–20.00.*
Maria Codena, now in her eighties, has the only Paris restaurant to feature in the *Guinness Book of Records*. The reason is that her three-course lunch or dinner, including wine, still costs just 5 francs! Only thirty-two people can be accommodated at either session and there are sometimes long queues; arrive well before 12.00 or 19.00. Maria is a philanthropic *emigrée* from Barcelona, 'In a world of plenty, hunger is a sin', but the merely curious, who may well be dining later at Maxim's, now tend to outnumber the needy. The main course is usually a choice between couscous and lentils. Obviously, this is not a place for gourmet food, and

fuller-bodied wine does exist elsewhere – it's the thought that counts.

42 Chartier (map page 139) *7 Rue du Faubourg Montmartre (47 70 86 29) M Rue Montmartre. Daily until 21.30.*
Chartier's, the most famous and spectacular budget restaurant in Paris, is its last '*bouillon*' (people's restaurant) to survive. A long, incredibly low-priced *à la carte* menu is served in a vast, turn-of-the-century, balconied hall. Tables are shared and the atmosphere is lively. Only with great difficulty can 80 francs be exceeded for three courses with wine. Queues may be long – if too long proceed to the nearby Druout restaurant, owned by the same establishment (see No 44). The customer is expected to write out his or her own bill on the paper table cover: the waiter sometimes checks it!
Specialities: simple French dishes as cooked in thousands of homes throughout the country.

43 Chez Ginette (map page 95) *101 Rue Caulaincourt (46 06 01 49) M Lamarck-Caulaincourt. Closed Sunday, August.*
Conveniently sitting above the Métro entrance, Chez Ginette's is one of Montmartre's best-value restaurants, partly because it is off the main tourist route. A *table d'hôte* menu is offered lunchtime only, but *à la carte* prices are reasonable.
Specialities: classic French dishes; home-made fruit tart.

44 Le Druout (map pages 28, 139) *103 Rue de Richelieu (42 96 68 23) M Richelieu-Druout. Daily until 22.00.*
Chartier's sister establishment, but less well known by tourists, and consequently less crowded. Clients tend to be 'regulars'. Menu and prices are practically identical to Chartier's, but last orders are taken thirty minutes later: at 22.00.

45 L'Incroyable (map pages 28, 139) *26 Rue de Richelieu (42 96 24 64) M Palais Royal. Closed Saturday evening, Sunday and Monday evening. Last orders 14.15 (14.00 Saturday) and 20.30.*
The *table d'hôte* menu includes three courses plus wine or mineral water. Quality is always excellent and this chintzy bistro is still hard to beat for sheer good value although not quite so outstanding since it changed owners in 1989. A small supplement will permit a speciality to be added to the choice. A pity that the bistro closes three evenings a week and last orders – strictly enforced – are so early.
Specialities: confits de canard, tripe à la mode de Caen; home-made fruit tarts.

46 Le P'tit Gavroche (map pages 154, 168, 188) *15 Rue Sainte Croix de la Bretonnerie (48 87 74 26) M Hôtel de Ville. Closed Sunday lunch.*
Situated in the heart of the ancient Marais quarter, this is the quintessential Paris bistro. Best to reserve a table from its small bohemian bar, where wine by the glass is amazingly cheap. Draft lager appears to be drawn from a goldfish bowl, but the fish survives and the brew is excellent. Old posters are a feature of the establishment, including, of course, an endearing portrayal of Victor Hugo's Gavroche from *Les Misérables*. Within the dining area, the *patron* bravely displays a huge chart, graphically describing what over-indulgence in alcohol does to the victim's appearance and liver. *A la carte* prices are amongst the capital's lowest and there is an economical lunch and dinner *table d'hôte* menu.
Specialities: steak with Roquefort sauce; coq au vin; maigret de canard (rare duck breasts); mousse au chocolat.

47 Le Petit Prince (map page 241) *12 Rue de Lanneau*
(43 54 77 26) M Maubert Mutualité. Open daily.
Some of the Latin Quarter's best-value food is served within
ancient stone walls and beamed ceilings. *Table d'hôte* two-course
menus are offered for lunch and dinner.
Specialities: macaroni au gratin; duck, spare ribs.

48 La Sourdière (map pages 49, 138) *4 Rue de la Sourdière*
(42 60 43 07) M Tuileries. Closed Saturday lunch and Sunday.
Excellent value food, *à la carte* or from the *table d'hôte* menu.
When entering La Sourdière it is advisable to conceal this
guidebook, as the patron, although welcoming tourists, is
paranoid that they might come in droves and upset his local
clientele (why then does he display an English translation of the
menu outside?).

49 Le Trumilou (map pages 154, 168) *84 Quai de l'Hôtel de Ville*
(42 77 03 98) M Pont Marie. Closed Monday.
Paintings cover the walls of this riverside bistro. It is always
packed and service may be slow at peak times. The menu here is a
little more ambitious than at most of the lower-priced restaurants,
and care is needed to keep within a 100-franc limit. The food,
however, is worth the little extra.
Specialities: canard aux pruneaux (duck with prunes); ris de veau
(calves' sweetbreads).

BARS
*(NB When ordering a beer (bière), ensure that it is pronounced
bee-air, otherwise you may be served a Byrrh, which is a sweet
apéritif.)*

50 Au Sauvignon (map pages 49, 208) *80 Rue des Saints Pères*
(45 48 49 02) M Sèvres Babylone or St Sulpice. Open 09.00–23.00.
Closed Sunday, August.
Undoubtedly the prettiest wine bar in Paris, Au Sauvignon is
decorated with paintings and giant, decorated envelopes. A
brightly coloured ceiling adds to the impression of drinking within
a Laura Ashley store. There is a small outdoor terrace.
Specialities: charcuterie; Bordeaux; Beaujolais.

51 Blue Fox (map pages 105, 138) *Cité Berryer (approached*
through 25 Rue Royale) (42 65 10 72) M Madeleine. Closed
Saturday evening and Sunday.
An easy-to-miss courtyard, under restoration in 1990, houses this
bar/restaurant, established by the English wine guru Steven
Spurrier, now personally managed by Mark Williamson. Very like
a London wine bar, with food always available, its summer
terrace will be even more pleasant once the extensive building
work has finished.
Specialities: first-rate wines from most regions; particularly
impressive is the exceptional range of Côtes du Rhône.

52 L'Ecluse (map pages 2, 209, 240) *15 Quai des Grands*
Augustins, M St Michel. Open until 02.00. Closed Sunday.
This riverside bar was formerly one of the smallest cabaret halls in
Paris, where performers included the young Marcel Marceau. An
ancient, woody atmosphere prevails, but prices are very modern,
i.e. high, as only vintage wines are served. Not, therefore, the
place for a lengthy session on plonk.

53 L'Entreacte (map pages 28, 139) *47 Rue de Montpensier, M Pyramides or Palais Royal. Closed Sunday.*
A popular, centrally placed bar just behind the Palais Royal. Its bright, tucked-in-the-corner site permits views looking up two 18C streets, which include the New Orleans-style Palais Royal theatre. Foreign banknotes are suspended from the ceiling, while the zinc bar gleams enticingly.
Specialities: charcuterie; salads; oysters and the hot dish of the day.

54 Le Fouquet's (map page 82) *99 Avenue des Champs Elysées (47 23 70 60) M George V. Open until 02.00.*
Le Fouquet's is a world-famous bar, with its terrace partly screened from *hoi polloi* by a hedge. Inside, wood panelling and a copper bar contribute to the atmosphere of genteel well-being. Cocktails are renowned, but cost the earth. Thankfully, Fouquet's has resisted the espresso machine, its coffee being served from *cafétières*.

55 Harry's New York Bar (map page 138) *5 Rue Daunou (42 61 71 14) M Opéra. Open daily 10.30–04.00.*
Harry's is a Paris institution. See page 148. Cocktails, although not cheap, are a generous size and always of the required alcoholic strength. In December a help-yourself Stilton cheese from England is placed in the bar every lunchtime. Arrive before 22.00 on Friday and Saturday, otherwise be prepared to queue.
Specialities: Bloody Mary (it was created here); Mint Julep; frankfurters.

56 Taverne Henri IV (map pages 2, 209) *13 Place du Pont Neuf (43 54 27 90) M Pont Neuf. Open 11.30–21.30. Closed Saturday, Sunday, mid-July–mid-August.*
This narrow bar, the most popular on the Ile de la Cité, is very crowded at lunchtime and early in the evening, when all is bonhomie.
Specialities: Loire valley wines; cheese; *charcuterie*.

57 Jacques Mélac (map page 288) *42 Rue Léon Frot (43 70 59 27) M Charonne. Open 08.30–19.00 Wednesday, Friday, Saturday; 8.30–24.00 Tuesday and Thursday. Closed Sunday, Monday, July.*
The handlebar-moustached Jacques presides over this, the most authentic of Paris wine bars: a must for every lover of the genre. See page 289.
Specialities: plat du jour, usually an Auvergne dish (every lunchtime and Tuesday evening); vin jaune.

58 Juvenile (map pages 28, 139) *47 Rue de Richelieu (42 97 46 49) M Pyramides or Palais Royal. Closed Sunday.*
A recently opened off-shoot of Willi's Wine Bar (No 63), most of Juvenile's friendly bar staff are English. Hot and cold food is available lunch and evening.
Specialities: château-bottled wines by the glass – list changed weekly.

59 Le Rubis (map pages 49, 138) *10 Rue du Marché St Honoré (42 61 03 39) M Tuileries. Open 07.00–22.00. Closed Saturday, Sunday, August.*
Many people's favourite central Paris bar: posters, price lists, bottles, polished glasses, all combine to evoke a Kurt Schwitters collage. The serpentine neon lighting, a feature of many Paris bars, is particularly successful here. Although small, and very crowded at lunchtime when businessmen order the hot dish of the

day (not available evenings), service is always efficient.
Specialities: casse croûte of assorted cheeses or *charcuterie*; home-
made rillettes; Roquefort.

60 Tabac de l'Institut (map page 209) *21 Rue de Seine,
M Mabillon. Open 08.30–20.00. Closed Sunday, August.*
A favourite with the English painter Francis Bacon, this is a tiny
tobacconist/newsagent with a surprisingly spacious bar behind.
Ancient beams and stone walls create a country-town
atmosphere. Surprisingly, students from the nearby Beaux Arts
don't take over.
Specialities: Macon; coffee (even though espresso).

61 La Tartine (map pages 155, 168) *24 Rue de Rivoli (42 72 76 85)
M St Paul. Open 08.00–22.00. Closed Tuesday, Wednesday a.m.,
most of August, Christmas week.*
A unique 'old Paris' atmosphere prevails in what is one of the
city's largest, but most reasonably priced bars. Great mirrors and
dark paintwork have been little altered since Trotsky and Tito
drank here as young men. Around fifty wines are available by the
glass.
Specialities: Beaujolais fort (very strong cheese); tartines;
Cheverny Rosé, Beaujolais.

62 Le Val d'Or (map page 83) *28 Avenue F. D. Roosevelt,
M St Philippe du Roule. Open 07.15–21.00. Closed Sunday,
August.*
A bright, friendly bar where snacks are served; in the basement is
a popular lunchtime brasserie.
Specialities: bœuf Bourguignon; ham on the bone; tarte tatin
(caramelized apple tart).

63 Willi's Wine Bar (map pages 28, 139) *13 Rue des Petits
Champs (42 61 05 09) M Pyramides. Open 11.00–22.00. Closed
Sunday.*
English bar staff are generally available to advise customers on
the never less than outstanding wines. Many are available by the
glass, thus providing an opportunity to sample superb vintages
without spending a fortune. Bar snacks or a wide range of dishes
in the attractive, beamed restaurant at the rear, are offered. The
day's *Financial Times* is usually available for perusal.
Specialities: wines from Burgundy and Provence; old Armagnacs;
exceptional desserts.

Index

Location descriptions, with their translations, are as follows: arc, arch; banque, bank; bibliothèque, library; bois, wood; bourse, exchange; cimetière, cemetery; chapelle, chapel; colonne, column; court, courtyard; école, school; église, church; ferme, farm; fontaine, fountain; galerie, gallery; hôtel, mansion; institut, institute; jardin, garden; lycée, grammar school; maison, house; musée, museum; palais, palace; parc, park; place, square; pont, bridge; porte, gateway; rue, street; tour, tower; vigne, vineyard.